Building Nineteenth-Century
Latin America

Building Nineteenth-Century
Latin America
Re-Rooted Cultures, Identities, and Nations

Edited by
William G. Acree Jr. and
Juan Carlos González Espitia

Vanderbilt University Press
Nashville

This book is printed on acid-free paper
made from 30% post-consumer recycled content.
Manufactured in the United States of America

Library of Congress Cataloging-in-Publication Data
Building nineteenth-century Latin America : re-rooted cultures,
identities, and nations / edited by William G. Acree Jr., Juan
Carlos González Espitia.
p. cm.
Includes bibliographical references and index.
ISBN 978-0-8265-1665-7 (cloth : alk. paper)
ISBN 978-0-8265-1666-4 (pbk. : alk. paper)
1. Latin America—History—19th century.
2. Latin America—Intellectual life—19th century.
3. Publishers and publishing—Latin America—
History—19th century. 4. National characteristics, Latin
American. 5. Nationalism—Latin America—History—19th
century. 6. Popular culture—Latin America—History—19th
century. 7. Gender identity—Latin America—History—19th
century.
I. Acree, William G.
II. González Espitia, Juan Carlos.

F1413.B85 2009
306.098'09034—dc22
2008045633

Contents

Acknowledgments

This book was born out of the activities and experiences of a working group within the Consortium in Latin American and Caribbean Studies at the University of North Carolina at Chapel Hill and Duke University. Created in 2004 as "Latin America in the Nineteenth Century" and continuing through the 2006–2007 academic year, this group held regular meetings and brought scholars from across the United States to give talks on themes that appear throughout this volume. All of the contributors participated in one way or another in the working group's activities, and without the support of the Consortium, as well as that of the Department of Romance Languages and Literatures at UNC Chapel Hill and Duke's Department of Romance Studies, this intellectual exchange among faculty and students would not have been possible.

We are also extremely grateful to Michael Ames, the staff at Vanderbilt University Press, and the anonymous readers of a previous version of this manuscript for their careful, expedient, and professional handling of this project from start to finish. The readers provided us with valuable comments to improve the book, and the staff at the Press responded quickly to all of our many queries. In short, we could not have hoped to work with a better editorial team.

Several individuals and institutions deserve our thanks, too, beginning with the contributing authors who believed in the importance and usefulness of this book and its goals from the very beginning. Our colleagues read multiple drafts of different parts of the manuscript and shared insightful advice along the way. The Intendencia Municipal de Montevideo, the Museo Blanes, the Museo Nacional de Artes Visuales, and the Museo Histórico Nacional in Uruguay, the Banco de la República and the Casa Museo Quinta de Bolívar in Colombia, and the Nettie Lee Benson Latin American Collection at the University of Texas at Austin all kindly granted permission to use images throughout the book and on the cover.

As is always the case with big academic endeavors, our family members gave us time and their steadfast support to make this project a reality.

Thank you all, and thank you to the readers who want to know something more about nineteenth-century Latin America.

Building Nineteenth-Century
Latin America

Introduction

William G. Acree Jr. and Juan Carlos González Espitia

In Latin America, national origins and national histories began with independence. Independence was nation building, or the beginning of the process of nation building, as could be seen one hundred years later in the displays of centennial celebrations of independence. These celebrations recreated the patriotic spirit of the *fiestas cívicas* (civic celebrations) that occurred throughout the nineteenth century. They brought meanings of independence to the surface of historical memory in hopes of providing ex-colonial communities with the material to form national ones.

Celebrations of the bicentennial of independence of Latin American nations are geared to serve the same function. That is why Chile has ambitious plans to design new bridges and bring renewed life to Santiago's nineteenth-century buildings, and why, before ending his presidency in 2006, Vicente Fox created an Office for the Organization of the Bicentennial in Mexico that is planning a special anniversary of the *Grito de Dolores*, the now festively honored call to arms of Miguel Hidalgo. Independence and its ramifications were likewise behind the events in Argentina and Uruguay that marked the two hundredth anniversary of the defeat of British forces in 1806 and 1807—a milestone recognized as an initial step on the road to sovereignty for the provinces of the Río de la Plata. Suffice it to say that the long list of festivities that have occurred and that are planned for the next decade will showcase what *Building Nineteenth-Century Latin America* explores: the process of and meanings that resulted from nation building throughout the nineteenth century.

The Long Road from Independence to Cultures, Identities, and Nations

The wars of Latin American independence ended, for the most part, around 1825. They helped establish legal frameworks for new republics, cemented the role liberalism would play in Latin American political culture, and promised much in the way of social change. The political landscape of the region was drastically altered, too, with more than a dozen incipient republican governments standing in the place of former colonial administrative units, but the consequences of the wars left many of the promises unfulfilled. Social hierarchies remained largely unaltered until the middle of the century. Spanish American society remained militarized after independence, and areas of Venezuela, Colombia, Bolivia, and Peru suffered large-scale destruction.[1] For the next half-century, political factions emerged and strove to be distinct while cultural institutions struggled to establish themselves. In Brazil, independence was achieved without much of the devastation of warfare, thanks largely to monarchy. While Spanish America struggled to implement republicanism, Brazilians were mostly comfortable under their king until the end of the century.[2]

Despite the challenges that resulted from the wars, it is clear that the period of independence constituted an opening toward a new future, but it was a confusing way forward surrounded by the complex relationships between people in positions of political authority and those who wielded political power. These were not one and the same. Charismatic landowners who could round up armies in no time often determined the agenda of elected officials at both the local and national levels, which in turn generated strong opposition and partisan warfare. Most Latin Americans were caught in the middle, and their loyalty to one side or the other impacted not just political culture but how new group identities would form, and how national communities would later evolve.[3]

Writing, symbols, and spaces that fostered social interaction were central to the period of independence and the nation-building process that followed. With the exception of the cities of Lima and Mexico, which were already established printing centers during the colonial period, the years 1810–1830 saw printing revolutions in the Río de la Plata, Caracas, Santiago, and Bogotá. Elites crafted new, national symbols, such as coats of arms and flags, as well as patriotic poetry that introduced *América* as the central rhetorical focus and were the first contributions to national literatures, from the gauchesque verses of Bartolomé Hidalgo to the more romantically inclined ones of José María Heredia and Andrés Bello. Yet widespread illiteracy up to the 1870s meant that the orality-print divide had to be bridged through various modes of reading in group settings, through visual culture, and at public spectacles. Dance and varieties of religion forged other bonds that would be critical to the formation of identities. Building nineteenth-century Latin America was a daunting process, and one that was far from uniform.

There was no blueprint for building nations at the outset of the 1800s. Liberalism and the dream of republican systems provided some guidelines, but they were not enough to make for a trouble-free merger of ideals with reality. In fact, this process fragmented into civil wars between liberals and conservatives (and federalists versus centrists); debates on race and the integration of ethnic groups into national communities; a fierce competition for predominance over national imaginaries; and, among other splinters, complex and often tense relationships of popular classes with people in positions of power. Intellectual male elites composed just one of the participating social sectors in this process. Africans and Afro-descendants, indigenous groups, poor creoles, women, and mestizos also defined Latin America in these years. They could be abused and mistreated by elites, but not ignored.

In the last third of the century, state institutions became stabilized and were thus able to consolidate their power, which translated into support for building armies, creating public school systems to instill "proper" values and codes of behavior, and urban development projects fueled by export-based economies and the entrance of Latin American products into the world economy. Visions of national identity could be promoted like never before, but they also ran into several hurdles. How could immigrants who arrived in massive numbers to places like São Paulo, Buenos Aires, and Montevideo be integrated into national cultures? Would the notion of a unified, national identity be able to triumph over other forms of collective identity that citizens subscribed to? What could be done to align faith in science and progress with groups of people considered to be obstacles to both because of race or disease? State institutions were not the only forces generating messages and symbols of collective identity and cultural representation at the end of the 1800s and the beginning of the twentieth century. They were challenged by multiple parties: ethnic communities, anarchists, and a growing sector of the population that resented immigration in some areas and modernization in others, to name just a few.[4] These competing discourses resulted in continued daily negotiations that fed the formation of cultures and identities within Latin America.

Recent scholarship has explored precise topics in nineteenth-century Latin America such as violence, portraits of everyday life, reevaluations of periodization, political institutions, and the contradictions of progress and modernity.[5] Political culture, popular participation in state formation, and subaltern communities have likewise attracted contemporary scholars' attention, as has the idea of the public sphere and its evolution through the 1800s.[6] The existing edited volumes on Latin America in the nineteenth century have focused similarly on narrowly defined subjects. These have provided valuable glimpses into social history, as can be found in the collection of *The Human Tradition in Latin America*, in-depth studies of visual culture, a critique of Benedict Anderson's *Imagined Communities* as it applies to Latin America, and voluminous editions on political culture and history.[7]

Building Nineteenth-Century Latin America has a different starting point. Its chapters aim to communicate an organic view of society, the components that were part of nation building throughout the century, and the political consequences of culture. What does this mean? Broadly speaking, they present snapshots of these components, grouped together in thematic sections that facilitate the linking of individual parts to create a vision of the whole. By virtue of this layout, readers will have access to the symbolically charged images exchanged on paper money throughout the century together with a look at homosexuality and gender on the eve of the twentieth century in Mexico. They will be able to establish connections between the transgressive games of carnival and the role of print media during wartime. Readers will experience the disparate meanings of religiosity and ideological war in the Yucatán alongside the war of words that filled the trenches during the Paraguayan war. And they can read about serial novels in early independent Mexico in tandem with a study of the historiographical narratives that were on display at the first National Fair in Venezuela.

Several common themes and concepts promote connections between the chapters and sections of this book. Print media and the roles they played make for one common theme among several authors. Visual culture, explored in foundational images as well as in the records of fairs, is another. War and the rhetoric of war are threads that run throughout this volume, and race and gender are central themes as well. From the racial slurs of the Paraguayan war to the cultural and racial mixture of carnival, this book's authors explore these two major components of life in nineteenth-century Latin America. Tied to race is the notion of marginal populations and how they were treated, as can be seen in the chapters that deal with disease, homosexuality, and gender roles in Latin American-U.S. relations. The performance of power is another theme that several authors engage here, and the roles of popular culture—at times co-opted by the state and at others in opposition to state power—is a thread woven into all three sections. The contributors make use of concepts such as the *lettered city* (referring to Angel Rama's idea of a limited group of people who, from the colonial period up through the early 1900s, monopolized power largely through writing), *foundational texts* (stemming from Doris Sommer's idea of novels being foundational for the emergence of nationalist sentiments), and Benedict Anderson's eponymous *imagined community*, as well as cultural *mestizaje*.

Lastly, many chapters employ archival material ranging from nineteenth-century newspapers and loose-leaf publications to unpublished documents and images. Others rely on a different type of "archive"— namely published literary works and historical accounts from the period that are read in innovative ways here. This juxtaposition of different modes of analyzing material allows for textual analysis to complement historiography; the dynamics of print culture to illustrate those of visual culture; and political and popular cultures to be better understood through multiple studies of their distinct facets. Likewise, the different perspectives of the contributors highlight the lack of scholarly consensus regarding some of the subjects and concepts that are studied, such as cultures, identities, and nations. The word *cultures* in the title of this book and in many of its chapters refers as much to popular culture as it does to political culture, and it encompasses visual and print cultures alike. *Identities*—or more explicitly, *social identities*—are explored in the multiple manifestations, too, from incipient national identity to partisan political identity to gender identities. And the complex notion of *nation* is engaged throughout the volume as a political and cultural entity that is constantly being molded and reinvigorated.

The three thematic sections dialogue with and build on each other. They adhere generally to the overall chronology of the period, with the first scenes staged at the outset of the 1800s and the closing acts focusing on years surrounding the 1910 centenary celebrations of independence.

The first of these sections, "Lasting Impressions," concentrates on print culture and the power of images to build part of nineteenth-century Latin America. The wars for independence were accompanied by a revolution in forms of communication that was led by print. Despite the earlier activity of the colonial printing centers in Lima and Mexico City, the period of independence ushered in the first large-scale printing revolution in the region. For the first time in Latin America, the technologies of print were engaged in a symbiotic relationship with politics and the fight for partisan identities. In fact, as the authors of this section show, printed words and images—appearing in newspapers, paintings, novels, loose leaves, and paper money—gave legitimacy to new states and the ideology of republicanism. They also gave a voice to popular discourse. These new forms of communication replaced colonial symbolism with representations of independence and the nation. After 1830, the quantities and types of print media grew exponentially throughout the rest of the century. Of course, some regions experienced this process much more intensely than others, but in all the places where this new mode of communication took hold, it left lasting impressions.

In the second section of the book, we move from print culture to parties—the transgressive quality of dance and social mestizaje, performances, and exhibitions. These chapters deal with topics ranging from the excesses of carnival in Rio to the first National Fair in Venezuela, where technology intersected myth and military metaphor, and performances in Mexico during the Porfiriato. Like the power of print, these forms of cultural production were critical to shaping social identities and building part of nineteenth-century Latin America. After all, who can imagine Rio without carnival? But what about carnival activities in Lima, a city less known for its carnival tradition? How did the jockeying of nations for prominence at the World's Fairs play out in Latin American exhibitions? What kinds of spectacles helped maintain Porfirio Díaz in power for so long? "Cultures on Display" posits some answers to these questions.

The last section of the book transports us to the turn of the century. Its chapters treat ideologies that had been present since the wars for independence, and that grew in strength as the years passed; revelations; and "hidden nations" that were marginalized within larger national communities. Liberalism was undoubtedly one of the defining forces of the nineteenth century, and its tenets were reinvigorated during the second half of the century, this time accompanied by positivism, new directions in scientific thinking, and a dramatic increase in foreign investment in Latin America. Liberalism was also at work in the lengthy Caste War that pitted indigenous inhabitants of Yucatán against the Mexican state. This was one of the many manifestations of the tensions between the liberal spirit, folkways, and popular culture that occurred throughout the century. War, indeed, was not missing from this last period in the building of nineteenth-century Latin America. There was the Caste War; there was the Argentine military's war against Indians to control southern territories; and then there was the Brazilian state's battle against millenarians following a messianic discourse in the backlands town of Canudos. The end of the century also saw wars that resulted in the loss of Spain's last colonies and the first incursions of the United States into the Caribbean. All told, war was a major contributor to social change and cultural formation as the new century approached, despite all the "progress" in the air. Reactionaries and groups whose behaviors seemed against the norm made news, too. This was the case of the revealing conduct of dandies who flouted a way of life that foreshadowed open manifestations of homosexuality, as we will see in the case of Mexico. There was a different kind of war waged against the internal enemy embodied by disease. Aside from wreaking havoc on populations, disease revealed characteristics about the nation, as did men who did not appear to know the "right" gender codes. In most cases, these were undesirable traits that needed to be kept hidden or corrected through urban planning and medical technologies.

Read together, the contributions to this book showcase groundbreaking research in some of the most exciting areas of study within current scholarship on nineteenth-century Latin America. In addition to providing what we think are engaging topics that will keep you turning the pages, the contributors share new ways to approach this period in Latin American history that invite further exploration. We hope the result will allow readers to experience the richly textured process of what building nineteenth-century Latin America was all about.

NOTES

1. On the militarization of Latin America following independence, see Tulio Halperín Donghi, *The Aftermath of Revolution in Latin America*, trans. Josephine de Bunsen (New York: Harper and Row, 1973).

2. For outstanding treatments of the period of independence, see John Charles Chasteen, *Americanos: Latin America's Struggle for Independence* (New York: Oxford University Press, 2007); Richard Graham, *Independence in Latin America*, 2nd ed. (McGraw-Hill, 1994); and Jay Kinsbruner, *Independence in Spanish America: Civil Wars, Revolutions, and Underdevelopment*, rev. ed. (Albuquerque: University of New Mexico Press, 2000).

3. See John Lynch, *Caudillos in Spanish America, 1800–1850* (New York: Oxford University Press, 1992) on these charismatic figures.

4. The "rougher" side of progress was studied by E. Bradford Burns in *The Poverty of Progress: Latin America in the Nineteenth Century* (Berkeley: University of California Press, 1980).

5. Some examples include Dale Torston Graden, *From Slavery to Freedom in Brazil: Bahia, 1835–1900* (Albuquerque: University of New Mexico Press, 2006); John Charles Chasteen, *National Rhythms, African Roots: The Deep History of Latin American Popular Dance* (Albuquerque: University of New Mexico Press, 2004); Stuart F. Voss, *Latin America in the Middle Period, 1750–1929* (Wilmington, DE: Scholarly Resources, 2002); Ricardo D. Salvatore, Carlos Aguirre, and Gilbert M. Joseph, eds., *Crime and Punishment in Latin America: Law and Society since Late Colonial Times* (Durham: Duke University Press, 2001); Hilda Sábato, *The Many and the Few: Political Participation in Republican Buenos Aires* (Stanford: Stanford University Press, 2001); Mark Wasserman, *Everyday Life and Politics in Nineteenth-Century Mexico: Men, Women, and War* (Albuquerque: University of New Mexico Press, 2000); Chasteen, *Heroes on Horseback: A Life and Times of the Last Gaucho Caudillos* (Albuquerque: University of New Mexico Press, 1995); David Bushnell and Neill Macaulay, *The Emergence of Latin America in the Nineteenth Century* (New York: Oxford

University Press, 1994); Doris Sommer, _Foundational Fictions: The National Romances of Latin America_ (Berkeley: University of California Press, 1991); and Adolfo Prieto, _El discurso criollista en la formación de la Argentina moderna_ (Buenos Aires: Sudamericana, 1988).

6. See Jens Andermann, _The Optic of the State: Visuality and Power in Argentina and Brazil_ (Pittsburgh: University of Pittsburgh Press, 2007); Pilar González Bernaldo de Quirós, _Civility and Politics in the Origins of the Argentine Nation: Sociabilities in Buenos Aires, 1829–1862_, trans. Daniel Philip Tunnard (Los Angeles: UCLA Latin American Center Publications, 2006); Ricardo D. Salvatore, _Wandering Paysanos: State Order and Subaltern Experience in Buenos Aires during the Rosas Years_ (Durham: Duke University Press, 2003); Guy Thomson, _Patriotism, Politics and Popular Liberalism in Nineteenth-Century Mexico: Juan Francisco Lucas_ (Wilmington, DE: Scholarly Resources, 1999); Charles Walker, _Smoldering Ashes: Cuzco and the Creation of Republican Peru, 1780–1840_ (Durham: Duke University Press, 1999); and Florencia Mallon, _Peasant and Nation: The Making of Postcolonial Mexico and Peru_ (Berkeley: University of California Press, 1995).

7. Judith Ewell and William H. Beezley, eds., _The Human Tradition in Latin America: The Nineteenth Century_ (Wilmington, DE: Scholarly Resources, 1989). On visual culture, see the recent example of Beatriz González-Stephan and Jens Andermann, eds., _Galerías del progreso: Museos, exposiciones y cultura visual en América Latina_ (Rosario: Beatriz Viterbo Editora, 2006). A fresh critique of Anderson can be found in Sara Castro-Klarén and John Charles Chasteen, eds., _Beyond Imagined Communities: Reading and Writing the Nation in Nineteenth-Century Latin America_ (Washington, DC: Woodrow Wilson Center Press; Baltimore: Johns Hopkins University Press, 2003). A sample of recent studies on political culture and history includes François-Xavier Guerra, Antonio Annino, and Luis Castro Leiva, eds., _De los imperios a las naciones: Iberoamérica_ (Zaragoza: IberCaja, 1994); Annino and Guerra, eds., _Inventando la nación: Iberoamérica siglo XIX_ (Mexico, DF: Fondo de Cultura Económica, 2003); and Hilda Sábato, ed., _Ciudadanía política y formación de las naciones: Perspectivas históricas de América Latina_ (Mexico, DF: Fondo de Cultura Económica, 1999). More in line with cultural history are Ivan Jaksic, ed., _The Political Power of the Word: Press and Oratory in Nineteenth-Century Latin America_ (London: Institute of Latin American Studies, 2002); and Paula Alonso, ed., _Construcciones impresas: Panfletos, diarios y revistas en la formación de los estados nacionales en América Latina, 1820–1920_ (Mexico, DF: Fondo de Cultura Económica, 2004).

PART I

Lasting Impressions

I

Foundational Images of the Nation in Latin America

Hugo Achugar

Nation and *nationalism* have made their mark on scholarship in the most divergent disciplines, fueling debates that have focused on connections to literature, history, memory, narrative, ethnicity, sexual identity, gender, and culture. Scholars of visual arts and communication studies have also actively engaged in these debates. Indeed, few and far between are the academic disciplines that have not been affected by conversations on nation and nationalism. This essay reformulates, in part, an argument on the nation in Latin America that I have been developing over many years. In a previous attempt to make the case, I concluded by claiming that in addition to the *lettered city*, and long before the apotheosis of the *televised city*, there was a *visual city*.[1]

The notion of visual art as an expression of national identity is common currency in intellectual circles, or at least it has been during multiple historical moments. This old idea was based on the premise that the nation—and consequently all things national—preceded all artistic production. *Nation* and the *national* enjoyed an ahistorical existence.[2] This romantic scheme gave birth to the concepts of "the spirit of a people," *volkgeist*, and folklore, which nourished stories that have attempted to explain the deep roots (or the beginnings) of nations and communities.

Among scholars, this "essentialist" understanding of *nation* has gradually lost support and been replaced by the widely accepted idea that *nations* and the meaning of what is *national* are social constructs. In other words, nations do not precede states; rather, they are shaped by them and their institutions, or the hegemonic social sector. This "constructionist" interpretation has been advanced fundamentally through literary analysis and by

---

This chapter was translated from Spanish by William G. Acree Jr.

studies of the printed word and written culture. In this spirit, Julio Ramos maintained that

> far from what literature could mean to us today—a relatively specialized activity, distinct from other discursive practices and from the everyday use of language—the longing expressed in Martí's prologue [to Juan Antonio Pérez Bonalde's "Poema del Niágara"] is a response to the crisis faced by a cultural system in which literature—or rather, letters—had risen to a place of utmost importance in the organization of new Latin American societies. Literature (with a capital L), the ideal expression of a rationalized and homogenous national language, became the space—perhaps fictitious— where models of behavior were communicated, and that projected norms for shaping citizens and citizenship, symbolic frontiers, social imaginaries, and even states in the process of consolidation.[3]

In spite of the emphasis on the "organization of new Latin American societies," this line of argument is not so much about *nation*. It deals more with the role the state plays in the construction of nations, focusing in particular on the significance of literature and the written word, similar to what Benedict Anderson and Doris Sommer have maintained.[4] In contrast, this essay aims to illustrate the importance of what I have decided to call *foundational images*. These images are no less fictional than Sommer's "foundational fictions" in the national imaginaries constructed by the state and Latin American lettered elites (or the hegemonic sector) throughout the nineteenth century and at the beginning of the twentieth century. The difference resides in the fact that their sustenance and materiality is visual and not written. In this sense, by studying a group of Latin American novels and privileging the written word, Sommer's argument leaves out components that are central to the construction of national, Latin American imaginaries, and that are intimately related to the visual, even when their visual quality is linked to writing. Furthermore, my claim modifies Benedict Anderson's well-known conclusions regarding the role of the press and narrative in the formation of imagined communities during the nineteenth century, and attempts to rethink the phenomenon of the construction of national imaginaries in the twentieth century, just as we are entering—so it would seem—a "post-national" period.[5]

Initially, my interest was to analyze those paintings, images, and icons of various countries that played or appear to have played a definitive part in the configuration of national imaginaries, such as Juan Manuel Blanes's *El juramento de los Treinta y Tres Orientales* (The Oath of the Thirty-three Uruguayans) in Uruguay, *El velorio* (The Wake) from 1893 by the Puerto

Rican Francisco Oller y Cetero (or Cestero), the image of the Virgin of Guadalupe in Mexico, and Goya's *El 2 de mayo* (May 2) in Spain. One of the first surprises (and challenges to consider) was discovering that not all countries could lay claim to visual artistic productions that helped shape the national imaginary, as was the case in Uruguay and, to a certain extent, in Puerto Rico. In reality, the image of the Virgin of Guadalupe in Mexico could and should be seen against the popular backdrop of mural paintings from the early twentieth century. In the case of Spain, *El 2 de mayo* did not have the "universal" national appeal that Blanes's *El juramento* held in Uruguay.

This gap becomes even more evident when looking at the cases of countries like Bolivia and Ecuador, where it is not possible—at least based on the evidence I have seen—to determine the existence of a foundational image of the nation. The only painting or image that could aspire to hold a similar role to *El juramento* is Emmanuel Leutze's *Washington Crossing the Delaware* (1851). It would appear that this work had a greater function than that of merely symbolizing a nation, for as the website *americanrevolution.org* states with candor, it is provincial and imperial at the same time: "With the possible exceptions of Da Vinci's *Mona Lisa* and *Last Supper*, this is perhaps the most universally recognized image in the entire history of art."[6]

The differences between the Uruguayan painting and that of Leutze's seem to revolve around historical veracity. In the case of Blanes, the attention to historical detail (and truth) went as far as bringing sand to his studio from the place he was depicting in the historical scene of *El juramento*, while Leutze completed his work in Germany and committed several "historical fallacies." In fact, this is not entirely true either, given that (as we will see below) Blanes composed racially and numerically the thirty-three Uruguayans of his painting not by following "historical truth," but according to a project of national representation. In any case, and aside from the particulars of each of these paintings, what is important about them both is their reproduction in public spaces and their use in programs of public (state-run) education. This is what allows us to understand how an image or its reproduction—independent of its historical veracity—becomes a foundation for the national imaginary.

In this sense, the idea that the visual—the *visual city* mentioned above—exercises a fundamental part in the formation of national imaginaries (possibly even greater than that of writing) still seems valid. However, the artistic images of high culture are not the only ones that give birth to and shape the nation; it is necessary to take into account other types of imagery and visual representation. Some research has been done in this respect. The work of Hans Konig on Colombia, for example, has looked at the images on coins appearing along the long road to national consolidation.[7] Taking a different approach, Lynn Hunt's scholarship on the French Revolution is another case in point.[8] It is precisely this other visual strategy, and this other imaginary, that should be considered when we study the construction of the nation.

Key in this respect is the visual universe of both paper money and metallic coins, as Konig demonstrates in the case of Colombia. In addition, monuments, architecture, the establishment and creation of cultural institutions, and especially the emission of national postage stamps should figure in the study of foundational images. It is clear that this visual universe constitutes a heterogeneous object of knowledge, insofar as it includes visual representations in general, and architectonic or symbolic ones in particular, and thus transcends the scope of a single discipline or methodology. But it is also a relatively homogenous field consisting of a set of representations that stem from the common processes and instruments of symbolization engaged by the state and hegemonic social sectors to construct the national imaginary.

This chapter considers a few examples of foundational images. We will explore Juan Manuel Blanes's *El juramento* in Uruguay first, and then consider the case of bills and coins in a handful of Latin American countries. Unfortunately, there is not room to consider the function of monuments in the construction of those sites that, loosely paraphrasing Pierre Nora, could be called "sites of nation" or "sites of nationalism" more than "sites of memory."[9] We proceed first with Blanes's *El juramento* since it represents an important example of the construction of a national visual imaginary in the context of the Americas. As noted before, it could be stated that there are similar, though not absolutely parallel, instances of paintings in the case of Puerto Rico and the United States. Moreover, it is the almost unique case of *El juramento* that, afterwards, will lead me to explore other visual representations—stamps, coins, etc.—of the nation-state, since the kind of iconic national image or imaginary that is Blanes's painting is not found in every country of the Americas with equal or similar functions or quality.

The Nascent Nation:
El juramento de los Treinta y Tres Orientales

Few historical paintings in Latin America have seen a trajectory like that of *El juramento de los Treinta y Tres Orientales* (Figure 1.1). Started in 1875 and

Figure 1.1: *El juramento de los Treinta y Tres Orientales* (1877) by Juan Manuel Blanes. Image courtesy of the Museo Blanes and the Museo Nacional de Artes Visuales in Montevideo, Uruguay.

completed in 1877, Juan Manuel Blanes's painting was part of the program of celebrations marking the fiftieth anniversary of what was then considered the beginning of Uruguayan independence—in this instance not from Spain, but rather from Brazil. Although, to be precise, the anniversary had taken place in 1875, the movement to celebrate the occasion had begun earlier, in 1874, with the decision to erect a commemorative monument in the Department of Florida, and lasted until the monument was inaugurated with the public reading of Juan Zorrilla de San Martín's poem "La leyenda patria" in 1879. The painting, the monument, and the poem—each in its own way and all together—configure the first image that aimed to renew the "dream nation" at the end of the century.[10]

The painting in question and Zorrilla's text would be converted into icons of the Uruguayan nation and of what it meant to be Uruguayan, thanks above all to actions of the state carried out in the field of public education. But state support was not the only form of endorsement they received. At least according to what has been preserved in the official historical memory, these icons were backed by the national community and, as historians have noted, by a show of popular support for both works. Put differently, both the painting and the poem interpellated, in the sense Althusser uses the term, the "us" of the Uruguayan community. But what scene does Blanes's painting construct?

The canvas stages the historical episode in which a group of Uruguayans initiates the war for independence against the Brazilian army governing the territory that would become Uruguay. More specifically, the painting documents (the term is not naive, for it hints at Blanes's style and representative will) the moment when the group takes the oath to fight for "liberty or death." The thirty-three Uruguayans portrayed include creole elites as well as mestizos, although evidence suggests that the number was perhaps greater, and there is speculation that "thirty-three" was chosen for its affinity with Masonic symbols.[11] In Blanes's version, neither blacks nor mulattos are represented, despite the fact that at least two individuals of African origin—possibly slaves—as well as Italian immigrants were part of the group of thirty-three. Thus, it is possible to claim that the universe Blanes designed gave the national imaginary a white, masculine, Uruguayan body in place of the classic feminine representation prescribed by the French Revolution's republican rhetoric, but that it also preserved ethnic and national characteristics as fundamental points of reference.

Blanes donated *El juramento de los Treinta y Tres Orientales* to the Uruguayan state in 1879 (the same year Zorrilla's poem was publicly read aloud), roughly a year after the work was put on display in the painter's studio in Montevideo. During the month of January 1878, more than 6,200 people flocked to see the historical representation.[12] The impressive march to view the work at the artist's studio—or, in the words of Agustín Benzano, the "boisterous event"—mirrored the attention residents of Buenos Aires paid to another of Blanes's paintings, *Un episodio de la fiebre amarilla en Buenos Aires* (An Episode in the Yellow Fever Outbreak in Buenos Aires) (1871).[13] With *El juramento*, Blanes saw not only relatives of the supposed thirty-three Uruguayans, who left bunches of flowers at the foot of the painting, but also a multitude who recognized the image—and saw themselves in it—as part of a "nascent nation." As Isabel Wschebor writes, "The painting was on display for more than a month, time enough for it to serve its purpose: it satisfied the 'necessity of nation' for which different social sectors and political figures longed. It created new gods whose first appearance (in *El juramento*) was so effective for the liberal imaginary that it would later become the watermark backdrop of bank notes or bills . . . and an icon of material support for the education of enlightened citizens."[14]

Wschebor notes the sustained deployment of the image of Blanes's painting through bills circulating as the newly printed national currency. As we will see later in this chapter, this use of such a foundational image points to the idea that the supposed "necessity of nation" was satisfied not only through fine arts (or high art), but also through the concrete, common, and not very glamorous material of paper money. This nascent nation, or this necessity of nation, is what Zorrilla celebrates in his poem "La leyenda patria." While there is no definitive evidence suggesting that *El juramento* inspired Zorilla to compose the poem, there is no doubt that the author had viewed the painting, and it is probable that he and Blanes maintained a constant dialogue. Independent of the more than likely conversation between these two artists, it is fair to claim that both the painting and the poem form part of the movement to rekindle the "dream nation" swirling around in the Uruguayan national community's collective imaginary at the end of the nineteenth century.

In any case, both "La leyenda patria" and *El juramento* deal with and are manifestations of the discourse of *patria*.[15] The focus on the group of the Thirty-three fulfils not only an ideological end where, like in the mystery of the Holy Trinity, the singular hero appears as one and thirty-three at the same time, but this visual concentration also operates in a way that achieves a homogeneous portrayal in which ethnic elements are blended into a general "Uruguayan" character, opportunely distinct from Brazilian and Argentine natures. The absence of a female figure in Blanes's painting could plausibly be explained by the fact that the work represents a military episode, and by the lack of historical evidence illustrating the presence of women in the landing of the Thirty-three on Uruguayan shores. Nevertheless, women appear in other historical paintings by the artist. In fact, Blanes paid close attention to the female figure and felt that it was necessary to recognize the role of female soldiers, especially when he began painting *La batalla de Sarandí* (The Battle of Sarandí) in 1881. This was also the case with the military paintings in the Palacio de Urquiza and in *La batalla de San Cala* (The Battle of San Cala) from 1876, where the dramatic image of a woman on horseback stands out from the rest of the composition. The same center of attention is visible in *El resurgimiento de la Patria* (The Resurgence of the Patria), where the semi-nude image of the republic (represented by the figure of a woman) wrapped in the national flag appears with an Indian at her feet. In the light of these examples, the absence of the female figure in *El juramento* reinforces the masculine image of the nation Blanes aimed to promote.

When they were unveiled, both Zorrilla's text and Blanes's canvas were recognized by a large group of citizens—as well as by supposed spokespeople for the popular classes—as representative of the national imaginary in force.[16] This did not mean, however, that the limits of this imaginary did not present or presuppose tensions with and fear of the Other. This Other, often constituted of popular classes, could have been embodied just as easily by foreigners, women, or those whose skin color was a little too dark for "national" standards. In this respect, Blanes and Zorrilla confirm the hegemony of an imaginary that is militarist, masculine, and white—one that hides or relegates to a position of secondary importance any representation of the body of the *patria* that does not promote this brand of imaginary. Indeed, the patriarchal paradigm and the metaphor of the family shared by Blanes, Hernández, and Zorrilla construct a disciplined space for women, a humiliating one (Hernández) or one of quasi non-existence (Zorrilla and Blanes) for blacks and Indians, and one in which foreigners are loathed.[17]

El juramento de los Treinta y Tres Orientales was reproduced throughout the entire twentieth century in school textbooks, on postage stamps, and on paper bills printed by the Uruguayan state. Thus, the reiteration of Blanes's image of the group of thirty-three—as important and influential as the icon he would create of José Artigas—allows us to consider the existence of foundational images of the nation in Uruguay. Now we will move on to the exploration of other visual forms and images.

Money and Nation, or the Difficulties of Coining the Nation

The greatest problem with the analysis of an emblematic painting like *El juramento* in terms of studying the construction of the national imaginary resides in the fact that somehow we remain trapped in the hegemonic sphere of "fine arts" in Rama's lettered city. Put differently, we remain inside the prestigious and privileged world of "high culture." The argument that guides this section of this chapter is that the power of the state or hegemonic social sectors in the configuration of national imaginaries is not limited to the realm of high culture, unless postage stamps and national currencies are considered (less dazzling) expressions of high culture. On the other hand, it is possible to argue that stamps, coins, and bills are part of a sub-division of art that would be "state art," in contrast to art produced in private or by civil society.

What were the decisions and actions Latin American states made and took around the middle of the nineteenth century that shaped the formation of emerging national imaginaries? What sources did they use? The so-called toolkit of national symbols—flag, coat of arms, national anthem—had already been created and was in circulation, but something more common that could be used on a daily basis was necessary. Parties, festivals, and commemorative events were staged, but these were not the only activities in which images contributed to the construction of nation. There were others that served the same end, although they revolved around an economic center or commercial message more than around the development of national symbols. These other activities and events became crucial to the endeavor of building foundational images exactly because they were part of the hustle and bustle of daily life and allowed state institutions to promote and consolidate national symbols in this context.

As in other centuries, dominant social sectors were aware of the fact that the majority of the population was illiterate, and of the problems the "unlettered" faced when approaching visual art and getting something meaningful out of the experience. Some studies on frescoes and bas-relief paintings from antiquity (the passage from the *Aeneid* where Virgil describes the relief painting that relates Aeneas's actions comes to mind) and the Middle Ages (one can recall the visual representation of Biblical stories in cathedrals across Europe) have focused on these problems. Yet, this type of image and strategy for connecting with the popular classes has not been limited to state efforts of long ago. Mexican mural paintings at the service of the Mexican Revolution at the outset of the twentieth century are prime examples of a visual enterprise similar to that of state education deploying images prior to the advent of mass media.

It is precisely in the context of daily life that the state intervened with the minting of coins, the emission of bills, and the printing of postage stamps. It is here, too, that the state found the appropriate site to carry out the task of consolidating the national imaginary. Moreover, it is in the dynamic character of the circulation of money where different "dream nations" become manifest and where we can observe the phases of different projects to build national imaginaries. Likewise, the emergence of postage stamps in Latin America—and throughout the rest of the Americas—sheds light on this process.[18] In this respect, by looking at the establishment of postal services and the images that Latin American stamps disseminated across countries and continents, we can see distinct moments leading to the formation of national imaginaries.

The slow unification of different, coexisting postal systems—even decades after the wars of independence—illustrates how the state had not yet gained control over all the corners of the territory under its watch. The first country in the Americas to have a national stamp was Brazil, in 1843. Stamps were issued around mid-century in various Spanish American nations, too, yet national postal systems and stamps that carried explicit nationalist messages—on scales not seen before—were developments that occurred during the last third of the century. Nowhere in Latin America was there a substantially developed postal service—led by the state at least—that reached all across the republic until this period. What is important to note here is that the analysis of these postage stamps provides insight into the imagery new Latin American states created and deployed. In various countries that achieved independence from Spain, the "May Sun" was the first image used to visualize local and or national identity. As time passed, other images materialized—images of independence heroes, of local flora and fauna, and of landscapes and monuments associated with self-perception and that supposedly defined a unique national character. Republican symbols, though not necessarily ones rooted in the French Revolution, appeared in these images as well as alone.[19] Postal discourse (the discourse of stamps) also reveals the late entrance into the postal system of Afro-Latin American and indigenous figures, even when (as we will see) the use of images of Indian and Amazonian women was frequent during the first years of the fight for independence in Brazil, Colombia, and Chile, among other new republics. A notorious exception is Haiti.

But if postal systems constitute one form of the effort to consolidate national imaginaries through visual representations that circulated on a daily basis and in the context of daily life, something different characterized the deployment of national currencies and their role in this process. For one, the process of minting coins and printing bills was neither linear nor homogenous. In many countries, the state's lack of political power during much of the nineteenth century resulted in the private sector taking over what would otherwise have been the work of state institutions and, in the process, thus acquiring political power. Private banks issued their own bills for much of the century, as did wealthy landowners. This was the case, for example, in Costa Rica, where the minting of coins—and pretty much all other forms of commercial exchange—was in the hands of coffee barons. These even produced coins with their own images.

In this light, it is appropriate to rethink the claims of the political scientists and economists who used to link the establishment of nation-states to real or potential economic arrangements that depend on state apparatuses whose raison d'être, in turn, is the pursuit of economic interests to maintain these arrangements, such as fencing in the countryside or exercising certain forms of judicial and police power. This question is equally important today, for one argument regarding globalization is that its economic components are what make possible the discussion of a "post-national" period—one in which regional communities are configured, like the South American Confederation or the European Community. In fact, the subject of a currency is central to the constitution and consolidation of these supra-national communities.

On the other hand, the desire and need to brand what was national can be observed on the coins and bills imprinted in various countries from

Figure 1.2: The revolutionary coin produced in Bogotá, known as the india or the china. Image courtesy of the Banco de la República, Colección Numismática, Colombia.

the very beginning of the movement for independence in Latin America. In Venezuela, for instance, following the declaration of independence, the Congress decreed on 27 August 1811 "a law calling for the printing of a million pesos in paper bills for the Confederation of Venezuela." According to Mercedes Carlota de Pardo, the idea was Francisco de Miranda's—one of the future heroes of independence.[20] There was a strong directive for the bills to be "marked with the seal of the Confederation, known as 'Miranda's seal,' displaying a sun whose rays are separated by seven stars representing the seven provinces that declared independence, and in whose center appears the number 19, for 19 April 1810 (for the establishment of the junta de Caracas). The slogan 'United States of Venezuela, 1811' surrounded the sun."[21] The short life of these bills (they were banned from use when royalists retook the government), combined with a public hesitant to confide in the new form of paper money, complicated both their political and economic functions.

In Colombia, patriots produced coins on an emergency basis on several occasions. The first ones were minted in Cartagena in 1811. Shortly thereafter, patriots in Santafé de Bogotá followed suit. Under the orders of Antonio Nariño, the coins minted in Bogotá were made of silver and decorated with the image of a woman (Figure 1.2). This coin "of little weight . . . was also called *de la india*, because the image of an Indian woman wearing a crown of feathers appeared on its obverse."[22] Its importance stems from the fact that it reveals a strategy that differed slightly from the ones behind the patriot coins of Cartagena (which depicted an indigenous figure holding a broken chain) and the paper bills in Venezuela. Mario Arango Jaramillo notes that this coin was "also known as the *china*, perhaps for the customary name *chinas* used to refer to female servants of indigenous descent in Bogotá households."[23] As Arango Jaramillo observes, the heart of the matter is about the transformation and replacement of symbolic codes: "Whatever the origin is of the coin's name, the Bogotá coin itself is a milestone in the history of Colombian coinage, for it substituted the effigy of the Spanish Crown with the head of a seemingly insignificant indigenous woman. It was a symbolic attempt to cling to the freshly-tasted sovereignty and affirm a new form of power. Years later, after the wars of independence, the china would be minted again."[24]

The symbolic acts of breaking with Spain and the colonial coinage bearing effigies of Fernando VII or the Spanish coat of arms took many forms. In Venezuela, patriots employed the celestial, republican symbols of the sun and the seven stars, while in Colombia they tried out a more vernacular symbolism with the image of the china. This duplicity—abstract-generic symbolism on the one hand and concrete-vernacular on the other—would be seen in the symbolic repertoires and the symbolism of independence in other countries. The case of the china or the india—first produced in 1813 and again at later moments—merits a bit more attention, for her image was not limited to the new coins (Figure 1.3). As Hans-Joachim Konig writes,

> [Creole patriots] chose the figure of a crowned and armed American indigenous woman—the figure of an india—as the allegorical representation of independence. This india appeared on coins, on the newly elaborated coat of arms, and imprinted on flags. She was generally portrayed with a crown of feathers, a quiver of arrows on her back, and her feet resting on a tamed caiman. One of the most well-known representations of the india as a symbol of independence is the painting of the Colombian artist Pedro José Figueroa, completed circa 1819, depicting Simón Bolívar with the crowned American Indian.[25]

The representation of women and the indigenous presence in newly independent Latin American nations is enough for an entirely separate study, especially if we add the case of Haiti to that of Colombia. In Haiti, the first image to appear on metallic coins was that of the notorious Henri Christophe, in 1807.[26] Paper bills, in contrast, displayed the predominant image of the Haitian coat of arms. It was not until around 1875 that the first image of a woman made its way into the symbolic repertoire of Haitian currency. What is important to note about the depictions of women is

Figure 1.3: The *india* presents the *Libertador* in *Simón Bolívar, Libertador y Padre de la Patria (Bolívar con la Alegoría de América)*, by Pedro José Figueroa, 1819. Photograph by Oscar Monsalve. Courtesy of the Casa Museo Quinta de Bolívar, Ministerio de Cultura de Colombia.

that they pictured women with "white" features, many of them accompanying figures like Geffrard or Domingue in presidential portraits—men of doubtless African origin.[27]

The case of Haiti, the example of the india in Colombia, and the patriot bills displaying republican ideals in Venezuela demonstrate that the symbolic repertoires of national imaginaries were governed by two schools of thought that utilized different strategies. In this regard, the use of the female image is revealing, for in some instances it corresponded to the representation of a white-looking or European woman established among the revolutionary symbols in the new republics of the United States and France. On many occasions, this female figure was presented as iconic and universal, often taking on features of Greco-Roman goddesses. A good example comes from the Haitian bills emitted in 1884, where the Roman goddess Ceres appears. In contrast, if we consider representations where the image is definitely American or displays local geographic and ethnic characteristics, as in the cases of Colombia and Brazil, then it becomes easier to see how projects of constructing national imaginaries followed different symbolic strategies and aimed to develop a possibly different set of meanings.

In Brazil, *mestiçagem* (the mixing of gene pools that began with Portuguese colonization) also characterized the blending of Latin American and European symbols. In the early 1830s, in what has been considered an allegory of the "discovery" of Brazil, an image appeared of an indigenous couple accompanied by a wooden cross.[28] This representation suggests that the Latin American imprint—the indigenous couple—points to the spirit of independence, even when paired with Christianity's greatest icon. Nevertheless, because of the particular process whereby Brazil became independent from Portugal, the use of images of Brazilian Indians is not a product of republican independence. In fact, between 1810 and 1813, shortly after the Portuguese royal family arrived in Brazil, the recently created Banco do Brasil followed the king's orders and produced bills displaying the image of an Indian and his bow in the upper left corner.[29] This image strains, if not dismantles, the exclusive and necessary relationship between the presence of Latin American symbols and the construction of independent, national imageries. It is also the case, however, that the arrival of the Portuguese court in 1808 has been understood as one of the factors leading up to the process of Brazilian independence.

Another element must be taken into account when studying the role coins and bills played in the construction of national imaginaries. The majority of Latin American states did not begin to centralize and homogenize the emission of currencies until decades after the end of the wars of independence. In Colombia, for example, the state began to centralize the production of currency in June 1846, when the law regarding national currencies was passed. Even then, monetary stability and the elimination of a double system where gold and silver standards were used would not be achieved until the end of the nineteenth century. In this sense, coins and bills follow a course that differs from that taken by symbols such as flags, national seals, and national anthems. It is a course that is at least much more dynamic than the paths leading to the making of traditional symbols, although the permanence of these in Latin America has been much less stable than what is generally believed.[30]

Part of the long process of monetary homogenization in nineteenth-century Latin America was the issue of sovereignty. Much of the conversation about the emission of currencies has revolved and continues to revolve—as demonstrated by the process of dollarization in Ecuador and by the establishment of the euro in Europe—around national sovereignty. References to sovereignty can be found in some of the decrees mandating the creation of *casas de moneda* (the sites where currencies were controlled, if not produced) and regulating the emission of currencies in various countries. But until the homogenization of currencies was complete, sovereignty expressed in the use of coins and bills was somewhat porous. An interesting example comes from Colombia, where the state authorized the circulation of foreign currencies—primarily from France and Belgium—until the end of the nineteenth century. This fact challenges the way we understand the impact coins and bills had on the consolidation of the national imaginary, despite the indias, chinas, granadinos, and cóndores whose images crisscrossed the country on Colombian money.

Although I have highlighted the case of Colombia, the circulation of foreign currencies has been a consistent phenomenon in most Latin American countries, from the time the first coins were minted up to the present, as illustrated in Fidel Castro's pronouncements regarding the circulation of the U.S. dollar in Cuba. Independent of the economic motivations that led and lead to the authorization or prohibition of the use of foreign currencies in a given country, it is clear that their presence (or lack thereof) fulfills a symbolic role in the construction of national symbolism.

The way the Banco de Buenos Ayres came together and functioned provides another example that is intimately related to the question of national sovereignty and tests the way we think about links between currencies and the state-driven construction of the national imaginary. The Banco was a private stock company of sorts promoted by and formed under the auspices of the provincial government of Buenos Aires in the 1820s. Here it is worth citing a description of the bank:

> At the beginning of 1822, a group of Buenos Aires residents gathered to discuss the project of establishing a bank. . . . Doctor Manuel José García, minister of the Treasury, had sent out the invitations and assumed the title of president of the new institution. The participants in the meeting agreed to set up the bank as a place to make deposits and to organize it as

a private stock company under the name of "Banco de Buenos Ayres." ...
Representatives of diverse social sectors were among its founding inves-
tors: the Anchorena brothers, Bernardino Rivadavia, Juan Manuel de
Rosas, Vicente López y Planes, the priest Domingo Belgrano (Manuel
Belgrano's brother) ... British residents ... Italians, Frenchmen, Germans
... estate owners, businessmen, military officials, [and] priests.[31]

That notorious figures of the fight for independence were cofounding investors with foreigners, soldiers, priests, businessmen, and people whose
reputations had not yet been made (like Rosas and the Anchorena brothers) is in itself noteworthy. This blend of figures from different social sectors also helps us understand the nature of the images on the bills emitted
by the Banco.

In 1826, the Banco de Buenos Ayres would be replaced by the Banco
de las Provincias Unidas del Río de la Plata (known more commonly as
the Banco Nacional), but the new institution would continue using the old
name, even a year after the change and on the new bills printed in 1827.
These were porters of a curious symbolism. Bills whose value ranged from
one to fifty pesos included illustrations of the well-known allegorical female figures as well as portraits of Simón Bolívar. In the context of the wars
of independence, this was not necessarily strange; what made it so was that
San Martín's image—more in line with the Rioplatense context—did not
appear on any of the new bills. On the flip side, the inclusion of Bolívar's
image affirms the presence of a Hispanic American anti-Spanish sentiment that permeated various levels of the independence process. However,
the visual scenario was more complex, for in addition to Bolívar's portrait,
which only appeared on the one- and twenty-peso bills, there were also
bills with portraits of George Washington and Benjamin Franklin joined
by the image of an eagle, a horseman (most likely a gaucho or a soldier),
and different female forms.

The inclusion of heroes from other countries on these bills emitted
during the first decade of Argentine independence seems best explained as
an effort to solidify the republican and Spanish American character of the
fight against Spain, and by the intellectual and political influence of U.S.
independence leaders in Spanish America. In the decades immediately following the end of the wars for independence, nation-states had borders and
identities that were much broader and inclusive than the ones they would
build by the end of the century, and this reality was reflected in their foundational images. This was true of not only Argentina and Uruguay, but
also of Central American countries and the ones that constituted Gran

Colombia. What the bills emitted in Argentina in 1827 illustrate is that along with the impulse to create an imaginary in tune with the affirmation of national sovereignty, the state was also concerned with reinforcing the republican and American character of its actions.[32]

Several conclusions can be drawn based on what we have seen up to this point. First, the images on coins and paper bills as well as their processes of elaboration demonstrate that the state has not been the only actor in the development of a foundational discourse of national imaginaries. Second, this discourse was neither homogenous nor lacking tension. Nevertheless, it is highly productive to reexamine and rethink the visual representations that circulated with these currencies, for they allow us to observe how the state negotiates—and the use of this verb is not innocent—national imaginaries beyond the realm of literature or the periodical press. But perhaps this reexamination should not be limited to the images displayed in paintings or on coins, stamps, and bills. Among the other components to study are the politics that oriented the construction of monuments for the centenary celebrations that took place across Latin America during the first decades of the twentieth century—a task for another occasion. Such monuments—even ones that were erected at the end of the nineteenth century, as in the case of the 1883 National Fair in Venezuela—are also central to the foundational images of a nation.

Again, a Provisional End

The process of constructing national imaginaries was extremely rich—much richer than what would appear if we limited the analysis to the lettered discourse of high culture. This richness is behind how regional interests—as well as the presence of private actors (banks and landowners above all)—and the economic transformation of Latin America in the nineteenth century (which included the circulation of counterfeit currencies) made the discourse of nation that its states formulated a very dynamic and colorful one. In this sense, the images that circulated during a large part of the nineteenth century and in the centenary celebrations at the beginning of the twentieth century deserve special attention. This attention means problematizing historical periodization, too, given that in order to consider the process of establishing these images as foundational images of the nation, it is necessary to go beyond the chronological limits of the nineteenth century.

Moreover, to advocate for an instance of foundational images created, stimulated, or deliberately constructed by the nation-state implies an acknowledgment of the power of the state to build the nation through all kinds of means, and not only with words. Art, monuments, clothing, and outfits (e.g., "national outfits" similar to the ones that identify gauchos, llaneros, guajiros, and so on) as well as paintings, stamps, coins, and other cultural products that are co-opted by the state are illustrative or significant of the process where images and art are used to construct national images, thus configuring the nation through a "visual city."

Today, the "body of the patria" is much more related to the bodies of professional athletes (soccer players, in particular)—a predominantly masculine universe in Latin America, and to the body-objects of the "Misses"—the models, actresses, and women who participate in the "Miss" pageants. The images of these figures have little in common with the representations of the heroes of independence or the republican allegories of the nation as a woman wrapped in the national flag and baring a single breast. The new bodies of the nation destabilize the official representations inherited from the nineteenth century; perhaps they do not topple the pillars of the patriarchal paradigm, but they definitely affect other aspects of these imaginaries. Yet these sporty and flashy images are not the only ones that challenge nineteenth-century imaginaries or the ones officially promoted throughout the twentieth century. Today there are other bodies and bodies of the Other that destabilize as well the representation of the body of the patria established at the end of the nineteenth century.

In several Latin American countries, the "absent body" of the disappeared and their children—presented in movies, photographs, monuments, painting installations, protests, stories, and other discourses—became a central figure in the public sphere at the end of the twentieth century, highlighting that the renewal of the dream nation contains a corporal void that is a sign of the violence done to the nation still in formation. Likewise, the absent body of migrants—those who emigrate to the United States, as well as those (perhaps more numerous) who migrate to neighboring countries in Latin America or to Europe and Australia—points to another type of corporal void that does not necessarily become a diaspora population.

Thus, by referencing the diasporic body of the nation, and by including and alluding to the absent body that has been a constant in the second half of the twentieth century, the representation and treatment of the bodies of the patria in film and other artistic productions evidence some of the transformations taking place in the body of the nation. For this reason, what was once a nightmare for the dream nation now integrates a new version of the dream nation in many Latin American countries, converting the once-revered heroic military body into a nightmare (as a result of its dictatorships and practices of torture) for the dream nation configured at the end of twentieth century.

NOTES

1. "The transformation in the description of thoughts and images of the 'dream nation' illustrates that, along with Angel Rama's lettered city, and before the rise of mass-televised culture, there was a rich and extremely effective visual city." Hugo Achugar, *Planetas sin boca: Escritos efímeros sobre arte, cultura y literatura* (Montevideo: Trilce, 2004), 198. See also Angel Rama, *La ciudad letrada*, with a prologue by Hugo Achugar (Hanover: Ediciones del Norte, 1984).

2. For an example on the ahistoricity of nation, see Inman E. Fox, *La invención de España: Nacionalismo liberal e identidad nacional* (Madrid: Cátedra, 1997).

3. Julio Ramos, *Desencuentros de la modernidad en América Latina: Literatura y política en el siglo XIX* (Mexico City: Fondo de Cultura Económica, 1989), 8.

4. Benedict Anderson, *Imagined Communities: Reflections on the Origins and Spread of Nationalism* (London: Verso, 1991); Doris Sommer, *Foundational Fictions: The National Romances of Latin America* (Berkeley: University of California Press, 1991).

5. The eventual "post-national" stage opens up the possibility of a new periodization that would include the "pre-" and "post-" national stages, as well as the "colonial" and "post-" national moments. The period in which the foundational "machine" of imaginaries functions spans the space between "pre-" and "post-" national moments.

6. See *www.americanrevolution.org/delxone.html*.

7. Hans-Joachim Konig, *En el camino hacia la Nación* (Bogotá: Editorial Banco de la República, 1994); and Hans-Joachim Konig, ed., *El indio como sujeto y objeto de la historia latinoamericana, pasado y presente* (Frankfurt: Vervuert; Madrid: Iberoamericana, 1998).

8. Lynn Hunt, *Politics, Culture, and Class in the French Revolution* (Berkeley: University of California Press, 1984).

9. *Les Lieux de mémoire*, 3 vols., under the direction of Pierre Nora (Paris: Gallimard, 1984–1986).

10. Stathis Gourgouris, *Dream Nation: Enlightenment, Colonization, and the Institution of Modern Greece* (Stanford: Stanford University Press, 1996).

11. See Oscar Antúnez de Olivera, *Lista oficial de los Treinta y Tres patriotas* (Montevideo: Estado Mayor Conjunto del Ejército, Departamento de Estudios Históricos, 1975).

12. Isabel Wschebor, "Fe y razón en la pintura patriótica: Blanes y la Sociedad de Ciencias y Artes," in *Catálogo Juan Manuel Blanes: La nación naciente, 1830–1901* (Montevideo: IMM, 2001), 104.

13. A chronicler of the period wrote of the crowds that viewed the work, "The entire town—men, women, and children—marched in procession to admire the excellent piece of art. For days, a growing throng of people surrounded the painting." Agustín N. Benzano, *La obra pictórica de Juan Manuel Blanes: Reseña bibliográfica—exposiciones—conferencias—homenajes* (Montevideo: Impresora Uruguaya, 1947), 5–6.

14. Wschebor, "Fe y razón," 104.

15. Translator's note: the Spanish *patria* roughly translates into English as "fatherland" or "homeland." It comes from the same root as *patriot* and *patriotism*. One of the main differences between *patria* and its English equivalent is that *patria* is represented by a feminine image—usually the same sort of figure that stands for republicanism and that comes from the French Revolution's iconography—while the English version has male overtones. Since images and icons are at the heart of this chapter, *patria* is used throughout to convey the most accurate spirit of the original Spanish.

16. This is the case, for instance, of the poetic letter "sent" by Martín Fierro to Blanes. See José Hernández, "Carta que el Gaucho / Martín Fierro / dirige a su amigo / D. Juan Manuel Blanes / con motivo de su cuadro / Los Treinta y Tres" (circa 1878), in *Poesía gauchesca*, ed. and with a prologue and notes by J. L. Borges and A. Bioy Casares (Mexico City: Fondo de Cultura Económica, 1955). See also "Blanes y el cuerpo de la patria: Apuntes acerca de las imágenes fundacionales," in Achugar, *Planetas sin boca*, 181–200.

17. See José Pedro Barrán, *La historia de la sensibilidad en el Uruguay*, 2 vols. (Montevideo: Banda Oriental, Facultad de Humanidades y Ciencias de la Educación, 1989–1990). A clear example also comes from the ridicule of the Italian called the *papolitano* in José Hernández's *Martín Fierro*.

18. Geoffrey Bennington claims that national postal systems were foundational elements of both the narration of nation and its very makeup. In "Postal Politics and the Institution of the Nation," in *Nation and Narration*, ed. Homi K. Bhabha (London: Methuen, 1990), 121–37.

19. Some of these republican symbols took root in the movement for independence of the Low Countries in the seventeenth century. For more on symbolic repertoires and republicanism, see Acree's chapter in this volume.

20. Mercedes Carlota de Pardo, *Monedas venezolanas* (Caracas: Banco Central de Venezuela, 1973), 37.

21. Ibid., 38.

22. Guillermo Torres García, *Historia de la moneda en Colombia* (Bogotá: Imprenta del Banco de la República, 1945), 32.

23. Jorge Child and Mario Arango Jaramillo, *Bancarrotas y crisis: Colombia, 1842–1984, América Latina, 1981–1984* (Bogotá: Biblioteca de El Espectador, 1984), 72.

24. Ibid.

25. Konig, *El indio como sujeto y objeto*, 20.

26. Christophe was brought to Saint Domingue as a slave, and later became president and then king. He was a leading figure in the coup against Jean-Jacques Dessalines in 1806. His reign grew unpopular, and he eventually committed suicide.

27. Nicholas Fabre Geffrard and Michel Domingue were both presidents during the second half of the nineteenth century.

28. See Neil Shafer and George S. Cuhaj, eds., *Standard Catalog of World Paper Money*, 9th ed., vol. 1 (Iola, WI: Krause Publications, 2002), 107.

29. Shafer and Cuhaj claim in *Standard Catalog*, 106, that the image portrays Neptune, although they do not provide any evidence to support their claim. One has to consider the possibility that the image does not depict an indigenous

inhabitant of Brazil, but the presence of Neptune on the new bills does not seem to fit.

30. See Javier Uriarte, "Las fechas y la invención del sistema simbólico nacional en América Latina," in *Derechos de memoria: Actas, actos, voces, héroes y fechas; Nación e independencia en América Latina*, ed. Hugo Achugar (Montevideo: Universidad de la República, Facultad de Humanidades y Ciencias de la Educación, 2003), 341–400.

31. Banco Provincial de Buenos Aires, *www.bapro.com.ar/museo/bco_fund.htm*.

32. According to the Gran Logia de la Argentina (Argentine Masonic Lodge), however, there is another explanation for the inclusion of heroes from other countries in Argentine symbolic imagery: supposedly all of them were members of different Masonic lodges.

2

Words, Wars, and Public Celebrations

The Emergence of Rioplatense Print Culture

William G. Acree Jr.

By 6 December 1779, the deal had been sealed. After sitting inactive for more than a dozen years in the dark, dank basement of the University of Córdoba, the first and only printing press of the Cordoban Jesuits was unearthed and packed up to make the journey over to Buenos Aires. When the Jesuits were expelled from Spanish America in 1767, the press had only been in use for a year, producing materials for the acclaimed Colegio de Monserrat. It had been disassembled and hastily stored in the basement, with no care taken to prevent moisture from penetrating the wood or to package properly the lead type blocks. Only in 1779 was new interest shown in the press, ironically by a representative of the Spanish Crown—the newly appointed viceroy of the Río de la Plata, Juan José de Vértiz y Salcedo. Vértiz, whom the historian and one-time Argentine president Bartolomé Mitre later praised as the most progressive colonial official the colonies had seen, had the notion to create a *casa de niños expósitos* (orphanage) in Buenos Aires. After all, at the end of the eighteenth century, the city's population (and number of orphans) was rapidly expanding with the growing importance of Buenos Aires as a commercial port. Vértiz recalled that there was a press in storage in Córdoba (confiscated from the "ex-Jesuits," as the viceroy called them), and thought that he could finance this humanitarian venture by establishing a print shop in Buenos Aires in the same locale as the future orphanage.[1] He argued the case to Charles III, though nearly a year after the press had arrived in Buenos Aires and printing activity was well underway. The king approved and, in proper formal style, dispatched a royal certificate to Vértiz in which he wrote that the press would be "very useful and even necessary in that city," lavishing praise on him for "all you have done regarding this matter, giving you thanks for the notorious zeal with which you labor in the service of

God, and for me."[2] Neither the king nor the viceroy imagined that they were laying the foundation for the print shop that would be the birthplace of revolutionary print media during the wars of independence.

In mid-September 1779, Vértiz wrote to the rector of the Colegio Convictorio—formerly de Monserrat—in Córdoba to inquire about the condition of the press and to ask what it would be worth. The rector wrote back in a humble tone, stating that Vértiz could of course have the press, pay the Colegio what suited his fancy, and that, since there was no inventory detailing the parts of the press, it was hard to tell what was missing. Its condition, however, was not beyond repair, which was what the viceroy was looking for. On 16 October, Vértiz wrote back, saying he would take it, pay the Colegio what the ex-Jesuits had spent in the early 1760s, and asked him to set things in order for the press's voyage.[3] Finally, in December, the wooden boxes packed full of the press's parts were loaded into a covered cart owned by a certain Félix Juárez. Juárez directed his oxen along an old colonial commerce route traversing the pampas and arrived in Buenos Aires in February 1780.[4]

There, at the newly created orphanage-print shop named the Casa de Niños Expósitos, the viceroy financed the press's renovation, and before long it was turning out publications. By 1810, over 1,200 publications had been printed, including letters, official edicts, textbooks, Rousseau's *Social Contract*, bills of sale, and the Río de la Plata's first newspaper.[5] With the May revolution of 1810, the Niños Expósitos press became an instrument of the patriots. During the next decade, it fired off thousands of circulars, poems, newspapers, official documents, letters, patriotic songs, and books, all aimed at waging rhetorical war on the colonial power. By the early 1820s, the old press's type blocks were well-worn. It was time to move on. In 1824, Bernardino Rivadavia signed into law the new Imprenta del Estado, which would take over the work and some of the materials of the Niños Expósitos print shop. The old press at the shop was taken to Salta by the provincial commissioner Victorino Solá, who had recently celebrated a new contract with the up-and-coming writer Hilario Ascasubi.[6] Up in Salta, a remarkable occurrence of transubstantiation took place: in the late 1860s, the lead type blocks taken by the Salta commissioner were melted into a few hundred bullets that were used to fight off some of the last bands of *gauchos* (Rioplatense cowboys) then wreaking havoc in the northwest, led by Felipe Varela.[7] The historian and bibliographer Antonio Zinny lamented the trajectory—literally—of the type blocks of the old Niños Expósitos press. It began with the blocks as messengers of civilization, he wrote, and ended with them piercing the bodies of "barbarians."[8]

The "biography" of the Niños Expósitos printing press—from its birth during the late colonial period and its vigorous days of revolutionary youth in Buenos Aires to its old age and death among gauchos in Salta—outlines the two key moments during which Rioplatense print culture emerged, namely the wars for independence and the most profitable years of cattle culture. The revolutionary moment, spanning from the British invasions of the region in 1806–1807 to a time of relative peace in the early 1830s, saw the birth of print culture in the Plata and is the focus of this chapter.

This revolutionary moment of Rioplatense print culture imparted enduring characteristics. First, writing was employed as a weapon of war, used with aims to convince and condemn, with words of independence driving a veritable printing revolution as well as a revolution in forms of communication. Second, the newly sown emphasis on the importance of the printed word—promoted as a tangible sign of legitimacy—began opening up a new public sphere or meeting place that encouraged greater public interaction between the lettered classes and those (literate or not) who occupied lower positions in the social hierarchy, such as freed blacks, women, and slaves. Public libraries and patriotic celebrations were a part of this new meeting place. Lastly, print culture during the revolutionary moment was critical to the elaboration of new symbolic repertoires to accompany new republics that were evident in poetic military marches, national anthems, coats of arms, and constitutions. Throughout the wars of independence, the *letrados* (those who could manipulate the technology of writing) were the ones setting the parameters that the budding culture of print would follow. But even with the grip of the lettered classes on the shape of print culture during these years, the *unlettered* (so to say) interacted closely with print media by listening to public readings of wartime newspapers, participating in public celebrations where print was central, and by associating with new symbolic icons disseminated through print.[9]

By looking at a sample of oral and written components of print during the revolutionary moment in the Plata, we will see that the emergence of Rioplatense print culture is a story that begins with words and wars, is elaborated at patriotic celebrations, and is further transmitted with the creation of repertoires of national symbols spread through print. This story not only helps us understand a variety of reading practices whereby print affects behaviors and senses of identity, it also points to the beginning of a relationship between written culture and the public sphere in the Río de la Plata that to this day manifests itself as a uniquely clear public concern with reading and writing.[10] If the revolutionary moment defined this emergence, the reach of the wars, the notion of "independence" and the initial efforts to create "national" and "republican" discourses were in turn indebted to the words, celebrations, and symbols that gave life to print culture in the Plata.

Words and Wars of Independence

The history of Montevideo's first printing press is not as exciting as that of the "ex-Jesuit" press that ended up fighting gauchos, but it was a wartime press from the start. When the British invaded the Río de la Plata in 1806 and 1807, they were driven out of Buenos Aires to the surprise of all. In the rival port city of Montevideo, British soldiers were able to establish a foothold that, while lasting only six months, allowed the occupying forces and merchants to launch a print shop. In his colorful and casual style, the self-taught Uruguayan man of letters Isidoro de María relates "public opinion" toward the press in the early nineteenth century: "Bah! There was no need to speak of that. . . . For some broadsheet or almanac, the *factory* over at the Niños Expósitos in the viceregal capital was more than enough . . . to teach the *Christ* to one or another young fellow."[11] But things changed in 1807. "By chance, or maybe by the luck of the devil," De María tells us, referring to the establishment of the British print shop, "its first birth was a little newspaper titled *The Southern Star*. . . . 23 May 1807 was the day of the birth, but the little fellow was short-lived, because he gave up the ghost in July of the same year."[12] Indeed, the press the English brought was only active for a couple months; yet, during this short stint, the writers of the *Southern Star* introduced a new liberal, mercantilist attitude toward commerce in the port city and aimed to discredit the Spanish Crown's capacity to rule the colonies.[13] So effectively incendiary were its pages, published in English and Spanish, that the Audiencia of the Río de la Plata charged Mariano Moreno—one of the intellectual heroes of independence—with the task of writing a refutation of the paper's claims. Given that he agreed with most of them, this put Moreno in a difficult position, which he got out of by advising that silence was the best way to put an end to the spread of the *Southern Star*'s propaganda.[14]

The Audiencia did not leave things at that. In June 1807 it issued an edict—published of course by the Niños Expósitos press—that prohibited the sale, possession, or reading in public or private of the *Southern Star*, judged to be the most "pernicious," "seductive," and effective weapon for the achievement of its "evil" designs.[15] Anyone who came into contact with the paper or who had knowledge of others possessing or reading the damned *Southern Star* without immediately reporting it to the proper authorities would be judged a "traitor to king and state, and would face the irreversible punishment corresponding to this atrocious crime."[16] Words of independence were not taken lightly.

With the Niños Expósitos print shop doing a fair amount of business, and with its presses in need of spare type blocks, the prospect of acquiring the *Southern Star* press—abandoned by the British when they left the Plata—looked promising. The war between England and Spain had made the shipment of new parts from Europe to the Plata impossible. More importantly, the Audiencia believed that if it could wrench the press from Montevideo, it could put an end to the threat of malicious propaganda being spread in print in the future. So in September 1807, the *Southern Star* press, having been disassembled and packed up, was taken by boat across the river to Buenos Aires. There it gave new life to the Niños Expósitos shop, soon to be printing revolutionary material again (not what the Real Audiencia had in mind when it purchased the press), which made its way back into the Banda Oriental—the territory that would become Uruguay.[17]

The newspapers that appeared in the Río de la Plata during the wars of independence constitute our first stop. During the wars, daily, weekly, and monthly newspapers sprang up on both sides of the Plata river, and not just in the port cities of Buenos Aires and Montevideo. Interior provinces acquired printing presses and produced newspapers, broadsheets, and poems. The printing revolution was, in effect, a revolution in modes of communication.

For nearly a decade before the local junta provisional in Buenos Aires declared its representative authority over the provinces of the Plata in May 1810, the Niños Expósitos press had a monopoly on printing in the viceroyalty of the Río de la Plata. With the English invasions of the Plata and the crisis of the Spanish monarchy, politically charged publications grew in number and severity.[18] It was not difficult, then, for the sole press in Buenos Aires to change from being a royal press to a wartime press and instrument for the new governing junta. Its new role became quickly evident, publishing on 28 May 1810 the announcement of the removal of then-viceroy Cisneros, along with the junta's first official proclamation.[19] A little over a week later, Mariano Moreno's *Gazeta de Buenos Aires* entered circulation and served as the mouthpiece of the junta. The *Gazeta* was the longest-lived paper of the revolutionary moment in Spanish America, lasting until September 1821, but its printed version was not very accessible to the masses it had hoped to reach.

For the unlettered who could not access the *Gazeta* in print, its messages were publicly pronounced in churches and squares, and often in cafés and *pulperías* (country stores), too. In the same way citizens professed loyalty to their faith in church and learned religious doctrine, they likewise needed to learn about the junta in order to show due reverence, or so goes the circular sent by the junta to the provincial dioceses. Since many rural inhabitants would be unaware of the changes taking place in Buenos Aires, and since many lived in conditions that did not facilitate reading the paper, the junta ordered that priests "bring together the parishioners after mass and read them the *Gazeta de Buenos Aires.*"[20] This same vein of thought was present in Bernardo Monteagudo's call for "functionaries, enlightened citizens, those of the *delicate sex*, and *americanos todos*" to read the paper to workers, artisans, and soldiers. "Arms will not lead the way to improve our situation," writes Monteagudo in the 27 December 1811 issue. All citizens, he argues, must understand their duties to the patria in order to know and exercise their rights, but this hope will not be possible without educating those "whose humiliating heritage has always been ignorance. If only some passionate patriot would devote himself to writing a political catechism to be used for general education. Meanwhile, we do not have any other recourse save publicly circulated newspapers." What needs to happen, concludes Monteagudo, is for the central government to impose on local mayors "the strict obligation to bring together on holidays artisans and other workers in a public place known by all in order to read and explain to them the newspapers. Judges, too, should join priests in this commitment to share the papers with workers and people from the countryside."[21] Military leaders, likewise, should take care to have the papers read to soldiers wherever they are stationed.

Public readings of this type were not entirely new; they had occurred during the colonial era. What was new was their increased frequency, the *Gazeta's* revolutionary content, the reactions it provoked—specifically in the form of print media—and the *quantity* of similar publications that followed suit and were read publicly. Never before had the printed word filled the air as it did during the wars.

One of the earliest of these reactions came from the *Gazeta de Montevideo*, started in October 1810. The royalist holdout of Montevideo had been without a print shop after the *Southern Star* press had gone over to the other side three years earlier. Facing the growing threats of patriot forces from Buenos Aires and the cattle hands led by the caudillo José Artigas (who fought as much for independence from Napoleonic Spain as from the influence of Buenos Aires), and confronted with the propaganda filling the pages of the *Gazeta de Buenos Aires* and edicts printed by the Niños Expósitos, the *Cabildo* (town hall) of Montevideo decided that it needed a new press to combat the revolutionary words. Government leaders made a plea to Carlota Joaquina, living in Rio de Janeiro.[22] The *prospecto* of the paper, a common feature of many of the period's newspapers that served as a sort of introduction to the writers' purpose, sheds light on how the deal was struck between Carlota and the Cabildo. In light of the recent "popular commotion" across the river, one reads, the loyalty to Fernando VII demonstrated by the residents of Montevideo made it the subject of special recognition by the court of Brazil and Carlota. In order to make public the laudable character of Montevideans, Carlota sent a new press that was accordingly baptized as *La Carlota*.[23] As the prospecto goes on to say, and as epistolary exchanges between the Infanta and the Cabildo members manifest in the 13 October 1810 edition, Carlota was "interested in preserving the dominions of her august brother."[24] Thus, the new press was designed from its beginning to contribute to fighting the rebels in Buenos Aires and protecting the colonies for the dethroned Spanish monarch.

In this spirit, every Thursday the local government would publish the *Gazeta*, with news from Spain and its kingdom, royal edicts, and "all that could be of interest to the true Patriots."[25] In an early appropriation of the word *patriotas*—a term that would soon become the code name for those across América opposed to the royalists—the writers of the paper hoped to convince their readers to continue supporting the Crown and remain strong in the face of the changing tides coming from across the Plata. The prospecto continues, "This is precisely the goal the Government proposes with the paper that is here introduced to you . . . to gather news on all that occurs until calm is restored in the Viceroyalty, and publish it free from decoration and with the simplicity that characterizes truth, so that you see the outlines of your true Character."[26] If words were capable of causing a big enough stir in Buenos Aires to jeopardize the rule of the king, then words from Montevideo should have been capable of putting out the fire.

Words, writing, and print were precisely the theme of a short essay entitled "On the Press" that appears in the 6 November 1810 issue of the *Gazeta de Montevideo*. In this piece, a certain "Fileno" argues in a string of syllogisms that the *word* is the greatest form of exercising moral order, that *writing* is a way of fixing words, and that *printing* is the perfection of writing. According to this logic, claims Fileno, printing is a "moral" activity, necessary for the proper maintenance of human societies.[27] Given the importance of the word, writing, and print, "we can deduce that writing and the press cannot and should not serve to spread gossip or slander" against a person's moral character or, perhaps more urgently, one's government. Fileno argues that a free press should exist, but "the press should be free insofar as it is necessary to promote the positive side of our civilization" (that is, the side opposed to the trash emanating from Buenos Aires). When the free press is employed to speak ill of people, "healthy traditions," or "the decency of government," then it loses its moral character.[28]

Fileno's words, and those of other authors of the *Gazeta de Montevideo*, were part of the project to strike back rhetorically at the news coming from Buenos Aires and other parts of Spanish America that were on the verge of declaring self-rule. The *Gazeta*, however, was not the only paper printed in Montevideo or Uruguay during the revolutionary moment. From the establishment of the *Southern Star* press in 1807 to the signing of the constitution in 1830 (a year of short-lived peace in Uruguay), close to sixty different newspapers were published.[29] Even though most of these only lasted a few months to a year, and it was not until 1826 that printing presses produced newspapers outside of Montevideo, the proliferation of newspapers was significant for the war-torn Banda Oriental, as was the fact that by 1830 nineteen print shops had been or were still printing newspapers and other print media in Uruguay.[30]

Meanwhile, back in Buenos Aires, the presses were still hot, and the word *independence* was becoming more present in revolutionary rhetoric. In July 1812, the Niños Expósitos press began printing a new weekly paper—*El grito del Sud* (Cry of the South). *El grito* was the creation of the recently-founded Patriotic and Literary Society of Buenos Aires (a significant name for a group devoted to joining written culture to patriotic causes). The paper came off the press with guns blazing, as could be read on the first page, which was dated "1812, third year of liberty."[31] Opposed to every word printed in royalist papers like the "insipid rags" of the *Gazeta de Montevideo*, and speaking openly and without reservation of independence, the prospecto opens bluntly: "Whoever thinks that human suffering derives from origins other than those of slavery and ignorance is either a stupid imbecile or an impudent impostor."[32] As the prospecto continues, there is no mistaking who the target of this statement is: the Spanish Crown, responsible for bringing slavery, misery, and sadness to America. "But the time has arrived to throw off once and for all the weight of oppression," the writer goes on, "and for us to begin to enjoy and exercise those sacred rights that tyrants have so long denied us." In the good liberal spirit, these rights are enumerated as property, in the first place; liberty; and security. If the readers are disposed to make an effort "worthy of Americans" to maintain what had been achieved on 25 May 1810, then the miserable yoke could be cast aside forever. Of course, reading *El grito* was crucial to keeping the May spirit alive (or etching its meaning into tradition) and remaining free from misery. After the scathing attack on Spain and what the colonial years had done to Latin America, the writer concludes, "I have thus sketched the plan for a newspaper that some members of the Patriotic

Society of the Río de la Plata have pondered sharing with the public, convinced that print is the only means to propagating knowledge among the people."[33]

El grito, like the *Gazeta de Buenos Aires* started by Mariano Moreno, was written by lettered elites, most likely including the author of the future national anthem, Vicente López y Planes. The epigraph in Latin at the head of every edition is sign enough to suggest that the paper was not for the average reader.[34] That said, the authors of the *El grito* were aware of the need to reach those who could not understand the epigraph or, in many instances, even read the paper's contents. It was sold outside the city of Buenos Aires, which allowed for its messages to travel a certain distance into the interior provinces. Like the *Gazeta* and the decree announcing the importance of a free press, read publicly on 1 December 1811, *El grito*, too, was read aloud to crowds in cafés and on occasion in church.[35] In the 21 July 1812 issue, the editors even published a patriotic song titled "Marcha patriótica with Notes for the Intelligence of Vulgar People," followed indeed by five pages of notes.[36] How accessible they were to "vulgar people," or the unlettered, is another question. If none of these measures helped the masses to absorb *El grito*'s messages, they could drink in the patriotic spirit with a stop at the Niños Expósitos print shop to check out a portrait of the "republican patriot" and "sage magistrate" Mariano Moreno that was for sale there.[37] They might even catch on to the wonders of the printed word while there.

During 1815, a year before independence was formally declared for the provinces that would become Argentina, a handful of short-lived newspapers were started that called for independence once and for all. One of these was the appropriately titled *El independiente*. Like *El grito del Sud* and the *Gazeta de Montevideo*, *El independiente* paid tribute to the power of the printed word in its prospecto, recognizing that the paper's value relied on "the divine art of writing that gives permanent life to human knowledge."[38] Attributed to Mariano Moreno's brother Manuel, the prospecto highlights the importance this new form of print media: "Newspapers have become the touchstone of the national education of a people. . . . It is not so much the distance separating America from the center of knowledge [Europe] that has been the cause of its overdue enlightenment, as much as its lack of good newspapers."[39] *El independiente* only lasted four months, despite its editor's goal to write in a style accessible to all types of readers and its claims that the paper would live as long as a free press existed.[40] A similar venture of the same period was the newspaper *Los amigos de la patria y de la juventud*, a monthly that lasted six months. The introduction to the paper stated its main concern to be education. But the editor was more in-

clined to provide space for (French) literary selections, usually illustrative
of some moral point, and for questions dealing with war, even though the
paper was an advocate of peace. This presentation aimed to temper the hot
attitudes coming from papers like *El independiente*.[41]

The short lifespan of papers like *El independiente* and *Los amigos de la
patria* complicates assessment of their impact on readers. Their creators
had envisioned them reaching beyond the closed circles of lettered elites,
but with few issues circulated, *El independiente*'s epigraphs in Latin, and
Los amigos' urban tone, it is hard to imagine how their words would have
taken hold in the countryside or among illiterate city dwellers. Further
research on the newspaper publications of these years could help paint a
clearer picture of how they were consumed. Nevertheless, these papers,
along with scores of others, were central to the spread of information during the revolutionary moment. As such, they were part of print culture's
first inroads to opening a new public sphere linking lettered elites to the
popular classes. The quantity of papers that appeared in the public landscape and the multiple ways in which they were read were critical to the
dissemination of revolutionary rhetoric.

Throughout the decade stretching from May 1810 to the defeat of
the weak forces of central authority operating in Buenos Aires in 1820,
over forty newspapers (printed by the Niños Expósitos and other, newer
presses) appeared in the provinces that would form Argentina. During the
years that followed, leading up to Juan Manuel de Rosas's rise to power in
1829, almost two hundred more newspapers entered the scene, eighty of
which were published and circulated outside of Buenos Aires.[42] For lettered elites eager to spread republican values, the press became a symbol
of liberal progress, with the printed word lending legitimacy to their messages and hence their endeavor. Newspapers were key messengers of words
of independence and framers of Rioplatense print culture, but they were
not the only ones. They had help from new public libraries and patriotic
parties where print enjoyed a privileged, public place.

Print Culture, Public Places, and Patriotic Parties

The creation of the Río de la Plata's first public libraries was central to
the emergence of a culture of print during the revolutionary moment. If
newspapers took the first major step in this process by spreading words
of war, libraries aimed to broaden the reach of print and cement its connections to republicanism by opening a new public sphere where greater
public interaction could take place between lettered elites and the popular

classes. Patrick Joyce has studied this process in the case of nineteenth-century England. He stresses the importance of performing in public—the display of self—that was central to the creation of a public sphere in the early part of the century, claiming that freedom and the success of liberalism rested on the creation of "political legibility and visibility, meaning that each member of society could see the other. The idea of the *free* library," he argues, "was central to the creation of a new sort of public, one constituted in a civic, urban public sphere. . . . Open, and therefore transparent. . . . Transparency was also the key to its particular function as one variant of liberal community." Libraries, continues Joyce, extended the culture of self-knowledge and self-help to create liberal citizens—or at least that was one of their main objectives—and thus played into "a liberal ethics of governance."[43] These bonds between the legitimacy of republicanism, public access to knowledge, and a new kind of citizen operated in the creation of libraries in the Plata.

The first of these libraries to appear was the Biblioteca Pública de Buenos Aires, which became the foundation of the future national library. There is debate on whether or not Mariano Moreno deserves credit as the founder of the library, but something most scholars of Argentina agree on is the simple fact that setting up a public library during a time of war was a significant symbolic event.[44]

Moreno took charge of requesting book donations for the library's collection, as well as financial contributions from those who had the money and were willing to give to this new cause of public enlightenment. By the end of 1810, he had raised a considerable sum to pay librarians and gathered close to four thousand books, maps, and other materials for the initial collection. Thus, the creation of the library, while supported by the junta and organized by its secretary Moreno, was in effect a public effort made possible by the donations and contributions of Rioplatense inhabitants, albeit wealthy lettered elites.[45] By buying into the public library, they took out stock in the new revolutionary culture of print that was advertised on a daily basis in the *Gazeta de Buenos Aires* and other patriot papers. In this sense, the library was a symbol of the May revolution and of the emergence of a new form of communication. It represented the effort to stake a claim on intellectual independence—a metaphorical imperative to accompany the political independence sought by patriots.[46]

After multiple changes to the date for opening the library, things were finally ready in March 1812. A week before the inaugural day, advertisements of the event were sent out in a circular to priests, military figures, judges, the administrator of post offices, and other government officials.

They were charged with notifying others and requested to attend this act.[47] The inauguration took place on 16 March 1812, and it was a well-attended public act, complete with a military band, lofty speeches, and the presence of the junta's central political figures, all welcoming the new public place where people could mingle with print. Juan Manuel Beruti, who lived through the English invasions of Buenos Aires, the wars for independence, and the Rosas years, tells us in his memoirs that "an infinite number of citizens" were present at the opening ceremony.[48] News about the event in the *Gazeta* is more reserved: a short note that appeared on 13 March to remind readers of the upcoming celebration was the only mention made of the whole affair.[49] The same brevity characterized the news of the library in the 17 March number of *El censor*, a weekly that was an offshoot of the *Gazeta*. Curiously, the note announcing the opening of the new library— an institution meant to embody the liberal spirit of May—was paired with an advertisement for the sale of a slave who knew "something about cooking" by the secretary of the Cabildo.[50]

The foundation of the Biblioteca Pública in Montevideo was a much more dramatic event, celebrated with more pomp and a wealth of symbolic performances, and inseparable from the 1816 *fiestas mayas* (May celebrations). These fiestas, which were also called *fiestas cívicas*, were modeled on those that first took place in Buenos Aires from 23 to 26 May 1813. These were declared an annual patriotic celebration at the General Assembly meetings in Buenos Aires that May. The preface to the legislation of the fiestas reveals their intended meaning: "It is the duty of free men to immortalize the day the patria was born and to remind future generations of the joyous moment when the strength of the most intrepid broke the idol and overthrew the altar of tyranny."[51] This held true for the fiestas in Montevideo, too. They were meant to celebrate the *beginning* of the nation's new history in the process of being defined, in part by print and in part by ceremonies. While similar to the fiestas of Buenos Aires celebrated in 1813, the fiestas in Montevideo from 24 to 26 May 1816 were nonetheless recorded with more zeal.[52]

The anonymously written description of these events begins with the relation of the occurrences on 24 May, when patriots decorated their houses and buildings in the city with tricolor flags representing Artigas and the separation of the Banda Oriental from Buenos Aires. The four corners of the main town square (what is today the Plaza Matriz) were adorned with arches made of laurel branches and flowers. Four broadsheets with patriotic verses hung from these arches. The first two spoke of the valiant efforts of Spanish America to end the oppression of the Iberian lion. The third and fourth broadsheets' verses go beyond merely singing the praises of those who have thrown off the colonial yoke and instead refer to the importance of inscribing the incipient collective history of the Banda Oriental. Upon reading the verses of these last two broadsheets, passersby were encouraged to remember "the divine month of May" and consider the feats of soldiers from the Banda Oriental as a beacon for fellow Americans fighting in wars for independence.[53]

These publicly displayed printed verses did not go unaccompanied that day. From 7:00 a.m. to noon there was music and food, and around 8:00 a.m. schoolchildren from Montevideo entered the scene, prepared to sing patriotic tunes. After lunch, prisoners were released from jails, and, partaking in the day's ceremonies, "some black dancers appeared in the plaza . . . emulating each other in decency and dancing to express their gratitude for the festive day."[54] Later that afternoon, government officials, soldiers, and denizens attended a church ceremony, and at night they watched fireworks and a good "liberal" tragedy. Printed words appeared again the next day, albeit engraved in a symbolic pyramid rather than impressed on broadsheets. Composed by Bartolomé Hidalgo, author of the cielitos and diálogos that introduced the voice of the gaucho in print, the pyramid's verses celebrate 25 May as the day that "shackles and tyranny disappeared." More important than recognizing the date as the beginning of independence for Rioplatenses was the notion of creating a common history that had *started* on that day: Schoolchildren encircled the pyramid at dawn. In proper patriotic spirit and saluting the sun, they intoned a song that vocalized the gist of the monument's verses—thanks to that glorious day in May, oppression had ended for Americans, and since then inhabitants of the Banda Oriental have sung praise to the great patria. Activities continued throughout the afternoon and night and into the next morning, with a theater performance of Bartolomé Hidalgo's *Feelings of a Patriot*, food, and dance.[55]

On 26 May, the schoolchildren again huddled around the pyramid and chanted their patriotic songs from 10:00 a.m. until noon, at which time the Cabildo members augustly announced the inauguration of the Biblioteca Pública. Dámaso Antonio Larrañaga was a priest, a political representative of Artigas, and the newly appointed director of the Biblioteca. In his inaugural speech, he proclaimed that the doors of the library would open for all who were present: "Every class of people has the right and liberty to learn from all the sciences, no matter how noble they are. All will have access to this august repository of knowledge. Come all, from the most rustic African to the most learned European."[56] Aside from a place where citizens could "become enlightened," the new library would serve as a bedrock for republican ideals. That the library offered a new place of learning for citizens was true, but uncertainty about attendance and the beginning of the period of Brazilian and Portuguese occupation of the Banda Oriental in 1817 suggest that this quality was more rhetorical than concrete.[57] Recent scholarship on Afro-Uruguayans and lettered culture, however, lends weight to the notion that white males were not the only ones capable of taking advantage of the library's collection.[58]

Both the description of the fiestas and Larrañaga's inaugural speech were published in 1816 and sent throughout the Banda Oriental. Artigas acknowledged receipt of copies of both, musing that the fiestas and the library were means of properly forming men who would bring glory and happiness to the nation.[59] First with words of war and now with words of patriotic celebrations, print was becoming an embedded social practice open to more people than its mere producers. Indeed, textual production of both the poetic and documentary sort was a key part of the fiestas, transforming the momentary celebrations into more permanent symbolic events.[60]

Other patriotic ceremonies and celebrations organized during the revolutionary period further illustrate the role of print culture in constructing a new public sphere. José Antonio Wilde provides some valuable examples from Buenos Aires. During the fiestas mayas of 1823, the Literary Society, which had been created the previous year, offered a prize for the person who could best respond *in writing* to a set of questions loaded with the Society's view of indigenous groups in the Río de la Plata.[61] The compensation for the winner was a mere medallion, but then again, the reward of the competition was to come from sharing one's ideas through writing. Public display of pride through print was also part of the festivities held in Buenos Aires two years later, following the arrival in January 1825 of news on the battle of Ayacucho. As the printed word was deeply entrenched in the beginnings of the wars for independence, it was part of the fiestas marking their end (at least in most of Spanish America). On the night of 22 January, a "dramatic representation" was put on in the Teatro Argentino, after which the crowd went wild upon singing the national anthem. Then, in an act that was meant to lend legitimacy to the news, a certain Colonel Ramírez stood on one of the theater's balconies and read the official report of the battle. Wilde recounts that the crowd applauded this public reading with the same "frenzy" that filled people's hearts when they had sung the national anthem.[62]

Revolutionary Symbolic Repertoires

The floundering new government institutions that replaced the control of colonial ones over provincial affairs in the United Provinces and the Banda Oriental required new symbolic representations. Revolutionary print culture made possible the elaboration of symbolic repertoires. Furthermore, it was through print that these symbols reached "official" status or became *national* symbols. In turn, they gave another dimension to Rioplatense print culture in the revolutionary moment. The words of war allowed new forms of communication to take root (figuratively and literally) in the Plata. A second dimension came with the role of print in public ceremonies and institutions like libraries. The elaboration of symbolic repertoires privileged print media as the premier form of communicating national iconography. These repertoires included poetic compositions and songs as well as thematic anthologies called *parnasos*, national flags and seals, and legal documents such as declarations of independence and constitutions. Whether or not such symbols successfully represented "the nation" and the diverse communities that were grouped as *Argentinos* or *Orientales*, they were widely disseminated through print.

Loose-leaf poems, publicly posted verses, and thematic tomes such as *La lira argentina, o colección de las piezas poéticas dadas a luz en Buenos Aires durante la guerra de su independencia* (The Argentine Lyre, or Collection of Poetic Pieces Published in Buenos Aires during its War for Independence) helped to establish a set of dates for the construction of national history and cultivate a symbolic vocabulary to describe oppressive tyrants, valiant military heroes, and reverence for the patria. Patriotic verse was central to what some scholars identify as the first stage on the road to the construction of national symbols in Spanish America. From the outbreak of the May revolution to 1830, creole elites attempted to put in place a new set of symbols to replace those that had accompanied colonial power.[63] Revolutionary newspapers chipped away at the old set of symbols, but their news sections, convoluted essays, and reprints of foreign newspapers did not provide the necessary material (concisely packaged) to craft new symbols. This is where verses came into play—sometimes in the very same newspapers, sometimes as loose sheets, and sometimes as songs.

Independence generated a wealth of verse that went hand in hand with the efforts of new government institutions to develop policies on "national" culture.[64] These poetic constructions both appropriated the colonial past to craft it into a new national history, and spoke of the birth of nations during independence, each with its own tabula rasa. Indeed, establishing a national poetic discourse and imaginary was as important as drafting laws for the new republics.[65] This was the case in Argentina, where the massive *Lira argentina* and a constitution were published in 1824. Similarly, in Uruguay the 1830 constitution was followed by the *Parnaso oriental* of 1835. More than just compilations of poems written by compatriots, suggests Hugo Achugar, these collections of symbolic verse constitute an ideological and cultural referent that only lettered elites had the power to shape, yet whose contents were beacons of collective identity for all social sectors.[66]

A case in point comes from the origins of *La lira argentina*. In 1822, Bernardino Rivadavia—a champion of liberalism in all its manifestations and at the time minister of the nascent United Provinces government—issued a decree outlining the government's plans to celebrate independence by publishing a volume of all the patriotic poetry written in the United Provinces since 1810—a year that, thanks to the verses, grew to mark a starting point for referring to "national" history. The goals of this initiative were clearly expressed: "Presenting poetic productions under this patriotic light will not only contribute to animating public sentiment, but it will also illustrate the level of good literary taste our country has achieved in its early stages. . . . Such a collection . . . is without doubt a monument of the most appropriate sort to celebrate the anniversary of the declaration of our independence."[67] The decree goes on to say that Rivadavia will be in charge of selecting the poems "worthy" of publication, that the collection will be printed in a distinguished volume, and that the government will foot the bill for the printing costs.[68] Rivadavia's plan did not come to fruition. However, his idea inspired the supposed editor of *La lira*, Ramón Díaz.

According to the note that opens the anthology, the collection is meant to nourish public spirit with the distinguished efforts of the editor's compatriots, and "pay due homage to the decision of a people to remain steadfast in the fight for independence."[69] The editor was serious about paying homage: some two thousand copies of *La lira* were printed in Paris and then shipped to Buenos Aires.[70] All of the compositions had been printed before—many in newspapers or pamphlets put out by the famous Niños Expósitos press—but their re-collection in *La lira* gave them renewed vigor and raised their status to that of official verses. Authors included Esteban de Luca, author of the popular "Canción patriótica" around 1810, Bartolomé Hidalgo, and Cayetano Rodríguez, who had been involved with the creation of the public library in Buenos Aires. Also among the group was Vicente López y Planes, whose "Marcha patriótica" had already become part of the national symbolic repertoire by being declared Argentina's national anthem.

José Antonio Wilde described the debut of the "Marcha" at the 1813 fiestas mayas, but his observations do not point out the reach of the poem's vocabulary or the significance of its performance. In Susana Poch's formulation, national anthems—more than just military tunes or patriotic poems—are efforts through writing to develop a set of meanings for a community, and this was certainly true of López's "Marcha."[71] This type of writing was often first shared with the public in fiestas patrias or through songs in collective ceremonies. Through their performance, thanks to their messages, and with the force of the law behind them, these songs became sacred written and sung tributes to the nation, providing emotional content for the foundation and maintenance of community. López y Planes's poem was published in loose-leaf by the Niños Expósitos, with a headline at the top stating it to be the *only* "marcha patriótica" for official use in the United Provinces.[72] It was later performed as part of the fiestas mayas. From there, as the official anthem (of a nation that did not yet exist), the "Marcha" accompanied San Martín as his troops spread to fight royalists throughout what would become Argentina, Chile, and Peru.[73]

The year 1813 was fruitful for symbolic production in Buenos Aires, for in addition to the marcha patriótica, the General Assembly ordered up a "national" seal or coat of arms (Figure 2.1). The seal was first used on official documents in place of the colonial seals, and then given a larger role as the representative emblem of the Assembly, which in turn claimed to collectively represent the nation.[74] This seal underwent modifications throughout the nineteenth century, but its initial character is still intact, blending European influence with reference to indigenous American societies. In Estanislao Zeballos's friendly history of the seal, he remarks that "the ideals that were on all our minds were *Liberty*, *Equality*, and *Fraternity*; they inspired the *National Anthem*, and they are synthetically embodied in the coat of arms."[75] Though an exaggerated statement, he touches on the importance of liberalism as a source of inspiration for both symbolic verses and seals.

The new coat of arms quickly made its way from the Assembly's printed communications to the public sphere. Beruti records that in May 1813, a "superior order" called for the removal of all the Castilian coats of arms dotting schools, forts, and government buildings. The "great coat of arms of the nation of the United Provinces of the Río de la Plata" was supposed to go in their place.[76] The elements of the new seal were not just confined to paper, either. From the printed page the seal was brought to life, so to say, guiding people's mode of dress at the fiestas mayas that year. During the fiestas, members of the Buenos Aires government wore red Phrygian hats just like the one depicted in the seal. The public joined in the performance too, "donning Phrygian caps for hats. The effect of this on good patriots, men and women alike, was that all continue wearing the cap. When not worn on the head, men use it as a cockade with other hats, and women do the same or pin it to their bosom."

In July of the same year, the Assembly printed an edict announcing to the public that the seal would be disseminated through yet another medium—"national" coins. The new coins, minted in the silver town of Potosí, had the seal without the sun on the front side; the sun covered the reverse side and was encircled by the words "In union and liberty."[77] This so-called national currency was short-lived, but it attests to the ways in which print culture was diffused throughout the Plata. What began as a seal to be used on official documents of the General Assembly became a national coat of arms and the basis of a design for a currency that began putting symbolic content in the hands of lettered and unlettered classes. By the end of 1815, shortly before independence was officially declared in Argentina, the seal had become one of the defining characteristics of the *Gazeta de Buenos Aires*, appearing at the top of the front page of every number of the *Gazeta* until its last impressions in 1821 (Figure 2.2).[78]

Similar to the Argentine one, the seal that appeared in the Banda Oriental during Artigas's time also portrayed the rising sun, though presiding over a scale of justice instead of a pike and Phrygian cap (Figure 2.3). "Provincia Oriental" is inscribed at the top, and encircling the sun and scale is the motto "With liberty I neither offend nor fear." This seal, too, was part of public ceremonies. The schoolchildren who animated with song the fiestas cívicas in 1816 carried the tricolor flag and wore tricolor Phrygian caps.[79] According to the anonymous author of the *Descripción de las fiestas cívicas*, the last night saw the debut of "a first-rate flag, and the coat of arms of the Banda Oriental was placed on the main façade" of the Cabildo.[80] The coat of arms was also stamped on documents and circulated through print, like the description of the fiestas and Larrañaga's speech inaugurating the library.

This seal was used on and off from 1816 up to the design and implementation in 1829 of what would become, with few modifications, the current Uruguayan coat of arms.[81] During this period of close to fifteen years, the seal represented provincial independence from Buenos Aires, resistance to and independence from Portugal and Brazil, the celebrated arrival of the Thirty-Three Uruguayans to the shores of Uruguay in 1825 (see Chapter 1), and the declaration of independence in the same year. In early 1829, the General Assembly established a special commission to come up with a new seal in preparation for the upcoming events to swear in the constitution. And in a display of the spirit of Uruguay's new national symbolic repertoire, the seal was stamped on copies of the *acta* (declaration) of indepen-

Figure 2.1: 1813 Argentine coat of arms, from Estanislao S. Zeballos, *El escudo y los colores nacionales* (Buenos Aires: Imprenta, Litografía y Encuadernación de J. Peuser, 1900), 46–47.

Figure 2.2: The new national seal at the head of the *Gazeta de Buenos Aires*, fascimile ed., vol. 4 (Buenos Aires: Compañía Sud-Americana de Billetes de Banco, 1912), 409.

dence, distributed during an "allegorical" performance of the declaration put on during the festivities to celebrate the signing of the constitution in 1830.[82]

Declarations and constitutions (both dependent on writing and print) were central to the elaboration of symbolic repertoires, too. These types of legal documents legislated patriotic fervor expressed in symbolic verse and bound citizens to the written and printed letter of the law. The declarations are unique in this regard. They serve as the hinge, suggests Susana Poch, "between the official poetic discourse of national anthems and the judicial discourse of constitutions."[83] The Argentine declaration, issued in July 1816, was a publishing phenomenon for declarations of independence. The congressional session that drafted the document and signed it into law ordered it to be printed in Spanish (1,500 copies), Quechua (1,000 copies), and Aymara (500 copies)—not a bad run for this period.[84] It is questionable how many Quechua and Aymara speakers could read the versions printed in these languages, but they were surely read aloud.

Figure 2.3: *Escudo de armas de la Provincia Oriental*, from Andrés Lamas, *El escudo de armas de la ciudad de Montevideo* (Montevideo: Talleres de A. Barreiro y Ramos, 1903), 56–57.

In addition to declaring independence from Portugal, Brazil, and any other tyrant, the Uruguayan declaration called for the need to destroy written and printed documents that bore any mention of the occupation of the Banda Oriental from 1817 to 1825. Given how Uruguayans abhor even the memory of the documents that correspond to that period of despotism, stated the declaration, government representatives of the towns that have archives of these memories "will gather on the first holiday with the parish priest, residents, and the notary, secretary, or whoever it is that records in writing events for the court, and, following the public reading of this decree, will erase from the first line to the very last signature such documents."[85] After this ceremony was performed, the same representatives had to send to the provincial government proof (written or printed) that they had indeed destroyed the documents. That holidays were chosen for these celebrations to occur is significant, for it was then that the largest public could join the representatives, priest, and notary in the collective act of erasing the traces of memories and past symbolic repertoires and preparing for a new one to accompany the independent Banda Oriental. Fortunately for scholars today, not all the documents were destroyed. The symbolic copying of this declaration was part of the public ceremonies organized for the 18 July 1830 signing of the constitution.

Isidoro de María, who told us about the first press in Montevideo, was present for the scene of merriment in the Plaza Matriz that July. The plaza was well-decorated, with national flags dotting every corner. Foot soldiers and cavalrymen were decked out in their color-coded uniforms (white and blue, like the flag). Government leaders stood on the balconies of the Cabildo and onlookers packed the plaza and covered rooftops despite the chilling cold of mid-July (Figure 2.4). Religion was also part of the ceremony, with a *Te deum* sung to accompany government members as they walked toward the cathedral. After performing their religious duties, they headed back to the Cabildo to sign the constitution.[86]

What followed was truly a spiritual act, blending religion with a newly established reverence for written culture as the legitimate embodiment of the infant state. After the leaders of the government swore their allegiance to the constitution in the main salon of the Cabildo, soldiers were called in from the plaza, followed by the "sovereign People" to make their pledge to the constitution. There they stood in front of a state official who asked them, "Do you swear to God and promise to the Patria that you will fulfill all the obligations that correspond to you as a citizen and on which depends the Constitution of the Uruguayan State, sanctioned . . . by the representatives of the Nation? Do you swear to uphold and defend the Representative Republican form of Government that the Constitution establishes? If you do, God will be on your side; if not, He and the Patria will demand as much."[87] The crowds of people pushed and shoved to have their turn to take this oath and pronounce the moving "yes, I swear"— some demonstrating their faith in God and patria, and others probably out of fear of saying no and having God and patria "demand" from them the proper respect.

The ceremony ended with cannon fire that mightily signaled the power of the printed word as rule of law, but that was not the end of the celebration. That afternoon and night the party continued, and "there

Figure 2.4: Sketch for the *Jura de la Constitución de 1830* (1872) by Juan Manuel Blanes. Image courtesy of the Museo Histórico Nacional, Montevideo, Uruguay.

was not a soul alive . . . that did not make his way to the plaza to watch the lovely *comparsas* [theatrical groups that would become key performers at carnival] . . . that . . . performed on the stage decorated with arches and sky-blue ribbons." One of the participants read a poem by Acuña de Figueroa, author of the future national anthem, admonishing citizens to live by their freshly sworn word to the grave. Commemorative medals were distributed, and loose leaves of patriotic poetry "were thrown like flowers to that world of spectators bent on catching one." In the San Felipe theater, which according to De María's description was overflowing, two poets read patriotic verses. Thus, like the morning ceremony, the night ended with the crowd joining in the collective act of praising the written word, which in turn contributed to solidifying the foundation of print culture in Uruguay.[88]

The emergence of Rioplatense print culture dovetails with and is defined by the wars of independence. It is the story of words of independence, patriotic parties, and the creation of new symbolic repertoires that combined to initiate a revolution in forms of communication. Beginning with words as weapons of war printed in revolutionary newspapers, poems, and edicts at the outset of the nineteenth century, presses like the Niños Expósitos in Buenos Aires and the *Southern Star* and La Carlota in Montevideo sparked a printing revolution in the Plata. While these print media presented news on the developments of the wars, they also affected public sentiment and public behaviors by inspiring patriots and condemning royalists, when not the other way around. The press and the printed word represented liberal notions of progress and lent legitimacy to republicanism, too. Print culture was further elaborated at patriotic parties and public ceremonies, where print was central. Whether at the fiestas mayas or the opening of the library in Buenos Aires, or the signing of the constitution in Montevideo in 1830, these ceremonies and the events and institutions they celebrated provided a new meeting place where lettered elites communicated with the unlettered. Print was central to the creation and spread of new symbolic repertoires as well. Symbolic verse such as national anthems, national symbols such as the coat of arms, and legal documents such as declarations of independence and constitutions—all depended on print for their messages to be successfully communicated.

In sum, Rioplatense print culture was defined by the revolutionary moment—but the claim is incomplete without remarking that print, in turn, defined the reach of the wars and the initial meanings that *independence* and *nation* would take on in Argentina and the Banda Oriental. By 1830, words, wars, and patriotic parties had laid the foundations for print culture in the Plata. For roughly the next forty years, until state institutions became stable around 1870, Rioplatense print culture would be taken in new directions, defined by new words, new wars, and gauchos.

NOTES

1. Bartolomé Mitre, *Ensayos históricos* (Buenos Aires: La Cultura Argentina, 1918), 200; José Torre Revello, *Orígenes de la imprenta en España y su desarrollo en América española* (Buenos Aires: Editorial Araújo, 1940), 214; Juan Canter, *La imprenta en el Río de la Plata: Síntesis histórica* (Buenos Aires: Imprenta de la Universidad, 1938), 38–39.

2. Canter, *La imprenta en el Río de la Plata*, 43.

3. Archivo Histórico de la Provincia de Buenos Aires, *Orígenes de la imprenta de Niños Expósitos* (La Plata: Taller de Impresiones Oficiales, 1941), 1–4.

4. Ibid., 5–6; Mitre, *Ensayos históricos*, 201, 208.

5. Guillermo Furlong, *Historia y bibliografía de las primeras imprentas rioplatenses, 1700–1850*, vol. 3 (Buenos Aires: Librería del Plata, 1959), 14. See also examples in Carlos Heras's introduction to Archivo Histórico, *Orígenes de la imprenta de Niños Expósitos*, xxi–xxiii; and Juan María Gutiérrez, *Origen y desarrollo de la enseñanza pública superior en Buenos Aires*, rev. ed. (Buenos Aires: La Cultura Argentina, 1915), 388–93.

6. Canter, *La imprenta en el Río de la Plata*, 67.

7. Miguel Solá, *La imprenta en Salta: Cien años de prensa (1824–1924) y bibliografía antigua de la imprenta salteña* (Buenos Aires: Tall. Gráf. Porter Hnos., 1924), 42–45. See also Canter, *La imprenta en el Río de la Plata*, 67–68. In *La edición de libros en la Argentina* (Buenos Aires: Editorial Universitaria de Buenos Aires, 1995), 29, Leandro de Sagastizábal suggests that the melted lead formed the

bullets used to pursue the montoneras headed by the mythic Facundo Quiroga, but with Quiroga acting in the early 1830s, this claim does not fit well with the press's fifty years of production in Salta.

8. Solá, *La imprenta en Salta*, 44.

9. For scholarship on the history of printing in the Plata, see Mitre, *Ensayos históricos*, 181–99; Canter, *La imprenta en el Río de la Plata*, 15–26; and Torre Revello, *Orígenes de la imprenta*, 117–22. More recent work includes that of François-Xavier Guerra, Rebecca Earle, Iván Jaksic, and Paula Alonso. On the broader subject of print in Latin America, the most widely cited analysis is Benedict Anderson, *Imagined Communities: Reflections on the Origin and Spread of Nationalism*, rev. ed. (London: Verso, 1991), 47–65. Anderson's model for understanding the connections between print media and incipient national communities during the wars of independence has been a constant point of reference for scholars dealing with this period of Latin American history. Critical assessments can be found in John Charles Chasteen, introduction to *Beyond Imagined Communities: Reading and Writing the Nation in Nineteenth-Century Latin America*, eds. Sara Castro-Klarén and John Charles Chasteen (Baltimore: Johns Hopkins University Press; Washington, DC: Woodrow Wilson Center Press, 2004), ix–xxv; and Claudio Lomnitz, "Nationalism as a Practical System: Benedict Anderson's Theory of Nationalism from the Vantage Point of Spanish America," in *The Other Mirror: Grand Theory through the Lens of Latin America*, eds. Miguel Angel Centeno and Fernando López-Alves (Princeton: Princeton University Press, 2001), 329–59.

10. This argument is fleshed out in William G. Acree Jr., "From Reading to Reality: Print Culture, Collective Identity, and Nationalism in Uruguay and Argentina" (PhD diss., University of North Carolina at Chapel Hill, 2006).

11. Isidoro de María, *Montevideo antiguo, tradiciones y recuerdos*, vol. 2 (Montevideo: Ministerio de Instrucción Pública y Previsión Social, 1957), 61.

12. Ibid., 61–62. *The Southern Star / La Estrella del Sur*, facsimile ed., with a prologue by Ariosto D. González (Montevideo: A. Barreiro y Ramos, 1942).

13. Juan Canter, introduction to *Gazeta de Montevideo*, facsimile ed., vol. 1, Biblioteca de Impresos Raros Americanos (Montevideo: Facultad de Humanidades y Ciencias, Instituto de Investigaciones Históricas, Universidad de la República, 1948), xxxix, xlix.

14. Ibid., l. See also Acree, "La otra batalla: *The Southern Star*, la *Gazeta de Montevideo* y la revolución de las formas de comunicación en el Río de la Plata," in *En torno a las "invasiones inglesas": Relaciones políticas y culturales con Gran Bretaña a lo largo de dos siglos*, eds. Ana Frega and Beatriz Vegh (Montevideo: Facultad de Humanidades y Ciencias de la Educación, 2007), 13–22.

15. *Bando de la Real Audiencia de Buenos-Ayres*, 12 June 1807, Impresos de los Niños Expósitos, Tesoro, Biblioteca Nacional, Argentina.

16. Ibid.

17. Canter, introduction to *Gazeta de Montevideo*, lvi. The name *Banda Oriental* refers to the "eastern bank"—the territory located east of the Uruguay river. Inhabitants of the Banda Oriental identified themselves as *Orientales*. After the declaration of Uruguayan independence in 1825, this adjective was—and still is—used as a synonym for "Uruguayans."

18. Examples can be found in Furlong, *Historia y bibliografía*, 141–43, 216–17, 228–30.

19. Ibid., 240–44, 321–25.
20. Narciso Binayán, ed., *Ideario de Mayo* (Buenos Aires: Editorial Kapelusz, 1960), 137.
21. *Gazeta de Buenos Aires*, facsimile ed., vol. 3 (Buenos Aires: Compañía Sud-Americana de Billetes de Banco, 1911), 71.
22. Carlota, daughter of the Spanish king Charles IV and Fernando VII's sister, had been married at age ten to the Portuguese prince João (later João VI as king).
23. *Gazeta de Montevideo*, facsimile ed., vol. 1 (Montevideo: Universidad de la República, 1948), 3 [8 October 1810].
24. Ibid., 7–8.
25. Ibid., 3.
26. Ibid., 4.
27. Ibid., 42 [6 November 1810].
28. Ibid., 42–45.
29. Wilson González Demuro is doing groundbreaking research on the press in the Banda Oriental during this period. See his "*El sol de las Provincias Unidas*: Un comentario sobre el periodismo, la revolución y la difusión de ideas en Montevideo a fines de la época colonial," *Colonial Latin American Historical Review* 13, no. 1 (2004): 53–87; and "Un gallego en los orígenes del periodismo independentista: Antonio Díaz y la prensa montevideana, 1814–1823," *Anuario del Centro de Estudios Gallegos* (2006), 87–104. See also Antonio Praderio, *Indice cronológico de la prensa periódica del Uruguay, 1807–52* (Montevideo: Instituto de Investigaciones Históricas, Universidad de la República Oriental del Uruguay, Facultad de Humanidades, 1962), 3–40.
30. Between 1826 and 1830, seven presses sprang up outside the city of Montevideo. The parts and type blocks for these presses, as well as for the new ones appearing across the river, came from a complex combination of sources. Many components were inherited or bought from print shops that had folded—ones that had acquired materials from the United States and, after the wars, Europe. Other parts were made from scratch by carpenters and ironworkers.
31. *El grito del Sud*, facsimile ed., with a prologue by Guillermo Furlong SJ and a preliminary study by Enrique de Gandía, Periódicos de la Epoca de la Revolución de Mayo (Buenos Aires: Academia Nacional de la Historia, 1961), 45.
32. Ibid., 47. The 27 October 1812 issue (173–80) directly addresses what was printed in "esos insulsos papelorios"—that is, in the *Gazeta de Montevideo* (173).
33. Ibid., 48–50.
34. The epigraph, from the first book of Tacitus's *Histories*, reads, "It is at rare moments of good fortune when one can think how one wants and say what one thinks," an appropriate choice of words for the moment of independence.
35. Enrique de Gandía, preliminary study to *El grito del Sud*, 16.
36. *El grito del Sud*, 63–68.
37. Ibid., 255.
38. *El independiente*, facsimile ed., with an introduction by Guillermo Furlong and a preliminary study by Enrique de Gandía, Periódicos de la Epoca de la Revolución de Mayo (Buenos Aires: Academia Nacional de la Historia, 1961), 33.

39. Ibid., 33–36.
40. Ibid., 41.
41. Enrique de Gandía, preliminary study to *Los amigos de la patria y de la juventud*, facsimile ed., with an introduction by Guillermo Furlong, Periódicos de la Epoca de la Revolución de Mayo (Buenos Aires: Academia Nacional de la Historia, 1961), 19.
42. Juan Rómulo Fernández, *Historia del periodismo argentino* (Buenos Aires: Librería Perlado, 1943), 219–26.
43. Patrick Joyce, *The Rule of Freedom: Liberalism and the Modern City* (New York: Verso, 2003), 100, 129–30.
44. See José Armando Seco, "Los primeros tiempos de la Biblioteca Pública," in *Anuario de historia argentina, año 1941* (Buenos Aires: n.p., 1942), 602–5; and Ricardo Levene, *El fundador de la Biblioteca Pública de Buenos Aires* (Buenos Aires: Ministerio de Justicia e Instrucción Pública, 1938).
45. Levene, *El fundador de la Biblioteca*, 34.
46. Ibid., 34, 64.
47. Ibid., 115–16.
48. Ibid., 61, 114. Juan Manuel Beruti, *Memorias curiosas* (Buenos Aires: Emecé, 2001), 210.
49. *Gazeta de Buenos Aires*, vol. 3, 146.
50. *El censor*, facsimile ed., with an introduction by Guillermo Furlong SJ and a preliminary study by Enrique de Gandía (Buenos Aires: Academia Nacional de la Historia, 1961), 92. For more on the discourse of advertisements, especially regarding marginalized communities, see Chapter 11.
51. *El redactor de la Asamblea de 1813*, facsimile ed. (Buenos Aires: La Nación, 1913), 30, 35–36. See also José Antonio Wilde, *Buenos Aires desde 70 años atrás* (Buenos Aires: EUDEBA, 1950), 196–97.
52. *Descripción de las fiestas cívicas celebradas en Montevideo, Mayo de 1816. Oración inaugural pronunciada por Larrañaga en la apertura de la Biblioteca Pública de Montevideo, 1816*, facsimile ed., with an introduction by Edmundo M. Narancio (Montevideo: Facultad de Humanidades y Ciencias, Instituto de Investigaciones Históricas, Universidad de la República, 1951).
53. Ibid., 6–7.
54. Ibid., 7.
55. Ibid., 9–11, 13–14.
56. Ibid., 29–30.
57. In *Montevideo antiguo*, vol. 1, 122, De María tells us that the library had two thousand volumes by 1818.
58. See Acree and Alex Borucki, eds., *Jacinto Ventura de Molina y los caminos de la escritura negra en el Río de la Plata*, with a prologue by George Reid Andrews (Montevideo: Ediciones Linardi y Risso, 2008; 2nd ed. forthcoming); Alejandro Gortázar, "Del aullido a la escritura: Voces negras en el imaginario nacional," in *Derechos de memoria: Nación e independencia en América Latina*, ed. Hugo Achugar (Montevideo: Facultad de Humanidades y Ciencias de la Educación, 2003), 189–263; and Gonzalo Abella, *Mitos, leyendas y tradiciones de la Banda Oriental* (Montevideo: BetumSan Ediciones, 2001), 49–103.
59. *Descripción de las fiestas*, 66–69 [letters from Artigas to Larrañaga and from Artigas to the Cabildo de Montevideo].

60. Clara Paladino, "Fiesta y contrapunto: Miradas en las celebraciones de la independencia en América," in *Derechos de memoria*, 126, 135.
61. Wilde, *Buenos Aires*, 212.
62. Ibid., 179.
63. José Emilio Burucúa and Fabián Alejandro Campagne, "Mitos y simbologías nacionales en los países del cono sur," in *Inventando la nación*, eds. Antonio Annino and François-Xavier Guerra (Mexico City: Fondo de Cultura Económica, 2003), 433–74.
64. Hugo Achugar, "Parnasos fundacionales, letra, nación y Estado en el siglo XIX," in *La fundación por la palabra: Letra y nación en América Latina en el siglo XIX*, ed. Achugar (Montevideo: Universidad de la República, Facultad de Humanidades y Ciencias de la Educación, 2003), 43.
65. Ibid., 50.
66. Ibid., 54.
67. Quoted in Pedro Luis Barcia, "Estudio preliminar," in *La lira argentina*, ed. Pedro Luis Barcia (Buenos Aires: Academia Argentina de Letras, 1982), xii–xiii.
68. Ibid., xiii.
69. Ibid., 7–8.
70. Barcia, "Estudio preliminar," xxi.
71. Wilde, *Buenos Aires*, 195–96; Susana Poch, "Himnos nacionales de América: Poesía, estado y poder en el siglo XIX," in *Fundación por la palabra*, 79–133.
72. Impresos de los Niños Expósitos, Tesoro, Biblioteca Nacional de Argentina.
73. Poch, "Himnos nacionales," 99.
74. Estanislao S. Zeballos, *El escudo y los colores nacionales* (Buenos Aires: Imprenta, Litografía y Encuadernación de J. Peuser, 1900), 10. See also Binayán, *Ideario de Mayo*, 228; and Luis Cánepa, *Historia de los símbolos nacionales* (Buenos Aires: Editorial Albatros, 1953), 129–54.
75. Zeballos, *El escudo y los colores*, 13.
76. Beruti, *Memorias*, 231.
77. Ibid., 232, 234–35.
78. See the *Gazeta de Buenos Aires*, vol. 4, 409 and after.
79. De María, *Montevideo antiguo*, vol. 1, 121–22.
80. *Descripción de las fiestas*, 17.
81. See Andrés Lamas, *El escudo de armas de la ciudad de Montevideo* (Montevideo: Talleres de A. Barreiro y Ramos, 1903), 56–58; Ricardo Goldaracena, *El libro de los símbolos: Escudos y banderas del Uruguay* (Montevideo: Arca, 1995), 69–94; and "Escudo de armas de la República Oriental del Uruguay, ley de su creación," Archivo General de la Nación, Archivos Particulares, Caja 333, Carpeta 1.
82. Javier Malagón, ed., *Las Actas de independencia de América*, with a preliminary study by Charles C. Griffin (Washington, DC: Unión Panamericana, 1955), xv.
83. Susana Poch, "Aura de inicio, trazas de escrituras: Actas de independencia de América (1776–1903)," in *Derechos de memoria*, 77.
84. Malagón, *Las actas de independencia*, viii.
85. Ibid., 131.
86. De María, *Montevideo antiguo*, vol. 2, 342–44.
87. Ibid., 344–45.
88. Ibid., 345, 347–51.

3

Novels, Newspapers, and Nation

The Beginnings of Serial Fiction
in Nineteenth-Century Mexico

Amy E. Wright

Serial novels constitute the majority of narrative fiction written in Mexico from the 1840s to the 1870s. While in literary histories these novels are often relegated to a category of inferior literature, I argue that these texts functioned as important instruments for the construction and dissemination of national models, and thus served as a fundamental tool in the early phases of the nation-building process in Mexico.[1] In this chapter, I explore the circumstances surrounding the appearance of the first serial novels in Mexico, as written by Justo Sierra O'Reilly and Manuel Payno, in order to begin to establish the similarities and differences between this occurrence in Latin America and Europe.[2] In this transmission of cultural codes, the concepts of *nation* and *novel* were intertwined in a relation of near-symbiosis: by the second half of the nineteenth century, "civilized" nations were supposed to produce novels as an increasingly important component of national expression, while novels had their own crucial role to play in the creation of nations.

As a form of communication, narrative has been privileged as a powerful mode of persuasion. Communications theorists have proposed that messages provided in narrative form are more effective than direct, didactic persuasion.[3] This principle is not by any means a new discovery; in the first half of the nineteenth century, intellectuals in Mexico, like their Latin American and European counterparts, began to place new value on narrative messages and discuss the merits of the novel as a powerful means for reaching a broad public.[4] Conversations between Hispanic classicists and romantics during the first half of the nineteenth century reveal an ideological divide with regards to the fledgling genre. While classicists tended to reject the novel as an upstart genre—an illegitimate mix of the classic forms of epic, drama, and poetry—intellectuals with progressive aesthetic and political tastes more frequently embraced its possibilities in form and function.[5]

The classicists' disdain for the novel as a young genre left it open to definition at the hands of the authors who chose to cultivate it. The Mexican intellectual Vicente Riva Palacio quipped that during the 1840s, writing novels in Mexico "was the work of Romans," referring to the "heroic effort" involved in the difficult and marginalized task.[6] Though an uphill battle, it was a worthy one for those with energy and inclination, for the novel's popularity among readers was impossible to ignore. This made it an appealing vessel for the articulation of progressive visions of nation—a great concern of the historical moment in which the novel entered the culture of Europe and the overseas colonies.

Like their European contemporaries, Mexican elites were in search of ways to cultivate a sense of nation within the country's territorial borders. Official freedom from Spain after the long wars of independence translated into an immediate need to unite a vast territory notable for extreme geographical and cultural diversity. But as daunting as these physical realities were, the internal landscape of colonization was equally imposing. As was the case in the other former Spanish colonies, nation-builders in Mexico were confronted with a populace that had been trained by several hundred years of colonial rule, and the roots of the mental colonization of these subjects went much deeper than the more immediate changes to Mexican laws and political systems would indicate. Thus, the elites faced the monumental task of preparing the horizon for the conception of a cohesive nation in the minds of the Mexican people.[7]

For the first time, the inhabitants of the lands now called *Mexico* were to be considered constituents, as opposed to subjects. Thanks to the new Enlightenment forms of thought, often termed in writings of the time as the *spirit of the century*, Mexicans were thought to be newly liberated from the bonds of oppression and tyranny. The connection between the new republican government and citizens hinged on a common spirit and interests emanating from a so-called inherent national "character," rooted in the romantic school of thought in vogue among liberal elites of the time (see Achugar's chapter in this volume). Citizens needed to be able to recognize enlightened government over tyranny, and, in order to do so, they first had be educated in the ideas of "self-governance." This imperative arose around the middle of the century, when educational infrastructure was lacking, literacy rates were low, and the average citizen had had little exposure to the concepts of republicanism or national sovereignty. Sociopolitical chaos had, in fact, been the norm since the beginnings of the fight for independence.[8]

The elites were in search of national models that would unify the linguistic, religious, and ethnic differences that marked their country. Finding consensus around these models, however, was no simple endeavor. Since the outbreak of the movement for independence, Mexican elites had been deeply divided over what form of government the new nation should adopt.[9] While most intellectuals agreed that a consensual idea of nation was paramount to order and a prerequisite for their country's progress, the exact terms of how to achieve these goals were unclear. By the middle of the century, the serial novel would have a large part to play in the proposal and exploration of ideas of nation for the broadest audience possible.[10] Given its flexibility as a container for multiple discourses and its possibilities for mass dissemination—inherent in its very conception as a hybrid between literature and journalism—this new narrative format was particularly poised to play a role in the nation-building process.

The story of the serial novel is traditionally considered to have begun in Paris in the mid-1830s, on the front pages of newspapers such as *La presse* and the *Journal des débats*. French editors initiated the form for the purpose of increasing readership of the newspaper. This first manifestation of the nineteenth-century serial novel was called the *feuilleton*, or *folletín*, and was typically published in the bottom portion of newspapers' front pages. Since its appearance, critics have tended to use the terms *novela por entregas* (literally, a novel in installments) and *folletín* interchangeably, when in reality they refer to two different phenomena.[11] As the nineteenth-century European serial novel was first conceived and published in the folletín format, it is natural that the two terms have come to substitute one another. Yet, the distinction of the *folletín* as a type of serial novel is significant because not all serial novels were published in periodicals.[12] In fact, by the time Spaniards began writing and publishing serial novels around the mid-1840s, editors and bookstore owners had appropriated the lucrative *folletín* concept and turned it into a new commercial phenomenon: they contracted the author they deemed to have the most potential for guaranteeing subscribers, and the serial novel began to be published in pamphlet-type installments that were delivered to subscribers' homes.[13] By this time, the serial novel was nonetheless associated with the newspaper format in which it first appeared. This ongoing association would continue to shape the understanding of the novel as a genre, influencing authors' conceptions and readers' expectations as well as editors' marketing strategies, for the serial novel was intimately linked to the lively world of the nineteenth-century newspaper. The boundaries between the news and the novel in early newspapers were remarkably permeable, and serial novels frequently featured the same mixing of multiple discourses as the nineteenth-century newspapers.[14]

Mexico provides a fascinating case study of the early association of novels, newspapers, and nation that predates significantly the first European serial novels, in the particular case of Fernández de Lizardi ("The Mexican Thinker") and *El Periquillo Sarniento* (The Mangy Parrot), widely recognized as the first novel of Mexico and Latin America.[15] *El Periquillo* was first distributed in serial form, thus anticipating the French serial novel by exactly twenty years.[16] It had been, however, created under entirely different circumstances and constituted a different creature than the nineteenth-century European serial novel. While the latter was conceived by French editors to increase newspaper sales, Lizardi's project had been conceived by the author himself, who operated in the simultaneous roles of newspaper editor and novelist and chose to write "fictional" prose in order to avoid the strict censorship that his nonfictional writings had begun to attract. Lizardi's project was an outgrowth of the thriving pamphleteering press that had arisen during the struggle for independence from Spain and the spread of printing technologies, a process that was described in detail in Chapter 2 in relation to the Río de la Plata. In short, Lizardi conceived his project as a way to address a wider audience in order to influence their thoughts and behaviors in new ways.[17]

The success of Lizardi's *El Periquillo* created a link between the Mexican novel and the early newspaper journalism from which it arose.[18] The newspaper symbolized freedom of expression, and so the first Mexican novel was by association a site for the exposition of progressive social ideas. The bourgeoning press industry in late colonial Mexico created an energetic space for creativity and insurgency that is credited with fostering and supporting the debate surrounding the Mexican struggle for independence. The urgency of the information in these papers—news that spoke directly to the realities of the Mexican people—attracted a public that consisted of readers as well as listeners, for it included the literate as well as the large illiterate population of Mexico City. Beginning in the late colonial period, these newspapers were read aloud regularly in public spaces such as taverns and plazas, as well as in private spaces, such as in the evening around the fire or by candlelight before going to bed.[19]

Indeed, Lizardi initiated more citizens than ever before into reading novels. Before *El Periquillo* reached the city streets, novels had been scarcely available to a limited readership of Mexican elites who read European works such as Surville's *Emilie* and Goldsmith's *The Vicar of Wakefield*.[20] These novels were published in book form, and since they were imported, they were expensive and subjected to a strict system of censorship before their late arrival in the Spanish colonies. By the time the censorship was lifted, book prices remained high relative to those in Europe due to the poor quality and expense of local paper production, as well as the high price of importing better-quality volumes from Europe.[21]

Public perceptions of the book format in Mexico were likely shifting during the period in which *El Periquillo* appeared. Vogeley hypothesizes that the colonial reader would associate the material object of the book with Europe; thus the reactions of individual readers towards the book would depend on their political views, which played a part in the determination of their relationship to the written word. For creoles who were critical of colonial domination and desired cultural liberation, the book would be seen as an expression of the colonializing power of print, thus making the publication of a Mexican novel in periodical form more appealing given its association with the popular and often revolutionary medium of the newspaper.[22] With the innovation of publishing an original creole novel using the printing press with which he had issued numerous political pamphlets and newspapers, Lizardi revolutionized the literary scene in Mexico City, making the novel more accessible to elites as well as to the small middle and large lower classes that made up the majority of the city's population. The serial novel's connection to the newspaper made it more affordable for the general populace, who saw the news as a necessity, as opposed to the novel in book form, which was seen as a luxury. Its ephemeral form also made it easier to pass from reader to reader, a common practice in those days.[23] The novel's division into easily readable sections made it more manageable for those who worked (the incipient middle class), in addition to making it more convenient to read out loud to others. Thus, the first Mexican novel's publication in serial form granted it a far broader readership than the European novels that had been previously imported to, published, and read in Mexico.

With the consolidation of independence in the decade of the 1830s, Mexican cultural life began to shift from what Vogeley terms a pervasive "colonized discourse" toward more open expression.[24] *El Periquillo Sarniento* was published for the first time in its entirety, for example, in the year 1830 (its first and second editions had been truncated due to prohibitions from the Mexican Inquisition, illustrating that Lizardi's efforts to avoid censorship through the use of the novel form were not entirely successful). The lifting of commercial restrictions imposed by Spain during the colonial period and the gradual establishment of steady trade with various European nations meant that literary currents arrived more freely and in a more timely manner. Romantic tendencies began to influence Mexican tastes and culture beginning in the early 1830s, and associations for the promotion of culture and based on the freedom of assembly began to flourish in post-independence Mexico.[25] The most established groups at this time were tertulias in the Mexico City homes of Francisco Ortega and the Conde de Cortina, and the Academia de (San Juan de) Letrán, founded in 1836 by Guillermo Prieto and others, brought these early groups together into an organization whose overarching purpose over time was seen as the "Mexicanization" of literature.[26] The Mexican serial novel of the 1840s would come out of the literary efforts of these associations, which followed in the spirit of Lizardi and reinforced the connection between early narrative fictions and the newspaper.

Mexican elites, like their Spanish counterparts, had been reading works in French and English or in translation well before the advent of the serial novel, but beginning in the 1830s, French and English novels that had been translated into Spanish were more available than ever before.[27] Their demand in Spanish America was sufficiently high that the French publishing houses recognized a business opportunity, hiring French-to-Spanish translators to work from France so that they could release the newest novels in the Spanish-speaking world at the same time they were introduced in Paris.[28] Both Spain and the new republic of Mexico were equally dependent on the French publishing houses for novels. This fact did not go unnoticed by Mexican intellectuals, who began to decry the lack of a national novel written for, by, and about Mexicans. Literary associations such as San Juan de Letrán formed the nuclei of the earliest complaints.[29]

These literary associations provided an environment that fostered collaboration and provided the support of a group, and it was in this creative haven that post-Lizardi narrative got its start. The gatherings provided a necessary space for authors to discuss and develop their ideas on formal issues such as style, genre, and influences, as well as on issues involving national cultural needs. The group environment facilitated writers' camaraderie and productivity within a larger sociopolitical climate that otherwise proved difficult for artistic production.[30] These groups often included members of all aesthetic and ideological persuasions; this was certainly the case with the Academia de Letrán. It was in these groups, too, that the first native narratives were cultivated—the fruit of the disputes aired between classicists and romantics over literature's nature and purpose. In sum, the majority of literary activity in the 1830s came out of these associations, with the members of Letrán becoming the most prominent journalistic and literary figures of the day.[31]

The members of these new literary associations began to publish periodicals, sometimes called *revistas*—another tangible result of the cultural freedom of the new decade.[32] These journals varied widely in content and reinforced the early association of novels and periodicals in Mexico. They also fomented the idea of fictional narrative as a space for musings on the nation, contained in the ephemeral press. Like earlier newspapers, cultural revistas often mixed scientific information with news and anecdotes, though most privileged "literary" content.[33] They published long short stories and novellas alongside poetry and theatre reviews. Most of the narrative fiction was translated, but toward the end of the decade the first Mexican narratives began to be published.[34] One of the first revistas to include Mexican narrative was Ignacio Rodríguez Galván's *El año nuevo ... presente amistoso* (1837–1840), a literary periodical in which some of Letrán's more progressive members (like Rodríguez Galván himself) had begun to publish their own romantic-inspired narrative. These short stories and novellas were the precursors of the full-length serial novel in both form and content. Since books remained expensive even some fifteen years after *El Periquillo* had been published in newsprint, the serial format was more viable and attractive for readers and editors.

Manuel Payno is most often credited in literary histories as the first Mexican novelist after Lizardi. He stands out as one of the most frequent contributors to literary periodicals during the 1840s, and is a prime example of how authors conceived of their role during the post-independence period. Payno first published his work regularly in various revistas like *El siglo diez y nueve* (1841–1896), *El museo mexicano* (1843–1844), *El ateneo mexicano* (1844), and *Revista científica y literaria de Méjico* (1845–1846), and he exhibited the frequent combination of letters and politics so typical among nineteenth-century elites.[35] His prolific contributions to the revistas were interrupted only by voyages abroad in service of the government.[36] These trips increased his exposure to literary currents outside of Mexico, particularly in Europe and more specifically France. In 1844, Payno wrote a review that praised the accomplishments of the French serial novel as practiced by Eugène Sue.[37] A year later, Payno published the first installment of his serial novel *El fistol del diablo*.[38] It is this publication that has earned Payno the title, among literary scholars, of "the first Mexican novelist after Lizardi." The first edition of the novel was left unfinished, however, when the *La revista científica literaria* ceased publication in 1846, and *El fistol* was not published in the version read today until 1887.[39]

Meanwhile, in the Yucatán, Justo Sierra O'Reilly (1814–1861) had co-founded a regional cultural newspaper whose inaugural edition featured the initial installment of a novel called *Un año en el Hospital de San Lázaro* (A Year in the Hospital of San Lázaro), completed in 1849. This novel is rarely discussed or recognized as the first to be completed in Mexico after Lizardi; Payno, not Sierra, is most often credited as the first Mexican novelist after Lizardi in national literary histories. There is evidence of some resentment towards Sierra O'Reilly in Mexico City and among Mexico's centrists for his having gone to the United States to plead for help during the Yucatán's *Guerra de las Castas*, so it is possible that the lack of national attention to Sierra is related to his image as a turncoat or traitor to Mexico.[40] For the remainder of this chapter, my purpose is to highlight Sierra's preeminent role in the creation of the Mexican novel through an exploration of the circumstances in which Sierra's first novels arose, as well as his regional and national political involvement. In Justo Sierra O'Reilly we can immediately recognize the combination of novels, newspapers, and the nation that we have seen beginning with Lizardi in 1816 and continuing through the formation of literary associations and cultural revistas in the 1830s.

From 1840 to 1850, Justo Sierra O'Reilly emerged as the most prominent figure in Yucatecan letters, during the same period in which he became involved intensely in local and regional government.[41] From a respectable though modest background, Sierra O'Reilly attended both the Universidad Literaria de Mérida and the Colegio de San Ildefonso in Mexico City on scholarship before receiving his doctorate in law in 1838. While in Mexico City during the 1830s, it is likely that he was exposed to the literary associations and cultural revistas that were thriving during that decade.[42] Two years after his return to the Peninsula, he co-founded the literary association recognized as Yucatán's first, El Museo Yucateco. Shortly thereafter Sierra O'Reilly and the co-founders of El Museo began to publish a revista with the same name, which entered circulation in 1841 with the stated purpose of promoting letters, arts, and science in the region.

El museo yucateco, printed from 1841 to 1842, is the Yucatán's first literary newspaper. In the words of the twentieth-century Mexican novelist and statesman Agustín Yáñez, the publication was "extremely important, and until this day [the mid-twentieth century] one of the most excellent literary reviews of the Peninsula; one of its objectives was to 'encourage our compatriots to cultivate a fondness for the study of literature.'"[43] In this inaugural cultural newspaper, Sierra O'Reilly shows some of the first literary indications of his intense interest in Yucatecan history, for he authored several short stories and novellas based on historical traditions of the region.[44] Though Yáñez stresses that *El museo* contained "not one word about politics," it is notable that Sierra O'Reilly's cohorts in his early literary efforts were also leaders in Yucatecan government.[45] Two of his most frequent collaborators in the 1840s were Manuel Barbachano—at one point the acting governor of the Peninsula—and Vicente Calero Quintana, who held various positions in the regional and national governments. The members of this group—of whom Sierra O'Reilly has been recognized as the "most enthusiastic collaborator and the soul of the publication"—collectively shaped the aesthetic and cultural currents emanating from the urban centers of Yucatán.[46]

The early 1840s also saw the beginning of Sierra O'Reilly's entry into Yucatecan political life, as secretary to don Sebastián López Llergo in his fight against the centrists in the 1840 siege of Campeche. With the initiation of the publication *El museo yucateco* in 1841, Sierra O'Reilly's long-term balancing act between literature and politics began. Speaking of this combination, Yáñez writes, "In addition to this work of superior quality [his literary production during the year and a half *El museo* lasted], political obligations had him editing *El espíritu del siglo*, a revista that served as the messenger of the Mendista party during the 1841 electoral campaign."[47] Sierra did not always view his decision to enter politics at that time as a positive one. At least one biographer has suggested that Sierra's cultivation of literature and history served as a refuge from and compensation for his political activities, which were tied to the combination of circumstance and necessity caused by the sociopolitical crises of the Yucatán in the early 1840s, as well as the sense of duty inspired by Sierra O'Reilly's close relationship with his father-in-law, Santiago Méndez Ibarra, a principal actor in Yucatán politics during the tumultuous period from 1833 to 1858.[48] Simply stated, Sierra O'Reilly had married inextricably into the chaotic political life of his region and nation.

Indeed, Sierra O'Reilly began to write novels during some of the most tense times in the history of the Yucatán Peninsula. He started composing his first full-length novel in January 1845, *Un año en el Hospital de San Lázaro*, the flagship folletín of the new literary paper that he had co-founded and edited, *El registro yucateco*. The years of *El registro's* publication, 1845–1849 (the years during which Sierra wrote the novel), saw a continual threat to the very sovereignty and social existence of the Peninsula.[49] Federalist and centrist conflicts had escalated since Santa Anna assumed Mexico's presidency in 1844, causing Sierra O'Reilly to express clear concern for the future of his patria chica by 1846: "I suffer greatly . . . thinking about my country, its fate, my future, my shortcomings, and everything that points to the fatal position of our disgraced Yucatán."[50]

In 1847, the infamous period of ethnic uprisings associated with Yucatán's Caste War began.[51] Studied closely in Terry Rugeley's chapter in this volume, the Caste War would last until the beginning of the twentieth century. It was in 1847, too, when Sierra O'Reilly's father-in-law Méndez Ibarra reassumed the governorship of the Peninsula. Due to ongoing conflicts between centrists and federalists, President Santa Anna refused to respond to Yucatán's pleas for help with uprisings, so in 1848 Méndez Ibarra sent his son-in-law as a diplomatic envoy to the United States, where Sierra O'Reilly stayed for close to a year. His requests for aid were ultimately futile, and it was then that he began to rue his initial involvement, commenting upon his impotence and appearing permanently embittered with politics as a means of helping the Yucatán.[52] Centrists operating in Mexico City were quick to condemn Sierra O'Reilly for having accepted this mission. It should be remembered that at the time, inhabitants of the Peninsula did not yet consider their region to be part of the Republic of Mexico.[53] It seems natural, then, that Sierra O'Reilly's concerns for his country would be focused on the Yucatán, and that his effort towards a national novel would therefore focus on the known territory of his patria chica.

The novel that Sierra O'Reilly was writing during these years asserted Yucatecan reality through narrative fiction. An epistolary novel set in the 1820s, *Un año en el Hospital de San Lázaro* describes the plight of Antonio, a Yucatán youth straying from the path provided to him by his upstanding father. His rebellious acts lead him to temporary social perdition when he finds himself quarantined in a Campeche leper colony. The novel serves as a sort of bildungsroman of its protagonist, Antonio, a nineteenth-century version of the prodigal son.[54] At the same time, it deals with specific social issues that had plagued the Peninsula from the time of its 1542 conquest by the Spanish to Sierra O'Reilly's day.

First and foremost, the epidemic of piracy is examined as symbolic of the Peninsula's abuse at the hands of "greedy 'foreigners'" who selfishly pillage and pilfer its wealth. This motif is carried over into the numerous misguided authority figures who do more harm than good to the community they supposedly serve. These agents of Spanish colonial power are embodied in the thoughtless administrators of the Campeche leper colony where Antonio is imprisoned. *Un año* also critiques the generalized ignorance and lack of education among all the social classes on the Peninsula, particularly in the area of human health and hygiene. This ignorance causes the egregious mistreatment, and even persecution, of those who are sick. Combined with the evil machinations of the outsider pirate Frasquito, Antonio's own naiveté and desire for rebellion are the explicit causes of the illness that has taken over Antonio's body, just as cancerous social ills have invaded the Yucatán Peninsula and threaten its demise. The protagonist offers a telling description of himself and this tragedy: "A youth of good birth, educated with great care and attention, who suddenly sees himself converted into the hero of an odious drama of pirates, adventurers, bandits, and prostitutes, finding himself condemned to await the final catastrophe of exile, far away from that which he most loves, abandoned and banished from society."[55]

While the victim Antonio bears the autobiographical signs of Sierra's impotent sojourn in the United States, his story is most strikingly the story of the Yucatán Peninsula itself, a body torn apart from within by conflicts between centrists and federalists and the violence of the Caste War. Like Antonio, the Yucatán Peninsula was abused from without, having suffered for centuries at the hands of outsiders as an outlying territory that received all the negative effects of Spanish rule but was frequently overlooked in the Crown's distribution of benefits to the colony. During the nineteenth century, Yucatán appeared more than ever as an isolated pariah, dismissed by Santa Anna's Mexico in its requests for autonomy and then abandoned by Mexico and ignored by the United States in its pleas for defense from the Indian uprisings.

The response of the victimized Antonio is to defy the spurious authority of his keepers—the doctors at the leper colony—and flee. Rather than accept his ordained destiny to die in quarantine, the rebellious hero escapes with the hope of wrongful diagnosis, believing that his true illness, syphilis, is scientifically curable (syphilis and regulating diseased communities are focal points of González Espitia's chapter in this book). At the end of the novel, Antonio is vitally redeemed for these efforts to save himself from misinformation and repression. Notably, the happy ending is made possible through the help of a small circle of stalwart friends from the same social class as Antonio, representative of the core group of Enlightenment thinkers on whose *hombría de bien* Peninsular progress depends.[56] The novel's overall mood is one of prolonged threat and longed-for conciliation: the patriarchal order is restored in the end after numerous twists of plot and unexpected coincidences designed to build suspense. In the fashion of the quintessential serial novel, Sierra O'Reilly uses suspense to keep readers interested until the very last page of the last installment.

It is crucial to note that in the same year this serial novel began to appear, one of *El registro's* editors, Vicente Calero Quintana, dedicated two essays to the history of the novel and its purposes in society.[57] In "Reflections on the Novel," Calero Quintana offers praise of the increasingly popular form of the serial novel, which he credits with giving the novel a philosophical weight so sublime that it approaches the force of religious teaching. This assertion may seem sacrilegious for its time and context, but Calero Quintana is speaking solely in terms of the serial novel's didactic power. "Understood in this light," he commented, "its study is imminently moral, and for portraying traditions and customs as they are, and proposing the example of how they ought to be, it is clear beyond any doubt that societies have much to gain from the novel in public and private spheres." Calero Quintana holds forth optimistically on the future of the novel in Mexico, citing the authors who had written for Mexico City's *El año nuevo* (by then defunct) as deserving of laurels from the patria. He closes with an appreciation of the possibilities that the Yucatán offers for the cultivation of the novel, for "in the incursions of the pirates, there are memories and traditions and news that are worthy of conservation."[58]

Calero Quintana's article serves, among other purposes, to justify the publication of *Un año en el Hospital de San Lázaro*, a tale that would speak graphically of the ills of syphilis and the "immoral" acts by which it was acquired, most likely to the great shock of the revista's subscribers. Calero combats potential reaction by tacitly inscribing the serial novel and those who would cultivate it into a long lineage of moral servants to the patria, citing the legacy of the Academia de Letrán and stressing the gravity of the serial novel's purpose in society. He also emphasizes that the simultaneous depiction of extreme good and extreme evil, far from encouraging the latter, is meant to educate readers in the consequences of vice and the codes of appropriate behavior. If the author succeeds in this task, says Calero, the highest possible purpose of the novel has been achieved. Calero's second essay, "The Novel, Theater, and Christian Morals," also published in 1845, reiterates many of the previous essay's arguments, while emphasizing at least one additional idea: Horace's precept of *dulce et utile*. The novel can be considered useful and complete if it successfully combines the critical teachings of philosophy and religion with the entertainment of its readers.[59]

Both pieces by Calero Quintana are intended to guide readers toward a full appreciation of the purpose of the serial novel that they are reading. In its lively presentation of past "reality" and captivating versions of Yucatán heroes and villains, *Un año* succeeds in painting a picture of what life in the nation should and should not look like. In addition to its evocation of the past, the novel produces a future space in which readers can imagine a different version of their society. Both spaces are carefully mediated by the narrative voice, which provides consistent commentary and guidance in the interpretation of images. These lessons are offered in close conjunction with the elite intellectuals' ideas on the forms that progress and modernization should assume on the Yucatán Peninsula.

With *Un año en el Hospital de San Lázaro*, Sierra O'Reilly offers a new kind of contribution to his region and to the nation of which it would later form a part. The presence of an autochthonous novel was increasingly seen as a contribution to the nation: civilized nations had prominent novelists, and the novel was on its way to being considered as an important accessory to national culture—a sign of its sophistication, power, and progress. The elites would also find empowerment in the cultivation of a form—the novel—that was European in origin but could be successfully adapted to subjects and concerns that were distinctly Latin American. This process of appropriation and adaptation would also symbolize the elites' ability to take charge of and master their own representation both to themselves and the outside world. In the same year of *Un año's* publication, Prieto decried the lack of a national novel, lamenting that Mexicans would rather read about the French than their own social reality, which he felt they wrongfully disdained.[60] Meanwhile, Sierra O'Reilly was writing a novel that would show, as Calero Quintana had indicated, Yucatán's possibilities for *nation* and *novel*: the "beautiful material" it offered for fictional representation was intended to guide its readers in the ways of modernity at the same time it strategically emphasized an abundance of characteristics that distinguished the culture as first "Yucatecan" and then "Mexican."[61] Indeed, it was this affirmation of a unique set of national characteristics that legitimized the nation's very existence.[62] Sierra O'Reilly's second novel, also published in the folletín format and considered the first historical novel written in Mexico, demonstrated similar characteristics. Appearing in Sierra O'Reilly's third literary newspaper, *El fénix*, from 1848 to 1851, *La hija del judío* (The Jew's Daughter) examines Yucatán's colonial past in search of explanations for the conflicts and difficulties of its present, again providing readers with heroes, heroines, and villains to emulate and avoid in order to progress toward a better future.

In closing, the first Mexican full-length novels after Lizardi's *El Periquillo Sarniento* appeared in 1845, almost simultaneously with the serial novel's appearance in Spain in the years between 1840–1845.[63] The authors of these first novels built directly on the foundation of Lizardi's legacy; they too envisioned, yearned for, and actively worked toward the creation of an enlightened nation. Their life stories were a mix of public work and literary contribution through their involvement in cultural associations and their interest in fictional narrative. This simultaneous cultivation of letters and participation in government reiterates the intimate relationship between the novel and the nation in the early days of both. So from the matrix of newspaper culture and the example of Lizardi, and from the literary associations that fostered the first romantic-inspired novellas alongside the European traditions of historical, costumbrista, and serial novels, a novelistic tradition in Mexico arose.

The strength of the serial novel as a tool in nation building was born out of the genre's initial connection with the already established and in-creasingly powerful newspaper industry. As Angel Rama argued, news-papers played an essential role in the evolution of the nation, for they eventually allowed authors to achieve economic—and thus ideological—independence from the state or state-related patronage.[64] As figures who to a certain extent achieved this independence, Manuel Payno and Justo Sierra O'Reilly were precursors to the later nineteenth-century leaders who, in the words of Jean Franco, changed the "sites of struggle" over na-tionalism: "A secular intelligentsia—whose base was the press and pub-lishing houses—were to become the main force in defining the nation and its future."[65]

As most Mexican serial novelists were public figures or government officials, all would use the serial novel to expound on their ideas of na-tional "essence." The content of their proposals vary, but in all the cases one element stands out: serial novels written in Mexico in the first half of the nineteenth century were geared toward proposing an imaginary repertoire—a new language and structure of behavior for their readers. Authors like Sierra O'Reilly intended for their narratives, delivered in the form of the serial novel, to play a crucial role in the most subjective and elusive piece of nation formation: the cultivation of a subject's willingness or desire to form part of a nation. This creative, imaginative component of the nation goes beyond the establishment of territory and government, and requires a willingness on the part of diverse individuals to sacrifice their own needs for those of the group.[66] The understanding of what it means to be French, Spanish, or Mexican, and the desire to associate with that iden-tity requires conscious inculcation. In the case of Mexico in the 1840s, the elites were at the stage in the nation-building process of proposing and cir-culating competing repertoires for the supposed national "essence." With the serial novel, an author could carry this debate into a broader circle than before and influence readers with his (and only occasionally her) particular proposal for national identity. The majority of nineteenth-century novels in Mexico were first published in serial form; yet, despite significant read-ership from the mid- to late-nineteenth century, they have been frequently dismissed in twentieth-century literary histories. The serial novel and the authors who cultivated it merit closer attention for their foundational role in the nineteenth-century construction of the modern nation throughout the Hispanic world.

NOTES

1.   See critics' discussions up to the 1940s as described in Mariano Azuela, *Cien años de novela mexicana* (Mexico City: Ediciones Botas, 1947), 15–20; J. Lloyd

Read's overall assessment of the period in *The Mexican Historical Novel,*
1826–1910 (New York: Instituto de las Españas, 1939), 80–133; and Anthony R.
Castagnaro, *The Early Spanish American Novel* (New York: Las Americas, 1971).

2. This effort is part of a larger project where I examine the transatlantic
dissemination of nineteenth-century ideals of nation and novel between Europe
and the overseas European colonies: Amy E. Wright, "Subscribing Identities:
The Uses of the Nineteenth-Century Serial Novel in Spain and Mexico,
1840–1870" (PhD diss., Brown University, 2006).

3. See Walter Fisher, *Human Communication as Narration: Toward a Philosophy of*
Reason, Value, and Action (Columbia: University of South Carolina Press, 1987);
and Stephen W. Littlejohn, *Theories of Human Communication* (Albuquerque:
Wadsworth, 1999).

4. Two Mexican intellectuals writing on this at the time were José María Heredia,
"Ensayo sobre la novela," *Miscelánea: Periódico crítico y literario* (1832) 3:65–70,
4:97–107, 5:129–35—who affirms that the novel was "the favored reading of
all social classes"—and Guillermo Prieto, "Literatura nacional: Cuadros de
costumbres," *Revista Científica y Literaria* 1 (1845): 27–29. In *Introducción a*
una historia de la novela en España en el siglo XIX, seguida del esbozo de una
bibliografía española de traducciones de novelas (1800–1850) (Madrid: Castalia,
1966), 47, José F. Montesinos comments that "the novel . . . triumphed in such
a way among readers that it was impossible to ignore." In 1822, an anonymous
Spanish author observed, "There is one certain and irremediable fact: Young
people do read and will [continue to] read novels with preference to other books
because they must be interesting and entertaining. . . . The writer can scorn a
genre that cannot aspire to the heights of Parnassus as much as he pleases; [but]
the moralist and the politician will commit a grave mistake to scorn it, for it is
a reliable and powerful means of influencing young people. It is vain to prohibit
young people from reading novels" (quoted in Montesinos, 49, citing *El censor*
15, no. 85 (16 March 1822): 24–26).

5. The discussions between classicists and romantics regarding the novel are well
documented. In *Hacia la novela: La conciencia literaria en Hispanoamérica, 1792–*
1848 (Medellín: Editorial Universidad de Antioquia, 1998), 257–58, Flor María
Rodríguez-Arenas refers to this division within one of Mexico's most influential
literary associations, the Academia de (San Juan de) Letrán, founded in 1836 by
Guillermo Prieto. Another take regarding the discussions around 1830 comes
from Montesinos, *Introducción a una historia:* "An amusing irony of history
made it possible for the novel—spurious substitute for the epic according to
the preceptistas that came before, triumphant now—to annex in all kinds of
narrations in prose and verse, independent of their aesthetic class" (78).

6. Vicente Riva Palacio, *Los Ceros: Galería de contemporáneos* (Mexico City: Díaz
de León, 1882), 279.

7. I use the terms *Mexican elites* and *nation-builders* to refer to the small minority
of creole *Ilustrados* (Enlightenment thinkers) principally concentrated in urban
centers such as Mexico City, Puebla, Guadalajara, and Mérida-Campeche.
Their sociological positions were firmly rooted in the figure of the intellectual
inspired by Voltaire in his seminal configuration of the *homme de lettres:* a
politically engaged author and thinker. See Pierre Bourdieu, "Fourth Lecture.
Universal Corporatism: The Role of Intellectuals in the Modern World," *Poetics*

Today 12 (Winter 1991): 655–69. On elites and the shaping of culture, see Itamar Even-Zohar, "Idea-Makers, Culture Entrepreneurs, Makers of Life Images, and the Prospects of Success," in *Papers in Culture Research* (2005), 184–202, *www. tau.ac.il/~itamarez/works/books/EZ-CR-2005.pdf*.

8. See Anne Staples, "Panorama educativo al comienzo de la vida independiente," in *Ensayos sobre historia de la educación en México,* by Josefina Zoraida Vázquez et al. (Mexico City: Colegio de México, 1981), 101–14; and Silvia Arrom, *The Women of Mexico City, 1790–1857* (Stanford: Stanford University Press, 1985), 5–10.

9. See Timothy E. Anna, *Forging Mexico, 1821–1835* (Lincoln: University of Nebraska Press, 1998) for an in-depth analysis of the issues plaguing consolidation—particularly the question of federal versus central government.

10. Serial novels would have a larger readership compared to earlier forms of literature due to their publication on the front pages of newspapers at a time when newspaper readership was steadily rising.

11. The second term would later signify certain traits of a novel's style and content, such as melodrama and moral dualism. These are perhaps the most benign of a host of negative characteristics that critics associate with the serial novel as a genre and subgenre. All too frequently these characteristics express a moral dimension—a tendency that began in the nineteenth century and has continued to this day: frequent metaphors are *corruption, venality, materialism, commercialism,* and *feminism.* See Wadda Ríos-Font, *Canon and Archive: Configuring Literature in Modern Spain* (Lewisburg: Bucknell University Press, 2004).

12. The use of the English term *serial novel* lacks the specificity of both *folletín* and *novela por entregas* in Spanish. A serial novel, defined on the most basic level, is a narrative that arrives to its readers in serialized fashion, typically at regular intervals of monthly, biweekly or weekly installments. The folletín is a specific manifestation of the serial novel, delivered to readers in the pages of a nineteenth-century periodical, while the novela por entregas is delivered to subscribers in separate installments (and is often written week by week), and is usually associated with the commercial apparatus of advertising and subscriber "bonuses" such as "luxury" bindings and *láminas* (engravings).

13. An example of this situation is humorously described by one of the first Spanish serial novelists, Juan Martínez Villergas, in the prologue to *Los misterios de Madrid* (Madrid: Establecimiento Artístico-Literario de Manini y Compañía, 1844). His editor visits him at home, accompanied by a group of partners/ investors, with the "mutually advantageous proposal" of undertaking a serial novel. Both parties will benefit economically, as long as the editor provides good publicity and guarantees subscribers, and the author starts writing immediately (v–ix).

14. The variety of types of discourse found in Mexican newspapers are discussed both in Malcolm Dallas McLean, *El contenido literario de "El siglo diez y nueve"* (Mexico City: Imprenta Mundial, 1938), 19–22; and Aníbal González, *Journalism and the Development of Spanish American Narrative* (Cambridge: Cambridge University Press, 1993), 16–17.

15. See Benedict Anderson, *Imagined Communities: Reflections on the Origin and Spread of Nationalism* (London: Verso, 1991), 29–30. *El Periquillo's* first edition appeared in 1816. The uncensored complete edition dates from 1830–1831.

16. Though this is not the emphasis of Vogeley's work, she does imply the serial nature of *El Periquillo*'s first publication on several occasions. See Nancy Vogeley, "Defining the 'Colonial Reader': El Periquillo Sarniento," *PMLA* 102, no. 5 (1987): 784–800; and Vogeley, *Lizardi and the Birth of the Novel in Spanish America* (Florida: University of Florida Press, 2001).

17. See Fernando Unzueta, "Scenes of Reading: Imagining Nations/Romancing History in Spanish America," in *Beyond Imagined Communities: Reading and Writing the Nation in Nineteenth-Century Latin America*, eds. Sara Castro-Klarén and John Charles Chasteen (Baltimore: Johns Hopkins University Press; Washington, DC: Woodrow Wilson Center Press, 2004), 115–60.

18. See Vogeley, *Lizardi*; and Ralph E. Warner, *Historia de la novela mexicana en el siglo XIX* (Mexico City: Antigua Librería Robredo, 1953), 7.

19. See Vogeley, *Lizardi*, 35–41; González, *Journalism and the Development*, 17; Luz Elena Galván Lafarga, "Leer es aprender: Una práctica del siglo XIX," in *Debates y desafíos en la historia de la educación en México* (Mexico City: El Colegio Mexiquense, 2002), 194–98; and Staples, "La lectura y los lectores en los primeros años de vida independiente," in *Historia de la lectura en México*, Seminario de Historia de la Educación en México (Mexico City: Colegio de México / Ediciones del Ermitaño, 1988), 96–101.

20. Staples, "La lectura," 95, 108, 117.

21. McLean, *El contenido literario*, 14–15; Staples, "La lectura," 94–96. This would not change until later in the 1840s when local paper production improved considerably and book prices dropped. Staples reports that affordable paper of good quality was not produced in Mexico until 1845.

22. Vogeley, "Defining the 'Colonial Reader,'" 786–87.

23. Vogeley, *Lizardi*, 35–41.

24. Ibid., 3–4.

25. Alicia Perales Ojeda, *Asociaciones literarias mexicanas: Siglo XIX* (Mexico City: Imprenta Universitaria de la Universidad Nacional Autónoma de México, 1957), 31–35. The relative scarcity of literary associations before independence indicates that freedom of association was limited during the colonial period, especially since the first groups of rebels came out of "literary groups" such as the one in which Padre Hidalgo participated.

26. Ibid., 49–52; and Rodríguez-Arenas, *Hacia la novela*, 255–58. As Perales Ojeda points out in *Asociaciones literarias mexicanas*, the association lasted from 1836 until 1856 (218).

27. The Abadiano collection in the Sutro Library (San Francisco) reveals the number of translations that were imported into New Spain before independence (Vogeley, *Lizardi*, 54). One of the most widely-read and influential authors in the rise of the novel across Europe and the overseas European colonies was Sir Walter Scott. His so-called rival James Fenimore Cooper was particularly popular in the Americas. In *Introducción a una historia*, 53, 57–58, 63–64, Montesinos refers directly to the growth of the market for translated novels in Spanish America.

28. See Shirley Brice, *Telling Tongues: Language Policy in Mexico (Colony to Nation)* (New York: Teachers College Press, 1972); and Mary Kay Vaughan, "Primary Education and Literacy in Nineteenth-Century Mexico: Research Trends, 1968–1988," *Latin American Research Review* 25, no. 1 (1990): 31–66. Translators were often recruited from among Spaniards exiled in France. The phenomenon

was sufficient to generate the commonplace within Spain's borders that the employment of their literatos as translators of French novels was gradually corrupting the integrity of the Spanish language itself. See, for example, Montesinos, *Introducción a una historia*, 52–54, 78; and José Álvarez Junco, *Mater dolorosa: La idea de España en el siglo XIX* (Madrid: Taurus-Historia, 2001). On the phenomenon of the transatlantic book trade between Europe and independent Spanish America, see Eugenia Roldán Vera, *The British Book Trade and Spanish American Independence: Education and Knowledge Transmission in Transcontinental Perspective* (Burlington, VT: Ashgate, 2003).

29. See, for example, Prieto, "Literatura nacional."

30. Perales Ojeda, *Asociaciones literarias mexicanas*, 16–17.

31. Ibid., 11; and Rodríguez-Arenas, *Hacia la novela*, 254–58. The group was known for including classicists such as Pesado and Carpio, as well as a different generation of romanticists such as Calderón and Rodríguez Galván.

32. See Perales Ojeda, *Asociaciones literarias mexicanas*, 237–45.

33. Though Ignacio Cumplido's Mexico City paper, *El siglo diez y nueve* (1841–1896), is not one of these ("literature" constitutes one of nine sections: "official," "unofficial," "scientific," "historic," "literary," "political," "mercantile," "economic," and "variety"), it provides an interesting description of what its editors designated as literary content: "Curious and interesting questions, articles about monuments, non-religious poetry, and anything related to theater, music, playwrights, and composers." See McLean, *El contenido literario*, 20–21.

34. Ibid., 23.

35. Jefferson Rea Spell, "The Literary Work of Manuel Payno," *Hispania* 12, no. 4 (1929): 348. Payno's prolific production consisted of short stories, novellas, and a good deal of nonfiction, including theatre reviews, travel literature (ranging from the United States to Mexico and Cuba), historical pieces, and articles (on such diverse topics as agriculture, colonization, and prison reform), as well as translations and satire. In one year alone (1845–46), he published thirty pieces in the *Revista*. In *El contenido literario*, 27–28, McLean considers him the most prolific contributor to *El siglo diez y nueve* (Guillermo Prieto is ranked second).

36. These began in 1842, when Payno visited South America and Europe as a secretary in the diplomatic service. In 1844, the Mexican government sent him to the United States to study the penitentiary system, but he returned to Mexico in that same year to help defend his country from the imminent U.S. invasion.

37. This article was written for *El museo mexicano* in 1844, the same year that Sue's *Les mystères de Paris* (1842–43) was available in Spanish translation. Jacqueline Covo, "Le roman feuilleton français au Mexique: Influence et interprétation; *El fistol del diablo* de Manuel Payno," in *Nationalisme et littérature en Espagne et en Amérique Latine au XIXe Siècle*, ed. Claude Dumas (Lille: Université Lille III, 1982), 240.

38. The installments first appeared in 1845, in the August/September edition of *La revista científica y literaria*, founded by the past editor of *El museo mexicano*. Aurelio de los Reyes, "Precisiones sobre El Fistol del Diablo de Manuel Payno," in *Del fistol a la linterna: Homenaje a José Tomás de Cuéllar y Manuel Payno en el centenario de su muerte*, 1994, ed. Margo Glantz (Mexico City: Universidad Autónoma de México, 1997), 186.

39. Ibid. *La revista científica y literaria* ceased publication in April 1846. In "Literary Work," 340, Spell hypothesizes that the revista was suspended due to the events of the Mexican War.

40. This attitude is patently clear in Marte Rodolfo Gómez, "Sobre Justo Sierra O'Reilly," *Historia mexicana* 3 (January–March 1954): 309–27.

41. Sierra was hailed as a pioneer by later literatos of the Peninsula. In *Don Justo Sierra: Su vida, sus ideas y su obra* (Mexico City: Universidad Nacional Autónoma de México, 1950), 15, Agustín Yáñez calls him the "Plutarch, father, patriarch, and king of Yucatecan literature."

42. Sierra O'Reilly's biographers do not give much information on this period, and little is known about his activities or interests during the time he spent in Mexico City.

43. Yáñez, *Don Justo Sierra*, 15. Yañez (1904–1980) was an educator, politician, and journalist known for his contribution to Mexican letters in the two novels *Al filo del agua* (1947) and *Las tierras flacas* (1967).

44. These include "El duende de Valladolid," "Don Pablo Vergara," "La Tía Mariana," "Doña Felipa de Sanabria," "Los bandos de Valladolid," and "El filibustero." The length of these stories strongly supports the possibility that they were first published in installments. In fact, some have referred to "El filibustero"—begun in 1842, but perhaps never completed—as a novel, ideal for a serial publication. See Rodríguez-Arenas, *Hacia la novela*, 288; and E. Abreu Gómez, *Clásicos, Románticos, Modernos* (Mexico City: Ediciones Botas, 1934), 99, 103.

45. Yáñez, *Don Justo Sierra*, 15.

46. Matilde Guerra Peón, *Justo Sierra O'Reilly y los orígenes de la novela en Yucatán* (Mexico City: UNAM, 1963), 40.

47. Yáñez, *Don Justo Sierra*, 15–16.

48. Ibid., 8, 15.

49. The novel began with the first edition of the paper, on 1 January 1845, and seems to have lasted for its duration, until the paper ceased publication in 1849. *El registro* was published regularly from 1845 until 1848, when it stopped for a time (most likely during the period when Sierra was in the United States), then resumed again in 1849. There were long intervals between the novel's installments, which suggests that Sierra composed the novel as he went along.

50. Quoted in Yáñez, *Don Justo Sierra*, 11.

51. See Nelson Reed, *The Caste War of Yucatán* (Stanford: Stanford University Press, 1964). The Caste War began with the revolt of the native Mayas against the population of European descent, the Yucatecos, and was triggered by specific conflicts over the changing of communal lands to private ownership. The lengthy war divided the Peninsula between the northwest position of the Yucateco forces and the Maya strongholds of the southeast. It officially ended in 1901, but skirmishes continued for another full decade.

52. See Yáñez, *Don Justo Sierra*, 10–15; and Gómez, "Sobre Justo Sierra O'Reilly," 320–21.

53. Gómez, "Sobre Justo Sierra O'Reilly," 311.

54. The German term *bildungsroman* signifies "novel of formation" or "novel of education." The subject is the "coming-of-age" of an individual (the development of the protagonist's mind and character, in the passage from childhood through

varied experiences and often through a spiritual crisis into maturity, which usually involves recognition of one's identity and role in the world. Most importantly for our case, the hero of the bildungsroman can also represent in allegorical fashion the parallel growth of a group of individuals such as a nation. See Doris Sommer, *Foundational Fictions: The National Romances of Latin America* (Berkeley: University of California Press, 1991).

55. Justo Sierra O'Reilly, *Un año en el Hospital de San Lázaro*, vol. 2 (Mérida: Ediciones de la Universidad Autónoma de Yucatán, 1997), 74.

56. This is the Spanish term for a classical concept that was revived in the Enlightenment. It refers to a constellation of honorable traits associated with fraternity and brotherhood, and encompasses virtues such as probity, integrity, generosity, and honesty.

57. In *Hacia la novela*, Rodríguez-Arenas documents the contributions of the Yucatán contingent in the creation of a national Mexican novel by including Calero Quintana's essays and Sierra O'Reilly's novels in her broader examination of the genre's development in Latin America from 1792 to 1848.

58. Vicente Calero Quintana, "Reflexiones sobre la novela," *El registro yucateco* 1 (1845): 64–70.

59. See Calero Quintana, "La novela, el teatro y la moral cristiana," *El registro yucateco* 1 (1845): 241–47.

60. See Prieto, "Literatura nacional."

61. Calero Quintana, "Reflexiones," 69–70.

62. Much of the prolific scholarship on nation since the 1960s has emphasized the degree of invention involved in establishing national traditions and a shared history. Kedourie, Hobsbawm, Gellner, and Anderson, for example, are considered to be "modernists": the first two see the nation as principally a tool of manipulative elites or ideological masks that disguise interests, while the last two tend to see the nation as tools of the elites as well as authentic expressions of identity. See *The State of the Nation: Ernest Gellner and the Theory of Nationalism*, ed. John A. Hall (New York: Cambridge University Press, 1998).

63. The simultaneity surrounding the dates of the serial novel's appearance in both Spain and Mexico suggests that the mode was transmitted directly from France to Mexico, with little mediation from Spain.

64. Angel Rama, *The Lettered City*, ed. and trans. John Charles Chasteen (Durham: Duke University Press, 1996), 43–44.

65. Jean Franco, *Plotting Women: Gender and Representation in Mexico* (New York: Columbia University Press, 1989), xvii.

66. In *Mater dolorosa*, 12, Álvarez Junco describes nationalism as that "feeling" of identification that individuals have towards the community in which they were born—a loyalty that carries them to make extreme sacrifices if the collective entity so requires. This is the idea of nationalism that I am using here; the collective, sociological phenomenon of the twentieth century, of course, does not yet exist. What does exist are national programs and definitions produced by writers, such as those contained in the serial novels, and a social reality that remains fragmented by multiple languages and regionalisms, among other obstacles.

4

Toikove Ñane Retã!

Republican Nationalism at the Battlefield Crossings
of Print and Speech in Wartime Paraguay, 1867–1868

Michael Kenneth Huner

B y the early months of 1867, writing was a difficult task in the
Paraguayan encampment of Paso Pucú. The Brazilian warships
that blockaded the Río Paraguay, the single viable trade artery in
a landlocked country, exacerbated the privations of warfare. Paper and ink,
among many other things imported, were scarce. The Paraguayan army
only a year before had turned this sparse, dusty elevation along a grove
of orange trees into a bustling military headquarters. It now had the appearance of a small town. The straw houses that lodged Paraguayan army
commanders formed characteristic urban blocks, and a web of telegraph
wires converged upon the village, spreading throughout the Paraguayan
earthworks. Although it lay in an isolated swampland, Paso Pucú was now
a center of administrative control. Writing was a logistical and ideological necessity. With the supply shortages, the Paraguayans took to ration-
ing and innovation. Military officers penned their correspondence in pre-
ciously small handwriting on reused parchment. Meanwhile, technicians
manufactured paper from the fibers of one native plant and extracted ink
from another. A printing press at the encampment used these materials
to continue to publish military orders, political proclamations, and even a
newspaper.[1]

Paso Pucú resembled a curious *lettered city*.[2] This idea, first developed
by Angel Rama, recalls the urban centers of administrative and judicial
power that were pillars of rule in the colonial empires of Latin America,
forged through assiduous control of the written word. Living in prominent
towns and cities, cadres of lettered men and sometimes women—clerics,
nuns, notaries, lawyers, and poets—had manipulated the pens that inked
the essence of social and political power in illiterate societies. They produced the legal scripture for wills and testaments declared, property deeds

consolidated, lawsuits filed, testimonies given, judicial rulings issued, and government proclamations decreed.[3] Later, in the heady days of the post-colonial world, with independent countries now strewn from shattered empires, lettered officials preserved the scripted elements of state power and even further reconstituted them with printing presses and upstart newspapers, often operating in far less-formal settings than old provincial capitals. In this regard, the Paraguayan encampment at Paso Pucú featured the typical concentration of political authority in an urban landscape where lettered bureaucrats exploited the technology of writing to exercise their power of the state. It was indeed a rustic military headquarters whose lettered officials nonetheless included scribes who fought as soldiers, rough-speaking military officers who served as judges, and priests freshly ordained in the trenches. Amid gray mud, trenches, and cholera, these lettered officials operated the telegraph lines and worked the printing press. They also conducted meticulously documented tribunals, putting to death alleged traitors and deserters.[4] It was a lettered city on a war-footing in a desperate struggle for national survival.

More than two years before, the Paraguayan president Francisco Solano López had made a bid for geopolitical power in the Río de la Plata region of South America and invaded Brazil and Argentina on the pretext of defending American republicanism against the machinations of the Brazilian monarchy. In 1864, Brazil had invaded Uruguay with the tacit support of the Mitre government in Buenos Aires. López launched his attacks with the alleged purpose of rescuing Paraguay's "sister republic" from imperial domination. Yet in 1865, Argentina, Brazil, and its now client-state Uruguay quickly formed an unlikely alliance to destroy the government of Francisco Solano López. Their forces soon repulsed López's armies and by 1866 began a protracted invasion of their own into Paraguayan territory. Their advance stalled later that year, however, and combat operations settled into the grim stalemate of trench warfare. Deep in the swamplands of southern Paraguay, disease and hunger killed off more soldiers and camp followers than the constant barrage of bombs and bullets. For his part, López realized that his main hope lay in standing firm and wearing down the allies. More than ever, the López government required the active support of the population that it claimed to represent.[5]

The rustic lettered city of Paso Pucú churned out print propaganda that tactically exploited the intersection of written and oral cultures. Its newspaper—a satirical publication with the Guaraní title *Cabichuí*—employed humor, images, and song to rouse the patriotism of the mostly illiterate Paraguayan soldiers and camp followers who occupied the trenches. In so doing, it mobilized the native Paraguayan vernacular Guaraní in prose and verse. Most Paraguayans could not read or speak Spanish, the traditional language of the state. Yet their lettered compatriots shared with them the common language of Guaraní, and with the print propaganda of *Cabichuí*, lettered agents of the state linked this indigenous American tongue to elite discourse on the nation, going so far as to promote Guaraní as the national language of Paraguay.[6]

The encampment at Paso Pucú featured a fierce battlefront struggle for hearts and minds in Guaraní-language print. The struggle, in fact, infused specific Guaraní words with potent nationalist meaning. More specifically, this effort attempted to reformulate the terms by which regular Paraguayans experienced politics and war. It thus rhetorically fused the defense of home against a foreign invader to the defense of the Paraguayan nation and, by extension, American republicanism against a hated racial Other. The maneuver effectively articulated the grandiose ideals of a patriotic cause in the familiar expressions and crass phrases running current in the trenches. Between 1867 and 1868, Paso Pucú was a lettered city whose officials embraced the oral culture of ordinary Paraguayans and filled their spoken Guaraní with songs of patriotic republicanism and nationhood.

The Print Combatant *Cabichuí*

In the early months of 1867, Francisco Solano López handed the assignment of publishing a popular satirical newspaper to the young lettered agents Juan Crisóstomo Centurión and Natalicio Talavera. Since adolescence, both had been favored pupils of the state and received European-style educations. The government even sent Centurión to study five years in England and France before the conflict.[7] Their worldly education and experience made them fluent in the broad political ideals allegedly at stake in the war. Serving as a sort of "embedded" war correspondent on the front lines for the state newspaper in Asunción, *El semanario*, Talavera wrote an article in March 1867 that mocked the "Brazilian cowards" as the ideological enemy of Paraguay. "The slave of a monarchy," he warned, "can never conquer the citizen of a free republic who defends until death his honor, his flag, and his government."[8] For it was in contrast to the manumitted slaves and black soldiers imperial Brazil used to prosecute the war that Talavera and Centurión were constructing their idea of Paraguayan republican liberty under threat of extinction.

Through the popular satirical newspaper, Talavera and Centurión sought to impress these ideas on their illiterate compatriots in the trenches. To do so, they counted on a number of resources. Talavera was quite skilled in verse and had a knack for composing rousing *coplas*, popular songs with an important lyrical component and, potentially, a political message.[9] For his part, Centurión had a talent for writing prose enlivened by soldiers' humor. They also relied on a team of amateur soldier-artists to produce lithograph illustrations for the newspaper. Proving handy with old knives and blocks of wood, the artists helped to put images in dialogue with the words on the page.[10] Priests were also available to help write the prose and verse of the newspaper and confirm to their soldier parishioners that their enemies were going to hell. Finally, this unlikely team of combatant publicists drew upon their familiar knowledge of the vernacular to place the printed word at the service of a dynamic culture of spoken Guaraní. They actively sought to make the printed Guaraní of their battlefront newspaper the jokes and songs the soldiers traded in the trenches.

The title of the newspaper proved crucial in this endeavor. Talavera and Centurión decided on the Guaraní word of *Cabichuí* for a black wasp known in Paraguay for its small size and swarming ferocity.[11] The intent was clear. The words of the newspaper were not to remain static but to swarm off of the page, entering the currents of speech. And indeed in the Guaraní prose and verse that filled its pages, *Cabichuí* became the combative printed word personified. He was to be a character in the songs and stories flying along the battlefront, listening, chatting, and passing all the gossip along to the ears of his audience.[12] He was also a fellow soldier, inflicting violence on the enemy with the printed word. One lyric sang in June 1867,

> Cabichuí flew
> through the middle of a bombardment
> and despite it all
> he stung the dirty monkeys.
>
> His stinger stuck them
> up to its very root.
> It made the kamba [the blacks] and their leaders
> shit themselves.[13]

Such themes were clear from the first issue of the newspaper published on 13 May 1867. The opening article in Spanish introduced *Cabichuí* to its readers through the wasp metaphor, echoing the animal imagery common to rural speech; the personification of animals and animal-like figures is common in the folklore of the Latin American countryside.[14] The article disclaimed pretensions of literary excellence, highlighted the importance

Figure 4.1: Note the *cabichuí* (wasp) in the center of the image, listening in on the conversation. Also, the soldiers are barefoot. *Cabichuí*, 8 August 1867, 3.

of the paper's illustrations, and pledged to publicize the deeds of the brave fighters who sustained "the war of the free against the slaves." Adopting a markedly popular tone, *Cabichuí* promised to huddle figuratively with the soldiers around their campfires "to speak with them in their typical light and joking tones."[15] With its broad humor and vulgar ridicule of the enemy, the publication clearly aimed to draw from, stimulate, and contribute to conversations in the Paraguayan trenches.

A woodcut illustration from August 1867 depicted this very process (Figure 4.1). In the picture, an officer reads *Cabichuí* aloud to four barefoot soldiers who listen intently and laugh. The Guaraní caption indicated that such group readings were almost mandatory. "Listen up good," commands the officer, to which the soldiers respond, "Yeah, we hear you!" An accompanying article narrates the details of such a group reading, in which the

Figure 4.2: *Cabichuí*'s unsubtle logo.

soldiers comment on the articles—all, of course, in Guaraní. The session ends with the soldiers vowing to protect their womenfolk from the invading forces. Ultimately, the group bursts into patriotic song, just as the authors of *Cabichuí* hoped would happen with their published lyrics.[16]

In fact, the illustrated logo of the newspaper, which adorned the first page of each issue, further visually demonstrated *Cabichuí*'s role as an active print combatant (Figure 4.2). The drawing portrayed a hairy, black, ape-like character holding a stick and futilely waving his arm to dispel a swarm of wasps. This unsubtle image received more explicit elaboration in the racialized prose and verse that followed it. A Guaraní-language song ended each issue of *Cabichuí*, and these verses went to work making obscene ridicule of the enemy. The first song from May 1867 told how the Brazilian emperor Pedro II had foolishly sent impressed recruits to the battlefront. Stupid and cowardly, the Brazilian troops had dived into their trenches at the first sight of a Paraguayan and, cowering at the bottom, they had uselessly fired their cannons towards the clouds until an annoyed God, clearly on the Paraguayan side, sent them off to hell.

The lyrics referred to this condemned enemy as *kamba*, the Guaraní slur for a black slave. Brazilian troops were "the kamba of Pedro II," and it was the "many ugly kamba" who were carried away by Satan. The song then lampooned the kamba eyes that glowed monstrously in dark faces.[17] The slur betrayed a colonial legacy pregnant in the use of Guaraní itself, for *kamba* was not originally a Guaraní word, its semantic branches in the Paraguayan vernacular springing from unknown regions. It instead infiltrated the language as part of the colonial experience of slavery and caste, wherein the black slave sat at the bottom of the official racial hierarchy of imperial Spain. It is crucial to note in this regard that the word *kamba* is not found in the seventeenth-century Jesuit Guaraní dictionaries, suggesting the slur came into usage with the introduction of African slavery into the territory by the Spanish. Supporting evidence for this assertion comes from the very Guaraní-language songs and articles found in *Cabichuí*. References to *kamba* were often coupled with the word *tembiguai*, which indicated "servant" or "slave." The songs thus reinforced a close semantic association between the words, with *kamba* carrying the extra racial bite. They evoked the links between the colonial practices of slavery and racial caste that were fused in the everyday language of Paraguayans.[18]

These words still resonated with the social reality of nineteenth-century Paraguayans. By the end of the colonial period, the Paraguayan territory had had a sizable population of free blacks, mulattos, and African-descended slaves. Slavery even persisted as a legal practice in independent Paraguay through the 1860s, with the majority of slaves traded and owned by the state.[19] Well into the 1850s, regular Paraguayans had continued to evidence keen familiarity with the labels and restrictions of a still-breathing caste hierarchy, whereby blackness suggested the inferiority of the slave. Brothers fearful of the racial stain on a legally-white family lineage had still objected to potential black suitors pursuing marriages with their sisters. Meanwhile, fugitives apprehended by police officials had continued to toy with colonial-era racial labels to their best legal advantage. Paraguayans made caste distinctions in their everyday interactions, and the common sense of racial hierarchy persisted. The slur *kamba* spoke to this prevalent social logic.[20]

The incorporation of the word *kamba* into Guaraní thus reflected how the language, as it was spoken and written in mainstream Paraguayan society, was itself a product of colonial times. The use of Guaraní had long fallen unhinged from the social caste identity of *Indian*. Elites and peasants alike, with varying strains of indigenous descent, spoke the language in their homes and on the street. For the sake of preaching and converting,

Catholic clergy had disciplined its sounds to the written expression of the Latin alphabet. This process forever altered what once had been a purely oral language of the indigenous Guaraní people. Spanish and other foreign words entered common usage, further assaulting the pre-Columbian purity of Guaraní. Yet such impurities were also evidence of the language's sustained vigor and cultural power. Spanish words incorporated into Guaraní speech were heavily modified, becoming detached from their original contexts. The assimilated Spanish words were even conjugated according to Guaraní rules. For example, the Spanish term *guapo*, meaning "handsome" or "tough," became *iguapó* (ee-wa-pó), meaning "laborious." The verb *disparar* signified in Spanish the discharge of a firearm; meanwhile, its "Guaranized" offshoot, *odispará* meant to run away. The Guaraní of mainstream Paraguay bore the impact of the colonial experience with an exuberant hybridism. It was, in sum, a colonial language with indigenous roots.[21]

The publicists of *Cabichuí*, Juan Crisóstomo Centurión and Natalicio Talavera, exploited Guaraní as such for its permeable boundaries between the worlds of print and speech. They drew from the predominately oral nature of Paraguayan Guaraní to write their songs and jokes, and in turn sought to channel such lyrics into the conversations and ballads of their compatriots in the trenches.[22] In so doing, they necessarily recalled a colonial legacy present in the language itself that was fraught with the slurs of slavery and caste. More than just familiar devices to engage an illiterate audience, however, such slurs and caricatures in the songs of *Cabichuí* also contained a nationalist vision with specific political aspirations.

Toikove Ñane Retã

To construct their nationalist vision in the Paraguayan vernacular, the editors and writers of *Cabichuí* seized upon the Guaraní word *retã* (and its derivatives *tetã* and *hetã*). Unlike *kamba*, *retã* was originally Guaraní. Seventeenth-century Jesuit priests recorded that *retã* referred to "place of origin" or "familial village." Typically, then, the impact of the colonial experience altered the meaning of *retã*, moving it closer to the Spanish concept of *patria*, one's country or homeland.[23] During the War of the Triple Alliance, the writers of *Cabichuí* made it an explicit synonym for republican nationhood. The related word *tetarã* indicated distant familial connection and "those from your patria." Many Guaraní words such as *tetã* had multiple forms, depending on their use in relation to the speaker. *Tetã* is the "original" form of the word. However, I use its derivative *retã* in the text because it pertains in most cases to the first person, such as "I" or "we."

The verses taught to the Guaraní-speaking combatants in the trenches around Paso Pucú, who came from many rural *patrias chicas*, that they nevertheless shared a common *retã*: the Paraguayan nation. When a Guaraní poem from May 1867 dismissed boastful Allied claims to conquer "our *retã*," the homeland in question was explicitly the Paraguayan nation. Another poem from January 1868 replied with boasting of its own. In each battle, the Allied forces got an object lesson in bravery. They learned the hard way what Paraguay, "our *retã*," was made of.[24] A song from September 1867 made *retã* and the Spanish *nación* directly synonymous, using the two words in adjoining lines of a stanza: "If only Pedro II / does not seize our *retã* / our *nación* will be laborious / and we will be prosperous."[25] Numerous songs in *Cabichuí* joined "vivas" for president Francisco Solano López with the proclamation: *Toikove ñane retã* (Long live our retã).[26] In response to this call, according to a verse from December 1867, President López received his loyal adherents as "sons of the *tetã*."

If *retã* bespoke the notion of nation and homeland, the natural mission of its defenders was to throw out the kamba invaders, with the word *kamba* serving as the common caricature for all Allied soldiers. Recall that *kamba*, as the Guaraní slur for a black slave, was the derisive reference to the Brazilian soldiers of color. Presumably the Paraguayan soldiers exchanged other ugly names for their enemy combatants, particularly those from Argentina and Uruguay. Historians have suggested that *kurepi* (pig-skinned), the present-day derogatory term for an Argentine (especially for a *porteño*, or denizen of Buenos Aires) had its origins in the war.[27] If the combatants of Paso Pucú used the word, though, the editors of *Cabichuí* avoided putting it in print. In passage after passage, *kamba* stood metonymically for the invading forces. In part, this usage reflected the reality of the Allied ranks. By 1867, comparatively few Argentine and Uruguayan troops constituted the front lines; it was mostly African-descended Brazilians who filled the Allied trenches. Yet it is difficult to believe that the preference for the epithet *kamba* in the Guaraní verses did not also respond to political designs, specifically to those prone to propagandistic racism.

Cabichuí's Guaraní jeers were replete with vulgar and pejorative racial characterizations of the kamba, whom they described as filthy and smelly. *Kamba ky'a* (dirty blacks) appeared in the songs as a sort of set phrase.[28] One poem from December 1867 pursued this theme at some length:

> There is no trash among them
> as dirty as those dirty kamba.

Not even pig sties compare
to those disgusting animals.

Even from far away
our noses burn intensely
from the stink
that those devil slaves carry.

Intimating the threat that such beasts posed to "the beautiful girls of Paraguay," the song promised to protect them from the smell of the kamba.[29]

The kamba were also constantly compared to monkeys, a common animal in Paraguay and one proverbially considered to be filthy. Simian references constituted traditional sort of ridicule in the country. The ensemble was part of a racialized assault upon the *kamba karaja ky'a* (the dirty black monkeys), and such depictions were applied not only to the African-descended Brazilian soldiers, but also to the lily-white Brazilian emperor and his European wife. Pedro II normally figured as the *macaco tuja* (the old ape), while his spouse was the *karaja guaigui* (the old monkey-woman). Together, these "old apes" sent their kamba legions into the trenches to die hopelessly in droves.[30] The songs repetitively derided the stupidity of the kamba in marching to their inevitable defeat and death, and they further delighted in the image of their dead enemies being cooked in the fires of hell.[31]

With the ridicule of their Guaraní verses, the editors and contributors of *Cabichuí* mobilized the derogatory language of racial hierarchy and caste, still-living vestiges of colonial society in a post-colonial world. Early in its production, the periodical clarified its appropriation of the word with a Spanish-language article that frankly stated, "The Guaraní word *kamba* is applied to blacks, and more generally and properly, to the slave." It then went on to explain using the slur against Argentine and Uruguayan soldiers, few of whom were African-descended and none slaves. They were, nevertheless, "true kamba," maintained the article, because they were the "kamba of the Brazilian kamba"—the slaves of slaves, having sold themselves to the political designs of the Brazilian emperor. As a result, the article proclaimed anyone *kamba*—even Germans, Frenchmen, and Englishmen—"who come and sell their souls to Pedro II to enslave a people."[32] The term's use as a general label for the Allies thus reinforced the rhetorical ideology of the editors who neatly defined the republican liberty of the Paraguayan *retã* against a derogatory slur for a black slave. Paraguayans were free republicans precisely because they were not kamba and pursuing a righteous war against the enslaving monarchy of Brazil.

Figure 4.3: Paraguay defending the republics of South America. Note
Uruguay and Argentina are also under "her" protection. *Cabichuí*, 16
December 1867, 2.

Contained in these messages, then, was the crass republicanism articulated by the lettered agents of the Paraguayan state throughout the
war. The Spanish-language articles and lithographs of *Cabichuí* were all the
more explicit in this regard. One article elaborated, "The ape monarch [of
Brazil] understands that with the victory of Paraguay, American democracy is saved. The Brazilian monarchy . . . will soon falter, collapse, divide,
and succumb like an exotic flower that with difficulty survives in the essentially republican world of Columbus." Paraguay sustained a heroic defense
at "the vanguard of American rights." Several lithographs were explicit in

depicting this republican identity, similar in some respects to the republican images studied in Chapter 1 (Figure 4.3). They often portrayed female images of Paraguay defending all of republican South America—even her enemies Argentina and Uruguay—against the threatening monarchic beast of Brazil. Other images depicted Bartolomé Mitre and Venancio Flores, the leaders of Argentina and Uruguay respectively, under the control of Pedro II and working against the true interests of their people. Pedro II, always shown wearing a crown, was the main focus of this propagandistic ire.[33]

The Guaraní verses in *Cabichuí* contributed to this message. They tangentially jeered Argentines and Uruguayans as political traitors who had sold out their republics. Two songs from February 1868 in particular were dedicated to the "ex-Argentines," now slavish traitors to their retã. As a result, the Argentines no longer stood at the figurative side of General José de San Martín, the republican hero of Argentine independence.[34] Still, the main target in the verses was Pedro II. In June 1867, Natalicio Talavera composed a *cielito*, a popular lyrical and dance genre of the Río de la Plata, to poke vulgar fun at the Brazilian emperor and his kamba.[35] The song claimed that at the roar of the Paraguayan artillery, the kamba urinated and defecated out of fear: "Those dirty apes / shit themselves bad / and the artillery / made them piss on themselves, too." Later, the cielito assured victory over the monarchic enemy: "On the ground already / is the old crown / of Pedro II, / king of the kamba."[36] Here was another triumph for republican America and the cause of freedom.

Through incessant contrast to the slavish kamba, the Paraguayan soldiers became republican heroes. They defended the very freedom of the Paraguayan retã, with the concept of liberty properly articulated in the Guaraní form as *ñande libertá* (our liberty).[37] The overbearing irony, of course, is that before and especially during the war, Paraguayans knew few of the political freedoms and practices of what might be understood as republican liberty. Since independence, autocrats had ruled their country with the proverbial iron fist. This idea of republican liberty contrived its meaning and relevance instead through the familiar slurs of a colonial racial category reinvigorated by the violence of foreign invasion and war. Centurión, Talavera, and the other officials of the rustic lettered city of Paso Pucú spoke to the reality of their fellow soldiers' war with their call to defend the Paraguayan retã against the kamba invaders, and it was the racist image of black hordes desecrating family, home, and country that effectively made republicanism and freedom ring true.

Conclusions

Consider the news story of Francisca Cabrera, as reported in *Cabichuí*, to ponder fully how the conjured image of these black hordes spoke to the reality of the Paraguayans' war. The story emerged from gossip and rumor around Paso Pucú and reached the ears of the combatant publicists of the newspaper. They in turn published the story in August 1867 as a propagandistic feature of selfless patriotism. It told how Cabrera remained in her home with her small children as Allied soldiers, bent on raping and pillaging, were descending on their village near the southern pueblo of Pilar. Brandishing the family machete, Cabrera steeled her children for the coming onslaught. The publicists of *Cabichuí* were careful to record her words in Guaraní: "Those kamba are coming to carry us off," she warned her children, "and I am going to fight them with this knife until I die." She then instructed them to pick up the knife after her death to continue the fight, "stabbing and slicing the bellies" of their enemies. Finally, she urged them to submit to death themselves before falling as "slaves to the kamba."[38] The editors of *Cabichuí* later produced a lithograph of the scene with Cabrera's famous words in captions (Figure 4.4). However embellished, the story of Francisca Cabrera tugged at the emotions of Paraguayan soldiers and camp followers worried about their own homes and families. The lettered agents of the Paraguayan state hoped that they too articulated their anxiety in the derogatory language invoking the fight for republic and nation.

By mid-1868, the Paraguayan defensive positions around Paso Pucú collapsed. Soon afterward in July, *Cabichuí* ceased publication after ninety-four issues. The rustic lettered city of Paso Pucú disintegrated as quickly as it was built. It had been the death of Natalicio Talavera in October 1867 that did not bode well for the encampment and its print combatant *Cabichuí*. Publication of the newspaper had limped onward into the next year without its most talented poet. Centurión, on the other hand, survived until the bitter end of the war. After the retreat from Paso Pucú, he fled with Paraguayan forces as they conducted a desperate guerrilla war in the northeastern part of the country and was present at the conflict's final battle when Brazilian forces killed Francisco Solano López on 1 March 1870. By that time, Paraguay had lost over half of its prewar population of nearly a half million.[39]

As unusual the story of Paso Pucú and *Cabichuí* may seem, lettered cities on battlefronts thrived in nineteenth-century Latin America. Indeed, the rash of civil and international conflicts, starting with the independence wars, created a fantastic demand for the words and narratives that necessarily accompany acts of political violence.[40] Printing presses were fre-

Figure 4.4: Francisca Cabrera instructing her children. Her Guaraní
words are recorded below. *Cabichuí*, 10 October 1867, 4.

quent companions of nineteenth-century Latin American armies. The
case of *Cabichuí* indicates that the social and cultural barriers of literacy
separating the printed word from the illiterate soldiers that largely filled
their ranks were hardly impermeable. In fact, wartime publishers actively
crossed them. In so doing, they placed the printed word into a constant
dialogue with the predominant oral culture of their companions. The spoken and printed word mutually influenced each other in what was often a
propagandistic symphony of song and dance.

The case of *Cabichuí* also demonstrates that upon reaching out to the oral culture of regular soldiers, battlefield presses in nineteenth-century Latin America also had to engage the vernaculars of indigenous origin. In these moments, notions of republic and nation gained some added currency within the logic of the languages themselves, though in Paraguay at least, it was a colonial legacy of caste, hierarchy, and deference that provided the flesh of their resonance. Insurgent and warring areas of Mexico, Bolivia, and Peru had their own mestizo interlocutors, versed in the languages of indigenous soldiers but also with connections to the lettered world of national politics.[41] Extensive questions remain, however, as to how such situations played out in these countries and their languages. The example of nineteenth-century Paraguay nonetheless suggests that the pressures of war and the interactions of print and tongue did encode the malleable ideas of republic and nation into the historical experiences of regular people.

NOTES

1. Juan Crisóstomo Centurión, *Memorias o reminiscencias sobre la Guerra del Paraguay*, vol. 2 (Asunción: El Lector, 1894), 120–23, 248–49. For another description of the "villages" at Paso Pucú and the female camp followers that tended them, see George Thompson, *The War in Paraguay* (London: E. and H. Laemmert, 1869), 155, 206.

2. Angel Rama, *The Lettered City*, ed. and trans. John Charles Chasteen (Durham: Duke University Press, 1996).

3. For exploration of notaries' manipulations of the *lettered city* and its documentary truth during the colonial period, see Kathryn Burns, "Notaries, Truth, and Consequences," *American Historical Review* 110, no. 2 (April 2005): 350–79.

4. For examples of the ordainments and tribunals in Paso Pucú, see respectively cura Francisco Pablo Aguilera, Libro de Orden Sacro, 1865–1883, Archivo de la Curia del Arzobispado de Asunción; and Relación del soldado paraguayo José María Curugua, desertor y espía pasado por armas, Paso Pucú, 1867, Archivo Nacional de Asunción-Sección Civil y Judicial, vol. 1797, no. 4.

5. For an overview of the tactical situation at the time, see Chris Leuchars, *To the Bitter End: Paraguay and the War of the Triple Alliance* (Westport: Greenwood Press, 2002), 155–68; Charles Kolinski, *Independence or Death! The Story of the Paraguayan War* (Gainesville: University of Florida Press, 1965), 137–42; Alfredo M. Seiferheld, "El Cabichuí en el contexto histórico de la Guerra Grande," introduction to *Cabichuí*, facsimile ed. (Asunción: Museo del Barro, 1984); and Thompson, *The War in Paraguay*, 196–243. For details on the cholera outbreak, see Centurión, *Memorias*, vol. 2, 255–57. For the origins of the conflict, see Thomas Whigham, *The Paraguayan War: Causes and Early Conduct* (Lincoln: University of Nebraska Press, 2002).

6. See "Idiomas," *El centinela* (Asunción), 25 April 1867, 2. Three popular-satirical newspapers were created during this moment of national emergency. Two were published in Asunción: *El centinela* and *Cacique Lambaré*, the latter of which was written entirely in Guaraní. The third publication, *Cabichuí*, was

published and distributed along the battlefront in Paso Pucú. I focus on *Cabichuí* in this chapter due to its proximity to the trenches. For an overview of Paraguay's wartime "combatant press," see Víctor Simón Bovier, "El periodismo combatiente del Paraguay durante la Guerra de la Triple Alianza," *Historia paraguaya* 12 (1967–68): 47–87.

7.　For these details, see Centurión, *Memorias*, vol. 1, 89–166; and Juan Pérez Acosta, *Carlos Antonio López: Obrero máximo* (Asunción: Editorial Guarania, 1948), 402, 523–40.

8.　Natalicio Talavera, *La Guerra del Paraguay: Correspondencias publicadas en el semanario* (Asunción: Ediciones Nizza, 1958), 128.

9.　Talavera is recognized today as one of Paraguay's great national poets. In fact, the anniversary of his death, 11 October, is officially commemorated as a national poetry day. For a hagiographic look at Talavera, see Juan E. O'Leary, *El libro de los héroes* (Asunción: La Mundial, 1922), 87–96. Carlos Centurión gives a brief biographical sketch of Talavera as well a list of his literary publications in *Historia de la cultura paraguaya*, vol. 1 (Asunción, 1961), 267–70.

10.　Testimonio de Juan Crisóstomo Centurión, Buenos Aires, 6 January 1888, Archivo de Ministerio de Defensa del Paraguay, Colección de Juan B. Gill, n. 118, 52. The late Paraguayan historian Josefina Plá lists the names of nine folk art contributors to the newspaper. They were Inocenio Aquino, M. Perina, Franciso Ocampos, Gregorio Acosta, Gerónimo Caceres, J. Borges, Francisco Velasco, J. B. S., and Saturio Ríos. See her essay in *Cabichuí*, facsimile ed., "El Grabado: Instrumento de la Defensa."

11.　Centurión, *Memorias*, vol. 2, 251–52.

12.　"De la vanguardia," *Cabichuí*, 24 June 1867, 4; "Actualidad," *Cabichuí*, 19 August 1867, 4; "Al 'Centinela,'" *Cabichuí*, 20 June 1867, 4; "25 de diciembre," *Cabichuí*, 26 December 1867, 4; "Diálogo," *Cabichuí*, 1 July 1867, 4.

13.　"De Chichi al 'Cabichuí,'" *Cabichuí*, 3 June 1867, 4. For another example of the newspaper "stinging" the kamba, see "Gratulación al 'Cabichui,'" *Cabichuí*, 16 May 1867, 4.

14.　For the case of Paraguay, see Dionisio M. González Torres, *Folklore del Paraguay* (Asunción: Servilibro, 2003), 69–85. Again, *Cabichuí* provides excellent evidence for this phenomenon, whereby monkeys, dogs, turtles, and ass were used to depict the allies or their leaders. See Heríb Caballero Campos and Cayetano Ferreira Segovia, "El periodismo de guerra en el Paraguay (1864–1870)," *Nuevo mundo mundos nuevos* 6 (2006), nuevomundo.revues.org/index1384.html.

15.　"A nuestros lectores," *Cabichuí*, 13 May 1867, 1.

16.　The lithograph appeared in the 8 August 1867 issue of *Cabichuí* on page 3. The accompanying article was titled "La lectura del 'Cabichuí.'" Both John Hoyt Williams and Thomas Whigham point out that the wearing of shoes was an indicator of class in Paraguay. See Williams, *The Rise and Fall of the Paraguayan Republic* (Austin: University of Texas Press, 1979), 75; and Whigham, *Paraguayan War*, 183–84.

17.　*Cabichuí*, 13 May 1867, 4.

18.　Antonio Ruiz Montoya, *Tesoro de la lengua guaraní* (Madrid: Juan Sánchez, 1639). For examples of *tembiguai* and *kamba*, see *Cabichuí*, 19 August 1867; and "Pobres negros," *Cabichuí*, 5 December 1867.

19. Milda Rivarola, *Vagos, pobres y soldados: La domesticación estatal del trabajo en el Paraguay del siglo XIX* (Asunción: Centro Paraguayo de Estudios Sociológicos, 1994), 87–91. The financial notary records of the pre-war Paraguayan government document the limited traffic in slaves by the state. See, for example, Libro de cajas, May 1858, n. 63, Archivo Nacional de Asunción. It should be noted that the government of Carlos Antonio López in 1842 decreed the gradual abolition of slavery with the *Ley de Vientre*, which declared all children of slaves to be legally free after their twenty-third birthday. Of course, the state and private individuals continued to partake in a limited domestic slave trade up until the war. See Jerry Cooney, "La abolición de la esclavitud," in *El Paraguay bajo los López*, eds. Jerry Cooney and Thomas Whigham (Asunción: Centro Paraguayo de Estudios Sociológicos, 1994), 28–33; and Ana María Arguello, *El rol de los esclavos negros en el Paraguay* (Asunción: Centro Editorial Paraguayo S. R. L., 1999), 88–93.

20. Disputes over proposed marriages among family members were common in Paraguay, just as in nineteenth-century Argentina. These *disenso* cases often involved rankling over "inequality of lineage" between the marrying couple and thus the perceived corruption of "pure white" lineage. In fact, in Paraguay the state had to concede to all marriages involving such inequalities, a testament to the still-living legal legacy of the colonial caste system. The litigants' prolific use of racial labels in these *disenso* cases, as well as in criminal cases, suggests their prevalence on the street. That is, regular Paraguayans continued to make racial caste distinctions in their everyday interactions and were keenly aware of the perceived inferiority of blackness. See, for example, "Caso de Marcos Presentado contra el pretenso matrimonio de José Villalva y María Rosa Presentado," Archivo Nacional de Asunción-Sección Nueva Encuadernación, vol. 2188, nos. 2–6. Also see "Causa judicial contra el pardo libre Bernardino Frasquerí, 1863–65," Archivo Nacional de Asunción-Sección Nueva Encuadernación, vol. 1646. For the case of Argentina, see Jeffrey Shumway, *The Case of the Ugly Suitor and Other Histories of Love, Gender, and Nation, 1776–1870* (Lincoln: University of Nebraska Press, 2005).

21. Barbara Ganson, *The Guaraní Under Spanish Rule in the Río de la Plata* (Stanford: Stanford University Press, 2003). Indigenous languages throughout the Spanish Empire became colonial institutions of the state and church. See James Lockhart, *The Nahuas After the Conquest: A Social and Cultural History of the Indians of Central Mexico* (Stanford: Stanford University Press, 1992); and Matthew Restall, *The Maya World: Yucatec Culture and Society, 1550–1850* (Stanford: Stanford University Press, 1997). For the case of Guaraní, see Bartomeu Meliá, *La lengua guaraní en el Paraguay colonial* (Asunción: CEPAG, 2003).

22. Aníbal Orué Pozzo emphasizes the mutually reinforcing influences of the spoken and written word in Guaraní in *Oralidad y escritura en Paraguay: Comunicación, antropología, e historia* (Asunción: Arandurã Editorial, 2002).

23. See Ruiz Montoya, *Tesoro*, 383–84. Ruiz Montoya gives the definition of *tetã* as "pueblo, ciudad."

24. "A los macacos convertidos en loros," *Cabichuí*, 23 May 1867, 4; and "Caxias y sus negros," *Cabichuí*, 2 January 1868, 4. For another explicit equation of the *retã* with Paraguay, see "Estratégia de Cachimbo," *Cabichuí*, 16 December 1867, 4.

25. "El 'Caba Aguará' al 'Cabichuí,'" *Cabichuí*, 12 September 1867, 4.
26. "3 de octubre," *Cabichuí*, 7 October 1867, 4; "25 de diciembre"; and "Caxias y la osamenta," *Cabichuí*, 13 January 1868, 4.
27. See Kolinski, *Independence or Death!*
28. See, for example, the first Guaraní song in the first issue of *Cabuchuí*, 13 May 1867, 4.
29. "Etopeya macacuna," *Cabichuí*, 9 December 1867, 4.
30. "Pobres negros," 4; "El 'Cabichuí,'" *Cabichuí*, 17 June 1867, 4; "3 de octubre" *Cabichuí*; and "Gratulación a 'Cabichuí," *Cabichuí*, 16 May 1867, 4.
31. "Impiedad y castigo a los negros," *Cabichuí*, 14 October 1867, 4; "A los macacos" and "Gloria y júbilo de 16 de octubre," *Cabichuí*, 10 November 1867, 4.
32. "El artículo negro," *Cabichuí*, 16 June 1867, 1.
33. "Situación de la triple alianza," *Cabichuí*, 9 September 1867, 3; "Venta de las repúblicas del Plata," *Cabichuí*, 3 June 1867, 2; and "La Guerra de la Triple Alianza contra el Paraguay," *Cabichuí*, 10 June 1867, 2. See Figure 4.3, which illustrates the republican rhetoric in the newspaper. Other poignant lithographs depicting republican themes appear in 15 July 1867, 2; 24 July 1867, 2–3; 16 December 1867, 2; and 5 August 1867, 2. For more on republican imagery and the nation, see Achugar's chapter in this volume.
34. "A los ex-argentinos," *Cabichuí*, 3 February 1868, 4; and "Para los pavos," *Cabichuí*, 6 February 1868, 4.
35. For a fascinating discussion of the cielito lyrical dance tradition in Argentina and Uruguay, see John Charles Chasteen, *National Rhythms, African Roots: The Deep History of Latin American Dance* (Albuquerque: University of New Mexico Press, 2004), 146–51; and his article "Patriotic Footwork: Social Dance, Popular Culture and the Watershed of Independence in Buenos Aires," *Journal of Latin American Cultural Studies* 5, no. 1 (1996): 11–24. By mid-century, the dance tradition had gained popularity in Paraguay. The Spanish playwright Ildefonso Bermejo, who was contracted by the López government, wrote a theatrical production in 1858 in which the opening scene portrays the dancing and singing of a Paraguayan cielito. See Ildefonso Antonio Bermejo, *Un paraguayo leal: Drama en dos actos y en verso* (Asunción: Talleres Nacionales de H. Kraus, 1898). Chasteen emphasizes that the cielito lyrics were especially susceptible to patriotic, if somewhat vulgar, renderings by their authors. Talavera obviously persisted in this tradition.
36. Natalicio Talavera, "Canción presentada al 'Cabichuí' en su visita al Paso Burro," *Cabichuí*, 6 June 1867, 4.
37. See, for example, "Caxias y sus negros" and "25 de diciembre."
38. "Francisca Cabrera," *Cabichuí*, 12 August 1867, 4; and 10 October 1867, 4.
39. The full extent of Paraguay's loss of population continues to be a subject of heated debate, due to the scarcity of documentary evidence. Thomas Whigham and Barbara Potthast, "The Paraguayan Rosetta Stone: New Insights into the Demographics of the Paraguayan War, 1864–1870," *Latin American Research Review* 34, no. 1 (1999) is the most accurate estimation. Vera Blinn Reber contends the casualty numbers were much lower than suggested by Whigham and Potthast. See her "Comment on 'The Rosetta Stone,'" *LARR* 37, no. 3 (2002): 129–35; and Whigham and Potthast's consequent response, "Refining the Numbers: A Response to Reber and Kleinpenning," ibid., 143–48.

40. John Charles Chasteen, "Fighting Words: The Discourse of Insurgency in Latin American History," *Latin American Research Review* 28, no. 3 (1993): 83–111. For the embattled Argentine dictator Juan Manuel Rosas's use of the printing press and his regime's engagement with popular culture, see Ricardo Salvatore, *Wandering Paysanos: State Order and Subaltern Experience in Buenos Aires During the Rosas Era* (Durham: Duke University Press, 2003) and William G. Acree Jr., "Gaucho Gazetteers, Popular Literature, and Politics in the Río de la Plata," *Studies in Latin American Popular Culture* 26 (2007): 197–215. On the broader subject of print and politics in the Plata, see Acree, "From Reading to Reality: Print Culture, Collective Identity, and Nationalism in Uruguay and Argentina" (PhD diss., University of North Carolina at Chapel Hill, 2006).

41. Recent literature on nineteenth-century popular politics in Mexico and Peru has focused on such figures. See most notably Guy Thomson, *Patriotism, Politics and Popular Liberalism in Nineteenth-Century Mexico: Juan Francisco Lucas* (Wilmington, DE: Scholarly Resources, 1999); Florencia Mallon, *Peasant and Nation: The Making of Postcolonial Mexico and Peru* (Berkeley: University of California Press, 1995); Charles Walker, *Smoldering Ashes: Cuzco and the Creation of Republican Peru, 1780–1840* (Durham: Duke University Press, 1999); and Cecilia G. Méndez, *The Plebian Republic: The Huanta Rebellion and the Making of the Peruvian State* (Durham: Duke University Press, 2005).

PART II

Cultures on Display

5

Forms of Historic Imagination

Visual Culture, Historiography, and the Tropes of War in Nineteenth-Century Venezuela

Beatriz González-Stephan

"Making history" is a practice. . . . If it is true that the organization of history is relative to a place and a time, this is first of all because of its techniques of production. Generally speaking, every society thinks of itself "historically," with the instruments that pertain to it. . . . History is mediated by technique.
— Michel de Certeau, *The Writing of History*

Clio's Closet

The relationships between the written word and visual culture throughout the nineteenth century were complex. They shared symbolic spaces, mobilized didactic forces, sought to delineate their respective domains, and fought over clientele. Both print and image competed ferociously to get ahead and achieve—each in its own way—the goals of the project of enlightened modernity. Of course, each embraced different meanings of this "enlightenment."[1] Nevertheless, written and visual cultures complemented and mutually contaminated each other. In most cases, words found support in images, on and off the printed page (see Chapter 1 in this volume).

I would like to draw attention to the levels of complexity of the interactions between words and images, especially the porosity of the sphere of letters (relating specifically to historical genres and historiographical practices pertaining to the realm of high culture), through a series of enormously popular manifestations that belong to the world of the visual spectacle. These manifestations include expressions and representations for

---

This chapter was translated from Spanish by William G. Acree Jr.

popular classes and the public at large and had little in common with elite preferences. After all, nineteenth-century Latin America was profoundly marked by a visual rhetoric—a rhetoric of the image—that required the world of letters to develop a form of textuality that made its references more visible, that worked to elaborate a more realist codification, and that, in sum, painted with words.[2]

The circuits of the written word and visual culture established lines of communication that were not exactly fluid or obvious, but that allowed for epistemic matrices to cross. Limiting oneself to the horizon of literary production, at least for the nineteenth century has impoverished the potential meanings of numerous cultural practices, including but not limited to the production of historical fiction.[3] In the words of Michel de Certeau, the practice of history occurs in a specific place at a specific moment, conditioned by other cultural practices and activities. For now, what is important to keep in mind is this larger context of other cultural practices (that could pertain to the realms of popular culture and scopic rituals, for example), and that the specificity of the practice of history is situated locally (obeying the logic of production determined by a given place's traditions).[4]

Cultural phenomena are complex, so it can pay off to engage in what has been called *cultural criticism*, a methodology that attempts to shed light on lineages and connections that traditional disciplinary approaches have ignored in favor of establishing discreet and discontinuous entities of knowledge. Reestablishing some of these nexuses could seem imprudent, but the benefits outweigh the risks. They permit us to rethink cultural phenomena from other vantage points and understand better their legacies.

I would like to invert the order, so to say, of the premises of our analysis of the interrelation and circulation of diverse cultural forms of the nineteenth century, avoiding from the beginning the question of the place of letters and focusing instead on the complex mediations of visual and material culture and the universe of the written word. Studying these mediations (historiographical panoramas, serial novels, print collections of so-called galleries of illustrious men, poetic albums) means asking about the dialogues among different modes of popular culture, public festivals and celebrations, fairs and exhibitions, the advent of a culture of technology, and daily consumption of decorative styles, as well as the emergence of literary genres that have enjoyed large reading publics. What is the genealogy that controlled historiographical production (the mechanism for producing a sense of the past) in a society trained to read visual formats? In a society that reads narratives based on images—from engravings appearing on loose leaves and "live" paintings to parades and dioramas—how was it possible to build a lettered repertoire capable of interacting with a visually inclined public? It is no surprise that newspapers and magazines incorporated rapidly the new technologies allowing them to reproduce images that would illustrate their pages and thus convert them into exhibitionary showcases. Progress was also measured through the reproduction of images of progress, challenging ocular competency. At stake was the issue of learning to see.

Let us begin by observing this process, which requires me to modify many of the reflections on historiography I have made in past years. Throughout the nineteenth century, dioramas and panoramas were enormously popular venues among a growing urban public used to watching (and often participating in) all sorts of scopic spectacles, including fairs, circuses, parades, varieties of fireworks shows, allegorical paintings, and a host of street performances. Many of these spectacles had roots in older traditions that filled the public sphere in colonial Latin America. Visual communication was key to these types of spectacles in the colonial period and more so following independence. Thus, playing with the effects of representation, producing illusions of what was real, substituting the appearance of an object for the object itself, exposure, illustration, and so on, were all new techniques of seeing. These techniques accompanied technological innovations like daguerreotypes, photographic cameras, microscopes, telescopes, and electric light, all of which revived a collective sensitivity to new modes of seeing and the devices that made them possible.[5] Taking into account other activities of cultural production invites us to establish bridges between lettered culture and popular culture.

Up until now we have drawn attention to the most common modality through which historical imagination materializes, namely written historiography (since tradition equates history with writing) and its possible exchanges with certain forms of visual culture. Nevertheless, the contents of the closet of Clio (the muse of history) are extremely varied, and her outfits are made of fabrics whose different textures do not necessarily obey the written text or the image that the text reproduces. The regime of historical imagination follows the logic of a specific time and place determined by a complex matrix of factors in which historical writing is only one outcome. The written word and iconic practices live in this matrix along with other expressions—such as architectonic ones or ones related to the decorative arts, for example, or scopic rituals such as visiting exhibitions and museums—that regulate the grammar of cultural politics and styles. The work of Hayden White and Michel de Certeau provide fruitful reflections on this point, but their analyses are limited by their conceiving of the historiographical event as bound to writing. I prefer the term *practices of historical imagination*, defined broadly as the body of rules that regulates cultural production of all sorts and that informs what a society perceives in a determined moment as historical memory, to refer to the same cultural phenomena. These rules controlled the range of themes as well as the rhetorical and stylistic repertoires of expressive modalities of both high culture and popular culture—in painting as much as in literature, and of public parties and celebrations and the decorative arts.

In what remains of this chapter, we will consider a key phenomenon in late nineteenth-century Venezuela: the context surrounding the first National Fair, organized on the model of the World's Fair. This first Fair led to the ordering and coining of culture according to a historicist fiction, and it was a space where manifestations of visual culture exercised a predominant role in the construction of a historical imaginary.

Learning to See

One of the "charms" of Venezuelan novelist Tomás Michelena's novel *Débora* (1884) is the sadomasochist mode of punishment the protagonist's husband, Adriano de Soussa, doles out to friends who happen to be his wife's lovers once he discovers their treachery and her double adultery. With her constant flirtation, Débora inflames the passions of her husband's friends and generates a triangular homoerotic tension that permeates the entire text. One of the scenes of punishment takes place in the style of a porno show. The husband forces Felipe Latorre, one of his wife's lovers, to look through a "magic eye" that was a skylight and watch the naked bodies of Débora and Alberto Cassard, the other lover. The two have been locked in a cellar and exposed to the excited eyes of the voyeurs above who enjoy—though not without some pain—the erotic spectacle going on below.

What is important to note from this narrative plot are the mechanisms that transformed seeing into a pleasure and the act of continuing to see into a permanent desire to see. In the case of the novel, the words attempted to take the place of the camera in order to present a striptease composed of images and the staging of reality. With the erotic images in view—at least for the reader and the two men peering through the skylight—the novel appealed to the new sensory pleasure that engaged cultural practices not necessarily regulated by the grammar of the written word. In reality, there was no torturous punishment for the insulted husband or for the lovers, for all enjoyed the exhibitionary game of watching and being watched.

There is no doubt that during the nineteenth century, the written word competed at a disadvantage against a wide range of forms of communication whose consumption was linked to seeing. In this sense, it is worth pointing out the different meanings of the term *ilustrado* throughout the 1800s. First, it referred to a person of great reason and knowledge—an *enlightened* person—or, with a more teleological end, the light that instructs and makes illustrious that person. *Ilustrado* was also used to speak of print media illustrated with plates or engravings, as well as the act of projecting light and making visible and intelligible an idea through an image. These meanings were intertwined—the one linked to rationality, the other closer to making ideas visible; the first born of a Cartesian and abstract conception of reality, and the second tied to a visual tradition of knowledge—and they shared in the production of cultural forms. So, for example, the images that appeared in print media "illustrated" the word and amplified its projection (in terms of both the meaning and the size of readership these media reached).[6] There was, nevertheless, a complex tension between word and image that revealed conflicts in the constitution of a "realm of letters" and the differences between high and low cultures. Likewise, this tension was made clear when it came to the reading public that, although more familiar with visual forms of cultural expression, was now faced with developing literary competency. These tensions led to the gentrification of certain fields of production, contrary to the general tendency throughout the century of preferring scopic modalities that undoubtedly prolonged a "phantasmagoria of equality."[7]

The poet Rubén Darío dedicated several chronicles to manifestations of visual culture—in particular, productions of technological reproduction like posters and postcards. His many lady friends showered him with hundreds of the "little cards" that were spread over his writing desk—"postcards from Spain and Latin America," explained Darío, "sent with the hope of me writing them something in return, even if it was just an autograph." Darío took pleasure in untangling the psychological relationship between the illustration on each postcard and the character of its sender. "To be in style," he noted, "they send the first postcard they have at hand: a statue, a view, a panorama, or a building from their home city."[8]

For his part, José Martí, during the many years he lived in the United States (1881–1895), developed a fondness for technological innovations. He was especially fascinated by mechanical and electrical gadgets, which he reviewed meticulously after seeing them on display at the grand exhibitions and fairs. These fairs of material culture pushed him to make adjustments in his projection of the "republic of letters." Martí appreciated the pedagogical advances achieved by these more democratic learning spaces, for by helping one to learn to see, fairs and exhibits could make education more effective and efficient for the masses. He insisted that "exhibitions and fairs are no longer just places to take a stroll. They are announcements; they are great, silent lessons; they are schools. . . . No book or collection of books can show teachers of agriculture what they can see with their own eyes at the fairground."[9] Martí was not speaking about learning to read the written word, but rather learning to see and read images—about a semiotics of things and about making practical inferences that would be useful in life.

In addition to his interest in Eadweard Muybridge's photos in motion, the photographs Richard Jahr took involving the light of the moon, and the developments of color photography, which he followed closely, Martí wrote in various chronicles of the popularity that panoramas enjoyed at the end of the century, especially those dealing with historical themes. For this particular moment, panoramas constituted the closest modality to what would later be documentary film. Martí felt that this form of "spectacular" entertainment, which often dealt with war and captured the attention of urban masses, could have an impact on the events rocking the world at the turn of the century, thus anticipating the advent of film:

> In Europe, the grand panoramas are still in vogue. . . . These panoramas are not mere views or canvases, but rather entire buildings or parts of buildings that represent, like in real life, memorable historical scenes with truth and art. The most well known is the Philippotteaux, on the Champs Elysées. It is a circular building whose interior walls are painted with scenes of the outskirts of Paris during the siege with great skill, science, and naturalness. The optical illusion is complete. . . . There is a moat filled with trenches, horses, spies, cannons, sand bags, cannon balls, cadavers. . . . Every detail is lovely. . . . The excess of color and sheen is bound to excite the anger of the French.[10]

The success of dioramas and panoramas was not just limited to metropolitan cities, either. In Latin America, they were in style before the arrival of the daguerreotype. For example, on Sunday, 31 December 1843, the Mexican newspaper *El siglo diez y nueve* published an announcement that commented on the frenzy caused by the new diorama in the Portal de Mercaderes. Given the tremendous turnout, it was imperative to find a larger locale capable of satisfying the demand of Mexico City's residents. The same announcement went on to mention news the diorama had generated in Havana and in the United States. While the panorama and diorama had in common mechanisms of optical illusion, the diorama did not need such an ostentatious building, and its transparencies allowed for more dynamic effects through the play of light and shadow. The diorama was closer to phantasmagoria; it bridged the visible and the invisible, and its effect, in the end, was more dislocating than that produced by the panorama.[11]

Although visual culture in nineteenth-century Latin America was deployed in multifaceted ways, I would like to emphasize on the one hand the efficiency of panoramas and dioramas in promoting social imaginaries that prepared the narrative of historiographical styles on different levels—from patriotic histories, historical novels, the apotheosis of heroes, and literary contests, to public monuments and architectonic forms. On the other hand, to enable this analysis and the intersection of practices, I would like to draw special attention to the first National Fair in Venezuela in 1883. Organized to celebrate the centenary of the birth of El Libertador, Simón Bolívar, the Fair was a highly concentrated symbolic space where cultural manifestations were channeled to endorse the power of the state. I am going to limit the focus to a handful of these, namely: the choice of architectonic forms for the main exhibition hall, resulting from a transatlantic dialogue between powers at the center and the periphery; the consumption of military fashion and new technologies; the logics that brought together Gothic styles with machines; and the epistemological mediators between the panoramas of the centenary and the series of historiographical narratives deployed at the moment.

Panoramas of the Rainforest

During the 1820s, Londoners could enjoy new artistic modalities that used simple forms to expand the horizon of their geographical imagination. One of these was Robert Barker's Leicester Square rotunda, where the freshest panoramas portrayed striking battle scenes along with views of European and Asian cities. Middle-class denizens could follow British imperial expansion and travel virtually to the far corners of the world without leaving London.[12] Derived in part from panoptic technologies, the ocular mechanism of the panorama did not impose the same restrictive politics of sight, and though it democratized certain geographies for the London public, the panorama also reintroduced the subjectivity specific to imperial control. After all, taking in views of landscapes from the elevated platform in the panorama gave spectators visual possession of a territory.

Around the same time, the Englishman Sir Robert Ker Porter returned to London after fifteen years in Caracas as the consul for Great Britain. He came back with various paintings of tropical Venezuelan lands. Shortly thereafter, the walls of Leicester Square would host the first panorama of the Valle de Caracas as seen from the Catuche river (Figure 5.1).

The scene portrayed a desolate landscape with vestiges of what could have been an ancient civilization. Porter sealed for the European imagination the vision of a land ruined by the 1812 earthquake and the fruitless years of a long period of coloniality. In short, he helped solidify the dehistoricized image of a deserted American continent. The panorama of the Valle of Caracas was not altogether different from the landscapes of Morocco and Kabul displayed in Barker's rotunda.[13] Panoramas of "depopulated" landscapes that corresponded to colonized regions served to both entertain observers and invite them to engage in the complex operation of comparing lands. Ultimately, the images implicitly illustrated the incompetence of certain empires (like the Spanish one, for example) whose management had been unproductive. The balance of their rule was ruin and a deserted landscape. Of course, many of these panoramas helped alert their viewers' sensibilities to the growing need to recuperate those territories for the sake of "civilization," this time through imperial powers that were less overtly "aggressive."[14]

Thus, Venezuela's image on the international stage did not find the same fortune as did that of Mexico, for example. During the same years, Mexico's image entered the European imaginary thanks to Mexico's pre-Hispanic civilizations, which "orientalized" the nation in accord with the "Egyptomania" in vogue following the Napoleonic campaigns. The taste for orientalism gained ground in the "Egyptian Hall" of the businessman and traveler William Bullock, who in 1824 had organized a popular exhibit of Aztec curiosities mixed with objects from Egypt and Turkey.[15] Bullock had visited Mexico around 1822 and taken calendars, codices, carvings, tombs, vessels, dissected birds, and precious stones back to London to display in his Egyptian Hall alongside curiosities from Egypt, including mummies. Thus, "Mexico" began to circulate with things from Egypt in the European imaginary and in the museological space. Later, this strange pairing became inevitable—for example, in the 1889 Paris World's Fair, where the Palacio Azteca was a pharaonic imitation.

Since it lacked a similar history of indigenous civilization, the young Republic of Venezuela incarnated the myth of uncultivated land in the repertoire of modernity's utopias. The two operations that, each in their own way, "orientalized" the continent—naturalizing it to fit a given narrative or through archeological exoticization—emptied it as well of its historicity. In the case of Mexico, the historical present was ignored in order to restrict the narrative of the country to its Aztec past, which ironically served as a motive for further archeological exploitation to fill the historical imagination of museums and imperial institutions.[16] Venezuela, on the

Figure 5.1: A view of Caracas's city center (1826). Drawing by Sir Robert Ker Porter for exhibition in London, in Graziano Gasparini, *Caracas: La ciudad colonial y guzmancista* (Caracas: Ernesto Armitano, 1978), 202. Although the 1812 earthquake demolished much of the city, romantic codes extended a set of standard images of desolation and ruin to other parts of Latin America. The new imperialism was interested in symbolically "emptying" the continent.

other hand and at first glance, was converted into a native land for a new "discovery."

Following the Industrial Revolution, the new imperial powers of the nineteenth century needed to reinvent America ideologically. America was recreated as a landscape, as an object of various discourses and disciplines, and above all as a source of wealth and resources. Europe needed America for its wide open and wild spaces, for the strange species that could satisfy Europe's museums growing thirst for collecting, and for the development of the humanities. The insistence of travelers and scientists upon reconverting American lands into "nature"—that is, lands without history, or with only a "prehistory" in ruins—kept pace with the growth in foreign investments in these latitudes. Suddenly America's historicity could vanish in order to appear "virgin" to Western eyes. Imagine the anxiety produced by the movements of Tupac Amaru in the Andes, José da Silva Xavier (alias *Tiradentes*, or tooth-puller) in Brazil, Toussaint Louverture in Haiti, Pedro Díaz Cuscat in Chiapas, José María Leyva Cajeme among the Yaquis, and Pedro Gual y España in Venezuela. Travelers and artists thus worked quickly to amend an esthetic of emptiness while philosophers were occupied with fine-tuning the universal categories of metaphysics. For their part, lettered Latin Americans—from Andrés Bello to Rómulo

Gallegos in the early twentieth century—perpetuated a Eurocentric vision of America by arranging their narratives around the theme of "civilization and barbarism."

Thus, the invention of the "tropical" rainforest was a strategic elaboration of the imaginaries of a body of lettered elites and politicians who needed silent support from both sides of the ocean. This support would serve to expand the tourist industry and function as the axis of the modernizing project. In what appeared almost as an orchestrated effort, the many stories of travelers who spent time in Venezuela in the nineteenth century practically subscribed to the vision of Sir Robert. Narratives like Pal Rosti's *Memorias de un viaje por América* (*Memoirs of Travels through America*, 1861); Edward Eastwick's *Venezuela, or Sketches of Life in a South American Republic* (1864); and *The Land of Bolívar, or War, Peace and Adventure in the Republic of Venezuela* by James Mudie Spence (1878)—just to name a few—gradually defined a tradition that crafted the same image of an uninhabited and savage region lacking in history but full of primary resources.[17]

Modified or not to be in line with reality, this image of a "savage" nation began to make the creole elite uncomfortable during the second half of the century. They were more committed to a process of efficient modernization and no longer identified with the portrait of a country full of alligators, mosquitoes, and Guajiro cannibals, and even less so when it came time to host the first National Fair in 1883. Toward the end of the century, the progress of nations was measured by the huge events of the fairs and expositions that arranged the symbolic capital of the country as an archive and showcase of culture. Thanks to the visual technologies that had quickly made their way to America, beginning around mid-century residents of Caracas could stroll Letras Patrias street and for a minimal price purchase postcards with panoramas of the World's Fairs that had been held in London, Paris, Vienna, and Bremen; they could enjoy the views offered by personal stereoscopes; and they could contemplate the lights and shadows of dioramas that at times projected Gothic structures.

A hidden dialogue between oligarchies on the American side of the Atlantic with their European counterparts would explain only in part the motives behind the construction of a Gothic palace as the main exhibition hall in a country with a tropical climate (Figure 5.2). What was the politics of selecting medieval nostalgias and knightly airs to communicate the spirit of modernizing forms? What anxiety led to the adoption of strict Victorian styles? In short, what historicist fiction guided the state to elect neo-Gothic forms for the Fair?

Figure 5.2: Colonial structures of the Convent of San Francisco were covered by a neo-Gothic façade for the 1883 National Fair Palacio. For weeks, massive crowds could visit the exhibition of all possible forms of material culture, illuminated by electric light, too. In front of the Palacio was the Guzmán Blanco square. In Graziano Gasparini, *Caracas: La ciudad colonial y guzmancista* (Caracas: Ernesto Armitano, 1978), 289.

Tropical ... *ma non troppo!*

Venezuelans had had significant experience in the way of anti-colonialist thought and revolutionary battles, and Venezuela had been a key site in the wars for independence, all of which supplied narratives to draw on in the projection of an alternative image of Venezuelan identity in the international arena. The signs of barbarism had to be covered with signs of civilization. After all, Venezuela had participated in World's Fairs and similar events—in London (1862), Paris (1867), Vienna (1873), Bremen (1874), Santiago (1875), Philadelphia (1876), and Buenos Aires (1882)—where the impact of symbolic representations could be measured. In addition, beginning in 1870, the government of Antonio Guzmán Blanco initiated a campaign to give Caracas a facelift in hopes of modifying opinions of "the crude tropics." In 1883, Guzmán Blanco invited the world community to the National Fair where the possibilities for businessmen and immigrants—the reaches of "progress" attained in arts and letters, handicrafts, and mechanics—

Figure 5.3: There were various neo-Gothic pavilions at the 1876 Centennial Exhibition in Philadelphia, perhaps inspired by the Crystal Palace at the 1851 World's Fair in London. In Philadelphia, there were buildings devoted to machines, sanitary devices, electrical appliances, communications, and agriculture; there was even a pavilion for women. In J. S. Ingram, *The Centennial Exposition, Described and Illustrated* (Philadelphia: Hubbard Bros., 1876), 111.

would all be on display. A fair could change the representations of Venezuela that had been in vogue up until then.

A fair like those mounted in Santiago and Buenos Aires could show how Caracas, a port of entry into South America, was home to sufficient infrastructure so that any participant and visitor could feel at home. An event of this magnitude was also destined to consolidate the Venezuelan state apparatus, and General Guzmán Blanco knew what we know today: namely, that the nation is a narrative, a performance. The Fair had to channel all available tools to create the effect of a single unified nation. The fabrication of nationalisms grew steadily in the second half of the century, and fairs were ideal spaces where the logic of progress governed a competition of nations.[18]

On 2 August 1883, the Palacio of the National Fair opened its doors to a much larger than normal crowd.[19] Of course, we cannot lose sight of the fact that Caracas then was a city with slightly more than fifty thousand residents (much smaller than Buenos Aires, Mexico City, Santiago, Lima, or Havana), but one that had developed a European atmosphere leaving little to be desired since Guzmán Blanco took power in 1870. Open day and night, and with cheap ticket prices (50 bolívar), the Fair attracted close to sixty-three thousand spectators. The press commented that many people visited the exposition more than once, making it difficult to calculate precisely the demographic flux. Yet there was a clear increase in movement of people in the city.

Venezuela presented itself to the international public with a "proven" style, via a neo-Gothic building that not only kept pace with the architectonic tendencies of the great fairs, but also endorsed the politics of style prevailing in seats of metropolitan power. Perhaps the most pertinent model in this respect had been the neo-Gothic pavilions of the Agricultural Hall at the 1876 Philadelphia World's Fair that had commemorated the centennial of independence in the United States (Figure 5.3).

The Venezuelan Fair's Palacio was an impressive, even extravagant, response to the various designs circulating among the "civilized" of the region, all of which were in line with Guzmán Blanco's fantasy and had very little of the tropical motif. The point was to demonstrate to guests that in the patria of El Libertador, one could find not only the most profitable gold deposits, the greatest variety of woods, and the best snakeskins; one could also drink the most bubbly Moet et Chandon. One of the emblems of this modernization was the inauguration of the Caracas-La Guaira railroad, timed to coincide with the centenary of Bolívar's birth. Foreigners arriving in the port of La Guaira could board the train in the low, hot lands of the coast and rapidly climb to the high lands of Caracas, the peak of progress. By that time, Caracas had donned the airs of Napoleon III's Paris.

Antonio Guzmán Blanco's eighteen years in office (1870–1888, known as the *Guzmanato*) changed substantially the face of Caracas. Many of the existing colonial structures were used by his administration and for the Fair with changes made only to their façades and visible exterior walls in order to accommodate the needs of "modern" life. This was the case with the Palacio, which had been the Convent of San Francisco. Guzmán Blanco expropriated the building in 1873 and converted it into the Universidad de Caracas, adopting the neo-Gothic look. The architect Juan Hurtado and the engineer Jesús Muñoz Tebar led the conversion and incorporated a museum into one of the building's wings. Around 1882, on the eve of the centenary, they annexed another structure destined specifically for the Fair.

Thus, under its pointed arches, the Palacio ordered the material culture of Venezuela and served as a pedagogical space. Venezuelan history—past and present—was arranged schematically in order to be learned at a glance. The neo-Gothic façade of the building conveyed symbolically and politically the modern discourse of the nation (Figure 5.4). It was probably the first time an old building's colonial structure had been metamorphosed in order to showcase in its niches modern technology and machinery. The languages of conversion and assimilation—from the Gothic to the tropic, from the Gothic to machinery, and from machinery to national heroes— underwent diverse processes of appropriation and semantic transculturation.[20] Yet if the Fair contained the nation, then how could the nation be understood in its Gothic codification?

Café con leche: Whitening the Nation

Now free from a period of civil war, both the emerging middle classes and the oligarchy supporting Guzmán Blanco learned quickly·that the politics of forms could guarantee social distinctions and better positions within the social hierarchy. Reproduction and mimicry were mechanisms that allowed for one to choose a position along this hierarchy. The Palacio created an "exportable" image of Venezuela that was profitable for investments, and its mimicry of metropolitan styles was a platform for dialogue between the center and the periphery with fewer inequalities. The reproduction of the neo-Gothic style was an imitation, but not in every respect: it was a mirage of metropolitan expansion following the grammar of new colonizing languages.

Let us recall that in Sir Robert's images of Venezuela, America appeared without a voice, as a place outside of history. The selection and transculturation of artistic languages was inscribed in a complex fabric of debates. Much of these processes involved struggles for interpretative power and the sociopolitical implications of adopting "proven" styles.[21] Undoubtedly the neo-Gothic style of the Palacio gave a more "civilized" face to the country. At least it denaturalized some imperial narratives by inverting their premises: Venezuela appeared not as an uncivilized region, but instead as a neurological center of modern historicity. The weight of this historicity was manifest in the most prestigious styles of metropolitan centers. The discourse that nationalized nature—that stereotyped Venezuela as a tropical rainforest—was exchanged for a discourse that nationalized history, linking the representation of the nation to heroes converted into myths and goods. If Venezuela had been previously identified with rivers and jungles, its new identity would be that of the patria of Simón Bolívar, starting from the time of the Fair. This new image was recrafted for export. Now the tropical country would be associated with prominent figures illustrating virility—Bolívar, Guzmán Blanco, then later Juan Vicente Gómez, Pérez Jiménez, Rómulo Betancourt, Carlos Andrés Pérez, and, at present, Hugo Chávez—leading to the identification of state agency with the masculine machine of war.

Figure 5.4: Detail of Martín Tovar y Tovar's *La Batalla de Carabobo*, designed to commemorate the hundredth anniversary of Simón Bolívar's birth. Tovar y Tovar's painting, which portrayed the war for independence, appeared in the dome of the capitol in Caracas. In Raúl Díaz Legorburu, *La Caracas de Bolívar, II* (Caracas: Editorial Los Próceres, 1983), 128.

It was imperative to produce enough narratives with historicizing effects—that is, with mechanisms to create pasts and genealogies. A majority of the Fair's exhibition halls housed displays regarding Bolívar and other leaders, the wars for independence, and the "origins" of the nation. The impulse to archive reunited in these spaces paintings, photographs, panoramas, machines, telephones, engineering plans, furniture, books, and other documents. The effort to establish genealogies sought to create traditions with a certain prestige. Logically, the modernizing thrust came draped in neo-Gothic garb, so a coffee grinder, for example, was adorned with Gothic arches, gargoyles, and lilies. Colonial styles in republican Venezuela were discounted because they were too reminiscent of a Hispanic model not in sync with the new styles of modernity, not to mention the overtones they carried of colonialism. Baroque styles did not fare much better. They were often tied to the "backwardness" and "primitivism" of pre-industrial countries, connecting Catholic heritage to precapitalist social structures. The evolution of the baroque grew more complex in the second half of the century when World's Fairs began associating the Hispanic baroque with new orientalist tastes. What resulted from this orientalist link to the baroque was an internationalization of stereotypical images that ultimately reproduced imperial hierarchies in the field of cultural exchange. Thus, the adoption of the Victorian Gothic in Venezuela—a style that recalled medieval and lordly traditions from northern Europe—was the most agreeable choice with the Napoleonic airs of national heroes and Antonio Guzmán Blanco himself, who, following the Prussian model, had his own personal guard (Figure 5.5).

In various registers of daily life, a military style took root, not only in masculine dress but also in the hypertrophy of the cult of heroes, the penchant for parades, artillery salutes, fireworks, military bands, and "live" scenes depicting epic stories. Young men were recommended to practice the art of fencing, and great care was taken to cultivate the genealogies of these activities and liken them to North Atlantic styles. In this respect, the Palacio assured the framework for a trusted historiographical image with real possibilities of temporal depth. In this climate of patriotic effervescence, Eduardo Blanco began publishing chapters of *Venezuela heroica* (Heroic Venezuela) in the magazine *Tertulia* in 1878. Having become what was probably the first best seller in Latin America, *Venezuela heroica* had gone through two editions by the 1883 centenary, the second one significantly revised with new scenes that satisfied the public's desire for epic scenes of imaginary wars in times of peace. Although the great Venezuelan battles were a thing of the past, more recent ones occurring in the Old World (the Crimean War, the Franco-Prussian War) were communicated rapidly thanks to the mechanical reproduction of print media and new visual technologies.

The circulation of this military esthetic and its impact on collective sensibilities (Venezuela was only trying to keep pace here with international fashion) optimized modern relations between the demands of the masses and the consolidation of states with both industrial and military goals.[22] Military themes—be they in historical painting, equestrian statues, historiographical modalities, historical novels, panoramas, portraits of generals for the stereoscope, or in other expressions of material culture—were potent cultural arguments. They fabricated traditions and ordered subjectivities according to a grammar for disciplining citizenries for work and the production of capital. In this sense, the revival of the Gothic, with its knightly fictions, forms of high art, and objects of popular culture, sweetened the state apparatus's new monopoly on violence and cloaked the new modes of imperialism. The Venezuelan nation thus appeared to have distant origins—origins that camouflaged the Hispanic past with North

Figure 5.5: Military fashion offered a model for a disciplined and orderly citizenry to be contrasted with ruffians from the countryside or workers who stirred up trouble. The dissemination of images like this one, such as the publication of patriotic histories and odes to heroes, naturalized the politics of the state for shaping a docile and obedient nation. In Carlos Eduardo Misle, *Sabor de Caracas* (Caracas: Ediciones Banco de Venezuela, 1980), 70.

Atlantic characteristics. In the overlap of violence to achieve this, at least one form of violence had to negotiate the question of race.

In the attempt to infuse the Hispanic past with medieval English fictions, the effects of the past were modified and complex operations of whitening remained hidden. For Latin American liberals during the second half of the century, the Spanish legacy was an obstacle in the way of achieving European modernization. In some intellectual circles, "Hispanic" was semantically equated with gypsies and nomadic peoples of eastern deserts, as well as with dark-skinned races. The stylized character of the neo-Gothic whitened and—at least in the game of appearances—allowed for one entertaining style to be substituted by another. There were probably many ghosts weighing on the conscience of new elites; one of these dealt with racial cleansing and the effort to distance themselves from "colored people," placing a white mask over mestizo skin. Another of these phantoms was related to the discontinuity of the traditional hegemonic social group—

that is, the replacement of white creole elites who led the fight for independence (those like Bolívar, for example) with new leaders from popular origins who had risen in rank during the wars for independence and subsequent civil wars (those like Páez and Guzmán). The rhetoric of forms took the place of family genealogies. Perhaps the insistence on Gothic fashions and medieval styles substituted for bloodlines and, to a certain extent, "dehispanicized" the faces of those who needed to speak with the interlocutors of Western modernity.[23]

During the Guzmanato, the number of imported styles rose sharply. These were masks that hid complex national and local histories. At the same time, they pointed to the desire to appear behind another different façade on the international stage, distanced from "exotic" and "backward" nations. Behind the adoption of imported styles was also the goal to establish distance from oriental styles that had been carefully appropriated by metropolitan powers. The neo-Gothic was ideal in this respect, for it was a cosmopolitan modality that allowed Caracas to be part of the center of western Whiteness, while at the same time transforming Simón Bolívar into an English lord or member of the Round Table. Moreover, the neo-Gothic functioned as an emblematic hinge connecting the old patrician elite with the new oligarchy. The Hispanic substrate was not discarded, however; it was reworked to reestablish links to Europe, as well as to the traditions of colonial creole elites. Nevertheless, Hispanism was not free from problems and contradictions. Hispanism, in the form of linguistic harmony, played a role in the territorial unity of the nation-state, for Spanish took precedence over twenty-two indigenous languages. Hispanism was also sustained through literary references to the Spanish literary canon as a way to legitimize national literature. And, the politics of the Spanish language illustrated the power of Hispanism when Latin American intellectuals claimed linguistic brotherhood with Spain in the face of a growing U.S. presence in the region toward the end of the century. On the other hand, the Hispanic legacy was rejected at the moment of articulating modernizing projects, and the Spanish language was not the most useful for commercial relations.

Deorientalizing the Torrid Zone

The choice of the neo-Gothic palace in the middle of the Torrid Zone was part of another agenda linked to the politics of the architectonic forms and styles behind the representations of Latin American identities at the World's Fairs. The styles conveyed strong ideological overtones, and in the case of the fairs, the pavilions were nations on display. The impact of the forms and façades determined the circulation of nations in an already global economy. The architectonic forms symbolized hegemony and subalternity; they embodied imperial styles and colonized ones.

Neo-Gothic styles gained favor between 1830 and 1870 as part of an effort to establish a more Christian and Western form to offset Byzantine and orientalist tendencies that had gained in attraction following recent English conquests. Designing an imperial architectonic style was a delicate matter for the agendas of both the imperial power and the colony. The architectonic forms, in fact, spoke directly to the control of a handful of nations over others. The assimilation of Byzantine and Islamic styles formed part of an initial strategy of alliances between empire and colony. Public buildings in England, for instance, incorporated elements of Islamic architecture, which softened imperial aggression through an inversion of the languages of domination. Ironically, England appeared dominated by its colonies.[24] This appropriation of the Orient and Europe's need to "orientalize" (for exoticism, libido, zeal for control) lasted beyond the turn of the century.

This situation stirred up a controversy among the members of the guild of English architects. They resented the excess of Islamic styles as an invasion of a colonial Other that was undermining the virile identity of the Empire. The architects—especially those who constituted the Ecclesiological Society, which counted among its members the founder Beresford Hope, John Ruskin, James Fergusson, and Edward A. Freeman—felt that respect for England was in jeopardy, and even more so considering that official buildings had adopted these imported styles. Beginning around mid-century, the members of the Society took to elaborating essentialist theories about the racial character of different architectonic styles, following a geopolitical scheme and gendered categories that opposed North and South, and Occident and Orient. It determined styles in line with Christian tradition to be virile, healthy, rational, and ordered. The styles of the Orient were qualified as feminine, bland, unstable, and irrational. In this framework, Islamic architecture was pegged as the opposite of all things the Empire represented.[25] English architecture, on the contrary, was by its very origins virile, rooted in strong medieval forms. According to the logic of the Society's arguments, it was up to this style to recover the "purity" of Christian tradition and reestablish through its vertical lines a spirit of rationality. If England wanted to become the capital of Western modernity, then neo-Gothic forms needed to gain architectonic primacy. Furthermore, England was the seat of the Industrial Revolution, exporting emblems of progress in its machines, steamships, and trains. Techno-

Figure 5.6: The grand Fairs had buildings devoted exclusively to the display of machines, as seen in this image from José Martí, *La edad de oro*, ed. Eduardo Lolo (Miami: Ediciones Universal, 2001), 292.

logical revolutions were a product of Western reason and by nature facilitated their own global expansion. The similarities between the premises of Christianity and those of the new, instrumental, technological reason combined forces. The neo-Gothic was one of their languages (Figure 5.6).

For several decades, industrial modernity was thus symbolized by forms evoking medieval architecture. The adoption of the neo-Gothic in the nineteenth century signaled a desire to be part of the Christian community's orbit. Deploying the neo-Gothic was a mark of a new evangelization whose catechism accompanied the expansion of economic liberalism.[26] The style of the Palacio at the National Fair, then, sought to distance the desire for modernity that it represented from any sort of orientalist gesture, holding to an imaginary of "high style" in order to diminish the image of the Torrid Zone. Ultimately, one of the driving ideas behind the Palacio was that it could *deorientalize* the region. It is important to point out here that the Western tastes that spread through orientalism—in architecture, decorative arts, fashion design, travel literature, painting, panoramas, and, later, film—did not have a solely negative relation to modernity. They were purveyors of a liberating and regenerative spirit in opposition to the destructive and alienating tendencies of the same modernity. Here, orientalist expressions celebrated the utopian quality of pre-capitalist spaces that, "primitive" and "effeminate," developed an ecological narrative to counteract the devastating forces of modernity, above all in the former colonies.

During the second half of the century, Latin American countries that sent representations to the series of World's Fairs carried the stigma of orientalism. The reader will remember that Mexico was already paired with Egyptian art in the European imaginary; at the 1884 New Orleans Fair, Mexico appeared in the Palacio de la Alhambra, and later, at the 1889 Paris Fair, the nation was on display in its Palacio Azteca.[27] Islamic styles appeared in numerous Latin American pavilions at the Fairs, thanks to the fact that they were aligned with contemporary cosmopolitan tastes and were not totally at odds with a certain Hispanic ancestry. In any case, Latin America was read through Asian styles as well, for the European imaginary continued perceiving the region as the West Indies.

While the Mexican and Salvadoran pavilions adhered to Egyptian and Asian styles respectively, Venezuela chose not to identify with the politics of exoticism. If the goal was to identify Venezuela with the land of virility, then it was important to distinguish the effeminate character of other architectonic forms from the military manliness of the patria's founders. This was achieved by adopting European architectonic forms. Moreover, the form of the Palacio at the Venezuelan Fair not only contributed to the whitening of urban styles in Caracas as well as of its residents, its feudal airs also hid the continued existence of a semi-feudal, semi-enslaved workforce that enabled the high profits for foreign capital. In a very real sense, the seignorial elegance erased the mestizo and indigenous nation, for whitening the façade reintroduced subliminally the hierarchy of a society far from democratic.

The War Machine and Historiographical Art

The neo-Gothic architecture of the Palacio was the symbolic framework in which the displays of culture would be interpreted. In the building's galleries, rooms, and patios, the seignorial tone of modernity would be present in different though equally significant ways. The historical conjuncture made possible substantial operations on the national imaginary, modifying the image of a "wild" country by presenting it as one full of historicity and constructing a new identity around a mythic hero. The transculturated meanings of the neo-Gothic worked toward this end, and motivated by the knightly overtones of the Gothic revival, national history began to be interpreted according to these epic codes.[28] It is no coincidence that it was under the neo-Gothic roof of the Palacio where Venezuelans saw for the first time Martín Tovar y Tovar's paintings *La firma del acta de la independencia* (The Signing of the Declaration of Independence) and *La batalla de Carabobo*. Also making their debut on display at the Fair were the second edition of Eduardo Blanco's *Venezuela heroica*, José Güel y Mercader's voluminous *Literatura venezolana*, the *Biblioteca de escritores venezolanos* by the Marqués de Rojas, and Felipe Tejera's *Perfiles venezolanos o galería de hombres célebres* (Venezuelan Profiles, or Gallery of Illustrious Men), as well as all the issues of the newspaper *El Zulia ilustrado*. These examples of print media were meant to be viewed as objects for visual consumption and part of the effort to construct a national imaginary along the lines studied in Chapters 1 and 2 of this volume.

Although for close to a decade Venezuelans had read the chapters of *Venezuela heroica* as they were published periodically in *La tertulia*—chapters conceived in line with epic battles—now the Fair gave new meaning to the text, not only in book form but accompanied by oil paintings and murals illustrating scenes of war and a heroic past. Those who were not able to read the chapters could, at the Fair, follow the historical narratives told through images. The effect of the images was such that it overshadowed the periods prior to and immediately following the moment of independence, converting that moment into a type of absolute present. Masculinities and the apparatus of war appeared to control the subjectivities of the moment and transform war into the great language of modernity. The panoramas of war provided documentary images for the public to visualize contemporary wars in Europe. Historiographical art, then, fulfilled the functions of recreating the past and informing the present.

The neo-Gothic style could also be seen in huge canvases on exhibit in the hall of fine arts. These included *El combate en el lago de Maracaibo* (measuring three meters in width) by José Manuel Maucó, Manuel Otero's *Entrevista de Bolívar y Sucre en el desaguadero de los Andes*, paintings depicting the deaths of generals and soldiers, and the panoramic fresco illustrating the battle of Carabobo on the inner dome of the capitol, now home to Parliament. The public space of this building became a space of relaxation and recreation where official painting was transformed into art for the masses.

Let us focus for a moment on this point to further highlight the logics of the cultural matrix connecting popular culture to expressions of high culture, including historiographical writing in the formats of patriotic histories and historical novels. This matrix constructed and channeled collective memory. The corpus of historiographical narratives emerging at the turn of the century—ranging from texts and images to performances, parades, and music that produced historical fictions—was marked by a grammar of linearity that owed much to the visual culture of panoramas presenting the masses with historical themes and dynamic scenes.

At this point, it is worth pointing out the difference between panoramas of vistas (landscapes and urban scenes) and panoramas communicating historical themes. Many historical texts found inspiration for their rhetorical mechanisms—specifically descriptive techniques—in panoramas. With both types of panoramas, the circular structure of the buildings functioned like a temple of illusions by introducing new perspectives of simulation and testing how viewers could see. Nevertheless, the scopic experience in panoramas portraying landscapes (see Figure 5.1) required viewers to maintain a certain distance from the painting in order to take in the entire view. An esthetics of geopolitics linked to ocular possession was at work in this view from a distance, from an elevated platform.

In the case of panoramas detailing historical scenes (see Figure 5.4), the mechanics of perception was reversed, attracting viewers not to distance themselves, but rather to get close, infuse, and wrap themselves in the actions represented. The spectator was part of the war spectacle, allowing for the fiction of the past to become naturalized in a melodramatic present full of emotion and lacking in critical distance.[29] These historical panoramas constituted a formidable machine for imagining history "such as it really happened." They naturalized history by eliminating its complexity, suppressing the contradiction, and enhancing facts and protagonists with a simplifying clarity. They appealed to emotions, shortening the distance between viewer and image. Techniques of realism produced the effect of a simulacrum capable of creating a precise duplicate of "reality." Furthermore, panoramas were a form of mass media that served a didactic purpose and played a part in the formation of collective memory. For this reason, they could be considered among the first means of industrial cultural production. Eduardo Blanco's *Venezuela heroica* functioned in a similar fashion, for its wide reception led to its conversion to a historiographical folletín (see Chapter 3 in this volume) with "weekly installments of battles." Its scenes inflamed the always incomplete desire for more, making for a text with the same circular structure as the panoramas with historical scenes.

The representation of war appearing on panoramas fabricated rewarding historiographies that alleviated the traumas of a troubled past. Here is an excellent example: the Napoleonic representation of independence blurred memories of the Guerra Federal (1858–1863) and replaced the popular hero Ezequiel Zamora with the whitened protagonism of Bolívar and similar figures. In this way, panoramas traded dangerously anarchic images of revolutionary mobs for illustrations of uniformed armies. Such panoramas offered an alternative trope to offset the threat of popular uprisings. In this sense, the glances made by observers on a stroll through the Fair, especially when viewing panoramas, disciplined bodies. The circularity of panoramas—there was no fixed beginning or end to their images—afforded a democratic experience that helped level differences between classes.[30]

The centrality of Bolívar's and Guzmán Blanco's protagonism in the culture of the Fair produced profitable images. One of these images was the increased value placed on military metaphor in times of peace, which in turn assured modern civic order for commercial transactions. The barrage of epic scenes favored military metaphor, presenting collective bodies synchronized in battle; such scenes depicted armies composed of professional soldiers and citizen fighters who shared the same will and marched in orderly fashion—disciplined armies working to achieve a common goal. These armies and battles were distinct from those of the wars for independence. They prepared popular sensibilities for future battles to be fought by armies of workers in the industrial workplace. The masses of soldier-workers appeared docile and obedient, and they would recognize, so the logic went, the natural authority of the strong man. The hypertrophy of heroic imaginaries was in sync with the showcasing of new technologies— motors and machines, telegraphs and telephones, grinders and threshing machines—all of which predicted the acceleration in the production of primary resources for export to industrialized nations, as well as the hard working conditions for dependent nations.

With this point in mind, the imaginaries being constructed were in accord with a hierarchy not very distant from a patriarchy. The language of the neo-Gothic reaccomodated modern patriarchal hegemonies, made legitimate by a new secular Christianity. There was no break with the Catholic sensibilities of Hispanism, which was evident in the Palacio with its modern façade built over a colonial foundation. Proponents of the *café con leche* idea of the Venezuelan nation needed whitened faces to negotiate the difficult languages of the process of recolonization wrapped in modernity. The hypertrophy of historical images and the proliferation of neo-Gothic detail led to a Gothic modernization of the nation. Today, the convergence of motors, machines, dynamos, and electric gadgets in a neo-Gothic space may seem strange, but technology was pertinent to the world of virile sensibilities. The muscular and heroic body of the soldier and the worker was the driving force behind the future nation. On the flip side, in addition to being evidence of material progress, machines also symbolized future wars.

The proliferation of a historicist esthetic that favored military metaphor and the trope of war was, from its visual and popular forms to the more elite modality of historiography, a key expression in the formation of nineteenth-century nationalisms. The impact of this esthetic did not stop with nationalism, either. It played in the disciplining of collective subjectivities and legitimized authoritarian regimes (as was the case of Guzmán Blanco in Venezuela and Porfirio Díaz in Mexico), and did much to pave the way for the future populisms and dictatorships of the twentieth century.

The Palacio of the National Fair harbored many promises. As a cathedral, it made sacred Venezuela's natural resources and hid the alienating power of commodification. As a factory, it welcomed the new world economy and offered a body of workers who did not yet know about industrial exploitation. It was a perverse Gothic: the "Saintly Chapel" in one of the Palacio's corners gave its benediction to the things on display. Lastly, the Palacio sweetened the new, complex relations that would accompany the exchanges of a culture that would soon become globalized. What would remain in the collective unconscious over the following decades would be the inclination of elites to recreate the same (but not the sole) heroic, neo-Gothic, virile, and military historiography that would rediscover new sources of wealth under the same ideology of liberalism.

Epilogue: Literary History Is a Panorama, Too

Literary fashions were mediated by new forms of consumption and thus had to be publicized. Several narratives were at play in this process, beginning with one that sought to make a certain cultural capital visible. Another hoped to show literature as a rich warehouse of pasts and resources in the present. Yet another narrative sought to produce images of national heritages through historiographical, museological, and exhibitionary discourses. All of these narratives were magnetized by the regime of *collectionism*.[31]

In the process of legitimizing the state apparatus and sectors that had embarked on constructing national fictions, the strategy of collection produced the effect of abundance and guaranteed entrance to the world market. In the same way that the Palacio served as a showcase for what Venezuela was capable of producing and storing as future resources, collectionist strategies accumulated symbolic artifacts—anthologies, dictionaries, encyclopedias, memoirs, documents, biographies—that spoke to the cultural capital of the nation. The cumulative effect and precise detail work that characterized the technique of panoramas lent their grammar to the display of numerous books at the Fair. The same taxonomy was applied equally to photography albums, portrait galleries, and battle scenes, on the one hand, and literary history and authors' "libraries," on the other.[32]

The same paratactic regime superposing biographical scenes—like portraits arranged sequentially in a gallery—ordered literary production. Just as the surface of the panorama aligned distinct historical moments in one continuous present, historiographical writing dissolved heterogeneity in the regime of narrative discourse.[33] What could have been oppositional or disjunctive was made compatible for the discursive space; opposites ended up together in the line of narrative progression. Thus, the story of evolution was endorsed by the practice of historiography, the same practice that was an agent of narrative time essential for creating the fallacy of teleology within the ideology of progress. It is no surprise that the Guzmanato saw the foundation of literary and political historiography in Venezuela. The material modernization that Venezuelans experienced during that period led to an ordering of culture.

Books were rare, luxurious objects in Venezuela. For this reason, many rooms at the National Fair celebrated the technology of print culture. Their displays consisted of mountains of books—enormous and thick volumes with sumptuous bindings in leather, gold print on their spines, and different types of paper. Books were there to be viewed and admired, and—of course—their selection was carefully made by organizers. After all, literature was the language that conferred legitimacy to the modern nation. It was therefore imperative to build a careful representation of a library (a collection), for the library represented the nation. Here, the Fair constituted a moment of foundational design of the canon of letters; it was a space that made possible the articulation of literary historiography and the canonization of texts that would form part of the capital of the literary institution. While the Fair popularized some forms of knowledge, the power of books still regulated discourses. States spoke through books, and female voices were rarely included.[34] Only "serious" genres were exhibited: memoirs, statistics, census reports, laws, annals, speeches, biographies, dictionaries, manuals, histories, stories, odes, and anthems—those that were thought to represent national heritage. Among these figured Ramón Azpúrua's fourteen volumes of *Documentos para la historia de la vida del Libertador* (*Documents for the Libertador's Life History*), a four volume collection of biographies of "notable men" in Spanish America, memoirs of ministers, and *Leyes nacionales*. "Literary" works included *Venezuela he-*

roica and *Zárate*; Arístides Rojas's *Orígenes de la revolución venezolana*; poetry by Ramón Yépez; the epic poems *La Boliviada* and *La Colombiada*; the drama *Triunfar con la patria*; Felipe Tejera's *Perfiles venezolanos o Galería de hombres célebres de Venezuela en las letras, ciencias y artes*; a dictionary of indigenous words; textbooks on morals, geography, and history; and religious instruction.

Preparations for the Fair created favorable conditions for cultural manifestations. In fact, the dates of the Fair, charged with the symbolic power of the centenary of Bolívar's birth, catalyzed the first attempts to produce a panorama of national literature. The Palacio and the books on display complemented each other; the building was, in effect, *Venezuela heroica* or *Orígenes de la revolución venezolana* in stone. Both the Fair and the books were animated by the same totalizing impulse, the same principle of accumulation, and the same reiterative grammar. Their voluminosity operated like a museum-warehouse, diluting temporal distinctions with the overflow of dates, works, and illustrious men. Full of the professional languages of positivism and liberalism, the rhetorical strategies did not have to justify the absence of the colonial period or difficult decades for the republic, for the mass of references and celebrities took the place of a historical narrative stage by stage. In line with this logic, historiography was controlled by the principle of accumulation, arranged in homogenous lineal sequences. Literary history was born under the influence of "panoramania" and the accounts of literary panoramas reproduced galleries and the logics of visual technologies.

In closing, let us return to the culture of panoramas. Although historiography was an exercise linked to the sphere of lettered culture, the monumental structure of historiographical content owed much to visual culture and the technologies of illustration. The "gallery of illustrious men" and the "literary panorama" were not easily derived from the more widely "read" panoramas of images, but both types of manifestations were tied to the same bourgeois spirit of capitalizing on symbolic goods and their exhibition.

The heyday of panoramania took place in the last two decades of the century. The masses flocked to see the illusory effects of the scenes. Not considered among the fine arts, panoramas were thought of more as manifestations of the cultural industry. In its different forms (cosmorama, georama, neorama, mobile panorama, cinerama), the panorama conjugated the technologies of the spectacle with the art of stage construction, photography, landscape painting, and above all, the operation of recreating reality and producing a simulacrum. The widespread public reception of panoramas blurred the frontiers between reality and its reproduction.[35]

Let us take a look at one last example. At the 1889 Paris World's Fair commemorating the centenary of the French Revolution, French businessman Théophile Poilpot's company Transatlantique presented a novelty in the genre of panoramas: a panorama titled "History of the Century." There, viewers could experience a synthesis of intellectual life, arts, and politics over the course of the century. A thousand people appear in the scenes. For a year, the creators of the panorama did research for the project under the direction of Hippolyte Taine; their fruit resulted in the development of seven similarly ambitious panoramas.

Thanks to the careful reproduction of portraits, the public was challenged to identify each individual represented. Here the exhibitionary complex was put to the test, as was dexterity of sight, for knowing how to read the images was also knowing how to recognize identities. It was also an exercise in selective memory that fixed some canonical faces while erasing others. This grand panorama offered an encyclopedic register that allowed viewers to access quickly a historical narrative. At the same time that viewers observed the images of the panorama, other observers came into sight, displacing the vertical and exclusive regime of the panopticon.[36]

This type of historical and biographical panorama was profitable, for it adopted the synchronic and accumulative scheme of the panoramas portraying war that were all the rage. Biographical panoramas updated the older tradition of the gallery of illustrious men. Historiographical imagination was, on the one hand, bound to genealogical archaeology—that is, the collection of wall paintings predating their written description that organized the relationship between space and time.[37] On the other hand, historiography was part of the phenomenon of art for the masses. It was for these reasons that the *Primer libro venezolano de literatura, ciencias y bellas artes* (1895) was organized like a historical showcase or museum. Years later, Walter Benjamin drew attention to the connections between "panoramic literature" and panoramas.[38]

How much do high culture and historiography owe to forms of visual and popular culture? There is no precise answer, but the fairs were no doubt spaces where the distances separating these realms were tested and where one field contaminated the other. The pavilions for the fairs were, for the most part, ephemeral. In most cases, only archives of documents and photographs remain. Yet the Palacio from Venezuela's 1883 National Fair still stands, and as the seat of the Academia Nacional de la Historia and the Academia de la Lengua, it continues to occupy an important place in the nation's cultural life.

NOTES

Epigraph source: Michel de Certeau, *The Writing of History*, trans. Tom Conley (New York: Columbia University Press, 1988), 69–70.

1. Translator's note: there is a play on words in the original Spanish, where *ilustración* means both "enlightenment" and "illustration." The same is true of *modernidad ilustrada*, which means both the project of modernity that grew out of enlightenment ideas as well as the illustrated images and visual culture of modernity.

2. See Jesús Martín-Barbero, *De los medios a las mediaciones: Comunicación, cultura y hegemonía* (Bogotá: Convenio Andrés Bello, 1998); *Galerías del progreso: Museos, exposiciones y cultura visual en América Latina*, eds. Beatriz González-Stephan and Jens Andermann (Buenos Aires: Beatriz Viterbo Editora, 2006); Paulette Silva Beauregard, "Un lugar para exhibir, clasificar y coleccionar: La revista ilustrada como una galería del progreso," in *Galerías del progreso*, 373–406; and Andermann, *The Optic of the State: Visuality and Power in Argentina and Brazil, 1870–1900* (Pittsburgh: University of Pittsburgh Press, 2007).

3. Hugo Achugar, ed., *Derechos de memoria: Nación e independencia en América Latina* (Montevideo: Facultad de Humanidades y Ciencias de la Educación, 2003).

4. Editors' note: the term *scopic* has recently become widely employed in the study of exhibitionary and visual culture. It comes from the film critic Christian Metz's notion of *scopic regimes* as a way of speaking about the intersection of technology and culture and culturally specific ways of seeing.

5. See Chris Jenks, ed., *Visual Culture* (London: Routledge, 1995); and Scott McQuire, *Visions of Modernity: Representation, Memory, Time and Space in the Age of the Camera* (London: Sage Publications, 1998).

6. Silva Beauregard, "Un lugar para exhibir."

7. Walter Benjamin, "La obra de arte en la época de su reproductibilidad técnica," in *Discursos interrumpidos*, vol. 1 (Madrid: Taurus, 1973), 16–60.

8. Rubén Darío, "Psicología de la postal," in *Obras completas*, vol. 5 (Madrid: Editorial Mundo Latino, 1917), 119–20.

9. José Martí, "Exposiciones," in *Obras completas*, vol. 8 (Havana: Editorial Nacional de Cuba, 1963), 368.

10. Martí, *Obras completas*, vol. 23 (Havana: Editorial Nacional de Cuba, 1963), 227.

11. Many writers at the end of the nineteenth century and during the first half of the twentieth felt attracted to technological innovation. This is the case of several of Horacio Quiroga's stories ("Miss Dorothy Phillips," "El espectro," "El puritano," "Una historia inmoral," "El hombre artificial"). Adolfo Bioy Casares questions the instability of reality by introducing phantasmagorias in the novel *La invención de Morel*.

12. See Stephan Oettermann, *The Panorama: History of a Mass Medium* (New York: Zone Books, 1997); Bernard Comment, *The Painted Panorama* (New York: Harry N. Abrams, 2000); and Robert D. Aguirre, *Informal Empire: Mexico and Central America in Victorian Culture* (Minneapolis: University of Minnesota Press, 2005).

13. Ker Porter worked primarily as a painter of historical and battle scenes. In Venezuela, he painted portraits of Simón Bolívar and José Antonio Páez. He painted on long canvases with the objective of showing his landscapes in the

Leicester rotunda. Ker Porter's is the only panorama of Venezuela that still survives, now in the British Library. Londoners had grown accustomed to views of Middle Eastern deserts as well as, in some circles, Aztec carvings and códices. On the other hand, French painters like Delacroix had helped make orientalism fashionable.

14. See Aguirre, *Informal Empire*; Thomas Richards, *The Imperial Archive: Knowledge and the Fantasy of Empire* (London: Verso, 1993); and Tim Fulfort and Peter Kitson, eds., *Romanticism and Colonialism: Writing and Empire, 1780–1830* (Cambridge: Cambridge University Press, 1998).

15. Richard D. Altick, *The Shows of London* (Cambridge: Belknap Press, 1978); Mauricio Tenorio Trillo, *Artilugio de la nación moderna: México en las exposiciones universales, 1880–1930* (Mexico City: Fondo de Cultura Económica, 1998).

16. Aguirre, *Informal Empire*.

17. Similar travel accounts include Karl Appun, *Unter den Tropen* (1871); Karl Sachs, *Aus den Llanos* (1878); and Anton Goering, *Vom tropischen Tieflande zum ewigen Schnee: Eine malerische Schilderung des schönsten Tropenlandes Venezuela* (1892).

18. Ivan Karp and Steven D. Lavine, eds. *Exhibiting Cultures: The Poetics and Politics of Museum Display* (Washington: Smithsonian Institution Press, 1991).

19. Guzmán Blanco wanted to draw attention to Venezuela after having transformed and "modernized" the capital. He invited diplomats from Europe, Africa, and the United States. At the Fair, they would have found a small Paris in the style of Napoleon III, a neoclassic capitol, a neo-Gothic palace, and a Guzmán Blanco theater, where the operas *Aida* and *Nabuconodosor* debuted. The officialist paper *La opinión nacional* was charged with reporting the preparations for the fair, and it served as well to measure the events of the inauguration. A valuable source for attendance and other details of the fair is Adolfo Ernst, *La exposición nacional de Venezuela en 1883*, 2 vols. (Caracas: Fundación Venezolana para la Salud y la Educación, 1983), originally published by the press of *La opinión nacional* in 1884.

20. Michael McCarthy, *The Origins of the Gothic Revival* (New Haven: Yale University Press, 1987).

21. Sylviane Leprun, *Le théâtre des colonies: Scénographie, acteurs et discours de l'imaginarie dans les expositions, 1855–1937* (Paris: Editions L'Harmattan, 1986); McCarthy, *Origins*.

22. George L. Mosse, *The Nationalization of the Masses* (New York: Howard Fertig, 1975); and Gillian Russell, *The Theatres of War: Performance, Politics, and Society, 1793–1815* (Oxford: Clarendon Press, 1995).

23. The project of modernity was manifest in complex sensibilities that pitted the different tastes of different elites—conservative liberals, bourgeois patricians—against each other regarding what program of modernization to pursue. So, *afrancesamiento* (the effort to align oneself with all things French) coexisted with a reaffirmation of Hispanic roots, especially during and after the Spanish-American War of 1898. In the final decades of the nineteenth century, and in light of an ever more frail grip on its last overseas territories, Spain engaged in a diplomatic "reconquest" of its colonies through an appeal to shared cultural heritage. With different interests at stake, both the metropolis

and creole oligarchies strengthened their ties, evident in Venezuela in the 1883 creation of the Academia de la Lengua (corresponding to the Real Academia de la Lengua Española) and manifestations of literary Hispanophilia. In Eduardo Blanco's *Venezuela heroica*, for instance, Simón Bolívar is compared to el Mío Cid. Literary Hispanism was filtered through Gothic codes, too, reinforcing the process of whitening through linguistic "purity."

24. Timothy Mitchell, *Colonising Egypt* (Cambridge: Cambridge University Press, 1988); and Mark Crinson, *Empire Building: Orientalism and Victorian Architecture* (New York: Routledge, 1996).

25. This orientalized vision was conveyed in similar ways by many lettered Latin Americans. In line with the Eurocentric episteme, they understood the pampas and the llanos from an exotic, imperial point of view. Domingo F. Sarmiento's *Facundo* is just one example where Argentine "barbarism" is filtered through an orientalist imaginary, with "American Bedouins" and gauchos who live like "nomadic tribes in the Argentine desert." The distinction with the case of Sarmiento was that this version of Argentine orientalism was aggressively virile.

26. Crinson, *Empire Building*.

27. Tenorio Trillo, *Artilugio de la nación moderna*.

28. Susan B. Matheson and Derek D. Churchill, *Modern Gothic: The Revival of Medieval Art* (New Haven: Yale University Art Gallery, 2000).

29. François Robichon, "Le panorama, spectacle de l'histoire," *Le mouvement social* 131 (1985): 65–85.

30. This display of patriotic narratives attempted to construct *one* of many forms of collective, national memory. Of course, there were other collective memories struggling to establish their prominence or, as the case may be, dominance. Eduardo Blanco, who wrote the immensely popular *Venezuela heroica*, published another novel in 1882 titled *Zárate* that was much less popular. The protagonist Zárate is a character operating in the margins of law; as a bandit, he demonstrates the fears the white oligarchy (of which Blanco was a member) held with respect to the popular classes, who were not well understood. Zárate's nomadic existence excluded him from the national project.

31. Editors' note: *collectionism* is a term used in museology to refer to the strategies and politics guiding the formation of a collection.

32. Beatriz González-Stephan, "Coleccionar y exhibir: La construcción de patrimonios culturales," *Hispamérica* 86 (2000): 3–17.

33. Michel de Certeau, *La escritura de la historia* (Mexico City: Universidad Iberoamericana, 1993).

34. This was the case even despite the contributions of female authors to the world of textbooks. Two who were key to the organization of juvenile imaginaries were Antonia Esteller and Socorro González Guinán.

35. Gillen D'Arcy Wood, *The Shock of the Real: Romanticism and Visual Culture, 1860–1860* (New York: Palgrave, 2001); and Ralph Hyde, *Panoramania! The Art and Entertainment of the "All-embracing" View* (London: Trefoil Publications and Barbican Art Gallery, 1988). Numerous authors and painters—José Martí, Rubén Darío, Juana Manuela Gorriti, Arístides Rojas, Eduardo Blanco, Julián del Casal, Manuel Ignacio Altamirano, Cristóbal Rojas, Martín Tovar y Tovar, and Arturo Michelena, to name a few—were fans of panoramas and appreciated their pedagogical qualities with regard to the popular classes. Diverse social

revolutions called for a democratization of knowledge, including a greater "visibility" of reality.

36. Various visual regimes coexisted throughout the nineteenth century. Both Jeremy Bentham's design of the panopticon (1791) and the plans for the Leicester Square rotunda (1801) were based on the same visual technologies, be they for policing a crowd, in one case, or creating enormous spaces where crowds could gather to see, in the other case. Both were disciplinary apparatuses—the first at the service of the state, and the second for rituals of cultural consumption. See Tony Bennett, *The Birth of the Museum: History, Theory, Politics* (London: Routledge, 1995).

37. De Certeau, *La escritura*, 116.

38. Walter Benjamin, "El flaneur," "Daguerre o los panoramas," and "Grandville o las exposiciones universales," in *Poesía y capitalismo: Iluminaciones*, vol. 2 (Madrid: Taurus, 1993), 49, 176–77.

6

Anything Goes

Carnivalesque Transgressions in Nineteenth-Century Latin America

John Charles Chasteen

Carnival is the time of year reserved specifically in the public life of Latin America for transgressive activities. Carnival happens during three main, "fat" days that are always a Sunday through Tuesday determined by the date of Easter, which must fall between 22 March and 26 April. Carnival Sunday is seven weeks before Easter Sunday. Carnival Tuesday, or Fat Tuesday (in French, *Mardi Gras*), is followed by Ash Wednesday, which marks the beginning of the somber season of Lent.[1] The most basic fact about carnival is that it precedes Lent, a period defined theoretically by self-denial and abstemiousness, by fasting or giving up a favorite food, and by prohibitions against gaiety or rowdy fun. The last three days before Lent are Lent's spiritual opposite, the last hurrah of the flesh. Carnival celebrates an absence of social control, including self control. Indulge yourself; anything goes.

Forget Bacchus, though. Pre-Lenten carnival has no traceable linear descent from Greek Bacchanals or Roman Saturnalia. Pagan references were suggested by nineteenth-century folklorists eager to find telluric survivals and then embraced both by revelers, who enjoyed the Greco-Roman imagery, and by moralists, who wanted to suppress the celebration and were glad to call it un-Christian. As a general European phenomenon, carnival's origins are not ancient but high medieval (between 1000 and 1300); its apogee, late medieval or early modern (1300 and 1600); and its general decline (between 1600 and 1800), "recent" only for historians. In the nineteenth century, as carnival faded in rural areas, and most urban ones, too, it nonetheless manifested itself with new intensity in particular cities. For the last two hundred years, carnival has tended to be a municipal festival, associated with particular localities: Venice, Cologne, and Nice in Europe, for example, and in America, Barranquilla, Veracruz, Santa Cruz,

Santiago de Cuba, Pasto, and Oruro, and also New Orleans and the Port of Spain.[2] Today, only in Brazil is carnival really a national festival, celebrated with official approval and greater or lesser enthusiasm throughout the country.

During the nineteenth century, practically every substantial city in Latin America had a carnival celebration that interrupted daily life for three days a year, which I noticed while researching the history of popular dance. Some of these cities—Buenos Aires, Santiago, Lima—would be on nobody's short list of likely carnival sites today, but they had in common a substantial population of African-descended people during the early and mid-nineteenth century. That historical population is precisely what attracted my attention in tracing the African roots of Latin America's "national rhythms."[3] Most of Latin America's popular music and dance genres, as is more-or-less well known, have a history linked to the African diaspora. The music and dance of slaves and their descendants were often repressed, of course—but not always, and especially not during carnival, when they were granted a public presence and usually received some mention in the newspaper. Poring through Rio newspapers from the 1860s to the 1890s, I realized that the three days of carnival were likely to yield more evidence on popular dance than any other moment of the year. I focused my subsequent research systematically on nineteenth-century carnival celebrations in Lima, Havana, Rio, and Buenos Aires. This chapter will explore the festival's nineteenth-century history with special attention to those cities, focusing on an understudied aspect of carnival in nineteenth-century Latin America—a practice that forced itself on my attention despite what seemed to me little promise of interpretive interest. I refer to the "throwing game" or "water game"—or as I prefer to call it (and you will see why), *the water fight*—that was unquestionably the most widespread and intense carnival activity after music, dance, drink, and sex.[4]

My main claim here is that carnivalesque transgressions can be generative of social change. Many decades before tango and samba reached their early twentieth-century apotheosis as national dances, carnival celebrations were facilitating fecund cultural contact across lines of race, class, and gender. Transgressive line-crossing is basic to the carnivalesque and it characterized even elements of the festival remote from dance. Carnival's transgressive urge explains how tango and samba—like jazz, originally expressions of the poor and downtrodden—gained a following among the well-to-do. It happened during carnival, when things got a bit out of hand . . .

From Inversions to Transgressions

The anarchy of our subject makes theoretical clarity essential. What goes on under the surface at carnival? Much can be said and has been said beyond the most basic fact of carnivalesque transgressiveness. The famous escape-valve metaphor, whereby people could "blow off steam" at carnival, was invoked as early as 1819 by a historian writing about Venetian carnival, probably Europe's most celebrated version of the festival.[5] The persuasiveness of this metaphor would seem to have diminished now that its referent, steam engines that often exploded from excess pressure, have disappeared from our experience. Still, the escape-valve metaphor raised a valid question. Does carnival preserve the very power structures it ignores for three days a year by preventing an explosion on the other 362 days?

Aficionados of carnival have viewed it quite differently, of course. Mikhail Bakhtin theorizes carnival as "a utopian realm of community, freedom, equality, and abundance," an ecstatic time-out-of-time, characterized by a unanimous, participatory ethos. Everyone must participate in carnival, according to Bakhtin, "because its very idea embraces all the people. While carnival lasts, there is no other life outside it. During carnival time, life is subject only to its laws, that is, the laws of its own freedom. It has a universal spirit; it is a special condition of the entire world, of the world's revival and renewal, in which all take part." A bit less subjectively, Bakhtin also highlights a commonly verifiable element of carnival, "the suspension of all hierarchical rank, privileges, norms, and prohibitions." He asserts (here echoing the logic of the escape valve) that the power and pervasiveness of hierarchy makes a break from it especially welcome. Whether or not carnival contributes to the stability of repressive regimes or to the renewal of the world, it must necessarily have been meaningful in notably hierarchical societies such as those of nineteenth-century Latin America.[6]

Carnivalesque inversions, a well-known phenomenon, have at times included the "topsy-turvy world" in which servants might dress up briefly in their masters' clothing. While the phenomenon has been studied primarily in the context of early modern Europe, such carnivalesque inversions certainly occurred in Latin America, too.[7] Jean-Baptiste Debret, the early nineteenth-century French visitor to Rio, described slaves "dressed as Europeans of old, aptly imitating their gestures as they waved to the balconies, left and right."[8] Dressing as European nobility has remained a costuming option ever since, although never among the most common. Even roughly simulating the clothes of rich people was difficult for the poor in the nineteenth century. The domino costume, with its all-concealing cloak and hood, was a privilege of the wealthy simply because it required so much cloth.

Cross-dressing—an inversive gesture as well as a transgressive one—was more common than any symbolic inversion of the larger social hierarchy, from quite early on. A Spanish poem mentions cross-dressing as characteristic of carnival there in 1605.[9] Usually men dressed as women. A company on Rio's fashionable main street, Rua do Ouvidor, advertised "breasts of senhora for dressing as a woman" at that city's 1835 carnival.[10] A Havana newspaper denounced the presence on the streets of "many women of both sexes" at carnival half a century later.[11] When the Buenos Aires police prohibited the wearing of carnival costumes not corresponding to the sex of the wearer, they revealed the presence of cross-dressing there as well.[12] The offending costumes may well have represented nuns. Another prohibition in Buenos Aires revealed the presence of satirical musical groups costumed as clergy.[13]

The most interesting frequent inversion in the carnivals I surveyed was blackface music and dance, as in U.S. minstrel shows. A group of ersatz "Negroes" performed at carnival festivities in Havana's principal theater in 1843, along with another of "Bedouins," and a third of "Valencians."[14] Late in the century, a Rio newspaper mentioned "white Africans" at that city's carnival celebration, and so on.[15] Probably no nineteenth-century carnival in Lima, Rio, Havana, or Buenos Aires was without some manifestation of blackface performance. Like cross-dressing, however, blackface performances might easily be lost from view in the larger picture of carnival reveling, with one arresting exception—the last three decades of carnival celebrations in Buenos Aires (and in nearby Montevideo), where blackface became a dominant carnivalesque theme. My ideas on that topic are elaborated elsewhere. Suffice it here to point out the highly inversive quality of the practice by which the elite sons of Buenos Aires dressed as slaves.[16]

Transgression is far more central to the carnivalesque. My own theorization of carnival follows Samuel Kinser on carnival's "removal and escape from social calculations through a variety of costuming and behavioral modes, of which inversion is only one." Kinser's discussion of the carnivalesque draws on Bakhtin and signals a pervasive doubleness, wherein everything contains the potential of its opposite—wherein, most especially, everything is and is not serious. Kinser talks about the intensification of perceptions and about emphasis on the body—especially the body from the waist down. Because its timing signals the coming of spring, carnival has always had sexual overtones. Most usefully for our look at carnival in nineteenth-century Latin America, Kinser talks about testing social boundaries.[17] Transgressing normal boundaries of class, race, gender, and approved social comportment was the permanent, ongoing activity of almost everybody who played carnival in nineteenth-century Latin America. If carnival has a larger social meaning, it must be embedded somehow in its predominant activity. A brief overview of carnival play will illustrate that point.

"Iberian" Carnival versus "Venetian" Carnival

Until the 1840s, carnival meant mostly one thing in Latin America, a kind of rough play called *entrudo* in Portuguese and *antruejo* in Spanish. This was the traditional carnival activity long played in villages throughout Iberia.[18] It included rowdiness and noise-making of various kinds, and cruel practical jokes. Killing someone's cat, for example, was a favorite carnival prank. In Spain, village lads put up swings and sent villages lasses soaring to expose their petticoats, but this carnival practice seems not to have crossed the Atlantic. The practice that did cross over, and then became the very definition of traditional carnival in late colonial Latin America, was what we might call most generically *the throwing game*.[19]

People threw various things at each other—flour and ashes, for example —the full effect of which cannot be imagined unless one keeps in mind that most people owned few changes of clothing. Most often, however, they threw water. In Lima, Rio, and Buenos Aires, the throwing game amounted to a water fight that became a generalized street melee lasting three days. Nor were those at home out of the fray: water flew inside houses, between houses, and between houses and the street. Those with resources to invest in the game prepared or purchased various kinds of appliances and projectiles, from large syringes that could be reloaded in a handy ditch to elegant wax "lemons" or "oranges" with brittle shells and a payload of a few ounces of perfumed water. This last refinement was especially Portuguese, and therefore normal only in Rio. The ammunition of choice in Buenos Aires, Lima, and elsewhere, on the other hand, was the intact shell of a hen's egg, its contents emptied through a small hole, replaced with water, and plugged with a drop of wax. Both households and businesses like bakeries made a practice of conserving egg shells in this way as they cooked during the weeks before carnival. Wax lemons and water eggs were advertised for sale in the newspaper as the three fat days approached.[20] The throwing game might be all about transgressing boundaries, as we will see, but there had to be some limit: ostrich-size eggs of the South American rhea, while available, constituted a rarely used sort of heavy artillery.

A second, contrasting style of carnival play began to appear in Latin

America during the 1840s. Its most frequent referents were the famous carnival celebrations of Venice and Paris. In the literature on Rio, the new style is often termed *Venetian carnival*, which will serve as a shorthand here as well, even though the more important model was probably Paris. Venetian carnival focused on music, dance, and costumes. Masked balls were its chief expression, promoted precisely as "the European way of celebrating carnival."[21] As with most aspects of European fashion in this period, Venetian carnival found its chief proponents among the upper classes, who created exclusive carnival societies, again on Old World models. Besides putting on masked balls, the elite carnival societies paraded in costume, often on horseback or on allegorical floats, for the whole city to see. Another new modality was the costumed musical group that moved through the street performing particularly at the houses of friends, who then invited the group in for refreshments. The elite blackface troupes of Buenos Aires, already mentioned, were of this sort. The costuming central to Venetian carnival provided many opportunities to engage in line-crossing transgressiveness—satirizing politicians or the clergy, for example. But Venetian carnival was romantic, above all. Costumes showed the romantic taste for the exotic Orient and for the Middle Ages. And the masked balls themselves, held amid decorations that made them a "cave" or "grotto," focused on romantic encounters between men and women. These encounters themselves might be transgressive, of course. Costumed anonymity cloaked extramarital and cross-class flirtations, and even cross-racial ones. Commonly, tickets were not sold at the door, so that the "decency" of the buyers could be ascertained while they were out of costume. In another variation, an "entrance committee" might demand that each costumed arrival at the dance momentarily lift his or her mask.[22]

   Venetian carnival was not for everyone, obviously. It was a diversion for the well-to-do—a game for them to play while the common people merely watched, admired, and envied them. Like many aspects of elite culture in this period, Venetian carnival brought with it the prestige of its French and Italian models. Costumes and masked balls seemed a clear manifestation of *progress* and *civilization* (in line with the expressions Beatriz González-Stephan studies in the previous chapter), in contrast to the rude backwardness of the throwing game. Here was "a real case of Sarmiento's civilization versus barbarism," according to a 1870 Lima newspaper reporter who was explaining why the old throwing game ought to be abolished.[23] As Venetian activities proliferated in the 1850s and 1860s, calls for the abolition of the barbarous throwing game became common. The Venetian-style concentration on costumes, music, and dance steadily gained popularity through the rest of the nineteenth century, moving gradually down the social ladder as costumes became more affordable.

The throwing game never disappeared, however. A Rio newspaper lamented the city's regrettable relapse in 1879: "It is better not to describe what went on in the streets, even those frequented by the flower of our distinguished society, where the entertainments of the moment were the same as those played in alleyways and tenements."[24] Water fighting spoiled the expensive costumes and therefore the fun of those interested in more elegant play. By the 1880s and 1890s, elite revelers had retreated from public masked balls, often held in theaters, to revel more securely among their social equals at the dances given by carnival societies exclusively for their own members and approved guests. In addition, young people of the popular classes had formed their own costumed musical groups, which competed for space and attention in the streets.[25]

When popular music and dance became central to carnival in Buenos Aires, in Rio, and in Havana, carnival's transgressive urge facilitated a momentous transition rather similar to the one that occurred when "black" rhythm-and-blues was repackaged as "white" rock-and-roll, though the more exact analogy would involve New Orleans, jazz, and Mardi Gras. In sum, carnival dances became occasions for middle-class experimentation with popular music and dance that was associated with people of African descent. The experimenters enjoyed themselves so much that the result, in each case, was a new "national rhythm"—a new musical emblem of national identity, distinctive to its birthplace and embodying collective idiosyncrasies and collective genius. The credibility of these ideological constructions rested largely on their claim to embody the identity of racially-mixed national populations. Learning to "dance black" (recall "Elvis the Pelvis") seemed transgressive, both racially and sexually, to many whites, which is why their experimentation occurred during carnival, when anything goes. Many white people experienced the "new" music and dance as a powerful personal liberation.[26] The dances they first learned at carnival became salient iterations of national myths of mestizo origin—by far the most pervasive and powerful national myths in Latin America. I have written about all this elsewhere.

Enough about dance and other "Venetian" carnival play. What of that enigmatic Iberian water fight that engaged such ubiquitous, enthusiastic energies among people of all social classes? To assess the larger social meaning of carnival in nineteenth-century Latin America, surely one must interpret the implications of the water fight.

Women versus Men

A very important fact about the throwing game—the central purpose of it, in fact—has so far not been mentioned here. Historians have seemingly missed it altogether, no doubt because contemporaries took it so for granted that they almost never comment on it directly. And here it is: beyond any question, the big water fight was "fought" primarily between men and women—especially boys and girls, of course, but including the amorously inclined of all ages. "The time has come to demonstrate amorous ideas using hen's eggs," announced a Buenos Aires newspaper of carnival 1865, giving rare direct voice to what normally went without saying.[27]

Domingo Faustino Sarmiento, oddly enough, offers important testimony in this regard. Contrary to what one might expect, Sarmiento was an enthusiast of the water fight. The quoted Limeño journalist who invoked Sarmiento's name in 1870 would surely have been astonished. The exiled Sarmiento may have endorsed *barbarous carnival* in a 1842 Chilean newspaper primarily for the purpose of excoriating his nemesis, Argentine dictator Juan Manuel de Rosas, who had just banned the celebration in Buenos Aires. Still, Sarmiento wrote convincingly about the pleasure of cornering and drenching the object of one's affections, enjoying the sight of wet clothes hugging sinuous bodies, and perhaps winning a kiss in a negotiated surrender.[28] The eroticism of a water fight is captured in this Peruvian journalistic appreciation: "In Lima, above all, where the women are so seductive, [carnival] is the favorite pastime of young people. We lay down the gauntlet before the severest disciplinarian or moralist, who finding himself in front of a pretty girl who challenges him to play with a smile on her lips, pleasure in her eyes, her hair slightly moistened and coming unbraided on her shoulders, her wet clothes revealing with seductive fidelity her beguilingly curved form." The breathless journalist then dares his (presumably male) reader, no matter how disapproving of the throwing game, *not* to want to wet that girl or kiss those ruby lips "panting with pleasure and exhaustion."[29] This does not sound like nineteenth-century bourgeois newspaper discourse—not the way we imagine people contemporary to the Victorians, who, of course, weren't the way we imagined *them*, either. In any other situation, such talk would be strictly off limits in a 1873 Lima newspaper. But this is carnival, when anything goes. Recreating a few more scenes will give the reader a fuller idea of the carnival spirit.

Lima, carnival 1859. According to *El comercio*, during the evenings of the fat days, you could hardly take a step downtown without running into groups of boys busily hurling water eggs at young women on the balconies and roof terraces of the houses. "The police resembled horse-and-rider soup, so dripping wet were they." One scene is recounted in affectionate detail: A group of young men arrives at a house where a dance will be given that evening. Penetrating into the patio of the house, they begin their assault. "But momentarily an emissary with a white handkerchief appears requesting a cease-fire. The parley is accepted and the owner of the house (for it was he) invites the young men inside so that they may fight on more even terms." (Or so that there would be less breakage, more likely.) Perhaps the homeowner's fears were exaggerated, for after token resistance, the girls capitulate and the dancing begins. Just an hour later, though, the playful water fight resumes inside the house, resulting in some broken crystal, soaked furniture, and a minor wound or two.[30] A year or two later, during a water fight in nearby Callao, some ladies reportedly "had to change dresses a dozen times."[31] Those were the ladies who had a dozen dresses, obviously, which was very far from the case for most women. We shall see how most people played in a moment.

First, however, there is another basic element of the throwing game to be discussed. Boys normally threw at girls in windows or on balconies that overlooked the street. The reverse positioning would have been considered ridiculous. Consider:

Buenos Aires, carnival 1865. Young "lions" on horseback, well-provided with water eggs, lay siege to a girl named Juana and her neighbor. Had the young "lions" come on foot, they might have brought with them a servant carrying a basket of ammunition, as was also done in Lima and Rio, where the servant might have been a slave. The warlike defenders of the balcony in question have at their side a half-barrel full of water and a good supply of old newspapers from which to fashion water bombs, in addition to several heavy packets filled with beans (rather than bonbons, an expensive alternative used by the wealthy). The young men in the street launch water eggs, actually aiming for the girls' faces. Juana has one eye closed. With one hand, she shields her face with a pot lid, and with the other, she heaves water down toward her fully drenched foe by the pitcherful.[32]

When water fights heated up, the boys occasionally tried to climb up to the balconies, often tearing their clothes in the process, while the girls continued to douse them with buckets "as if washing horses."[33] A group of Englishmen reportedly achieved "splendid triumphs" using the hose of a hand-pumped fire engine to strafe balconies on which young women had playfully raised a banner reading SEBASTOPOL, an allusion to the ongoing Crimean War. During that year's carnival (1855), *Russians* became a generalized term, it seems, for girls playing on Buenos Aires balconies.[34] Water fights also happened elsewhere, of course. For example, Rio papers chronicled the usual girl-wets-boy, boy-wets-girl on the crowded streets in the intervals between parades put on by the city's elite carnival societies.[35] Carnival there and elsewhere usually included organized carriage rides in which wealthy families showed off their expensive vehicles, their fine teams of matched horses, and their liveried servants. The girls in such carriages might well have concealed several perfumed wax lemons in their skirts in case the right young gentlemen approached them on horseback.

But besieging a balcony was the only way to wet most so-called "decent girls." Official regulations sought to control possible excesses. Homeowners might be fined if they ignored warnings to control women on balconies, and the besiegers might be sternly admonished "neither to force any windows or doors nor enter houses on foot or horseback in pursuit of the game." Nobody was likely to suffer much as a result of such dire warnings and admonitions, however.[36]

The transgressive possibilities of the water game should now be crystal clear. It allowed participants to cross the normal lines of comportment between the sexes and to straddle the social barrier between house and street. The water game allowed for playful explorations of the lines being crossed. Theoretically, social lines and categories were neat and clear; practically, however, they had to be negotiated in the give-and-take of daily interpersonal encounters.[37] Would such-and-such a girl in that big house (or boy on that fine horse) pay any attention to me? A perfumed wax water-lemon was a low-risk way to find out.

This freedom to explore must have been particularly important to middle-class women whose lives were so cloistered, relative to men's. No doubt that is why, according to the vox populi, women were "decidedly in favor of carnival, the only time of year that permitted them certain liberties."[38] Housebound teenage girls who spent countless hours silently watching passersby from their windows could, during carnival, reach out into the street and, by means of a folded-newspaper water bomb, take the initiative of calling the attention of strapping lads on showy horses. "The liberty that the three days of carnival offer to muchachas" was proverbial in Buenos Aires and most other sites in nineteenth-century Latin America. "Carnival neutralizes the timidity of the modest señora," intoned one Lima chronicler. "Who hasn't seen the most serious and modest young lady let her hair down at carnival?" asked another.[39] The 1876 carnival in Rio displayed characteristics totally in tune with the idea of feminine liberty, as crowding became so intense downtown that any kind of supervision was impossible and random physical contact was unavoidable: "The streetcars are completely packed. Their windows are a display of feminine elegance. In the streets, the crowds move now like ocean waves, now like flowing lava."[40]

The liberties that women took during carnival are most clearly indicated by the anxieties they aroused. A particular genre of stories, highly revelatory of these anxieties, frequently appeared in nineteenth-century newspapers at carnival season. The stories invariably involve a married couple and a carnival masked ball. One way or another, both spouses attend it separately and in concealing costumes. And, what else? They meet anonymously and flirt, with various outcomes that range from ironic husbandly outrage to a late variety in which the husband sagely accepts the difficult implications of gender equality.[41]

Race and Class

Social equality for people of various colors and social class was also at issue during carnival, and it too could be ludically explored and negotiated in the throwing game with minimum personal risk.

For the most part, as has probably already become evident, people sought to play with their social equals, particularly acquaintances. Occasionally, they made fun of foreigners who missed the point by "throwing at people they didn't even know." On the other hand, nothing is more central to the carnivalesque than disrespect for hierarchy and social distinctions of all kinds. "The leveling power of carnival is incredible," effused a mid-century chronicler who observed that even such august personages as priests and generals habitually got doused.[42] The assertion is constantly repeated by adepts of the festival, who invoke the recognition of common humanity that anthropologist Victor Turner termed *comunitas*.[43] A kingdom of equality without social distinction is carnival's idea of itself, so to speak—the myth that Momo's subjects annually reenact. Maria Isaura Pereira de Queiroz has persuasively argued about Brazilian carnival that, to the contrary, social distinctions are very much maintained, and that is true—although not the whole truth, to judge by the plaintive denunciations made by newspaper writers.[44] Somehow, during carnival, explains a mid-century Lima journalist,

The lower order of folk finds a way to rub elbows with people who, any other time of year, would have nothing to do with them. That's why the ill-bred and ill-behaved boast of wetting and touching beautiful señoritas of superior position in the social order. That's why the most ragged and disgusting zambo thinks he has the right to take the hand of a señora who may be, for some reason, by herself, and shatter water-eggs all over her. In fact, we have seen countless lower-class individuals with mean looks, ill-dressed and worse spoken, put their filthy hands on señoritas with humiliating intent. The fault belongs *not* to these men, however, but to the ladies supposedly of quality who, enjoying the game, allow themselves to be groped [*groseramente agasajadas*] by men who have no right even to approach or speak to them.[45]

Thus far, men of the "lower orders" testing their access to women "of superior position." The reverse possibility—an encounter between "decent" men and poor women—was less menacing to those norms, so it was denounced with scorn but without hysteria. A particularly incensed chronicler declared his sympathy for any "decent" man who ventured onto the streets of Lima during carnival:

> He moves through the streets timidly, as if through a besieged city, and upon raising this view to the balconies of las señoritas *x* or las señoritas *z*, expecting to see them there, what does he find? The Indian cook, Ña Peta, no less, and black Ña Nieves, the wet-nurse, with her mistress's babe in arms, and Ña Nicolaza, the zamba factotum, had taken over the balcony! There they were, armed with old saucepans and dented tin pitchers, even syringes. That house, like the whole neighborhood, was upside down. The common hand that peels potatoes and never touched a handkerchief dared insult the most dandified gentlemen.[46]

The family of the "upside down" house was evidently absent, probably having withdrawn to the country or the seashore, as many "decent" families did during carnival. Seaside recreational communities had their own water fights, but in a country-club atmosphere, in which the only zambas present were patiently holding trays of lemonade. The alert reader will have noticed that "upside down" [*patas arriba* in the original] suggests a carnivalesque inversion. But the writer evidently did not experience this moment as a sacred "time out of time" that, by inverting the hierarchies of daily life, allowed the regeneration of the world. Instead, like the "groping" of the "ill-dressed and worse spoken" men in the previous quotation, the presence of women of the popular class on the balcony—women carefully assigned a rainbow of non-white racial status—figures as a worrisome insult. Where might such behavior lead after carnival is over? Transgression—not inversion—is the dominant trope in such writings.

Concern at the transgressive carnival antics of the poor, colored majority appears in almost every issue of nineteenth-century newspapers reporting (or discoursing) on carnival. "The plebe, unbridled to an irritating degree, refused to pardon any decent person" whom they encountered on the streets of Lima in carnival 1853, "obliging them all to submit to a soaking with dirty water."[47] That same year in Rio, an alarmed journalist reported "bunches of blacks armed with syringes and pans of inky liquid, who strolled freely around the streets and stationed themselves on corners."[48] And twenty years later, the self-denominated "decent" people's lament was the same: "The lowest class of people goes crazy, escaping all law, bounds, and consideration."[49]

To imagine ourselves in the shoes, for a moment, of the journalist who went out in search of señoritas *x* or *z* and found instead their cook, wet-nurse, and factotum—how was he to react if they succeeded in wetting him? What should he do if drenched by the common women who clustered at the doors of tenements and "invaded the street" throwing water at "decent" gentlemen or threatening to, unless persuaded to refrain from doing so in return for a coin or two? Let us remember, as our hypothetical subject was sure to, that the water in question had most likely come from the open sewer that ran down the center of every Lima street. Violence toward such women, while not out of the question if he were angry or mean enough, would only discredit him. Should he then pay them? Or hurl a few water eggs at them, hoping to injure them but thereby ignominiously engaging them in play? Should he shout a superior-sounding insult? Or should he walk on stoically, knowing himself to be the object of public fun, cursing under his breath? A journalist, of course, had a final option. He could go straight to the office and write an angry sketch of Ña Peta, Ña Nieves, and Ña Nicolaza.[50] My heart does not go out to our annoyed journalist, but the implications of his annoyance are clear. The transgressive carnival play of lower class people did not appear as a harmless symbolic inversion to many "decent" (middle and upper class) city dwellers. To the contrary, it seemed to test the limits of the permissible and thereby, I would argue, contributed to the possible redefinition of those limits.

Conclusions and Implications

A redefinition of limits was, of course, unlikely. During carnival—and *not* during the other 362 days in the year—anything goes. This was the specific condition of carnivalesque transgression—a deal that absolutely everyone understood, even if they did not consider themselves personally signatories to it. Overall, carnival is clearly no roaring engine of social change. Nor, however, is it merely an "opiate of the masses." Rather, various carnival practices carry with them various implications, some of them contrasting.

I do intend to be less wishy-washy, but first I must backpedal a bit more. Carnival celebrations vary from year to year, from group to group, and from place to place. Havana, for example, did not have a water fight of anything like the generalized intensity of what took place annually in the other cities. The throwing game there, as one would have to call it, seems more often to have involved ashes or flour, and it was far less central to what went on, perhaps because absolutely nothing could compete at the Havana carnival with social dancing. Rio had the most "official" of carnivals—a contradiction in terms, but there it is. Lima never developed a "Venetian" carnival in the nineteenth-century at all. Buenos Aires carnival thrived through the turn of the century and then pretty much died. A different mix of activities characterized each city in each period. This chapter has merely explored and interpreted one important activity that rarely gets serious attention.

So, all caveats in place, what can one take away from this discussion of carnival transgressions in nineteenth-century Latin America, besides an amusing image of young nineteenth-century ladies and gentlemen soaking each other in a water fight? Perhaps the image itself is my main conclusion, because an emphasis on the gendered quality of the water fight—the fact that it was girls against boys—is totally absent, to my knowledge, from the scholarly literature on carnival in Latin America. That conclusion expands the social meaning of nineteenth-century carnival, showing how the water fight—so pervasive, so often described, and so rarely interpreted—fits coherently into an overall theorization of the festival. One could notice that this expanded meaning depends on a reading of carnival practices that highlights their frequent transgressiveness.

Transgressions, rather than inversions, lead to social change. Symbolic inversions may seem provocative but they are really conservative. When the elite youth of Buenos Aires sang "tangos" in blackface or slaves put on their master's garments for a day, the moment when such inversions might be realized came not one nanosecond closer. Inversions cannot be incremental, which makes them impossibly distant in practice. Furthermore, inversions may seem to be audacious reimaginings of the social order, but they are not. To the contrary, they merely reverse the signs, producing another hierarchy with precisely the same organizing characteristics as the old one. Carnivalesque inversions may lead to all sorts of existential insights, but if any kind of carnival play somehow affirms the social order it seems to challenge, it's inversions.

Transgressive carnival play, on the other hand, is more practical. Individuals used it to explore their own place in the social order. Cumulatively, men and women of all colors and social ranks used it to test and sometimes, very incrementally, to modify the prevailing norms of social comportment. What if women *could* initiate a flirtation year round, as they could during carnival? This might be a tough proposition in some settings, but it is not a utopian one. Wouldn't approaching a person of contrasting gender, class, or race often enough during carnival make it easier to approach such a person outside of carnival? Again, there is evidence to suggest that carnivalesque transgressions *can* occasionally help redefine the limits of permissible behavior generally. Middle-class people—especially women, who first experimented during carnival with "dirty dancing," like early tango—eventually dared to do it at other times of the year, too.

NOTES

1. Eneida de Moraes, *História do carnaval carioca*, rev. Haroldo Costa (Rio de Janeiro: Editôra Record, 1987), 13–17.
2. Samuel Kinser, *Carnival, American Style: Mardi Gras at New Orleans and Mobile* (Chicago: University of Chicago Press, 1990), 6–7.
3. John Charles Chasteen, *National Rhythms, African Roots: The Deep History of Latin American Popular Dance* (Albuquerque: University of New Mexico Press, 2004).
4. Almost all studies of carnival in nineteenth-century America mention the water fight as a colorful curiosity, without serious interpretation.
5. Julio Caro Baroja, *El carnaval (Análisis histórico-cultural)* (Madrid: Taurus, 1965), 147.
6. Mikhail Bakhtin, *Rabelais and His World*, trans. Helene Iswolsky (Cambridge: MIT Press, 1968), 7–10.
7. Among the most notable of these studies are those by Natalie Zemon Davis.
8. Moraes, *História do carnaval carioca*, 20. Another rare mention of poor people doing this: "Hechos locales," *La tribuna* (Buenos Aires), 11 February 1872.
9. The poem "Diálogos de apacible entretenimiento" (1605) by Gaspar Lucas Hidalgo says, "La mujer se viste de hombre / Y el hombre se viste de hembra." Another line mentions street rowdiness, including "harina por el rostro." Caro Baroja, *El carnaval*, 49.
10. Delso Renault, *O Rio antigo nos anúncios de jornais: 1808–1850* (Rio de Janeiro: José Olympio, 1969), 133.
11. "Carnaval," *El Fígaro* (Havana), 24 February 1887.
12. "Carnaval," *Diario de la tarde: Comercial, político, y literario* (Buenos Aires), 4 February 1837.
13. "Carnaval," *El nacional* (Buenos Aires), 9 February 1872. Cross-dressing in turn-of-the-century Mexico is at the heart of Christopher Conway's chapter in this book.
14. "Teatro de Tacón," *Faro industrial de la Habana*, 7 March 1843.
15. "Carnaval: As passeatas," *O paiz* (Rio de Janeiro), 22 February 1898.
16. Chasteen, "Black Kings, Blackface Carnival, and the Nineteenth-Century Origins of the Tango," in *Latin American Popular Culture: An Introduction*, eds. William H. Beezley and Linda Curcio-Nagy (Wilmington, DE: Scholarly Resources, 2000); and forthcoming work by George Reid Andrews.
17. Kinser, *Carnival, American Style*, 47, 127.

18. An overview of the development of carnival in Latin America may be found in Maria Isaura Pereira de Queiroz, "Evolução do carnaval latinoamericano," *Ciência e cultura* 32 (November 1980): 1477–86.
19. See Caro Baroja, "Actos propios del carnaval," chapter 3 of *El carnaval*, 47–66.
20. These basic outlines of the water fight have been often described. Moraes provides a detailed description of various accoutrements in her *História do carnaval carioca*, 128–36.
21. Ibid., 29–32.
22. Because they were initially activities of the elite, Venetian activities produced a lot of evidence. Newspapers included frequent descriptions of masked balls and elite paraders. See Chasteen, *National Rhythms*; and Enrique H. Puccia, *Breve historia del carnaval porteño* (Buenos Aires: Municipalidad de la Ciudad, 1974); as well as Moraes, *História do carnaval carioca*.
23. "Carnaval," *El comercio* (Lima), 2 March 1870.
24. "Carnaval," *A gazeta da noite* (Rio de Janeiro), 27 February 1879.
25. The attempt to impose "Venetian" practices at the expense of more popular traditional ones has been a principal topic of the historical literature on carnival in nineteenth-century Latin America, just as it was a principal topic of contemporaneous elite discourse in the nineteenth century. When Uruguayan historian José Pedro Barrán and his student Milita Alfaro apply the categories *barbarous carnival* and *civilized carnival* in discussing nineteenth-century Montevideo, they are consciously adopting categories used at the time. See Barrán, *Historia de la sensibilidad en el Uruguay*. Vol. 2, *El disciplinamiento (1860–1920)* (Montevideo: Banda Oriental; Facultad de Humanidades y Ciencias, 1990); and Alfaro, *Carnaval: Una historia social de Montevideo desde la perspectiva de la fiesta. Primera parte: El carnaval heróico (1800–1872)* (Montevideo: Ediciones Trilce, 1992).
26. Peter Wade, *Music, Race, and Nation: Música Tropical in Colombia* (Chicago: University of Chicago Press, 2000).
27. "Escena carnavalesca," *La nación argentina* (Buenos Aires), 21 February 1865.
28. Sarmiento is quoted in Puccia, from the original in *El mercurio* (Santiago), 10 February 1842.
29. "El Carnaval," *El comercio*, 26 February 1873.
30. "Los tres días de carnaval," *El comercio*, 9 March 1859.
31. "Cronica del Callao," *El comercio*, 14 February 1861.
32. "Figura carnavalesca," *La nación argentina*, 21 February 1865.
33. "Carnaval," *El comercio*, 10 February 1869.
34. "Las Rusas," *El nacional*, 22 February 1855.
35. "Carnaval," *A gazeta da noite*, 6 March 1878.
36. "Repartição de polícia," *Diário do Rio de Janeiro* (Rio de Janeiro), 9 February 1842; and Puccia, *Breve historia del carnaval porteño*, 21.
37. This is one of the principal insights from Pierre Bourdieu, *Outline of a Theory of Practice*, trans. Richard Nice (Cambridge: Cambridge University Press, 1977).
38. "Carnaval," *El comercio*, 23 February 1858.
39. "Carnaval," *El comercio*, 14 February 1863; and 1 March 1876.
40. "Carnaval," *Gazeta de notícias* (Rio de Janeiro), 27 February 1876.
41. The last example is admittedly not from the nineteenth century, but rather from Rio's fashionable First World War–era magazine, *Fon Fon*, 16 February

1918. Earlier examples can be found in Lima ("Crónica local," *El comercio*, 10 February 1875), where the story is presented as social gossip, and Buenos Aires ("Carnaval," *El nacional*, 16 February 1872), where the couple declare they will divorce.

42. "Carnaval," *El comercio*, 6 March 1867.

43. Turner's idea has been invoked by Roberto da Matta in *Carnavais, malandros, e heróis: Para uma sociologia do dilema brasileiro* (Rio de Janeiro: Zahar Editores, 1978).

44. Maria Isaura Pereira de Queiroz, *Carnaval brasileiro: O vivido e o mito* (São Paulo: Editora Brasiliense, 1992).

45. "Los tres días de locura," *El comercio*, 22 February 1860.

46. "El carnaval," *El comercio*, 2 March 1870.

47. "Carnaval," *El comercio*, 23 February 1859.

48. "Rio de Janeiro," *Jornal do comércio* (Rio de Janeiro), 9 February 1853.

49. "Carnaval," *El comercio*, 26 February 1873.

50. Descriptions of poor women throwing water at the doors of tenements: "Carnaval," *El comercio*, 14 February 1872; "Crónica local," *El comercio*, 10 February 1875; "Carnestolendas," *El comercio*, 17 February 1901.

7

Performing the Porfiriato

Federico Gamboa and the Negotiation of Power

Stuart A. Day

If the expression "Speak truth to power" still has a utopian ring to it, this is surely because it is so rarely practiced. The dissembling of the weak in the face of power is hardly an occasion for surprise. It is ubiquitous. So ubiquitous, in fact, that it makes its appearance in many situations in which the sort of power being exercised stretches the ordinary meaning of power beyond recognition.
—James C. Scott, *Domination and the Arts of Resistance*

A president comes to power under questionable circumstances with the support of conservative forces in Mexico and abroad. Pro-business and other major newspapers publish editorials in the United States that hail the newly-elected leader as a friend of progress, while in Mexico the political Left questions his legitimacy. Foreign ideals (and dollars) rule the political stage in a new but familiar context where words, and sovereignty, are once again lost in translation.[1] The distribution of land is more and more unequal every year, leaving campesinos—and their supporters in the metropolis and beyond—to consider raising arms as the only viable way to ameliorate centuries of oppression. An intellectual laments in his diary the discomfort of working for the "system"; his measured fury is made public with great care lest his livelihood and loyalties be compromised: "It is the old tacit agreement. For our living we count entirely on the government, and every government—from the viceroyalty to the present day—counts on the fact that we count on them."[2]

The title of this chapter helps to contextualize the preceding paragraph, placing it not in the here and now—where it might fit comfortably, despite the fact that present-day intellectuals in Mexico have more avenues of autonomy than their Porfirian predecessors—but on the cusp of two previous centuries, the nineteenth and twentieth. In the turn-of-the-century diary entry quoted above, Federico Gamboa (1864–1939) bemoans the power of patronage over his destiny at a time when politics in Mexico were dictated by Porfirio Díaz (1830–1915), who, as will be seen in Terry Rugeley's chapter, ruled Mexico with scant interruption for over three decades before leaving for Europe in 1911 from the port city of Veracruz (a destiny sealed by the arrival of the Mexican Revolution). Yet despite the criticism of the Porfiriato that Gamboa often penned in his diary, José Emilio Pacheco signals the issue that makes Gamboa such an interesting figure in Mexican intellectual history: "Gamboa is not, nor can he be, a radical critic; he is a Porfirian to the degree that when the regime disappears, he suspends his work as a novelist. . . . He needs the at once paternal and demonic shadow of don Porfirio."[3]

The life of Gamboa—the author, diplomat, professor, and public figure who literally stood by Porfirio Díaz until the end—offers an intriguing view of the negotiation of power that was performed in playhouses as well as on the national stage during the Porfiriato. Through a study of Gamboa's own writing and life, as well as the performances of the time (as seen in newspapers, political cartoons, and other historical accounts), it becomes clear that negotiation and acting, rather than the unadulterated domination by which political regimes are often characterized, are foundations of Porfirian hegemony. For Díaz, power could be blunt and brutal, of course, but also as malleable and acquiescent as the political situation demanded. In his oft-referenced *Domination and the Arts of Resistance*, James C. Scott offers one possible outcome in the face of domination: "Those obliged by domination to act a mask will eventually find that their faces have grown to fit that mask."[4] Another possible outcome, more auspicious in terms of revolutionary change, is seen in Scott's analysis of the character Mrs. Poyser in English woman novelist George Eliot's *Adam Bede*: "[Eliot's] claim is that the necessity of 'acting a mask' in the presence of power produces, almost by the strain engendered by its inauthenticity, a countervailing pressure that cannot be contained indefinitely."[5] Do the masks acted by the characters in Gamboa's play *La venganza de la gleba* (The Revenge of the Earth, written in 1904, staged in 1905, and published in 1907)—or the masks acted by Gamboa himself—fit the faces they cover?[6] That is, do years of domination control *thought* itself, or does one negotiate knowingly in order to navigate the prevailing power structure? To answer this question, it is useful to address *La venganza de la gleba* and the diaries of Gamboa, the consummate, complex man of letters in turn-of-the-century Mexico, as well as some instances of the performances of the Porfiriato. Thus, there are two layers to this chapter: the negotiations on the part of characters in *La venganza*, and then Gamboa's own negotiation of the political system. The purpose of this reading of Gamboa is to consider the effects of power relations on theatrical and national stages, with the hope of shedding light on both.

Foreign ideas (economic liberalism, naturalism, positivism, and social Darwinism, among others) flowed into Mexico under Díaz's watch. Economic ties with the United States and its robber barons opened the gate to foreign capital. Meanwhile, in Mexico's capital city, cultural connections to Europe were often facilitated by the wealthy (who could send their children to be educated in Europe) or diplomats like Gamboa (who had the luxury of traveling in an official capacity). Such was the case more than a decade before the first staging of *La venganza* in Mexico City's Teatro Renacimiento. In his diary, Gamboa recounts that he found himself in Paris at two in the afternoon on 4 October 1893. Knowing that his prospective host would not recognize his name, the Mexican public servant and writer left a note that expressed a desire to meet with the resident of the house in the Rue de Bruxelles. Later that day, Gamboa fulfilled what had been an important literary goal—indeed, a dream: he met with "Emilio" Zola, who greeted Gamboa in slippers and, after an extended discussion, commented that it was right of Gamboa not to offer him copies of his books since, in Zola's words via Gamboa, "I only read in Castilian, and with great difficulty, the newspaper articles that talk about me."[7] This is Gamboa's side of the story, of course. His exhilaration at meeting Zola had been diminished somewhat by a feeling that, while he had been treated properly by the French author, Gamboa himself "needed another, very different Zola—the one I had tenderly engendered in my own mind."[8] The influence of Émile Zola—the literary Zola of Gamboa's imagination—contributed to the biting social commentary in *La venganza*, which provides an exemplar of the paradox of Gamboa's life: as a writer who based his work on close observation (plus a dose of romance), he could ignore neither the Mexican milieu nor the hereditary, colonial tradition that binds one to the land and to a master. As a steadfast supporter of the Díaz regime, the ending of *La venganza* seemingly had to ignore both Mexican realism and the literary genius of the writer in the Rue de Bruxelles whose work Gamboa so admired. Perhaps the Díaz regime wins out in this piece, though based on reviews of the play, Gamboa's sociopolitical commentary might not have been lost on the audience. Indeed, one theater critic writes, "It is a thesis play. Socialist? A bit. Compassionate more than anything."[9]

The play is set in 1904. The hacienda where each of the three acts takes place is six hours by rail from Mexico City and belongs to the Pedreguera family—as do its workers, one might argue. The stage directions describe both the corrosion of the years and the wealth generated by the workers who are overseen by don Francisco Rayo, the hacienda's administrator. In more than one scene, the dialogue is interrupted by the Mayordomo as he calls out weights representing sacks of grain that will be transported via rail, ostensibly to Mexico City. On the hacienda, we also find *los de abajo* (the underdogs), a term used by Gamboa that, with the publication of Mariano Azuela's novel by the same name a decade later, became tightly tied to the Mexican Revolution.[10] The only member of the Pedreguera family who has been on the hacienda in recent years (the rest have spent over half a decade in Paris, in part due to the illness of the family patriarch) is Damián, the "illegitimate" child of the hacendado's son, Javier de Pedreguera, who has not been to the hacienda in eighteen years. Blanca, also Javier's biological offspring, arrives with her family from Paris. She is obviously the "legitimate" child and will—no surprise to the spectator or the reader of *La venganza*—fall in love with her half brother. The ending of the play will come only after a *pausa trágica* (tragic pause) and the death of her grandfather from a hereditary disease, from the sinful dishonor his son has brought upon the family, and/or simply from the shock of knowing that his granddaughter has fallen in love not only with a peón but with her half brother.

La venganza has been classified in many ways by many critics, though seldom do studies go beyond the requisite three or four pages the author of the incredibly successful novel *Santa* (1903) necessitates. For some, the text has touches of naturalism; for some, it is realism; and for others, it is simply and sometimes derogatorily "romantic" or "sentimental."[11] In "Zola's *L'Œuvre* and *Reconquista* of Gamboa," Robert J. Niess notes that Gamboa's "work provides only scattered examples of direct appropriation from Zola and the latter's influence on him was rather general than specific, bearing mainly on his choice of subject-matter, method of treatment and overall social outlook."[12] Though Niess goes on, as many others have, to argue the influence of Zola in Gamboa's work—in this case in the novel *Reconquista* (1937)—what interests us here is not classification (the play clearly represents a variety of literary currents) but rather, as noted above, the Zola imagined by Gamboa, and indeed *imagined* naturalism, both of which influenced the play at hand and may have led to the "naturalistic" title *La venganza de la gleba*—*The Revenge of the Earth*, specifically the cultivated earth, in its basic definition.

According to José Emilio Pacheco, a Mexican intellectual born the year of Gamboa's death, *gleba* (glebe) quickly leads, metonymically, to *los siervos de la gleba* (the servants of the land), "at least in the vocabulary of the political right in Mexico."[13] Definitions of *gleba* abound, and while most dictionaries initially define the term as "earth cultivated by a plough," subsequent definitions often include, for example, "serf," "fief," or "heritage." One dictionary indicates that *gleba* is also a "slave anciently joined to a piece of land and transferred with it to another owner," while another confirms that the "siervos de la gleba" could be sold along with the land they cultivated.[14] *Gleba* and *siervos de la gleba* are so tightly tied that under *siervo* in the *Diccionario del español usual en México*, "siervos de la gleba" is listed as the first example.[15] Notwithstanding the political implications of the title, however, Pacheco notes that "Gamboa seems to have thought more about the vengeance of Mother Earth than about the revenge of the humiliated and offended." This seems true, following Pacheco, especially given the final scene of the play: without knowing of the blood ties, Blanca proclaims to her ailing grandfather that she is in love with her brother Damián, and as the grandfather dies he declares that the land (*la tierra*—and not *la gleba*, with its broader implications) has taken its revenge. Yet in light of the relationship of the people (especially the peones) to the land, not to mention the explicit dedication of the play "to the wealthy people of my country," it is impossible to ignore the social—if not socialist—content of the work. Blanca's "shattered romantic interlude" in hindsight is also the shattered illusion that the Mexican elite could continue to own horses and to place bets at the racetracks in Mexico City (a well-known pastime of Mexican elites) while "los de abajo" were tied to land that they did not own.

Like the dedication of the play itself, the last line of *La venganza* is inescapably ironic. The administrator of the hacienda, don Francisco, reads a telegram from Javier de Pedreguera—the father of Damián and Blanca, the two siblings in love—justifying his delayed arrival at his father's deathbed: "Impossible to go today. I was triumphant, honoring the family name."[16] For Gamboa, at least in this play, there is no honor in exploitation; at the racetrack with the Porfirian elite and his winning horse, Javier represents the wealthy of Gamboa's country to whom this play is dedicated. Pacheco is right to draw attention to the unavoidable reality of Gamboa's play: "Gamboa passes through the haciendas like an English novelist would travel through India. . . . A novelist from a city that exercises its empire over the countryside, Gamboa sees in it the old barbarism opposed to urban civilization."[17] Gamboa not only puts the countryside and its workers on stage—half a decade before the Revolution, and well before Pancho Villa and Emiliano Zapata would sit in the Casa de los Azulejos (now a Sanborn's restaurant owned by Mexican multibillionaire Carlos Slim) where the Jockey Club and its racing aficionados had enjoyed their wealth and power—but he also lets us know what the novelist as tourist (in his own country) might see, and how he and other Mexicans might perceive the countryside now and in the future.[18] Indeed, he is the colonial writer in a "foreign" land.

While it would be imprudent to equate Gamboa with his contemporary, English writer Rudyard Kipling (1865–1936), or Mexico's sociohistorical context to that of the British Empire, Edward Said's observations on Kipling's poem "The White Man's Burden" (1899) are nonetheless pertinent:

> As happens in several poems, in novels like *Kim*, and in too many catchphrases to be an ironic fiction, Kipling's White Man, as an idea, a persona, a style of being, seems to have served many Britishers while abroad.... Kipling himself could not merely have happened; the same is true of his White Man. Such ideas and their authors emerge out of complex historical and cultural circumstances.... Reality is divided into various collectives: languages, races, types, colors, mentalities, each category being not so much a neutral designation as an evaluative interpretation. Underlying these categories is the rigidly binomial opposition of "ours" and "theirs."... This opposition was reinforced not only by anthropology, linguistics, and history but also, of course, by the Darwinian theses on survival and natural selection.[19]

From the very description of the dramatis personae in *La venganza*, the divisions of Mexican reality at the beginning of the twentieth century are clear, though Gamboa's text is more self-conscious (yet perhaps no less paternalistic) than the work of authors like Kipling. From the *harapos* (rags) and *sombreros de petate* (straw hats, made from the same material used for humble sleeping rolls) of the workers to the European dress (typical of wealthy Mexicans) worn by the Pedreguera family, the 1905 spectator as well as the contemporary reader would understand clearly the social divisions at play—and thus the effect of Porfirian hegemony. It is evident that the distance between the campesinos and, for example, the princess-like Blanca Pedreguera is, or should be, maintained based on societal norms.[20] In this case, natural selection is anything but natural, though the façade of heredity—biological, not colonial—performed by both the elites and the people who work the land might lead one to think otherwise. This is the discussion (tightly tied to negotiation) that Gamboa brings to the fore in *La venganza* and that makes the play revolutionary despite reviews to the contrary, Gamboa's ideas expressed in other venues, or Gamboa's "true" feelings, whatever they may have been. The scenes of negotiation in this century-old play—often metatheatrical and self-conscious—are, like the social strata mentioned above, communicated effectively through costumes.

However, instead of serving as disguises, these representations function to demonstrate purposely a stark, hierarchical reality.

The administrator of the hacienda, don Francisco, falls in-between the Pedreguera family (as does the character from Mexico City, Joaquín, who dropped out of college and works in the hacienda office) and the campesinos. Don Francisco visually (and verbally, as will be seen shortly) negotiates class structure: he wears a waistcoat and an unadorned hat—made of felt, not petate. Gamboa also specifies that this character's jacket and pants are "not for riding horseback." Make no mistake about his origins—the playtext does not—but don Francisco is, from the point of view of the Pedreguera family, one of "them" who understands "us." In the first act, when the administrator is accused by the young city slicker Joaquín of sounding like the "socialists" ("those who want the underdogs to rise to where the wealthy find themselves now"), he clarifies his liminal position: "That's just nonsense, Joaquín. Why would I want that if I'm not with one group or the other, and with what's left of my life it's the same to me whether those rise or the others go down? . . . What I was saying was that the masters should care more than they generally do about the people who work for them."[21] This quotation forms part of a dialogue commonly cited by critics and theater historians who signal the possibly revolutionary tone of *La venganza*. Don Francisco continues with what is the most potentially radical line of the play, at least according to one possible reading that is also cited often:

> Those of us who work the land, who water it with our sweat and with our tears, those of us who with the plow destroy its entrails so that everyone can eat, those of us from the campo and those of you from the cities. . . . We are not bandits, we're guerrillas . . . revolutionaries, precisely to defend the land from those from the outside and those from the inside—it's the same! . . . What does this have to do with the rich, with religion, and with governments? Even with bad governments![22]

In one of the most in-depth and insightful analyses of *La venganza*, Marcela Del-Río notes that don Francisco is one of the characters who serves as an intermediary from whom the play's "social prophesy" comes.[23] The above quotation demonstrates the ideological fissure between the campo and the city: one can infer either that the "bad governments" are hypothetical or that, as Del-Río affirms, "the author, as a member of the government of Porfirio Díaz, knew that a completely revolutionary discourse could bring him lamentable consequences." Yet it is probable that Gamboa was signaling the importance of social change that had nothing to do with radical revolution, but rather with increased social justice—just the right amount to maintain the government of Díaz. Del-Río is clear on this point: "In *La venganza de la gleba*, what [Gamboa] is trying to do is not to instigate the people through a subversive message so that they rebel, but rather the contrary: he is promulgating the avoidance of the social chaos that a revolution would entail, since it would lead to another dictator because of the ethnic fatalism to which, according to Gamboa, Mexicans are subject."[24] While it seems that Del-Río contradicts the statement quoted above regarding Gamboa's cautious stance as a member of the Porfiriato, it is clear that these contradictions also lie within Gamboa himself. He is both weary of the Porfiriato but also of what might replace it if there were a revolution. Gamboa negotiates political desires as well as his fear (expressed by the city slicker Joaquín, who expounds on socialism in the play) of an upheaval that would place the country, and his own position in the Porfirian government, at risk.

What brought on the accusation of don Francisco being a socialist, in addition to voicing his opinions regarding the rights of the workers, is the conversation he has with Marcos, the campesino who is raising Javier de Pedreguera's son as his own along with his wife Loreto, who is the mother of the child:

DON FRANCISCO: Who's there?

MARCOS: It's us, don Pancho, may God grant you a good evening! (*Removing his hat.*)

DON FRANCISCO: (*Removing his hat upon hearing the divine Name.*) Good evening, Marcos, who are you speaking with?

MARCOS: With Loreto, patrón . . . did you require [*mandaba usté*] something?

. . .

MARCOS: (*Turning his hat in his hands.*) Señor don Pancho, did you order something?

DON FRANCISCO: Have you already heard the news that the masters [*amos*] arrive tomorrow? . . . That you have to come greet them with those of us who eat their bread?

MARCOS: I won't be able to be there, señor don Pancho, because of my little animals, with your permission! They don't know about this and can't go a day without food. . . . I'll go into the hills [*m'iré al monte*], God willing, as always, in the morning, and your grace [*su mercé*] will tell the masters that . . . I don't know how to speak.

DON FRANCISCO: Why don't you have the herders drive the cattle, and you can join the rest, since you're a horseman, for the ride that will go and meet them at the train? ... Come on! And I'll let you ride my "Apache," with its new saddle ...

MARCOS: If your grace commands it ... but I don't know how to speak, don Pancho! ... and I have two sick cows ... and I'm the only one who can cure them ...

DON FRANCISCO: Look, man, don't be stubborn, it's not even a matter of talking, and you can cure the cows upon your return. Do you want to go or not? ...

LORETO: (*Quietly to Marcos.*) Come on, man, go! ...

MARCOS: (*Resolute.*) Well, if your grace commands it, but I'd rather go with my cows and bulls, don Pancho. ... I don't know how to speak ...

DON FRANCISCO: (*Turning benevolently toward Joaquín.*) I'm telling you, Joaquín, it makes you want either to kill them or leave them, because they don't understand even if you shoot at them! ...

MARCOS: (*Tugging on Loreto's shawl.*) Well, then, patrón, with your permission, and may your grace rest ... good evening, don Joaquín! ...

Loreto and Marcos exit.

JOAQUÍN: Goodness! Señor don Pancho, what patience you have with these brutes. ...

DON FRANCISCO: (*Reacting, within his nature, which is in the end that of a campesino.*) No, no, Joaquín, they're not so brutish, the man has his reasons ... I mean (*upon noting Joaquín's strange reaction*) he must have his reasons, but they're like that: very introspective, swallowing their desires and their suffering, more than anything if it has to do with the masters ... what I mean (*restraining his own discourse*) is that if they fear the masters will not take well what they do or what they say, yes sir, even thought itself! Because the respect that the earth breeds for the master ... encompasses even thought ...[25]

This extended quotation shows the masks worn both by the campesino and by don Francisco. Marcos cannot express himself in front of the "masters"; "I cannot speak" (*no sé hablar*), he repeats. He affirms, in effect, that he has no voice and no ability—but more importantly, no authority—to express himself to the Pedreguera family. The linguistic cues of his performance for don Francisco indicate that he also does not have the schooling or the power of Joaquín (though Joaquín did not finish his university studies) or of don Francisco (who went off to school before returning to the campo). *Su mercé* (your grace) implies, in a slightly different but appropriate connotation, dependence on the volition of another; *usté*, the formal "you" sans the final "d" (as is the case with *mercé*), serves as a sign of respect and as a rural social marker; and *patrón*, a person who mandates the actions of others, points to the total dependence of the campesino on his boss. What don Francisco knows that Joaquín does not (as the reader or spectator gathers when Joaquín reacts strangely to his comment that Marcos "has his reasons") is that Marcos does not want to see the father of the son he calls his own—though, in the end, Javier de Pedreguera never appears on stage. Marcos clearly fears the social situation, though it is also possible that he fears an *eruption* that would result from the bringing to light of what James C. Scott calls the *hidden transcript*—a "privileged site for nonhegemonic, contrapuntal, dissident, subversive discourse."[26] Marcos fears, perhaps, a revealing of truths generally spoken only among the campesinos during which the mask of a subordinate is removed to show that the face and the mask only appear to fit together, that disruption (personal or national) of the status quo is manifest, and that there is a desire for revenge that, according to Scott, can be shared by a community: "An individual who is affronted may develop a personal fantasy of revenge and confrontation, but when the insult is but a variant of affronts suffered systematically by a whole race, class, or strata, then the fantasy can become a collective cultural product. Whatever form it assumes—offstage parody, dreams of violent revenge, millennial visions of a world turned upside down—this collective hidden transcript is essential to any dynamic view of power relations."[27]

It is difficult to ascertain the position of don Francisco in the text, for he plays the part of defender of the campesinos (as seen in his discussion with Joaquín and in other sections of the playtext), but he also serves to keep the workers in check for their own benefit (at least from his point of view). He is one of them and should act as such according to the stage directions quoted above, where Gamboa affirms that his "nature" is, after all, that of a campesino. We see this in the text from don Francisco's point of view, though he clarifies the difference in status: "I, born here, right here, on this hacienda, although fortunately at a higher rank . . . I know what you know, and what you do not."[28] We also see subtle deference to the masters when don Francisco refers above to the campesinos who eat the food provided by the masters. This is in sharp contrast to the reference in a heated exchange with Joaquín, when don Francisco exclaims that the campesinos harvest food so that those in the countryside as well as those in the city may eat. The difference is clear: in don Francisco's conversation with Marcos, there is a façade to protect (that is, that the food, as with the hacienda and its inhabitants, is the property of the masters)—a façade that is upheld by the both dominant and subordinate entity in a given interaction. According to Scott, this is the public transcript, "a shorthand way of describing the open interaction between subordinates and those who dominate. The public transcript, where it is not positively misleading, is unlikely to tell the whole story of power relations. It is frequently in the interest of both parties to tacitly conspire in misrepresentation."[29]

The performance of don Francisco serves to maintain the status quo. Marcos gets what he wants, but the power relationship is reinforced in the line where don Francisco reminds Marcos of his authority, telling him, "You know me." In part, don Francisco has been kind and understanding; yet, without a doubt, he also feels the need to refer to acts of past violence or punishment so that his authority remains intact in terms of how he appears in front of both men. In a broader context, don Francisco sustains the balancing act of the hegemonic power structure by releasing steam (giving in while maintaining authority) at exactly the right moments. In this way, he helps Marcos escape a difficult situation and also avoids the possibility of an explosion of the hidden transcript. The manner in which Marcos regards don Francisco is potentially multifaceted. As Scott notes, "There is little doubt that acts of deference—for example, a bow of greeting or the use of a superior's honorific in addressing him—are intended in some sense to convey the outward impression of conformity with standards sustained by superiors. Beyond this we may not safely go. The act may be performed almost automatically as a ritual or habitual act; it may be the result of calculating its advantages; it may be successful dissembling; it may spring from a conscious desire to honor a respected superior."[30]

In the interaction between Marcos and don Francisco, we see a certain paternal admiration; the desire on the part of Marcos to achieve his goal, and thus perhaps the additional use of respectful words and gestures; and, of course, the habitual, natural-appearing removal of the hat. For don Francisco, it is in deference to God, whereas for Marcos it is a gesture of respect, real or feigned—or both.

As with any power structure, there are ranks that must be obeyed, and don Francisco, despite his power over the campesinos, shows deference not only to God but also to his patrón, don Andrés de Pedreguera. At the beginning of the second act, don Andrés speaks with don Francisco in order to ascertain whether or not the child Loreto and Marcos are raising is the offspring of Javier. The other child, the "legitimate" offspring of Loreto and Marcos, had died at a young age. Don Andrés suspects that the child is his grandson; his wife, doña Guadalupe Orto de Pedreguera, wants to know the truth in order to make amends and avoid divine retribution; and Marcos, under pressure, finally reveals that the child is indeed a Pedreguera.[31] Don Andrés, however, wants a different version of the story—one that will assuage his wife's concerns. Don Francisco must once again negotiate by hedging, employing standard tools of the social structure, to slowly achieve the desired result—avoiding a conversation with doña Guadalupe in which he, portrayed as ever so noble by Gamboa, would have to lie. Don Andrés employs his power to get his way ("Am I going to have to remind you that I am the master?"), but don Francisco is able to adhere to his desire not to speak directly with the wife of the hacendado, using his linguistic prowess and power of negotiation to do so.[32] Instead of *usté*, as when speaking with others, in this section of text don Francisco uses the full word. He clearly knows when and how to negotiate, though he is successful here in part because honor (don Francisco's desire not to lie) wins out in a play that is becoming more and more centered, by the second act, on an ethos of religion and less on the reality that one might experience in the campo, however idyllically and stereotypically that reality is presented.

"The power of the dominant," Scott writes, "ordinarily elicits—in the public transcript—a continuous stream of performances of deference, respect, reverence, admiration, esteem, and even adoration that serve to further convince ruling elites that their claims are in fact validated by the social evidence they see before their very eyes."[33] This reverential deference, always negotiated with care, becomes evident in numerous conversations in the play. Gamboa understood that maintaining the hegemonic power structure requires obedience without limiting opportunities (for advancement and honor, as in the case of don Francisco, and in the case of Marcos, good will from his patrón) so severely that no progress with personal goals or change is possible—a situation that would lead to revolution. Within *La venganza*, there is room to move, to advance, and to achieve at a minimum the respect of the administrator and even the Pedreguera family itself. The question becomes, then, to what extent are the campesinos operating in a colonial structure that they have internalized and that to them appears natural? Does one interpret, for example, Marcos and his actions as, to use the title of one of Scott's book chapters, "False Consciousness or Laying It on Thick?"[34] Or, to put it another way, are the face and the mask identical?

A review published in the newspaper *El imparcial* on 16 October 1905 makes reference to the most surprising element of the play: the Mexican *pueblo* on stage. The reviewer states, "*La venganza de la gleba* shows us how it is possible to bring to the stage our life, our blood, national customs and passions. . . . The play's peons speak like our campesinos, in a type of popular speech in which the Castilian words have archaic touches—colonial echoes—and phonetic alterations of a pueblo that for centuries has not heard spoken correctly the language taught to them by the conquerors."[35] The "us" here is the bourgeois class. It is clear that campesinos would not have been in the theater to see themselves represented on stage, though they were—history tells us—already rehearsing revolution in their conversations and defying in small ways the power structure. The "colonial echoes" are clear, too; the question is to what extent the gestures and words would have been so ingrained as to not be recognizable to the workers as a performance of self-preservation or advancement. While wary of hegemony, especially the variety that precludes agency on the part of subordinates, Scott indicates that gestures such as the tip of a hat or the use of pleasantries that hedge or honor a dominant interlocutor "may, in some cultural contexts, become as habitual as the ordinary conversational prefaces to complaints by subordinates who are not yet so alienated as to declare war." He goes on to argue that "any dominant ideology with hegemonic pretensions must, by definition, provide subordinate groups with political weapons that can be of use in the public transcript. . . . Historical evidence clearly shows that subordinate groups have been capable of revolutionary *thought* that repudiates existing forms of domination."[36] That is, there is room for negotiation and false consciousness, which is, at least in part, the illusion produced by perfected performances rehearsed for centuries.

In his conversation with Joaquín, don Francisco indicates to Joaquín's surprise that land breeds respect for the master, whose power of rule encompasses "even thought itself."[37] Yet the ritualized signs of respect seen repeatedly in the play are belied by the conversations among the campesinos; it is clear that we are dealing not simply with false consciousness but with self-preservation, prudence in the face of domination. As love and talk of marriage blossoms between Blanca and Damián, the "legitimate" and "illegitimate" Pedregueras respectively, one of their conversations offers insight into the hidden transcript—the words spoken off stage among the people who work the land:

> BLANCA: Silly, silly, didn't I tell you that with my grandpa I get everything I want, everything, everything? . . . And you'll see how he consents to let me marry you! . . . (*Juvenile.*) And imagine the look on the faces of the people from here the day we marry! . . . The look of Loreto's face, and that of Marcos! . . . Don't you like that?
>
> DAMIÁN: (*Somber.*) No! I don't like it, because it seems impossible! . . . My father has explained it to me many times: "The masters think we're different from them, and they consider us to be in every way worse than animals." . . .
>
> BLANCA: And if we're different, then why do we love each other? . . .

DAMIÁN: (*Pensive.*) I don't know ... maybe it's because nobody mandates love. ... There are things that nobody controls! ... things that are free![38]

While this is not a conversation among subordinates, Damián's reference to what his father has repeatedly told him, and what is clearly relayed—indeed quoted—based on conversations held in the absence of the powerful, give insight into a *literary* hidden transcript. This unveiling of Marcos's words contradicts his speech and actions in the face of power; namely in his conversation with don Francisco (in the presence of Joaquín) and in a later conversation with Blanca's mother, when he remains almost voiceless while interrogated regarding the paternity of Damián. Marcos "knows his place," as the audience of 1905 might have appreciated. What is also apparent, however, is that while Marcos may be controlled by "colonial echoes," this control does not necessarily extend to his thoughts—thoughts expressed in the hidden transcript.

Regarding the term *hegemony*, Sara Mills notes that instead of a strictly Marxist view of ideology that "implied a simplistic and negative process whereby individuals were duped into using conceptual systems which were not in their own interests," a view of discourse heavily influenced by Foucault "offered a way of thinking about hegemony—people's compliance with their own oppression—without assuming that individuals are necessarily simply passive victims of systems of thought."[39] Compliance implies choice, of course, and some "choices" bring about drastic consequences for subordinates in a given situation. For Marcos, this would surely be the case; we do not get to see the end Damián would have faced if it had not been discovered that he was related by blood to Blanca. Del-Río believes that the play is not about class structure "because what impedes the union of the siblings who, as they fall in love with each other, do not know what they are, is the blood relationship and not the social difference."[40] True, the reason that a campesino cannot marry Blanca happens to be, in this play, the blood ties they share. Yet what would the reason have been were this not the case? Without the reality of the Mexican Revolution, *La venganza* would have been a foundational fiction affirming divisions of class and race, not to mention the incest taboo common in many Latin American texts; because of the Revolution, it was, in short, a premonition. Damián, without a doubt, encroaches on the class divisions, on the domain of the White Man.

The importance of colonial (as opposed to genetic) heredity is shown numerous times in the text. For instance, when Blanca falls from a horse, Damián carries her—but only after getting permission from "the main or 'big' master."[41] Yet perhaps the best example is when Blanca and Damián are discussing their relationship. Blanca indicates that she will never run off with Damián (he cannot believe there could be another way), but promises to speak to her grandfather. At this point Blanca's mother, Beatriz, calls her from the window, and the stage directions make the situation clear: "As soon as the voice of Beatriz is heard, Damián, out of hereditary and centuries-old respect, instinctively removes his hat and moves away from Blanca, who, on the other hand, is unaffected, innocent and pure."[42] Beatriz has a "voice"—a voice Blanca can ignore at will. During the play, Damián, despite being so forthright as to use the informal "you" (*tú*) with Blanca because it seemed "natural," calls her formally by the name *niña Blanca*, *niña* being a sign of respect as well as marital status.[43] While Blanca is immutable, Damián should remain "mute," as in the scene described above, which brings to mind the theater term *mutis*—to remove oneself from the scene, to give center stage to another actor, or to remain quiet. Damián does so, and the myth of inferiority is shown to be pervasive. In *Mythologies*, Roland Barthes proposes that "myth has the intent of giving an historical intention a natural justification, and making contingency appear eternal. . . . The function of myth is to empty reality . . . Myth does not deny things, on the contrary, its function is to talk about them; simply, it purifies them, it makes them innocent, it gives them a natural and eternal justification, it gives them a clarity which is not that of an explanation but that of a statement of fact."[44] The actions and words of Damián and others in *La venganza* show both mythical iterations and understanding on the part of "los de abajo" that behaviors are anything but natural; they can be muted, but are also mutable. The face has not grown to fit the mask in the case of characters like Damián and Marcos.

"Natural," of course, is how reviewers saw the 1905 performance, and *naturalism* as a theatrical term (also from Zola) fits well with the assessment of the play. While reviewers who saw *La venganza* perceived that Mexico had been put on stage, critics since that time have rightly emphasized Gamboa's paternalism in his treatment of characters, especially the campesinos (Marcos, for example, abuses alcohol to dull the pain of his situation with Loreto). Gamboa clearly wants to influence his characters in a way that will, in turn, influence the audience. Carlos Solórzano ties this idea of paternalism to his classification of the play, which once again brings naturalism to the fore: "True, incisive naturalism, without being toned down, could not prosper in literary expression in which the author treats his characters and his public paternalistically."[45] This sentiment is also expressed with a slightly different take by Donald L. Shaw, who, writing on Gamboa's novel *Santa*, affirms that Gamboa was not a "real" naturalist and that he "retained his religious beliefs which, indeed, became stronger towards the end of his life. In other words, although he allowed himself to dive into the murky waters of *fin-de-siglo* existential negativism, he always kept firm hold of a life-line."[46]

Following the claims of Shaw and Solórzano, it is clear that Gamboa was negotiating literary currents as well as his own religious beliefs. For some critics, this results in watered down naturalism, though of course this ignores the work of many writers, beginning with that of nineteenth-century Spanish author Emilia Pardo Bazán, who was influenced (but not overtaken) by Zola, among others. João Sedycias highlights the combination of "Catholic" naturalism à la Pardo Bazán and social criticism, saying that Gamboa's "brand of naturalistic fiction is unique . . . in that with it the author sought to bridge two very different and distant worlds: the intellectual milieu of European letters and the social and religious ambience of his native Mexico."[47] What is clear is that there is room for redemption with Gamboa, and there is social criticism in his work that belies the seemingly objective tone of "real" naturalism. According to Bertolt Brecht, naturalism leads an audience to see the world as unchangeable and to see sociohistorical situations as natural. "Naturalists," states Brecht, "show human beings as if they were showing a tree to a passerby. Realists show human beings as one shows a tree to a gardener."[48] Because Gamboa does not aspire to (or achieve) "clinical detachment," we have a window onto a more intriguing subject than a faux laboratory experiment: the religious, political, and social debates of the Porfiriato. In the play, we see that Gamboa negotiated literary currents as well as his own religious and political positions. He negotiated, in short, Porfirian hegemony, and in the process his face grew to fit the mask—a mask of complicity, albeit coupled with compassion.

A newspaper review of *La venganza* points to one of the first calculated moves that Gamboa made—one of his first incursions in the power structure that would at once serve him and also require his services: "With regard to the execution of the play, we can assure that it was pleasing, although at times one noted a certain monotony in its delivery. . . . For us, the triumph of Mr. Gamboa is a great satisfaction, and we thank the chronicler from *El imparcial* for the affectionate words that he dedicates to him. We say this because the author of *La venganza de la gleba* began to brandish his first literary arms in the pages of *Diario del hogar* around the years 1885 to 1886."[49]

In addition to countering the claim made in the review quoted above and attributed to Urbina, we see that Gamboa had left the *Diario del hogar*. He would, from here on out, use his literary arms with great care, and this is perhaps where the face begins to grow to fit the mask. The tone of the review is amicable, as was Gamboa's departure from the paper when the editor, Filomeno Mata, decided to take a more critical stance toward Díaz and gave his staff the option of leaving.[50] The possible source of Gamboa's decision to support Díaz (as María Guadalupe García Barragán indicates, and for which there is ample evidence in Gamboa's *Diarios* [Diaries]) is his gratitude toward Díaz for sending a military escort for his father's funeral. In 1901, Gamboa writes that the act "sealed, forever, my gratitude toward [Díaz].... At times I have censured, in word and in thought, many acts of the governor ... but I have not stopped loving the man, Porfirio Díaz, nor have I ceased to be grateful."[51] García Barragán affirms that the memory of this gesture was Gamboa's reason for going to work at the newspaper *El lunes*, though it also seems clear that Gamboa perceived a fruitful future in the Díaz regime (as he would after the advent of the Revolution, when he and many of the incorporated Porfirian intellectuals would back the short-lived presidency of Huerta).[52] Thus began a long career in the Porfiriato—a career that ran parallel to, but was very different from, that of Filomeno Mata. In the end, Gamboa would make an unsuccessful bid for the presidency as a Catholic Party candidate, while the editor of the *Diario del hogar* would see the 24 May 1911 headline of his newspaper proclaim "Today General Díaz Resigns."

The story of the opposition newspaper *Diario del hogar* indicates the limited (but nonetheless extant) space for criticism in Mexican papers, and the Porfiriato's policies and actions related to the press offer one of the most useful examples of its negotiated performance. In his biography of Porfirio Díaz, Paul Garner addresses the case of the newspaper's editor in the years following its 1881 inception and Díaz's first re-election:

> Mata became an even more outspoken critic of permanent re-election.... He not only urged Díaz to resign his candidacy, but published a satirical poem which lampooned Díaz ... As a consequence, Cosío Villegas estimates that *El Diario del hogar* was subjected to an average of four prosecutions a year between 1885 and 1890, and that Mata himself spent a total of 47 days in prison in 1890 alone. He was imprisoned again in 1891 and 1892 and, even though he resigned as editor in 1892, the persecutions continued.... In 1907, Mata once again resumed the editorship ... and, again, his printing equipment was confiscated.[53]

Notwithstanding the government's actions regarding this and other newspapers—actions that varied over the long period of the Díaz regime and the Díaz-influenced government of Manuel González (1880–1884)—negotiation was consistently part of the official repertoire. John Charles

Chasteen describes the modus operandi during the Porfiriato: "Díaz offered just two alternatives: *pan o palo*, meaning roughly 'carrot or stick.' For example, he subsidized the press to keep it friendly, then jailed journalists who spoke out against him."[54] Many papers obliged Díaz out of fear, or because they were paid to do so. Enrique Krauze explains that "during Díaz's reign, the press was hobbled by the Ley Mordaza. . . . A journalist could be imprisoned for a 'psychological crime' or even through a report to the police of his 'intentions.'. . . Significantly, from 1896 on, *El imparcial*, subsidized by and representing the government, became the most widely read newspaper in Mexico."[55]

El imparcial was one of the many newspapers where one could find, daily, reports on the performance of the Porfiriato—a performance that focused on steady progress, even if that progress was often related to the (front page) news that a new Porfirio Díaz Park had been inaugurated, that Díaz had attended a play, or that a new street had been named in the leader's honor. On 12 July 1904, the headline read "Re-election of Señor General Díaz"; the paper made clear that there was "jubilation" in the entire country, and the first lines of the story buttressed the legitimacy of the regime by indicating that the elections were carried out in conformity with the constitutional laws of the country. On 14 September 1906, the front page headline highlighted Díaz's economic plan ("Capital: The Foundation of our Progress"); in that same month, the day after national celebrations of independence from Spain—celebrated on the eve of the anniversary, which happened to be Díaz's birthday—Díaz was once again applauded, the jubilant masses "invaded" a prominent park, and fireworks were enjoyed by all. On page one of the 17 October 1900 edition, there was an announcement that advised the reader of the next meeting of the Circle of Friends of General Díaz, which had as its goal a discussion of upcoming celebrations.[56] Garner explains that, given Díaz's understanding of the importance of ritual, and his desire to nurture a "cult of personality" and a performance of legitimacy, "Díaz's military exploits rapidly became incorporated into the public calendar of patriotic ritual." The aforementioned Circle of Friends was one of several formal groups that existed (and that were promoted in pro-Díaz newspapers) in order to organize specific public celebrations—all centered around Díaz, even if the link was a stretch, and all contributing to his persona of power and to the view of Díaz "as a classical republican nation-builder, a member of the pantheon of liberal heroes who had contributed to the creation of the patria."[57]

The mask of the Porfiriato was constantly reaffirmed publicly and available for consumption not only in newspapers like *El imparcial*, but also in public ceremonies, in statues, and on street names, among other ven-

Ya te conosco mascarita.

Figure 7.1: "I already know you, little mask" (Ya te conosco, mascarita). From Rafael Barajas Durán (el Fisgón), *El país de "El Llorón de Icamole": Caricatura mexicana de combate y libertad de imprenta durante los gobiernos de Porfirio Díaz y Manuel González (1877–1884)* (Mexico City: Fondo de Cultura Económica, 2007), 295.

ues. Yet dissent was also registered, as seen in the example of the *Diario del hogar*, and the mask of the Porfiriato was easily (if temporarily) uncovered—often by political cartoonists, who made sure that the heads of state understood that their impunity, hidden behind the legitimizing force of the constitution, was witnessed if not mitigated. In a cartoon whose idea of masking and pseudo-royalty would be used by other satirists in the future, Santiago Hernández portrayed Manuel González as a king, with a small crown topping the caricature of the president, who smiles deviously (Figure 7.1). In front of his face is the paper-thin mask of the constitution, though an old man representing the pueblo can recognize, by squinting and tilting his glasses, the colonial past. The caption "Ya te conosco, mascarita" (I already know you, little mask) demonstrates that the viceroyalty had not been forgotten, and that the González administration was nothing more (from the point of view of the cartoon) than an extension of the regal reign of Díaz. Shortly after Díaz was re-elected in 1884, another car-

Los Náufragos.—Por Fígaro.

Figure 7.2: *Los naufragios*. From Rafael Barajas Durán (el Fisgón), *El país de "El Llorón de Icamole": Caricatura mexicana de combate y libertad de imprenta durante los gobiernos de Porfirio Díaz y Manuel González (1877–1884)* (Mexico City: Fondo de Cultura Económica, 2007), 304.

toon depicted Díaz's manipulation of Mexican law, showing him ripping through the constitution head first and attacking the independent press (Figure 7.2).

The constant—if often suppressed—ability to articulate counter-hegemonic opinions during the Porfiriato is surprising, considering the care with which Díaz groomed his image (it is often said that he used makeup to appear more white) and the historical accounts that dominated post-revolutionary Mexico. It is more common (and equally accurate) to hear of the Díaz who ruled with an iron fist than the Díaz who negoti-ated, deferred, flattered, compromised, and offered gestures of support and even kindness to ensure loyalty. In order to hold numerous diplomatic positions in the Díaz administration, as opposed to spending time in jail, for example, Gamboa criticized the regime from the inside, always playing the subordinate role when necessary—just like the characters in *La ven-ganza*. The weak, fearful Díaz of the political cartoon seen above was not, of course, the Díaz that Gamboa witnessed. Gamboa's interactions with him were, in fact, representative of the public transcript—the carefully crafted performance of a leader. Garner refers to the "enigmatic persona" of Díaz and to Gamboa's perception of the leader: "Díaz was, according to Gamboa, 'always serious, always in control, unsmiling, his bearing and physique strong and upright: his features, which never revealed whether he is pleased or displeased, are perfectly enigmatic, and never betray him.'"[58] Gamboa's diary offers insight into the relationship Gamboa had with Díaz—one that led the author, shortly after *La venganza* was staged, to find himself questioning Díaz's use of the familiar, plural conjugation of a verb in a telegram: Gamboa was ultra-sensitive to the protocol of the pa-trón, as are the characters in his play.[59]

While Gamboa was clearly useful to the Porfiriato, as a diplomat and genuine devotee—albeit qualified—it is still surprising that *La venganza* could have made it to the stage. Though this could be seen as a change in the regime, it is important to note that in the same year a Mexico City audience could have enjoyed Gamboa's play, more traditional spectacles of power were available at the Teatro Principal. Armando de María y Cam-pos, for example, writes about the custom of staging theatrical pieces to honor the "Héroe de la Paz" (the Hero of Peace). He notes insightfully that "political theater was, without a doubt, that which authors wrote to eulogize President Díaz."[60] María y Campos offers the example of an eve-ning in 1905 when spectators were treated to a play about Díaz's military exploits: "The episode is pure fiction, but it gives the author a reason to ex-alt the . . . virtues of the President of the Republic. General Díaz does not appear—no one dared at that time to put him on stage—but he is alluded to."[61] Others were staging the exploits of Díaz, while Gamboa—with the political capital that comes with negotiation, the always extant tools of subversion inherent in hegemony—painted the exploitation of Díaz from the inside. To some degree, Gamboa's face grew to fit the mask, though his diaries, the volumes of which were always published years after the fact, always show that he was aware of his position—of the sacrifices he had made to gain relative political power.

Perhaps the best way to explain the compassion that Gamboa shows in *La venganza* is his return to religion. Despite all of the numerous racist comments in his diaries and in public speeches, to give one example, Gamboa seems to see a higher calling. He is willing to forgo "pure" naturalism for nature—nature that is shown to be, in *La venganza*, the creation of God.[62] By denaturalizing the colonial echoes on the hacienda of the Pedreguera family, Gamboa affirms that "even" the "indios" are equal, despite the textual undercurrent that works against this argument and may or may not be self-conscious. Such is the case when Blanca chastises her grandfather, "Don't be an Indian," or when Loreto—who proves to be more assertive in front of the masters than Marcos—indicates that Marcos is, in the end, more "white" (that is, good) on the inside than Javier de Pedreguera, who is the biological father of the son they are raising.[63] Loreto and doña Guadalupe are the two characters in the play who most present a religious interpretation of society. For Loreto, this stance is one of caution and resignation: "Remember that we are poor workers, very poor, without anyone who loves us except God! . . . and you will conform . . . as we have always conformed."[64] Loreto refers here to Marcos's drinking and the need to ask God not to abandon them, though later in the same scene Marcos's words have a revolutionary ring when he proclaims that there is no justice for the dispossessed.[65] Doña Guadalupe, on the other hand, presents at various points in the text a strong religious argument in favor of equality (even if her main purpose is to make it to heaven). For her, while social codes sanction behavior, "there is not a bit of conscience in any of the codes of the world."[66] She is concerned with righting wrongs (in this case, the possibility that her son has not taken responsibility for his actions, though clearly this is linked also to not leaving the family offspring in the campo) and is thankful to God for "miraculously" curing (temporarily) her husband of hemiplegia, which includes partial paralysis—a possible naturalistic reference to syphilis, a topic that will be taken up in the last chapter of this book.[67]

The negotiations in *La venganza de la gleba* mirror in many ways the negotiation of Gamboa. The play itself contains a significant message of social change, and the writing and production of the text is a significant social act that, with touches of naturalism, also leaves room for Catholicism and the social message the latter conveys through the words of doña Guadalupe. Gamboa was able to use the tools of hegemony to stage a play that criticized the Porfiriato at a time when Díaz's exploits were honored in ceremony after ceremony, play after play. Gamboa not only held a mirror up to a Mexican audience of 1905 but offered numerous examples that pointed toward the social construction of the status quo, showing the world to be anything but immutable. The mask did, in some ways, fit the face in the case of Gamboa, but he also knew how, and when, "to lay it on thick." On the first page of the playtext, where Gamboa dedicates his work to the wealthy of his country, there is also an epigraph from Marcel Prévost that summarizes the spirit of the play: "To write a play is an altruistic effort." In the history of Mexican theater, Gamboa stands out as a complex negotiator who staged the future. He "speaks truth to power"—the very power in which he is explicitly complicit.

NOTES

I would like to acknowledge the steadfast support of William G. Acree Jr. and Juan Carlos González Espitia throughout the writing and editing of this chapter. Epigraph source: James C. Scott, *Domination and the Arts of Resistance: Hidden Transcripts* (New Haven: Yale University Press, 1990), 1.

1. Jorge G. Castañeda, *Sorpresas te da la vida* (Mexico City: Aguila, 1994), 20.
2. Federico Gamboa, quoted in Enrique Krauze, *Mexico: Biography of Power; A History of Modern Mexico, 1810–1996*, trans. Hank Heifetz (New York: HarperCollins, 1997), 588.
3. José Emilio Pacheco, introduction to *Diario de Federico Gamboa (1892–1939)*, by Federico Gamboa (Mexico City: Siglo Veintiuno Editores, 1977), 28–29.
4. Scott, *Domination*, 10.
5. Ibid., 9.
6. Federico Gamboa, *Teatro*, ed. and with a preliminary study by María Guadalupe García Barragán (Mexico City: Universidad Nacional de México, 2000).
7. Gamboa, *Diario*, 42–45.
8. Ibid., 45.
9. Quoted in *El teatro en México durante el porfirismo*, vol. 3 (1900–1910), comp. and with a preliminary study by Luis Reyes de la Maza (Mexico City: Universidad Nacional Autónoma de México, 1968), 288. While this quotation is from *El teatro en México durante el porfirismo*, the majority of it can be found in Pacheco, where I first encountered both the quote and the documentation for the review itself. Pacheco affirms that the review was probably written by Luis G. Urbina. De la Maza places a question mark after the name in his text. A previous review that is attributed without question to Urbina repeats some of the exact language found in the review I have quoted, leading me to concur that Urbina was the author of both.
10. The term appears in Gamboa's work (including *La venganza*) well before

Mariano Azuela's homonymic novel of the Mexican Revolution was first published in *El paso del norte*, as García Barragán's preliminary study to Gamboa, *Teatro*, 22, points out.

11. For theater historian Antonio Magaña Esquivel, for example, *La venganza de la gleba* represents nothing more than "sentimental tribulations" (in *Medio siglo de teatro mexicano (1900–1910)* (Mexico City: Instituto Nacional de Bellas Artes, Departamento de Literatura, 1964), 21). For García Barragán, "it is not a naturalist play; it deals with a typically romantic theme: the love that becomes impossible when two lovers—lovers in the literary sense of the word—discover that they are siblings" (preliminary study to Gamboa, *Teatro*, 21).

12. Robert J. Niess, "Zola's *L'Œuvre* and *Reconquista* of Gamboa," *PMLA* 61, no. 2 (1946): 577.

13. Pacheco, introduction, 20.

14. *Velásquez Spanish-English Dictionary* (Englewood Cliffs, NJ: Prentice Hall, 1973), 342; and Ramón García-Pelayo y Gross, *Pequeño Larousse ilustrado* (Mexico City: Ediciones Larousse, 1993), 504.

15. *Diccionario del español usual en México* (Mexico City: El Colegio de México, 1996), 821.

16. Gamboa, *Teatro*, 211.

17. Pacheco, introduction, 21.

18. For more on the Jockey Club, see William H. Beezley, *Judas at the Jockey Club and Other Episodes of Porfirian Mexico* (Lincoln: University of Nebraska Press, 1987). Referring to social clubs, Scott indicates that "the seclusion available to elites not only affords them a place to relax from the formal requirements of their role but also minimizes the chance that familiarity will breed contempt or, at least, diminish the impression their ritually managed appearances create" (*Domination*, 13).

19. Edward Said, *Orientalism* (New York: Vintage Books, 1979), 227.

20. See Gamboa, *Teatro*, 136, for the dramatis personae.

21. Ibid., 144.

22. Ibid.

23. Marcela Del-Río, *Perfil del teatro de la Revolución Mexicana* (New York: Peter Lang, 1993), 31.

24. Ibid., 33, 41.

25. Gamboa, *Teatro*, 141–42.

26. Scott, *Domination*, 25.

27. Ibid., 9.

28. Gamboa, *Teatro*, 142–43.

29. Scott, *Domination*, 2.

30. Ibid., 24.

31. For other instances of elites seeking hidden truths, see González Espitia's comment on Claudio de Alas's novel *La herencia de la sangre* in Chapter 11.

32. Gamboa, *Teatro*, 162–63.

33. Scott, *Domination*, 93.

34. Ibid., 70.

35. Quoted in Reyes de la Maza, *El teatro en México*, 287–88.

36. Scott, *Domination*, 101.

37. Gamboa, *Teatro*, 142.

38. Ibid., 193.
39. Sara Mills, *Discourse* (London: Routledge, 1997).
40. Del-Río, *Perfil del teatro*, 41.
41. Gamboa, *Teatro*, 195.
42. Ibid., 196.
43. Ibid., 192.
44. Roland Barthes, *Mythologies*, trans. Annette Lavers (New York: Hill and Wang, 1995), 142.
45. Carlos Solórzano, "Algunos paralelismos entre la novela y el teatro hispanoamericanos de este siglo," *Actas de la Asociación Internacional de Hispanistas* 3 (1968): 854, *cvc.cervantes.es/obref/aih/pdf/03/aih_03_1_094.pdf*.
46. Donald L. Shaw, *A Companion to Modern Spanish American Fiction* (London: Tamesis, 2002), 30–31.
47. João Sedycias, *The Naturalistic Novel of the New World: A Comparative Study of Stephen Crane, Aluísio Azevedo, and Federico Gamboa* (Lanham, MD: University Press of America, 1993), 99.
48. Quoted in Patrice Pavis, *Dictionary of the Theatre: Terms, Concepts, and Analysis* (Toronto: University of Toronto Press, 1998), 302.
49. *Diario del hogar* (Mexico City), 17 October 1905, 2.
50. García Barragán, preliminary study to Gamboa, *Teatro*, 47.
51. Quoted in ibid.
52. Ibid.
53. Paul Garner, *Porfirio Díaz* (London: Pearson Education, 2001), 126.
54. John Charles Chasteen, *Born in Blood and Fire* (New York: Norton, 2001), 193.
55. Krauze, *Mexico: Biography of Power*, 9.
56. *El imparcial* (Mexico City), 12 July 1904, 1; 14 September 1906, 1; 17 September 1906, 1; 17 October 1900, 1.
57. Garner, *Porfirio Díaz*, 129.
58. Ibid., 76.
59. Federico Gamboa, *Mi diario IV (1905–1908)* (Mexico City: Consejo Nacional para la Cultura y las Artes, 1995), 55.
60. Armando de María y Campos, *El teatro de género chico en la revolución mexicana* (Mexico City: Biblioteca del Instituto Nacional de Estudios Históricos de la Revolución Mexicana, 1956), 39.
61. Ibid., 40.
62. Del-Río, *Perfil del teatro*, 35.
63. Gamboa, *Teatro*, 163.
64. Ibid., 149.
65. Ibid., 155.
66. Ibid., 174.
67. Ibid., 177.

PART III

Ideologies, Revelations, and Hidden Nations

8

The Imponderable and the Permissible

Caste Wars, Culture Wars, and Porfirian Piety in the Yucatán Peninsula

Terry Rugeley

Uring the second half of the nineteenth century, a specter haunted devout Mexicans: the specter of liberalism. Yet another revolution had taken place in 1876, but no one knew what it meant for the long run. The nation's new president, a war hero named Porfirio Díaz, had rebelled in the name of regular elections, but would he himself step down when his term expired? In cultural terms, too, a spirit of unresolved issues hung in the air. For two decades, despite invasions and civil wars, Mexico had adhered to a series of laws known as the Reform—laws that separated church and state, and that secularized social authority. Yet the vast majority of Mexicans remained at least nominally Catholic, and their commitment to a world disarticulated from spiritual beings remained doubtful.

This relative humidity of the uncertain could, at odd moments, condense into precipitation. At such times, people's actions showed that they remained tied to the old ways—especially the old ways of the spirit—in face of the new. One such place was San Sebastián, a southwest barrio of the city of Mérida, Yucatán. Here, in 1879, padre Irineo Muñoz went to jail for profaning the corpse of Baltazar Madera, the barrio magistrate. Although he had been Madera's political opponent in life, Muñoz did not want Madera condemned to the inferno because of his excommunication, and believed that by whipping the alcalde's cadaver he would remove the spiritual stain.[1]

Like so many glimpses into a people's hidden world, the paper trail starts and stops there. A brief note by the jefe político simply reports that it happened, nothing more. What did the magistrate do that had so tarnished his soul? His crime, presumably, had been enforcement of the Reform laws that had suddenly turned the imponderable into the permissible:

stripping the church of its control of cemeteries and life passages, expropriating its wealth, and ending the priest's role as a public voice. Indeed, town magistrates like Madera, and not national statesmen, served as the Reform's real enforcers. But the actual details elude us. There the anecdote stands, frozen in time: the dead magistrate, the persecuted yet determined and emotionally torn padre, and the act which seemed so brazen, so macabre, and so impermissible then, and so perversely comical a century and a half later.

For us, padre Muñoz's whip expels all the preconceptions we may have held about a place, a time, and a people. Instead, it forces us to look at unsuspected undercurrents of daily lives—undercurrents flowing through the realm of popular religion and beliefs. The rule of General Porfirio Díaz Mory from 1876 to 1911 constituted a key period for Mexico, for it brought stability, economic growth, the creation of infrastructure, a doubling of the population, and the expansion of both literacy and the middle class. Porfirians had a style all their own. In most aspects, their society resulted from a synthesis of old and new: liberal positivist sensibilities pasted over unreformed colonial practices. Porfirianism outwardly championed constitutionality and the rule of law, but in fact maintained power through a top-down administration that a colonial viceroy would have recognized instantly. The regime's strength rested more on appearances than reality, and as subsequent events were to prove, a relatively minor challenge was sufficient to bring down the whole structure.

Thus far, we know relatively little about the interplay of religion and popular cultures during the age of Porfirio Díaz. Tolerance toward religion clearly increased after 1876, even as the secularizing legislation of the 1850s continued on paper; at the same time, the Catholic clergy softened its own opposition to the 1857 Constitution, allowing citizens greater latitude in serving two masters. But as with the Porfirian economy, regionalism remained a major variable. In western areas, the post-Juárez clergy appears to have continued their roles as community leaders and enjoyed substantial church infrastructure, facts that contributed to the emergence of the 1920s Cristero revolt among freeholding mestizos.[2] Further to the northwest, church influence never entirely recovered from the 1767 expulsion of the Jesuits, and the region's serrano communities lived an intense folk Catholicism that often included a pronounced hostility to the clergy itself.[3] In regard to the southeast, the two studies that do exist can at best be categorized as preliminary. The late Hernán Menéndez's *Iglesia y poder* (1995) stresses clerical complicity in the construction of the repressive late-Porfirian cacicazgo of henequen baron Olegario Molina.[4] On the oppo-

site end of the ideological spectrum, Franco Savarino's *Pueblos y nacionalismo* (1997) interprets patriarchal and high-clerical cooperation as part
of a larger and basically positive project of regional development.[5] While
offering opposite visions of the role of religion in daily life, both tend to
view matters through institutional secondary sources, and both present a
largely top-down perspective without much emphasis on popular behavior,
widespread attitudes, or the frequent contradictions and countercurrents
that so often appear when dealing with a matter as baffling as religious
culture. Finally, both tend to overstate their case: Menéndez in imagining
bishops as behind-the-scenes puppet masters, Savarino in downplaying the
racism and violence of a plantation police state.

    This chapter rejects the notion of either a monolithic or an effica-
ciously constructive Catholicism. Instead, it explores religious strategies
and sensibilities in the Porfirian southeast, stressing that the tensions between surfaces and substrata remained a defining feature of the Porfirians'
world. Liberal ideologue Sebastián Lerdo de Tejada served as the leader for
positivists obsessed with urbanism, growth, technology, and stronger legal
institutions. In 1876, Lerdo fell, but the attitude he represented continued
as a veneer over persistent folkways and profoundly pietistic beliefs. How
then did a nation that began its life with three centuries of established
church and a total Catholic monopoly fall into a culture war centered on
religion? How did the political order of the late nineteenth century man-
age to knit together the strands of old belief and new materialism? And
what do we know about the ways of the spirit in the age of Reform and
afterward?

Yucatecan Religion in the Time of Trouble

The question of the Mexican church's nineteenth-century misfortunes
tears at some long and gnarled roots. The first fifty years of independence
presented a thorny path for Yucatecan Catholics. In 1833, the institution
lost its privilege of enforced tithing. The revolt against Mexican central-
ism (1836–1840) began the long destabilization of the religious head taxes
known as *obventions*. Then came the Caste War (1847–1901), which took
considerable national territory out of ecclesiastical supervision. As peace
and planters returned to the war zone, a series of state-overseen mortgage
adjustments systematically reduced the amount of paper wealth that the
church held. In the late 1840s, the state sold about a third of its provincial
church iconography in Cuba to finance the war. Finally, church interiors

had been gutted and pillaged by soldiers who had quartered there during the course of the many revolutions. The southeastern Catholic church thus ended the 1840s in truly deplorable circumstances.

Then came the Reform. During the 1850s, a new generation of statesmen attempted to impose their version of liberalism on classic nineteenth-century liberalism, that is, with emphasis on capitalism, individual rights, a secular state, and juridical equality. Then as now, ideologues fought the culture war, with the broad band of human beings caught somewhere in the middle. The conflict was not simply about an outside imposition, but rather built upon deep roots of anticlericalism that had proliferated at least since Bourbon times and probably far longer. The Reform had three major thrusts: expropriation of church wealth, secularization of basic records-keeping over life passages, and the elimination of clerical participation in politics.

The Reform's first project, the eradication of clerical wealth, grew out of the belief that the church held vast amounts of property in mort-main, thus preventing its circulation in a truly capitalist market. The reformers of 1855–1863 found little in the way of corporately held real estate, but did confiscate church-held mortgages amounting to some $900,000.[6] These mortgages were not always as they appeared on ledger sheets. As in pre-coffee Guatemala, their holders had seldom foreclosed; rather, clerics had perennially rolled over debts on property in exchange for modest if regular payments. In the early 1860s, the Reform stripped the church of these mortgages, and the vast debt owed to priests and clerical institutions mostly vanished in a puff of paper. Only a few bodies of loan capital cohered, such as the Uliburri fund, which became the endowment of Yucatán's first public university. Post-Reform War Liberals also did away with church taxes, and though functionaries of the conservative, French-sponsored Empire (in Yucatán, 1863–1867) made fitful efforts to revive the practice—the Empire was too strapped to worry about other people's tax rights—the emperor Maximilian's fall ended obventions forever. Meanwhile, the private clerically-owned haciendas that had been once a staple of the economic landscape now died by attrition as priests lost the ability to accumulate capital. The vast influx of money related to the sale of henequen fiber thus became concentrated in secular hands, with family-based commercial houses supplying most of the venture capital. Never again would the Catholic church be a significant financial player in southeast Mexico.

Once the Empire collapsed, reformers went to work expropriating the scattered remains of corporate property—mostly the indigestible morsels left over from the 1850s. In 1867, the state turned the last nuns out of their Mérida convent despite protests from prominent women who had received their education under the nuns there, but the property itself sat vacant for the next decade while the *cabildo* (town council) tried to decide what to do with it. The only other wealth that remained was the old Franciscan convents, which were more white elephants than red plums. Too large to serve as rectories, they were also so sprawling and dilapidated that no one wanted them. Liberal officials drew up a resumé of such buildings in nineteen other communities as well. Despite the unwieldy quality of this property, the functionaries pushed ahead, assessing values and posting the structures for sale. Little is known about the people who claimed these trophies, or what they thought about carving up pieces of an institution that had once been Mexico's soul.

The 1870s constituted the nadir of nineteenth-century church fortunes in the southeast. Financial support for parish activities became even more miserly than it had been during the darkest years of the 1860s. In the town of Uayma, to take only one of many examples, the citizens refused to pay and even insulted the cura when he solicited their help: "Such is their immorality, and on every occasion the progress of this disease is evident," he mourned.[7] The story was the same everywhere. When hacendados did not wish to cover their workers' *medio-real* contribution to the church, they could always take refuge in the old accusation that clerical services were lacking.

The second Liberal project, the secularization of records, also made headway. The state prohibited churchyard burials and created public cemeteries, both as a way of inculcating public health and to whittle away church authority. Then came the establishment of the Registro Civil, an institution that usurped clerical oversight of the critical life passages of birth, marriage, and death. Well into the 1850s, the Yucatecan bureaucracy had continued to rely on priests for basic demographic tabulations. The change was practical, since priests made for highly idiosyncratic census-takers, and the coordination of church-state initiatives often proved slow and complicated. But the change also had to do with lowering the church's status as the arbiter of human existence. The temporal heart of the culture wars came in the republican Restoration years of 1867–1876, a time that marked the rock bottom of church's nineteenth-century fortunes. The Juárez-era Reform laws arrived late to Yucatán, and their execution was quickly sidelined by civil war and the renewed Caste War. The eradication of political power also meant removing church authority over the life passages of baptism, marriage, and burial. Under the new system, priests intending to perform such ceremonies were to demand to see a *boleto* (paper certifying that the individuals requesting baptism or wedding ceremonies had first gone through civil channels). Priests who failed to do so suffered fines. In most cases, though, the question was irrelevant, since people had quit paying church support altogether, and conducted their lives, joined with their sweethearts, and buried their dead without benefit of formal services. Moreover, rural Mayas clearly were not the only ones to avoid religious services in favor of either the civil counterpart or simply cohabitation; in many towns and villages, everyone did so, including the Hispanic bourgeoisie.

The third Liberal goal was to pressure the church out of politics. Priests had long been public figures; they provided education, established boundaries for moral behavior, and participated heavily in the intrigues that surrounded Yucatecan independence. After 1821, clerics kept a lower profile but continued to oppose creeping secularization, first through membership in secret political organizations such as the reactionary Rochela group, then as willing allies to the French Empire. The triumph of Mexican republicans brought renewed repression. The Liberal party, now dominated by the more ideologically driven flank of Sebastián Lerdo de Tejada, went after the religious as punishment for their support for foreign occupiers. In March 1875, for example, the state issued "Regulations for the Ringing of Church Bells," an edict that forbade the ringing of church bells before 4:00 a.m., or for longer than ten minutes.[8] These prohibitions sprang from memories of church bells being used to herald revolts, as when rebels rang the chimes to gather their followers together. The directive was still enforced in the late 1880s, even in relatively remote locations. In this case, the Reform's durability reflected a larger initiative toward the regularization of town life. The cura of Motul went so far as to remove the church bells altogether—a smaller version of the lockout clerics later staged in the years 1926–1929, when priests withheld services to protest the anticlerical tack of the revolutionary government.[9]

Would religion have lost its influence over the public mind if the state had lived up to the claims it set for itself? The answer to this question cannot be known, for the Porfirian system remained patrimonial, corrupt, incompetent, and inefficient up to the moment of its demise. But as contemporary United States history shows, anti-intellectual and fundamentalist religions are fully capable of surviving revolutions of education, literacy, and technological progress. The chief example of this fact lay in the problem of cemeteries. Since the time of the Bourbon reformers, disposal of the dead had come to signal social power. The Yucatecan state aggressively claimed this right during and after the Reform War, but the follow-through remained sketchy. From the start, however, the state's actions failed to comply with the much-publicized expectations. As is well known, Mexican burial practices differ from those of the United States, in that arid remains are frequently disinterred to be placed in ossuary boxes, thus providing space for other family members. During the worst days of the civil wars, cemetery upkeep remained dreadful, and many villages witnessed the sad spectacle of pigs and dogs rooting up cadavers.[10] The matter improved somewhat with the advent of Porfirian peace, but in the leaky vessel of Porfirian finance, means seldom matched objectives. By 1905, Mérida's cementerio general—the former hacienda Xcoholté—had fallen into shambles. Not only had the population been outstripping capacity, but survivors had often failed to reclaim their loved ones' arid remains, causing a huge pileup of bones. Each outgoing cemetery director had left a swelling backlog of remains that had become increasingly difficult to identify.[11] Space was somewhat more abundant in the pueblos, but funds (as well as political autonomy) were correspondingly scarce, making it difficult to remodel, expand, or improve the facilities.[12]

These were the contours of the secular versus religious conflict in 1876: a politically discredited church, bankrupted in material wealth but with much claim upon popular hearts and minds; and a state victorious in arms, but typically without the wherewithal to make good on its claims as the supreme power. Economistic readings of the Porfirian revolution point to pressures from international capital and private Mexican ambitions, including plans to reactivate Mexico's mining industry, the need for railroad infrastructure, and the quest for border security. But the national changes in the late 1870s and early 1880s also partly owed their existence to the fact that the resumed Liberal reform under Sebastián Lerdo de Tejada tore Mexico apart at the local level, ultimately forcing provincial Mexican Catholics to adopt new strategies and an overall redefinition of religiosity.

The Return of the Gods:
Voluntarism, Gremios, and the Press

Southeastern church leadership took a while to find its path.[13] The aging bishop Leandro Rodríguez de la Gala, who beginning in 1863 headed the southeastern hierarchy in one capacity or another for twenty-four years, initially had little to offer except stiff-backed resistance to the new national currents.[14] His 1877 pastoral letter reads as if it had been clipped straight from the *Syllabus of Errors*, urging the faithful to make no concessions to godless liberalism, Masons, radicals, freethinkers, or spiritualists. Rather than seeing increasing secularism as a consequence of vast social and economic changes, Rodríguez jumbled cause and effect, positing that irreligiosity was the source of all other ills, and prescribing a return to sabbath-keeping and increased dedication to the Sacred Heart of Jesus.[15] The following year, Rodríguez mandated the reprinting of an Italian pamphlet—basically an institutional pep talk—that urged Catholics to keep heart in the battle against a brigade of enemies: "Protestants, schismatics, Jews, false Catholics, false politicians, unbelievers, rationalists, worldly men, false philosophers," all supposedly united in their efforts to undo the church.[16] These paranoid exhortations provided a weak alternative to a set of global changes springing more from industrialization, urbanism, increased literacy, and scientific innovation, but they were the best that the bishop had to offer.

Fortunately for the faithful, a more practical direction had begun to take root, one which proved successful in adapting Catholicism to the twentieth century and beyond. Leaders of the late nineteenth century manifested profound concern about the underclasses: their filth, their ignorant and immoral behavior, and their lack of reverence for the positivist changes that were gradually taking root throughout Mexico. Indeed, even the most casual perusal of court records and administrative papers reveal that fin de siècle Yucatán teemed with its share of depravity: murder, robbery, suicide, assault, incest, and fraud all figured into the landscape.[17] The problem of upgrading the hottentots preoccupied all Porfirian elites, but one strain of upper-class thinking favored advancement through secular institutions, while another saw religion as the only true medicine.

From these concerns sprang reform Catholicism, Porfirian-style. Some notion of the social role devout Porfirians imagined for their religion comes from the 1899 address that Yucatecan literati Néstor Rubio Alpuche delivered before the students of Salesian College in Mexico City.[18] Titling his speech "Regeneration of Mexico's Indians and Proletarians by Means of Christianity," Rubio fingered those he considered the anchors holding back national development: "The proletarian class, full of vices, and the Indian, indifferent to progress, form a heavy burden for the state and cause it to march but slowly." This racist delivery went on at some length, consistently ignoring the fact that the two groups in question were underwriting Mexican growth through land loss and forcibly lowered wages and living standards. But hope existed, Rubio explained. Catholicism offered the last, best chance for reclaiming the masses, and it was precisely this argument that allowed rhetoricians such as Rubio to open space for a way of thought and belief attacked by state-builders a half-century earlier.

Coupled with this change in orientation came a repertoire of specific strategies. First, there was a retreat from direct intervention in political matters. Anyone who has researched both the early national and Porfirian periods will be struck by the abrupt disappearance of priests from public affairs, particularly with the fall of the church's failed savior, the Empire. So complete was the change that based on governmental papers alone, one would almost conclude that by 1880 the church had ceased to exist. The reality was different. No longer financiers, census-takers, or the eyes and ears of the state, priests now concentrated on their spiritual mission, and as such they engaged in activities not readily apparent in state archival collections. The Liberal reforms had actually saved the Mexican priesthood, although quite against the will of most clerics.

More coherent and purposeful leadership emerged after Rodríguez's death. Crescencio Carrillo y Ancona (1837–1897), who succeeded Rodríguez as bishop until his death in 1897, labored to improve church-state relations, making a sort of peace offering by donating his own private antiquities collection to create what became the state archaeological museum.[19] Carrillo perceived the futility of political brawls and instead pitched his institution as a champion of science, progress, and patriotism. Next came Puebla-born Martín Trischler y Córdoba (1868–1942, and bishop for the last thirty-nine of those years); he brought back the Jesuits, made common cause with the henequen oligarchy, said little about the disguised slavery then proliferating on the estates, and opposed the Revolution tooth-and-nail. However, he also did everything possible to promote the doctrines of *Rerum novarum*, the papal bull in which Pope Leo XIII advanced his vision of a church committed to non-radical social engagement.[20]

The most critical decision may have been to stake the church's future on urban Hispanics. The church continued to respond to the funding problem through the voluntarist strategies begun in the late 1850s: subscription lists, moral suasion, and a monthly half-*real* quota for rural peons and a full *real* for free villagers. Private individuals were more susceptible than the state to pressure, and priests refused services to anyone who claimed what had been church property. Curas took subscriptions from those who were willing to support the faith, and then persuaded them to sign voluntary contracts to provide tithes or medio-*real* contributions. Each cura either carried out the collections himself or else relied on a local volunteer (a variation of *mayordomía*) to do so. Priests compiled long lists of willing payers that included Hispanics, Mayas, and even members of the local militia unit. They also tripled the price of such special services as masses said for the benefit of departed loved ones from one to three pesos; curiously, people would pay for masses but not for maintenance. The problem everywhere was that people fell behind on their intentions within a few weeks. Priests had no choice but to dismiss their ministers in order to cut costs. Public gatherings produced new pledges of support, followed by new resistance. But for all its weaknesses, voluntary funding became the way of the future.

The church also took advantage of the wave of lay organizations and urban cofradías that swept through Mexico during the century's last quarter. In earlier times, these organizations had leaned heavily toward mutualism, in which members anted up money to help generate a fund for health and burial costs.[21] Lay organizations had crumbled during the time of troubles, but made a slow yet certain comeback from the 1870s onward. During the initial months of the Restoration, the pious citizens of Ticul shelved plans to re-create their archicofradía that, like so many, had fallen into abeyance since 1854. At least 315 individuals were ready to join, but lingering bad feelings postponed the great revival of cofradías until the late 1870s. Under the new order, lay organizations split in their functions. While working-class organizations stayed true to their earlier function, the new archicofradías had less to do with the primitive insurance policies of older days—the Porfirian prosperous could now take care of themselves without recourse to mutualism—and more to do with prestige and ostentatious public spending.[22] Whether rich or poor, however, gremios and cofradías reflected a church revival based on activating a lay urban base.

Many examples of the revived lay groups crop up from 1876 onward. The Association for the Perpetual Cult of San José specifically guaranteed "a good death" and protection from the devil, but suffered from stiff rules: like its honoree, members were expected to maintain vows of chastity.[23] Catholic Youth groups also appeared, consisting not so much of young people themselves, but rather individuals who pledged money and time to help support Catholic education and fight the pernicious habit of smoking. Stealing a page from secretive groups like the Freemasons, Catholic Youth forbade its members from speaking to outsiders of their activities; religious paranoia apparently remained alive and well into the early years of railroads and telegraphs.[24] Many of the aims and activities of such organizations remain vague. Members of the Catholic Society were enjoined to take all opportunities to defend their faith, but most of their energies appear to have gone toward the support of various feast days, such as Corpus Christi (during that era, a major event) and the Immaculate Conception.[25] To those acquainted with the contours of Mexican religion, it will come as no surprise to find a women's organization dedicated to supporting the Cathedral's fiesta of the Blistered Christ. This group raised nearly $4,500—a substantial amount of money in those days—to provide for such components as flowers, fireworks, music, and priests' fees.[26]

But the arrival of the modern age brought more space than the church alone could fill. Indeed, increasing literacy and urbanization made the late nineteenth century the great age of civil associations, both secular and religious. The tendency to civil association found heightened impetus by the suppression of unions and by the highly precarious lives of the Porfirian working class, making nonpolitical mutualism an attractive option for many. The Artisan Society of Mutual Assistance kept faith with pre-Reform organizations whereby members pledged dues to contribute to their own health care and burial of participating individuals. Wages (and prices) had risen since the days of Iturbide, and workers now measured their dues in whole pesos instead of cuartos, medios, or any of the irregular folk currencies that had once circulated even in the cities.[27] Another primitive health insurance program emerged in the Unión Cosmopolite, which charged two pesos monthly coverage for members but also included an option to enroll family members for an extra fifty centavos.[28] Mérida's ill-paid and long-suffering teachers created their own mutualist organization in 1911, just as the Revolution was rippling onto Yucatecan shores. These individuals, who doubtless saw themselves as the cutting edge of science and progress, specifically renounced all religious affiliation.[29]

Other civic associations had a more distinctly middle-class flavor. The Liga de Acción Social championed the study and development of peninsular society through the promotion of a sense of "individual responsibility," evidently a slap at old corporatist tendencies.[30] The main goal of the Sociedad "La Unión" was to establish a civic center for meetings and cultural activities, but it also took an active hand in celebrating the February carnival.[31] Finally, Mérida's Art and Recreation Society promoted the enjoyment of art, literature, philharmonic orchestras, dances, and "legitimate diversions."[32] The men and women who led these organizations typically emerged from the educated middle and upper-middle classes, and their mission remained one of uplifting the masses, which they saw as degraded and ignorant. But what united them with Catholic organizations and worker mutualists was that they functioned above the level of the family and below the level of the state (laying aside formal permission), and they owed their existence in grand part to the more urban and literate nature of Porfirian Mexico.

As a related and equally important strategy, the church also embraced the press, which was critical, as we have seen in the first section of this book, for cultivating a more urban and literate base. Unthinkable fifty years earlier (the first printing press only arrived here in 1812), the decision to engage with both the state and the public through books, newspapers, pious literature, and polemical pamphlets turned out to be one of the shrewdest decisions the Mexican Catholic church ever made. In

1868, it launched a weekly titled *La caridad*. The editors shrewdly avoided confrontations they could not win; most of *La caridad*'s articles dwelled on the events of biblical times, while the editors went out of their way to eulogize Liberal statesman Cepeda Peraza following his death in March 1869. Maudlin items such as "The Conversion of a Princess," "The Death of Fratricide," and "The True Friends of the Poor" probably bored all but the fanatical, while heavy doses of pastoral letters made *La caridad* a Catholic version of *Granma*.[33] The journal provided regular updates on the pope, and cautioned its readers to shun the works of Honoré de Balzac.[34] Whatever their weaknesses, Catholic journals soon proved an indispensable part of church survival and recuperation in the Porfirian era.

To that end, much of the literary efforts of devout Catholics were aimed at making the permissible once more the imponderable. For example, the gremio of merchants and hacendados produced a four-page pamphlet on the importance of confession, trotting out the old stories of famous freethinkers who had supposedly confessed as their end drew near: Voltaire, Napoleon, Diderot, Montesquieu, and others.[35] One leading Catholic press of the time was A. M. de Cantón, which regularly produced such tracts as "Notes on a Visit to the Holy Land," "Consolation for Those Who Suffer," and "Catechism for Controversies." Almost all of these works were imports, but they found a ready market among the Mérida pious.[36]

Novenas remained a trusty standby of Catholic literature. The nine-part prayer cycle had formed a standard component of pre-Caste War piety, promising help for the innumerable ills that beset mankind.[37] Though of ancient European pedigree, the nine-part ritual touched sympathetic chords in Maya culture, where the number nine held significance. Pieces like the "Novena to the Most Holy Virgin of Caridad del Cobre" or the novena to Jesús Nazareno advertised themselves as means of help for the lame, leprous, and ill. They evoked the century-worn position of prayer as a combination of praise and petition for spiritual beings believed to keep watch over human affairs.[38] The genre also included a wide number of prayers to be used as spiritual exercises.[39]

This formula was a success. The combination of voluntarism, lay association, and the press may not have been what church patriarchs of ages past had imagined when they laid the groundwork for a universal institution, but it yielded the combination that mattered for a Mexico where industry, urban culture, and the increasing expectations of the individual defined how much one was willing to give to the world of the spirit.

Alternate Paths

Whatever else might have changed about the nineteenth-century church, it had not lost its intolerance of rivals. In olden times, this had meant Jews, Moors, and Native American shamans. But the nineteenth century brought a new lineup of enemies, and much of the era's print production was devoted to taking down would-be claimants to popular belief. Even while Catholicism moved toward a more moderate (and sustainable) position on matters of state and society, remnants of the anticlerical old guard still kept up the fight. Pablo García, the architect of Campeche statehood and in many ways the standard-bearer of Lerdo's more elite and intellectualized liberalism, was ultimately forced from power by the more moderate Joaquín Baranda. García dedicated the rest of his long life to a profitable law practice, but also found time to edit the newspaper *Libre pensador*, which pulled no punches in dealing with the church. The newspaper's discourse remained very much at a deist level, and while perhaps when pressed it acknowledged the existence of God, *Libre pensador* pretty much confined him to the making of cosmic-scale watches. Not surprisingly, warnings against unnamed freethinkers remained a standard rhetorical trope during the century's waning years.

The church also published periodic reminders that Protestantism was dangerous and to be avoided.[40] Yet relatively few Protestant forces appeared in Yucatán at this time, mainly owing to the area's geographic isolation. Those who did come were not the evangelical sects that foster so much of the religious change today, but rather mainstream faiths—above all the Presbyterian Church, which established a beachhead in Porfirian Mérida and branched out to tiny nuclei in surrounding communities.[41]

Yet often it seemed that Catholic thinkers were jousting more with the ghosts of foes past than with the more immediate, practical threats. The Freemasons lived on, and even into the 1920s were still reprinting hoary rule books handed down from the days of Louis XV.[42] The old Freemasons' call for universal brotherhood probably rang quaint by the standards of an age shaken by civil wars and the radical critiques of Karl Marx and the anarchists. With their appeals to reason and human perfectibility, the members' role as bourgeois shock troops against clericalism had become irrelevant, largely because they had carried the day. Liberalism was in some ways Freemasonry made politically incarnate, although without the utopian consequences that the Masons of long ago had imagined when they swore fealty to the ruler, the compass, and the all-seeing eye. But the mere whisper of Freemasonry still infuriated and scandalized religiously conservative quarters.

The greatest nineteenth-century ideological challenger to religion was spiritualism, that hydra-headed amalgam of religion, science, and fantasy that stressed human dialogue with spirit beings via seances and Ouija boards. The peninsular mouthpiece for spiritualist beliefs, the free-wheeling *Ley de amor* (law of love), closed its operations in 1876 when its founder moved on to dedicate himself to the more tangible project of railroad construction. But men still heard portentous voices from the Other Side. Spiritualism itself thus remained a threat, and in 1921, with revolutionary conflict swirling all around, Trischler took the time to reprint Cuban bishop Valentín Zubizarreta's "Instructions Concerning Spiritualism," a catechism-style pamphlet that supposedly exposed heretic lies and set the record straight. Zubizarreta took on spiritualism not for positing invisible worlds (hardly a tenable position for him), but rather for distorting the spirits' true nature and our relationship to them. As he patiently explained, only four types of spirits existed: God, the good angels, demons, and the souls of the dead, none of whom could or should be accessed without church supervision. Spiritualism was bad not only for the soul, but for the mind and body as well, since long-term practice tended to produce "nervous excitation." Most noteworthy in the pamphlet, however, is the rhetorical posture that the bishop assumed: unlike spiritualism, he claimed, the Catholic church was dedicated to "demonstrating scientifically the divinity of Jesus Christ and his ministry."[43] Whether such a point admits laboratory proof remains debatable. More undeniable is the fact that like spiritualism itself, mainstream Mexican religion had now learned to base itself on the scientific sensibilities of the Porfirian age, adopting its argumentation and rhetorical postures without the features of empiricism and reproducibility that were science's true essence.

Moreover, the ideological wars played out against a huge body of popular beliefs, many of which cut across ethnic lines. Well into the twentieth century, for example, it was common to cover up wells during moments of solar eclipse, least some evil force work its way into the water.[44] In the countryside, many people still engaged in the folk weather predictions known as *cabañuelas* or *xok k'iin*, in which the first twelve days of the year are believed to provide a forecast of the coming months. To compound matters, the church itself had its own strain of wonders. Essentially medieval leftovers, they nonetheless reflected a real component of nineteenth-century Catholicism that was often omitted in the discussions of gremios and social movements. Southeasterners, for example, could thrill to "La estigmatización," a forty-four-page pamphlet of what today would be deemed pseudo-science. In this work, Doctor of Medicine Imbert Gourbeyre went on at some length about mysterious stigmata, the phenomenon whereby human bodies take on the wounds of Christ. Groubeyre unearthed case upon case of hands perforated from one side to the other, levitating nuns, nails found imbedded in human hearts, cadavers that refused to decay, and saintly lives "of continual ecstasy," all verified by the testimony of Italian Jesuits.[45] To Gourbeyre, these marvels rendered nil the prospect of free thought, and doubtless carried much the same impact for peninsular readers, most of whom were self-selected anyway and hence predisposed to believe.

Scandalous behavior lived on as well, most notably in Mérida's carnival. This quintessentially medieval event, with its prancing devils, costume giants, and licentious behavior, had been a problem for proponents of dour and more orthodox Catholicism for many years.[46] The early years of the Mexican republic saw a decline in the boisterous popular behavior associated with Corpus Christi, but much of this same enthusiasm simply transferred to carnival, a liturgically-related event immediately preceding the onset of Lent. Mérida's own carnival never rivaled the licentiousness of its cousins in Rio de Janeiro, New Orleans, or Veracruz, but it did remove many of the barriers associated with public morality, as we learned in Chasteen's chapter in this volume. The spirit of Juan Carnaval represented happiness, abundance, and self-indulgence over the austere prudery of his counterpart doña Cuaresma ("Madame Lent").[47] The great parades became moments when Yucatecans shed their overabundance of clothing and walked down the street in skimpy costumes. Their (presumably victimless) sins have washed away in the river of time, but the revelers left us their carnival books, pocket-sized volumes of jokes and doggerel specially composed for the occasion. Much of the humor contained therein was simply nonsense unlikely to amuse today's reader.[48] Other items were more off-color; for example, the 1907 poem "La mujer y la casa" stretched out an elaborate metaphor of how women resemble houses, replete with sexual metaphors that only the obtuse could fail to perceive.[49]

Certainly the most numerous of the peninsular heterodox were the Maya peasants. Various factors kept the Mayas out of the church renewal process, the first and foremost being simple resistance. The Mayas had adopted much of the outward form and vocabulary of Christianity but injected their own religious sensibilities and reworked the colonial faith into something with space for themselves. The free villagers continued to manifest ambivalent relationships toward the divine institution and its magistrates, though noncompliance was now underscored by the peasantry's war-related poverty and social dislocations.

Second, the very strategies that guaranteed an institutional future—press venues, urban societies, Catholic education, and cautious national engagement—excluded rural Mayas altogether. The peninsular church produced neither anthropologists nor champions of the ethnic underclass. Perhaps, as has often been suggested, religions resemble water in that they assume the form of the cultural vessel into which they are poured, for upper-class Porfirians brought to Catholicism the widespread racist attitudes of their time. The one cleric who had manifested radical sentiments—Mauricio Zavala—was kept safely isolated in the port of Progreso, where his contact with the ethnic masses remained confined to literary explorations. Back in the 1870s, Zavala had led a failed uprising in the San Luis Potosí area with the aim of creating an indigenous nation; banished to Yucatán, he devoted his free time to writing a detailed if fanciful Maya grammar that is still retailed in area pharmacies.[50]

Third, the church now suffered a heightened inability to deliver on the services that purportedly justified its existence. Caste War upheaval destroyed many church registries of baptism, marriage, and death, forcing people to forge anew the records of their past. At the same time, padres had fewer forms of economic coercion, and less support from secular authorities. From the 1850s onward, town meetings turned into shouting matches in which priests could only force support by invoking veiled threats of military conscription.[51] Under these circumstances, ethnic peasants now enjoyed a permissiveness unimaginable to their grandparents.

At least three redoubts of Maya syncretic culture survived. There was the militarized Maya state of Chan Santa Cruz and its later splinter groups. But it would be a serious (if long tempting) mistake to read rebel society as a return to pre-contact religious practices. The Caste War had never been an explicit rejection of colonial Catholicism, but rather a conflict spun out of the more material issues of land, taxes, and political violence. For all its oracular exoticism, the world the rebels created was less a revival of ancient Maya culture and more an amalgam of different colonial institutions—the church, the town government, and the militias—all cobbled together to confront the Hispanic state. And few would suggest that the rebels were somehow responsible for perpetuating indigenous beliefs elsewhere on the peninsula.

Within the pacified areas, two other preserves shielded the sort of beliefs immortalized in later anthropologies. First, a growing number of Mayas were now peons on the henequen haciendas. Hacendados endorsed certain limited church services that they saw as useful in satisfying peons—ceremonies to bless buildings and oratories, for example. But beyond this, they remained hostile toward intrusions of the clergy. Hacendados seldom demanded that their workers attend days of religious instruction in neighboring villages. Or, if religious instruction was to be permitted, so-called *amos* insisted that Mohammed come to the mountain, rather than vice versa. Compounding the problem was that curas often called upon local Mayas, including hacienda peons, to perform unpaid labor in construction and refurbishing projects. Hacendados permitted such labor, but only on days normally reserved for doctrine classes. The curas understood that the arrangement turned holy days into workdays, but saw no alternative.[52] This sort of minor compromise characterized church survival during the worst years of the Reform. Second, and hacienda literature notwithstanding, both Yucatán and Campeche teamed with Maya small freeholders who quietly went about their old ways unmolested by orthodoxy. These syncretic religious practices enjoyed particular vibrancy in the south and east, but in fact could be found throughout the length and breadth of the peninsula.[53] Here Maya owners continued to do as they pleased, and found in private property an enclave for what had once been communal practice.

The relative openness regarding Maya folk religious practice, a tendency which Robert Redfield and Alfonso Villa Rojas observed in the 1920s, thus came after forty years of clerical retreat from rural society, initially through the Porfirian church's urban strategy and later under the anticlerical tendencies of the Revolution.[54] By the time of Trischler, the lack of hierarchical supervision over the countryside had become a dominant motif of church correspondence and reports.[55] As the official hierarchy declined in importance, so too did their Maya assistants, such as the members of the church staff that included *fiscales* (building superintendents), *maestros de doctrina* (catechism instructors), and the *maestros cantores* who chanted their amalgams of Spanish, Latin, and Maya at moments of life passage and community ceremony. Though early revolutionary indigenism typically presented ersatz visions of ahistorical Indian essences, the cultural ferment of the 1920s and 1930s made it more permissible to speak of the shaman known as the *h-men* (the "h" is silent), a figure previously confined to remote cornfields, private homes, and furtive whispers.

The Revolution and Beyond

The survival of religion in whatever form into the Revolutionary era and beyond is a subject that has thus far received very little attention. Without appending an entirely new study, it is still possible to offer some preliminary observations.

When Díaz finally did weaken, the mobilization of Mexican elites began over what many believed a dead subject: militant secularists (that is, old-guard Liberals) disgusted with the renewed pretensions of the Catholic clergy.[56] Over the next ten years, priest-bashing gave way to a more systematic critique of the Díaz system, and guerrilla mobilizations in the state of Chihuahua catapulted hacendado-turned-revolutionary Francisco Madero into the national palace. Madero spoke in golden generalities, and Catholics interpreted his rise as ushering in a period of genuine religious tolerance. In the context of the times, this did not mean a plea for threatened religious minorities, but rather an end to official state opposition to the Catholic church and, depending on who was speaking, a potential return to open church participation in politics.[57] Indeed, freedom of religion has always meant different things among cultures such as the United States and Mexico. In the former, it has referred to not allowing any single faith to gain advantage by protection of the state, while in the latter it has meant an active disassembly of a near-monopolistic religion, something accomplished only by force. The more deeply conservative Catholics disliked rebellion on principle, and hoped that the ferment would soon pass. More liberal-minded counterparts interpreted *maderismo* to mean more of a switch to U.S.-style freedoms, with hands-off state policies allowing the Catholic religion to reach once again for an openly hegemonic position.

Gremio activities were thriving at the time of the Madero revolution. In March 1911, even as maderistas were preparing for their final showdown with federal troops in Ciudad Juárez, the gremio and mutual aid society of Progreso dockworkers was preparing its triumphant procession in honor of San Pedro González Telmo, patron of navigators. Their march would include *bronceos* (cannonades) by day and fireworks by night.[58] Similarly, the Círculo Católico de Obreros (Catholic Worker's Circle) came into existence in the time of Madero, competing for the same clientele as anarchist-inspired groups like the Casa del Obrero Mundial. To outdo its more radical counterparts, the Círculo Católico had to come up with real benefits, which in this case included health mutualism, access to the Círculo's library, and participation in recreational activities such as bowling, chess, dominos, gymnastics, and more relevant to the new age, motion pictures.[59]

Dominos may have been an innocent enough pursuit, but peninsular Catholics failed to distance themselves from the murderous regime of Victoriano Huerta (1913–1914), and this mistake would cost them dearly. The Catholics championed a return to the status quo, while moderates kept silent or sounded crypto-huertista. While professing to be apolitical, padre Ramón S. Verdejo had no problem with rallying his flock to the cause of the usurper Huerta, who had overthrown and assassinated President Francisco Madero in February 1913. Verdejo was careful to couch his opposition to the U.S. occupation of Veracruz as a defense of Catholicism itself;

in his telling, northern Protestants who had been unable to win the Mexican people through persuasion had now come to impose their religion by force.[60] Bishop Trischler allied himself with regional henequen oligarchs against the Constitutionalist forces, and when General Salvador Alvarado arrived in 1915, he immediately implemented a persecution campaign that continues to rankle the hearts of Yucatecan Catholics today. Indeed, scandalous stories of a mounted Alvarado galloping into the Cathedral and lassoing santos still circulate among the devout church ladies of Mérida. Trischler twice found himself exiled to Cuba (in 1914–1919 and once more in 1927–1929). Alvarado's wing of the Revolution drew upon the support of an educated middle class who saw the Catholic church in much the same way as had José Martí: a colonial holdover that had managed the Inquisition, repressed women, hidden behind the superstitious Indians, cut a deal with hacendados, and done everything possible to foment ignorance. It was essential to suppress the Catholic influence, "because the only man who is truly free is he who has managed to liberate himself from the ominous yoke of dogma and tradition."[61]

The project met two banks of resistance: the urban Catholics whom the church had labored so diligently to cultivate, and rural folk Catholicism, which was far more syncretic and further removed from ecclesiastical supervision than was its city counterpart, but which had internalized so much of Catholic symbolism. A strident minority of homegrown regional atheists and anticlerics did exist, but as the revolutionary project lost momentum from the 1940s onward, the conservative and devout elements reasserted themselves, heavily supported by the Catholic education system and the *Diario de Yucatán*, the journalistic son of the *Revista de Mérida* and for many years virtually a hegemonic voice in peninsular news.

A handful of factors guaranteed the perpetuation of older forms of religious practice that revolutionary state-builders would not have approved. First, matters of political survival often forced Lázaro Cárdenas (president during the years 1934–1940) to form a pact with more conservative elements; though chiefly driven by hardball concerns like the need to check rivals and to safeguard more higher-priority projects like petroleum nationalization, the pro-conservative pacts also opened space for the very religious matters which revolutionary leaders had so detested. In Yucatán, this meant turning over the state to interests sprung from the former hacendado sector, now deeply entrenched in the bureaucracy and in commerce. Through a combination of interest and inclination, this sector brought its religion with it. Second, and perhaps more important, the post-revolutionary state consistently promised more than it could deliver—a problem that was to recur on a grand scale in matters of public education. Perhaps no political order could have scored more success in remolding a far-flung rural society speaking dozens of languages and above all hamstrung by poverty and its underpinning conditions, but the national public school system simply failed to meet the overall challenge, and privately run (and more often than not, Catholic) schools have typically remained the education of choice for those with the means to pay. Third, resistance—whether institutional or popular—simply proved too vast, too unyielding, and too dependent on long-cherished religious beliefs to yield. Modes of thought such as religion, nationalism, and ethnicity may indeed be less critical than basic economic needs, but they are also the repositories of humanity's deepest fears and aspirations, and for that reason command allegiance. Post-1940 leaders forgot about antifanaticization campaigns in order to get on with the business of industry and urbanization. Thereafter, the pious elements of the plutocracy occasioned little more than grumblings of the intellectual set, which was small indeed. From an institutional perspective, the post-Reform strategies for survival depended on twin tracks, addressing both a literate, urban clientele more directly under church supervision, and a more rural, folk Catholicism that had limited use for priests but which cherished the norms, symbols, and stories of Christianity like fragments of some fallen star, and which would fight to the death to retain them. The repeated post-1920 attempts to suppress Catholicism typically ended as what Adrian Bantjes has called "failed cultural revolutions": in Sonora, in Michoacán, and elsewhere throughout the Republic.[62]

None of this is to suggest a lopsided victory. Indeed, the Catholic church has lost much since 1940. Changing lifestyles, increased individual power, and expanded communication and travel have brought a Protestant challenge that dwarfed the one that padre Verdejo thought he'd detected in the U.S. invasion of Veracruz. The old ways have proven durable, but have had to share the stage with alternative modes of thought. More than anything, an increased material consumerism and sexual permissiveness occupy people's hearts and minds, a fact that anyone who has spent time in modern-day Mexico will readily confirm. Numerous practices unimaginable in earlier eras now help to define daily life: the list includes divorce, birth control, single-mother parenting, premarital sex, gay and lesbian relationships, and (since 2006) limited abortion rights for violated women. Eroticism in entertainment and advertising often exceeds levels found in the United States; in this sense, at least, Juan Carnaval has won the day.

Conclusion

We will probably never know what became of padre Irineo Muñoz, the man who whipped the magistrate's corpse. Nor will we know what effect, if any, this had on the alcalde's soul, or if such a thing as the soul even exists. Indeed, uncertainty may be our own condition, just as it was the condition for the Mexican peoples of 1879. But we can know about the world and the context around this imponderable act. A war that had sprung to life over explicitly material issues of land, labor, taxes, and politics nevertheless passed through the filter of popular customs and beliefs, and in turn modified those customs and beliefs. Forty years of violence changed—or in some cases failed to change—this world. It gave power to the jefes políticos, who subsequently became the bête noire of the Mexican revolutionaries. Liberal land alienation of communities was a far slower and more complicated process, and in fact tended more to follow the uncertain motions that characterized Central America. Maya elites, men who in earlier times sported the ancient titles of indigenous office, found a way to go on in spite of the changes, and now prospered as a class of Maya rancheros who brokered much of the later Revolution.

The two most important changes in the modern Mexican church were its loss of financial power and its related shift from a rural to an urban base. In particular, it was the decision to work through the press that helped the church along. Literacy rates in the peninsula today are high, but a large if undetermined number of people read nothing at all, while the extremely devout read only religious tracts and the conservative and strongly Catholic *Diario de Yucatán*. But these new strategies focused on individual urban piety, and in so doing left a vast space wherein older and more syncretic forms of Maya Catholicism could flourish unmolested.

Perhaps the clearest fact to emerge is the religious trajectory of a people long conditioned to an enforced ideological uniformity. All peoples have their norms and laws, but who knows what any of us will do once the eye of the ruler is no longer upon us? For some, at least, the answer proved too unsettling. Despite the continued health of other forms of control—coercive labor, patriarchal relations between men and women, and a near-universal consensus among Hispanics that Maya peasants were biologically inferior—this prolonged taste of a society without ritual and spiritual hierarchy showed the pitfalls of freedom. The civil wars had readied them for Porfirianism. Indeed, this generation could look back on the previous four decades as a study in what happened when prolonged violence, and a reform that seemed every bit as permanent as China's "permanent revolution," turned the imponderable into the permissible.

NOTES

1. Hemeroteca Pino Suárez (HPS), *Razón del pueblo*, 24 November 1879, 3–4.
2. Karl M. Schmitt, "Catholic Adjustment to the Secular State: The Case of Mexico, 1876–1911," *Catholic Historical Review* 48, no. 2 (1962): 182–204; and Paul Garner, *Porfirio Díaz* (Harlow: Pearson Education, 2001), 49.
3. Paul Vanderwood, *The Power of God Against the Guns of Government: Religious Upheaval at the Turn of the Nineteenth Century* (Stanford: Stanford University Press, 1998).
4. Hernán Menéndez Rodríguez, *Iglesia y poder: Proyectos sociales, alianzas políticas y económicas en Yucatán (1853–1917)* (Mexico City: Consejo Nacional para la Cultura y las Artes, 1995).
5. Franco Savarino Roggero, *Pueblos y nacionalismo: Del régimen oligárquico a la sociedad de masas de Yucatán, 1894–1925* (Mexico City: Instituto Nacional de Estudios Históricos de la Revolución Mexicana, 1997). Of the two studies, Savarino's is certainly the better written, but Menéndez's is the more interesting, owing to the author's deeper knowledge of Yucatecan society (often through the prism of the long Menéndez family history in journalism).
6. Information on corporately held funds appears in the elaborate breakdown entitled "Capitales impuestos manifestados por sus propietarios o administradores," originally found in the Archivo General del Estado de Yucatán (AGEY), Fondo Municipios, Ticul, Box 7, Legajo 9, Expediente 6, 1856. At the time this chapter was written, this important document was currently part of a massive reorganization for the years 1840–1876.
7. Archivo Histórico de la Arquidiócesis de Yucatán (AHAY), Decretos y Oficios, 2 February 1870.
8. AGEY, *Colección de leyes* (ed. Eligio Ancona), vol. 5, 24 March 1875, 58–59.
9. AGEY, Poder Ejecutivo 189, Milicias, 28 April 1875, Motul.
10. To take only one example of this surprisingly common complaint, see AHAY, Decretos y Oficios, 7 May 1859, Champotón.
11. AGEY, Poder Ejecutivo 485, Milicias, 1 February 1905, Mérida. Material classed in "Milicias" often had no relation whatsoever with military affairs. The confusion arises from the fact that jefes políticos also supervised guard service in their domains, and their papers often came to be jumbled into this catch-all category.
12. Matters of cemetery reconstruction crop up everywhere. See, for example, AGEY, Poder Ejecutivo 496, Gobernación, 17 May 1905, Ticul; and AGEY, Poder Ejecutivo 483, Gobernación, 25 January 1905, Tecoh. Funding and bureaucratic oversight always remained the catches.
13. The phrase "The Return of the Gods" in the heading to this section is a tip of the historian's hat to the late Hernán Menéndez: "El retorno de los dioses" was to be the title of his never-completed work on the return of Yucatán's Catholic hierarchy following the high tide of revolutionary radicalism.
14. On Rodríguez's career, see his biographical entry in *Yucatán en el tiempo*, vol. 5 (Mexico City: Inversiones Cares, 1999), 345–46.
15. Centro de Apoyo a la Investigación Histórica de Yucatán (CAIHY), Pamphlets, vol. 21, expediente 14, "Octava carta pastoral que el Illmo. Sr. Obispo Dr. D. Leandro Rodríguez de la Gala dirigió al venerable clero y fieles de su diócesis" (Mérida: Miguel Espinosa Rendón, 1877).
16. CAIHY, Pamphlets, vol. 31, expediente 2, "Deberes de los católicos en la

presente lucha de la iglesia. Traducido del italiano por un miembro de la Sociedad Bibliográfica" (Mérida: Miguel Espinosa Rendón, 1878).

17. See Allen Wells and Gilbert M. Joseph, *Summer of Discontent, Seasons of Upheaval: Elite Politics and Rural Insurgency in Yucatán, 1876–1915* (Stanford: Stanford University Press, 1996), 137–40.

18. CAIHY, Pamphlets, vol. 15, expediente 19, "Regeneración de los indios y de los proletarios de México por medio del cristianismo. Discurso pronunciado por el señor Lic. D. Néstor Rubio Alpuche en la distribución de premios a los alumnos del Colegio y Talleres Salesianos de la Ciudad de México el 3 de septiembre de 1899" (Mexico City: Colegio Salesiano, 1899).

19. "Carrillo y Ancona, Crescencio," in *Yucatán en el tiempo*, vol. 3 (Mexico City: Inversiones Cares, 1999), 108–9. On the origins of the Museo Yucateco, see CAIHY, Libros Manuscritos 190, "Libro con documentos relativos al Museo Yucateco," various dates. Carrillo y Ancona served as museum director until 1875.

20. "Trischler y Córdoba, Martín," in *Yucatán en el tiempo*, vol. 5, 621–23.

21. On the nature and practices of pre-1876 urban cofradías, see Rugeley, *Of Wonders and Wise Men: Religion and Popular Cultures in Southeast Mexico (1800–1876)* (Austin: University of Texas Press, 2001), 73–86.

22. Ibid., 97–100.

23. CAIHY, Pamphlets, vol. 30, expediente 2, "Asociación para el culto perpetuo del Señor Don José con las indulgencias concedidas por S. S. el señor Pío IX. Establecido en Mérida de Yucatán en la Santa Iglesia el día 26 de noviembre de 1872" (Mérida: Miguel Espinosa Rendón, 1877).

24. CAIHY, Pamphlets, vol. 32, expediente 14, "Reglamento de 'La Sociedad Católica.' Establecida en Mérida de Yucatán." (Izamal: A. Acosta C., 1879).

25. CAIHY, Pamphlets, vol. 37, expediente 15, "Reglamento de la Sociedad Católica Central Diocesana del Obispado de Yucatán" (Mérida: Gamboa Guzmán y Hermanos, 1883).

26. CAIHY, Pamphlets, vol. 42, expediente 18, "Fiesta del Stmo. Cristo de las Ampollas. Gremio de Señoras. Corte de caja del año de 1906" (Mérida: Gamboa Guzmán, 1906).

27. CAIHY, Pamphlets, vol. 44, expediente 11, "Reglamento de la Sociedad de Socorros Mutuos de Artesanos. Aprobado el 25 de febrero de 1901 y reformado el 16 de marzo de 1902" (Mérida: Tipografía y Litografía Moderna, 1902).

28. AGEY, Poder Ejecutivo 493, Gobernación, 30 December 1904, Mérida, "Reglamento de la 'Unión Cosmopolite' Sociedad de Socorros Mutuos reformado en la junta general celebrada el 30 de diciembre de 1904."

29. CAIHY, Pamphlets, vol. 84, expediente 22, "Reglamento de la 'Sociedad Mutualista de Profesores'" (Mérida: Imprenta La Luz, 1911).

30. AGEY, Poder Ejecutivo 638, Gobernación, 29 March 1909, Mérida, "Reglamento de la 'Liga de Acción Social.'"

31. AGEY, Poder Ejecutivo 638, Gobernación, 10 April 1909, Mérida, "Reglamento de la Sociedad 'La Unión.'"

32. AGEY, Poder Ejecutivo 638, Gobernación, 31 March 1909, Mérida, "Arte y Recreo."

33. Assorted numbers of *La caridad* (1868–1870) survive in HPS. *Granma* is the official news organ of the Cuban communist state.

34. HPS, *La caridad*, 10 March 1871.

35. CAIHY, Pamphlets, vol. 46, expediente 9, "Recuerdo del gremio de comerciantes y hacendados. La confesión en el Evangelio y en la historia" (Mérida, 1908).
36. CAIHY, Pamphlets, vol. 54, expediente 5, "Catálogo de la agencia de publicaciones religiosas, de A. M. de Cantón para 1896" (Mérida: R. Caballero, 1896).
37. Rugeley, *Of Wonders and Wise Men*, 71–73.
38. CAIHY, Pamphlets, vol. 99, expediente 4, "Novena a la Virgen santísima de la Caridad del Cobre" (Mérida: La Amadita, 1919); and vol. 30, expediente 11, "Jesús Nazareno" (n.p., 1877).
39. For example, see CAIHY, Pamphlets, vol. 29, expediente 19, "Piadosa práctica para el día diez y seis" (Mérida: Escuela Correccional de Artes y Oficios, 1876).
40. CAIHY, Pamphlets, vol. 29, expediente 8, "Edicto sobre la vigilancia en que deben estar los fieles católicos con motivo de la propaganda protestante" (Mérida: Revista de Mérida, 1885).
41. Rugeley, *Of Wonders and Wise Men*, 200–201.
42. CAIHY, Pamphlets, vol. 103, expediente 1, "Antiguos límites y preceptos de la masonería, y reglamentos generales, comparados con los antiguos registros, usos y costumbres de la fraternidad" (Mérida: Pluma y Lápiz, 1923).
43. CAIHY, Pamphlets, vol. 101, expediente 15, "Instrucción sobre el espiritualismo por el Iltmo. Sr. Obispo de Camagüey" (Mérida: E. G. Triay e Hijo, 1921).
44. A reference to well-covering appears in CAIHY, Books Collection, *Calendario de Espinosa para el año de 1879* (Mérida: Manuel Espinosa Rendón, 1878). However, the practice survived, if poorly documented, into the twentieth century.
45. This unusual and quite entertaining piece of literature appears in CAIHY, Pamphlets, vol. 29, expediente 13, "La estigmatización y los libres-pensadores. Por el Dr. en Medicina Imbert Gourbeyre" (Mérida: Juan F. Molina Solís, 1876).
46. On the history of Yucatán's carnivals, see Rugeley, *Of Wonders and Wise Men*, 86–96.
47. Apologies to *El libro de buen amor*, the early fourteenth-century work attributed to one Juan Ruiz, Arcipreste de Hita; in one of its passages, doña Cuaresma meets don Amor, with predictable results.
48. Consider the false advertisement found in the *Recuerdo del carnaval de 1900* (Mérida: El Eco de Comercio, 1900), located in CAIHY, Pamphlets, vol. 61, expediente 23: "Don Antonio Mimenza, agent without portfolio and instructor of Maya, graduate of the University of Hecelchakán, seeks woman to wash clothes and clean house." The idea of an instructor of Maya hailing from an imaginary university in tiny, rustic Hecelchakán apparently tickled turn-of-the-century funny bones, though it would likely fall flat today. Humor is a fleeting quality.
49. "La mujer y la casa" is found in CAIHY, Pamphlets, vol. 74, expediente 6, *Los que lloran serán consolados. Carnavalescos por Chan-Chi. Carnaval de 1907*.
50. On Mauricio Zavala's career as radical priest, see Mark Saad Saka, "Peasant Nationalism and Social Unrest in the Mexican Huasteca" (PhD diss., University of Houston, 1995). The fact that Zavala's confusing *Gramática maya* (Mérida: Imprenta de la Ermita, 1896) is still sold indicates how limited is the demand for serious pedagogical Maya language materials. Like many

early Maya grammars, it tends to hew too closely to the structure of romance languages. Perhaps the 1974 facsimile edition's persistence owes to the fact that its editor was José Díaz Bolio, noted peninsular reactionary and amateur archaeologist.

51. AHAY, Decretos y Oficios, 9 August 1865, Ticul.

52. From 1870 onward, hacienda oratories proliferated; see Rugeley, *Of Wonders and Wise Men*, 149. See also AHAY, Decretos y Oficios, 27 November 1872, Temax; 16 July 1872, Calkiní; and 21 December 1873, China. For sample (albeit early) cases of hacendado resistance to the clergy, see AHAY, Decretos y Oficios, 13 February 1872, Tunkás; and AHAY, Decretos y Oficios, 9 March 1872, Espita.

53. A thorough history of the Maya freeholders *outside* the Porfirian henequen zone remains to be written, but the existence of such properties is undeniable. For the Chenes region, see Wolfgang Gabbert, *Becoming Maya: Ethnicity and Social Inequality in Yucatán since 1500* (Tucson: University of Arizona Press, 2004), 84. For the Oxkutzcab region, see Margarita Rosales González, *Oxkutzcab, Yucatán, 1900–1960: Campesinos, cambio agrícola, y mercado* (Mexico City: Instituto Nacional de Antropología e Historia, 1988), 77–84. A more global (and contemporary) account appears in the massive 1905 property registry, found in AGEY, PE 520, Fomento. It includes most partidos, but unfortunately lacks information from Valladolid, where such properties surely abounded.

54. See Robert Redfield and Alfonso Villa Rojas, *Chan Kom: A Maya Village* (Chicago: University of Chicago Press, 1934); and Alfonso Villa Rojas, *The Maya of East-Central Quintana Roo* (Washington, DC: Carnegie Institute, 1943).

55. Savarino, *Pueblos y nacionalismo*, 223.

56. James Cockcroft, *Intellectual Precursors of the Mexican Revolution, 1900–1913* (Austin: University of Texas Press, 1968), 91–97.

57. See, for example, "La libertad religiosa, conferencia dada en la escuela nacional preparatoria de México la noche del 6 de febrero de 1912 en representación del Comité Mexicano de la Alianza Científica Universal por Francisco Barrera Lavalle," in CAIHY, Pamphlets, vol. 86, expediente 15 (Mérida: Empresa Editora Yucateca, 1913).

58. AGEY, Poder Ejecutivo 725, Gobernación, 22 March 1911, Progreso.

59. CAIHY, Pamphlets, vol. 87, expediente 14, "Reglamento del 'Círculo Católico de Obreros' fundado en 19 de noviembre de 1912 en el suburbio de San Cristóbal de Mérida, Yucatán" (Mérida: Empresa Editora Yucateca, 1913).

60. CAIHY, Pamphlets, vol. 89, expediente 5, "Sermón predicado en la Santa Iglesia Catedral de Mérida de Yucatán, por el presbítero D. Ramón S. Verdejo en el solemne triduo celebrado para impetrar de Dios la pas y la victoria para la nación mexicana" (Mérida: Empresa Editorial Católica, 1914).

61. The spokesman for these views was Rodolfo Menéndez Mena, and his chief work was "La obra del clero y la llamada persecución religiosa en México. Defensa de la política reformista y anticlerical del constitucionalismo," in CAIHY, Pamphlets, vol. 91, expediente 14 (Mérida, 1916).

62. Adrian A. Bantjes, *As If Jesus Walked on Earth: Cardenismo, Sonora, and the Mexican Revolution* (Wilmington, DE: Scholarly Resources, 1998), 6–21.

9

Birds of a Feather

Pollos and the Nineteenth-Century
Prehistory of Mexican Homosexuality

Christopher Conway

arlos Monsiváis has attributed the invention of homosexuality
to a 1901 police raid on a Mexico City ball in which forty-one
men, many of whom were dressed as women, were arrested for
indecency.[1] The sensational press that these arrests provoked, including broadsides by the popular engraver and lithographer José Guadalupe
Posada, publicly disclosed and disseminated the concept of the abject, effeminate invert. The Forty-One not only violated the gender norms that
Porfirian positivism had enshrined as natural and essential to progress,[2]
but also became the focal point for working-class critiques of consumer-
ist men of the leisure class who belonged to the Porfirian establishment.[3]
The Forty-One represented a break with the past because Mexican print
culture had never before disclosed or disseminated such transparent images of sexually deviant, effeminate men. Instead, the nineteenth-century
print media circulated ambiguous stereotypes of effeminate masculinity
that were continuous with centuries-old genealogies of male effeminacy
in Spanish and European culture. Although eighteenth- and nineteenth-
century effeminate men were transatlantic characters defined by a feminine obsession with fashion and its public display, they were not seen as
sexually deviant threats to the national order. Their "type" undoubtedly
represented a challenge to gendered categories of the self, and as such a
potential disruption to the social order, but they were never vilified as in-
trinsically alien. It was the scandal of 1901 that implanted the image of the
invert-as-deviant in the Mexican imaginary and established a long-lasting
relationship between the number forty-one and homosexuality, both as a
cornerstone of modern homophobia and modern gay identity.[4]

The question of what came before the public outing of the invert at the beginning of the twentieth century in Mexico is a difficult one. Robert McKee Irwin argues that nineteenth-century Mexican cultural history was predicated upon a privileging of fraternal bonds between men and by a deep suspicion of heterosexuality. His reading of nineteenth-century novels such as *El Periquillo Sarniento* by Fernández de Lizardi, *El fistol del diablo* by Manuel Payno, and *Los piratas del golfo* by Vicente Riva Palacio underscores that "heterosexual desire could contaminate racial purity, blur barriers of social class, corrupt virgins, destroy the institution of matrimony by means of adultery, incite the sin of incest, or even engender the infamy of pregnancy out of wedlock."[5] In contrast to the perils of heterosexual desire, Irwin notes how male homosocial relationships in fiction are depicted as a more constructive foundation for the national project. In this frame, men whose self-presentation was seen as feminine did not belong to a constructive, national fraternity of men but to the orbit of the weaker and more suspect feminine sex.

In Mexico, such men had many names, including *dandy*, *currutaco*, and *petimetre*, but one of the most prevalent and local labels at mid-century was that of *pollo* (chicken), a type that foreshadowed important aspects of the sensationalist stereotypes of the *joto* and *marica* that burst into print literature in 1901. It bears repeating that the *pollo* was not a sodomite, but his androgynous style was universally seen as implying a closer proximity to feminine qualities than to masculine ones. To be sure, the ridicule to which he was held by critics was generally not as virulent or hostile as the attacks that were directed at the Forty-One, but like his homosexual forebears of the fin de siècle, he was aristocratic, indolent, and harmful to the national order. In the pages that follow, I trace the multiple histories and meanings of the nineteenth-century Mexican *pollo*, noting the ways in which he paved the way for the image of the effeminate Forty-One who inaugurated the history of modern Mexican homosexuality. The *pollo* is not only key for understanding the more fluid and androgynous versions of masculinity that circulated at the dawn of Mexican modernity, but also for bringing into focus nineteenth-century anxieties about gender and its proper definition.

Effeminate Masculinity in Eighteenth and Nineteenth-Century Western Culture

The *pollo* belongs to a class of masculinity in Western Culture defined by an excessive interest in fashion. The most common eighteenth and nineteenth-century terms for this kind of man were *beau, petit-maitre* (*petimetre* in Spanish), *dandy*, and *currutaco*, all of whom shared an obsession with color and the adornment of their bodies. The term *beau* was coined in the seventeenth century and remained in use until the nineteenth century, signifying a "man who gives particular, or excessive attention to dress," as well as being the "suitor of a lady; a lover, sweetheart."[6] The English satirist Joseph Addison observed that what little soul the perfumed *beau* had (if any at all) was spent narcissistically gazing in a mirror.[7] This vanity is shared by the contemporaneous figure of the *petit-maitre* (from the French "little master"), who Denis Diderot described as "affected" and "drunk with self-love."[8] In eighteenth-century Spain, the *petimetre's* obsession with presenting himself as beautiful in society was equated with effeminacy or even the possibility of a third sex. In the *Cartas marruecas*, for example, Jorge Cadalso compared the *petimetre* to a bat because he was neither a mouse nor a bird.[9] The *petimetre* also symbolized French foreignness and served as a stylistic frame of reference for the emergence of the *majo* type, who embodied Spanishness in dress and gesture.[10] In contrast to *petimetre*, whose very name signaled a foreign provenance, *currutaco* (a synonymous, late eighteenth-century term for an affected or effeminate man) was derived from the combination of *curro* (the Andalusian *majo*) and *retaco* (short), which was either a literal reference to short dresses or a more figurative one to the belief that short people are more affected and arrogant than those of regular stature.[11]

The most universally recognized and enduring image of the conceited man obsessed with fashion is the *dandy*, a figure contemporaneous to the Spanish *currutaco* who emerged in Restoration England. The most famous of the Restoration *dandies* was the figure of George "Beau" Brummell (1778–1840), an aristocratic socialite and personal associate of the Prince of Wales whose impeccable taste, refined dress, and lack of romantic interest in the fairer sex came to embody an idealized vision of the style and demeanor of the late eighteenth-century masculine leisure class and its social rituals. Dandyism was redefined when it migrated to France at the beginning of the nineteenth-century; like the *petimetre*, who provoked nationalist anxieties in Spain, the French *dandy* at first represented regional Otherness—specifically qualities that the French considered "English": affectation, melancholy, a lack of civility, and an emphasis on external adornment.[12] At his most fundamental and most enduring, however, the *dandy* was simply a man who lived to dress for society, and as such, to display himself like an object of art. This conception of the masculine self made the *dandy*, like his predecessors the *beau* and the *petit-maitre*, open to accusations of effeminacy even if he undertook the task of conquering the affections of a woman. For example, in a caricature by the English caricaturist I. R. Cruikshank, "Dandies Dressing" (1818), several dandies are shown dressing in a room. Two of them in particular are represented as androgynous and inviting sexual contact with each other. They share a mirror while they dress, with one standing on the floor and the other on a chair behind him. The blouse of the dandy on the chair hangs in such a way that it looks like breasts, and he complains that his fool's cap collar is not "stiff enough" as he wraps a long scarf around it. The dandy below, whose trousers are puffy in the rear and who is also wrapping his collar, replies, "You'll find some to spare in my breeches."

While *beaus*, *petit-maitres*, *currutacos*, and *dandies* circulated at the dawn of the nineteenth century as conspicuous cultural types of non-procreative masculinity, developments in psychiatry and medicine began to cultivate models for describing pederasts that precisely matched the distinguishing features attributed to these cultural types. As early as 1857, the French doctor Ambroise Tardieu (1818–1879) was describing pederasts in his *Medico-Legal Study of Crimes Against Public Morals* as having curled hair and made-up skin, and wearing jewelry and perfume.[13] At the end of the nineteenth century, the image of the pederast and the invert in medical literature as a hysterical, effeminate man was quite common. Yet, these scientific constructions of effeminate men were not new in and of themselves, but rather built on long-standing arguments about the importance of keeping the categories of the masculine and the feminine separate. In *De officiis*, Cicero declared, "We ought to regard loveliness as the attribute of woman, and dignity as the attribute of man. . . . Therefore, let all finery not suitable to a man's dignity be kept off his person, and let him guard against the like fault in gesture and action."[14] In sixteenth-century Spain, *sodomy* was defined as any sexual act that was not procreative, and men who showed interest in the lace, fine linens, and ruffs and cuffs associated with the Italian style of dress were seen as having a propensity toward sexual immorality, including same-sex desire.[15] Finally, Enlightenment thinkers such as Jean-Jacques Rousseau drew links between the consumption of luxury goods—specifically clothes—to woman's sex and self.[16] As these arguments from different historical moments demonstrate, constructions of masculinity may be contingent on historical circumstances, but they have also been consistent in promoting binary thinking: men and women are different in appearance, dress, and self-presentation, and should remain so for the well-being of society.

Reconstructing the Mexican *Pollo*

The words *pollo* and *polla* and their English equivalent *chicken* have been used in past centuries to refer to human offspring and the young in general.[17] In nineteenth-century Spanish usage, the concept of *chicken fowl* had a resurgence as slang for "young lovers," whether they be male (*pollos; pollitos*) or female (*pollas; pollitas*), especially in the Spanish theater of the latter half of the century, which saw the production of a large number of comedies about the romantic misadventures of pollos. The origin of this usage can be traced to the eighteenth-century French term *poulet*, which referred to the winged, folded notes that young lovers exchanged with one another.[18] In fact, one Mexican critic observed in 1873 that arrogant pollos were a public nuisance because they pinched girls at social gatherings and tried to pass them love notes.[19] However, as I will demonstrate below, the Mexican pollos were more than simply young lovers. They were extravagantly dressed young men whose masculinity, good sense, and morality were questionable. This linking of youth with corruption may have been related to other etymological crosscurrents in the use and associations of the word *pollo*. For example, chicken-sellers were associated with prostitution in France, explaining why pimps were publicly humiliated by tying chickens to their legs.[20] In Spain, these sexual associations are referenced in Francisco Goya's famous *Capricho* "Que la descañonan," which depicts a young prostitute with wings under the cape of a magistrate and under attack by the predatory officers of the court.

It is also revealing to note the ways that the Mexican *pollo* echoed aspects of the etymologies and meanings of other words for foolish extravagant men, such as the sixteenth-century *coxcomb* (whose name derived from a fool's cap that looked like a cock's head); the seventeenth-century *maricón* (which, apart from "effeminate sodomite," has a secondary meaning that refers to the *curraca*, a green bird particularly adept at imitating the human voice); the *currutaco* (possibly related to *curruca* as well);[21] the *dandy* (also used to refer to a kind of bantam fowl); and *plumet* (a French variant of *dandy*, from the word for "feather"). The association of birds with same-sex desire between men has a long cultural history, hearkening back to the story of how Zeus took the form of an eagle to kidnap the boy Ganymede; the scene has sometimes been represented by the image of the boy riding a cock rather than an eagle.[22] In Spanish and Latin American culture, the words *pájaros, pajarito, pato,* and *ave* have been used to label gay men, and in North America, *chicken* has been used since the nineteenth century to refer to boys who serve as men's sexual partners and *chicken-hawks* to men who pursue such chickens.[23] Such usage was clearly unknown to the contemporaneous Spanish and Mexican commentators who used the term *pollo*, but it is still important for mapping the meanings of the *pollo* and his descendants. However difficult it is to label his sexuality deterministically, the *pollo's* place in this historical gallery of "queer" birds indicates that he was semantically and culturally situated within a long-standing genealogy of masculine types that were associated with effeminacy and same-sex desire.

In Mexico, *pollo* shared a semantic field crowded with other terms for extravagantly dressed men and was used interchangeably with them. In 1869, different commentators referred to *pollo* as synonymous with *dandy*, *sportsman, petimetre, lion*, and *merveilleux*.[24] In the decades that followed, *pollo* was treated as a synonym of *currutaco*,[25] *sietemesino* (a prematurely born man), *gomoso* (from *goma*, referring to moustache wax), and *catrín*.[26] By and large, however, it is clear that Mexican commentators understood that the *pollo* and other young men of his ilk were essentially cut from the same cloth: they were the ridiculous individuals defined by an obsession with fashion and by a lack of reason, wisdom, and good sense. The term *pollo* probably came to broad prominence in Mexico City's elite circles when the one-act comedy "Una ensalada de pollos" (1850) by the popular Spanish playwright Miguel Bretón de Herreros (1796–1873) was staged in the Teatro de Santa Anna in February 1852. Bretón de Herreros's humorous play, which was advertised in *El monitor republicano* as containing "the spiciest satire and saltiest jokes," provides a lighthearted snapshot of the witty repartee of insubstantial pollos and pollas pursuing each other at a ball. "Una ensalada de pollos" clearly left a mark on the city's theatergoing public because its libretto remained in print and for sale at the offices of *El monitor republicano* for at least a decade after its premiere at the Santa Anna.[27]

The currency of the *pollo* was also furthered by the writings of Mexico's most popular humorist and commentator on social manners, José Tomás de Cuéllar, whose series of costumbrista sketches were published under the title of *La linterna mágica* (The magic lantern) and the pseudonym of "Facundo." In 1869, while he was residing in San Luis de Potosí, Cuéllar was inspired by Bretón de Herreros to serialize a novel titled *Ensalada de pollos* in the magazine *La ilustración potosina*. Cuéllar's novel, which was republished in book form in 1871 and 1891, centers on a varied group of Mexico City pollos and their involvement in a seduction and a fatal duel. Shortly after the serialization, Cuéllar moved to Mexico City, where he edited the magazine *México y sus costumbres* (1872), in which he published multipaneled, full-page caricatures by José María Villasana of the *pollo* and the *polla*. The publications of Cuéllar, as well as the chronicles of several other contemporaneous commentators of Mexican culture, such as Ignacio Manuel Altamirano, Baron Gostkowski, and Francisco Sosa, underscore that by the Restored Republic (1867–1876), the *pollo* had become a well-established and notorious category of Mexican masculinity.

But who was the Mexican *pollo* and what did he signify? He is perhaps best understood as the masculine version of the nineteenth-century feminine archetype of the *coquette*, the flirtatious girl whose interests lie in amorous play and luxury rather than domesticity. The eighteenth-century satirist Joseph Addison drew explicit connections between men of fashion and *coquettes* in two essays published in the literary magazine *The Spectator*, both of which were reprinted in the Mexican newspaper *El siglo diez y nueve* in 1845. The first was "The Dissection of the Beau's Head" and the other "The Heart of a Coquette."[28] The dissection of the *coquette*'s heart reveals her vanity and obsession with social climbing. The examining doctors discover a tube in her heart that functions as a "weather glass," rising each time it is approached by feathers, embroidered coats, fringed gloves, and dandy-like figures in general, and falling in the presence of men of reason and men and women wearing unfashionable or ill-fitting clothes.[29] Most importantly, at the center of the heart, doctors uncover a small and extravagantly dressed figure. "The more I looked upon it," writes Addison, "the more I thought I had seen the Face before. . . . The little idol which was . . . lodged in the very Middle of the Heart was the deceased Beau, whose Head I gave some Account in my last Tuesday's paper."[30]

The image of the *coquette* was well-known in nineteenth-century Mexico, and many of her qualities were transposed onto the feminine counterpart of the *pollo*, the *polla*. The multiple panels of Villasana's caricature of the *polla* in *México y sus costumbres* underscored the superficiality and narcissism that Addison noted in the *coquette*, as well as her extravagant imagination: a polla lightheartedly powders her face before a mirror to cover her shame after being scolded by her father (for behaving improperly, we may assume); a polla sleeps contentedly, surrounded by cherubic angels representing her dreams of luxury goods; a polla sings an aria from *La traviata* on a piano, and in a separate panel asks the moon to admire her for being as beautiful as the titular protagonist of Vincenzo Bellini's opera *Norma*; and a polla disdainfully extending the exaggerated bows and wrappings on the backside of her dress as she rehearses her rejection of a suitor called Godofredo.[31] The extravagant self-image and susceptibility to luxury in the *polla* also appears in the description of the female protagonist of Cuéllar's *Ensalada de pollos*, Concha, whose fantasies of social ascent and romance ultimately result in the loss of her honor. She is overcome by pleasure when she pulls on a luxurious stocking that an affluent *pollo* suitor has given to her as a gift. "That electricity that rose from her feet," writes Cuéllar, "flooded the machine, dazzled Concha and she was lost."[32] The intoxicating, and ultimately sexual, seduction by luxury goods of women is also illustrated in Ignacio Manuel Altamirano's posthumous novel, *El zarco*, in which a fantasy-prone girl is seduced by the fictions and gifts of a murderous bandit. Subjugated by the world of color, status, and luxury represented by clothes and jewels, the nineteenth-century *polla*—the Mexican *coquette*—ultimately embodied desires that were sensual in nature, and which endangered her virtue and honor.

As a male *coquette*, and the embodiment of traits associated with femininity, the *pollo* may be read from the outset as a man who deviates from dominant concepts of masculinity. In representations of the *pollo*, this redefinition of gender is associated with the figure's physical immaturity, his interest in fashion, and his susceptibility to theatrics—what we might call his "operatic" self. These qualities underscore the mismatch between the *pollo* and more productive, virile forms of masculinity, such as that of the responsible husband or father, the honest worker, and the upstanding citizen. Let's begin by considering the youthfulness of the *pollo*. As stated before, one of the oldest meanings of *chicken* is that of a young person; in its nineteenth-century reincarnation, however, the *pollo's* youthfulness is the correlate of a lack of virility. In *Ensalada de pollos*, Cuéllar writes that the *pollo* is "the larva of the generation to come. . . . The biped of twelve to eighteen years, spent on immorality and bad habits."[33] That same year, one of the columnists of *El monitor republicano*—the Baron de Gostkowski—symbolically emasculated Roberto Esteva, a columnist from *La constitución*, for holding ideas contrary to his on the meaning of romanticism. Gostkowski speaks directly to his intellectual rival—whom he calls both a pollo and a dandy—and cruelly mocks the milk-white color of his skin, the curls on his head, his high-pitched voice, the faint moustache on his "infantile" lips, and the languidness of his gaze. These are attributes that Gostkowski considers useful for the public exhibition of "chic" and attracting pollas, but worthless for the more virile endeavors of intellectualism and "standing up to tyrants."[34] This version of the *pollo*, the effeminate adolescent, is in essence synonymous with the *sietemesino*, an early and vaguely medicalized term for an effeminate man. The Spanish novel *Los pichones y los sietemesinos (Memorias de dos señoras impresionables)* by the widely-read novelist Manuel Fernández y González, defines the *sietemesino* as a premature, petulant, ignorant, and sickly adolescent with a squalid and infantile look about him.[35] The disparaging nature of this category of masculinity, however, is best illustrated by the well-known example of José Martí's seminal "Nuestra América" (1893), in which the term *sietemesino* is used to disparage the effeminate weaklings with "painted fingernails" who lack the courage and vision to fight for Latin American unity.[36]

The most visible, public sign of the *pollo* and the failure of his virility is his penchant for fashion. In his landmark work *Sartor Resartus*, the English philosopher Thomas Carlyle writes that the *dandy* is a "Clothes-wearing Man, a Man whose trade, office, and existence consists in the wearing of Clothes." Carlyle memorably adds that this "Poet of the Cloth" lives to exhibit himself as a shiny "object" who craves the gaze of others.[37] Similarly, the Mexican *pollo's* obsession with presenting himself as an object of beauty likens him to women, whose feminine subjectivity is defined as a function of their weakness for beautiful things and their self-fashioning as objects of the male gaze. Two of the panels of Villasana's 1872 caricature of the *pollo* type in Cuéllar's *México y sus costumbres* are useful illustrations of the meanings ascribed to the *pollo's* self and body.[38] The titular panel that operates as the central image of the caricature presents us with the figure of a well-dressed man wearing a top hat, a wide tie, tight pants, and small, tight, high-heeled shoes (Figure 9.1). (*Pollos* and their ancestors—the *catrines*, *pisaverdes*, and *petimetres*—were associated with tight pants and constricted, high-heeled shoes.)[39] One of the pollo's bent arms ends in a theatrical and delicate hand (with extended pinky) that is holding a pair of spectacles.[40] The other bent arm is lower, with its hand holding the head of a thin cane to the body while its tip juts out away from the body. The position of both of these limbs signal a mannered and conspicuous economy of gesture: here is an individual who is unafraid to extend his limb outwards, and who is well aware of his need for space (hence the distance between his glasses and his face, and between his body and the furthermost tip of his walking cane). Moreover, the artificial positioning of the legs underlines that this pollo is posing. Neither walking nor standing, he places his left leg before him in a gesture that suggests rootedness and stability, while the right is turned to the right with the slightest hint of a bend in the knee, suggesting the possibility of movement.

It is in another panel of Villasana's caricature that the *pollo's* interest in fashion becomes more pointed with regards to its implications for gender, directly shifting the figure's interest in clothes from mere affectation to effeminacy. The panel, which is in the upper left of the caricature, shows a pollo being fitted into a corset by a servant boy, who is pressing his leg against the rear of his master. The pollo in profile is shown to be languid and delicate in comparison to the body structure of the servant, whose thick legs, arms, and torso contrast with those of his master. The pollo is extending his arms before him, looking toward a mirror and saying, "Squeeze, damn you, squeeze! I need to be in corset to be the Sylphide of Plateros Boulevard." The word *sylphide* invokes the romantic ballet *Sylphide* (1832) by Auguste Taglione, in which a magical female sprite falls in love with a Scotsman, only to die when he tries to keep her in his possession. The pollo is also queered through the mention of Plateros Boulevard, the French shopping district of Mexico City, well-known for its jewelry and pastry shops. Thus, Villasana's corseted pollo deviates from the norms of patriarchal, national virility because he performs a public, feminine identity (that of a sylphide) and because he is identified with jewelry, sweets, and foreign goods (Figure 9.2).

The *pollo*'s penchant for self-exhibition also relates to a theatrical sense of the self. Coquettes and other women of fashion were seduced not only by objects of luxury but also by shiny fictions—such as *La traviata*, *Norma*, and the lies of a colorful bandit—that turned them against the more modest expectations of domestic, respectable lives. Similarly, pollos had "operatic" selves that underscored their intellectual frivolity and inferiority in comparison to more measured men of reason. In an article titled "El pollo ridículo" (1875), in the children's magazine *Biblioteca de los niños*, one critic characterizes the *pollo* as a passionate follower of Dumas whose head is so full of novels that he believes he is a fictional character in one of them. This characteristic is echoed in Cuéllar's *Ensalada de pollos*, in which one character believes he is living the story of Zorrilla's *Don Juan Tenorio*, and others use the expression "¿Y bien?" from Dumas.[41]

Along these same lines, two of Villasana's caricature panels depict the *pollo* as a melodramatic subject. In the first, a stirred up pollo spreads his legs and bursts into an opera aria from *I puritani* (a scene that is also staged in *Ensalada de pollos*), while in the other a despondent pollo holds his head over a table and contemplates suicide (Figures 9.3 and 9.4).[42] In one newspaper chronicle from 1868, a pollo named Perico is approached at the theater by a friend who asks him what he is doing. "Nothing, I'm bored with life," responds Perico, "I'm tired already of living."[43] These examples underscore the ways in which the *pollo* lives as if on a stage, borrowing poses, exclamations, and even feelings from the theater and from literature. This imitative and theatrical nature alienates him from true feeling (such as love), true commitment (to any ideal other than his wardrobe), and true intelligence.

In her study of Spanish petimetres, Rebecca Haidt writes that pollos, like other fashionable men who blurred the line between masculinity and

Figure 9.1: Central panel from "El pollo" by José María Villasana, *México y sus costumbres*, 25 July 1872. Nettie Lee Benson Latin American Collection, University of Texas Libraries, The University of Texas at Austin.

femininity in the eighteenth century, were aberrations. The subversiveness of their style of self-presentation migrated inward from the adornments on their body, contaminating their capacity for rational thought.[44] Thus, the insubstantial self and foolishness associated with men who lived to dress extravagantly, whether it be the sixteenth-century English *coxcomb* or the eighteenth-century Spanish *petimetre*, presents continuities with medical representations of the male hysteric in the nineteenth century. Until the end of the nineteenth century, when Dr. Jean Martin Charcot's ground-breaking work on hysteria broke with long-standing beliefs about the condition, experts tended to view hysteria as a "female malady" that resulted from the sensitivity of woman's nervous system and disposition.[45] Within this broad paradigm, authors such as Thomas Trotter in *A View of the Nervous Temperament* (1807), Ernst Von Feuchtersleben in *The Principles of Medical Psychology* (1847), and John Russell Reynolds in *System of Medicine* (1866–1879), among others, underscored the emasculated nature of hysteri-

Figure 9.2: "Tighter, you wretch, tighter! I need to be
in corset to be the Sylphide of Plateros Boulevard."
Panel from "El pollo" by José María Villasana, *México
y sus costumbres*, 25 July 1872. Nettie Lee Benson Latin
American Collection, University of Texas Libraries,
The University of Texas at Austin.

cal men.[46] As Vernon Rosario writes, "Male hysterics were regularly found
to demonstrate physical stigmata of 'feminisme' (sparse beard, delicate
complexions, fine hair, weak constitutions, and underdeveloped genitals) as
well as familial histories of degeneration—in particular, hysterical mothers."[47] In early Mexican studies of hysteria, such as *La histeria en el hombre*
(1882) by Dr. B. Jiménez, and "La epilepsia y la histeria, neurosis heredi-
tarias y degenerativas" (1895) by Dr. J. Olvera, the nervous disease resulted
from a combination of factors, including heredity, the pressures of urban
life, and an overactive imagination sparked by reading the wrong kinds of
literature.[48] Although representations of the *pollo* per se did not belong to
the domain of medical epistemology in Mexico, it is clear that his feminine
penchant for theatricality and emotion made him a cultural analogue of
the effeminate male hysterical subject.

Figure 9.3: "Since that woman excites me, let us sing *I puritani*: Suone il violin intrepito!" Panel from "El pollo" by José María Villasana, *México y sus costumbres*, 25 July 1872. Nettie Lee Benson Latin American Collection, University of Texas Libraries, The University of Texas at Austin.

As a conspicuous consumer, and a promoter of consumption during the Restored Republic, the *pollo* cut against the grain of emergent notions of national identity and political subjectivity. The *pollo* did not perform a persona that could be identified as Mexican and virile, but rather was a throwback to the aristocratic and effete foreignness of the Hapsburg interregnum in Mexico. For commentators such as José Tomás de Cuéllar and his close friend Ignacio Manuel Altamirano, the *pollo* did not represent the nationalist prototype best embodied by the figure of the proud, productive, and dignified Mexican man of the working class. Cuéllar's *Ensalada de pollos*, published two years after the expulsion of the French from Mexico, explicitly weaves nationalist decolonization with the problems of class and gender through an archetypal pollo named Pío Prieto. This adolescent was born into a tinsmithing family in a working-class neighborhood of Mexico City, but he is seduced into the *pollo* persona and lifestyle when his father buys him a frock coat. Like Concha, who is too weak to resist the sensory pleasures of her new stockings, Prieto is unable to resist the cosmopolitan thrills promised by his garment. He abandons an honest, dignified apprenticeship under his father in favor of an idle life while loping about the city and its cafés disguised in his frock coat. The problem that plagues Mexico, then, is not a surfeit of wealthy dandiacal young men, but the social and cultural eclipsing of the ideal of a Mexican working class best suited to fulfill Mexico's nationalist potential. In Cuéllar's own words:

Figure 9.4: "Death. . . . Death! . . . I will kill myself early tomorrow!" Panel from "El pollo" by José María Villasana, *México y sus costumbres*, 25 July 1872. Nettie Lee Benson Latin American Collection, University of Texas Libraries, The University of Texas at Austin.

And when the boys of the middle class, as those of the people, favor the workshop and not the study of the law, mechanics and not medicine, the hammer and not contracts; when the use of lambskin gloves has as its object to interpose a smooth skin between the hand of a beautiful woman and the callus of the worker, then it will be difficult to buy elections; then clerks will begin to darken and be miserable in comparison to the gentlemen artisans; then the republic will begin to everywhere have dignified sons and free citizens, separate from the teat of the motherland, and who, emancipated by work from the tutelage of the government, and from the manic pursuit of public office as the only recourse, will be the legitimate representatives of democracy and the sincere defenders of free institutions.[49]

The pollos thus emerge from Cuéllar's important novel as a fictional or deluded leisure class composed of urban petit bourgeois and working-class youths who play the part of cosmopolitans while denying the virile promise of Mexico.

Such arguments surrounding the meaning of *pollo* during the Restored Republic faded away during the Porfiriato, when the term was replaced by others and "Clothes-wearing" men became a state-sanctioned symbol of cosmopolitan modernity.[50] Whereas the *pollo* of the past had been a relatively benign and underdetermined symbol of masculine theatricality, the *dandies* of the Porfiriato became symbols of degeneration that were

Figure 9.5: "Damn Englishman! Following me even
in my country walks! Trying to get me to give him
the price of my neck." Panel from "El pollo" by José
María Villasana, *México y sus costumbres*, 25 July
1872. Nettie Lee Benson Latin American Collection,
University of Texas Libraries, The University of
Texas at Austin.

satirically attacked in the working-class penny press. These forebears of
the *pollo* represented something more sinister than the embodiment of an
insubstantial and false leisure class. They were the grotesque embodiment
of femininity in man, and a symbol of the moral, social, and political bank-
ruptcy of the Porfirian elite. The effeminate man, medicalized and patholo-
gized by a steadily growing body of scientific literature on sexuality, could
now be "outed" as something worse than simply a colorful character. He
was a deviant (Figure 9.5).

The Sexual Enigma of the *Pollo*

> Pío Prieto was able to make an enigma of his life, which is the
> natural state of many Píos that we know.
> —Cuéllar, *Ensalada de pollos* (1869)

I have situated the *pollo* in the prehistory of modern, Mexican homosexuality because he cannot be neatly classified into the modern categories of sexual identity that began to emerge at the end of the nineteenth century. While an analysis of the gender of the pollo underscores that he was commonly seen as an androgynous figure, establishing a link between sexual orientation and his gender is difficult, if not impossible. While it is true that pollos were generally represented as pursuers of the fairer sex, their investment in seduction was mitigated by their overall superficiality. The narcissistic imperative to embody a style is anathema to male virility and true commitments of any kind, including love. And yet, several of the *pollo*'s qualities, such as his refinement, extravagance in dress, and high-pitched voice, made him a symbolic analogue of woman and foreshadowed the stereotype of the effeminate homosexual that emerged with the scandal of the Forty-One. In this regard, it may be useful to reflect upon early texts in which the "Clothes-wearing" men of nineteenth-century Mexico are more explicitly represented and condemned as transvestic or deviant figures. Such texts, although few, underline the sexual liminality of the *pollo* in ways that point to the image of the turn-of-the-century invert. The unraveling of such texts is daunting not only because they were composed without recourse to the modern categories of sexual identity but also because of their use of circumspection or humor, which assumes that some things cannot or should not be said directly. Although fragmentary, multivalent, and ambiguous, these representations suggest how pollos and other men of fashion did in fact embody the possibility of a different kind of desire.

In an 1842 chronicle published in *El siglo diez y nueve*, the pseudonymous Padre Calancha describes some of the social types and behaviors of Mexico City's theatergoing public to a religious superior he addresses as "Your Reverence." Padre Calancha's description of two precursors of the *pollo*, the *pisaverde* and the *lechuguino*, underlines their penchant for repeating the opinions of others (because they have none of their own).[51] In particular, he singles out the "Verde Gay de Verdegay" club of adolescents who, like the pollos of decades to come, pretend to be men of maturity. "Your Reverence will soon understand that the Verde Gay de Verdegay gang combs their gray hairs pretending to be of a mature age. For this very reason, Your Reverence will also be able to see them on holiday made up like pretty things . . . but Jesus! I become slanderous." This coded passage presents us with an unexpectedly literal example of the ways in which "Clothes-wearing" men fit into the genealogies of gay identity as early as the first half of the nineteenth century. The ellipsis with which Padre Calancha introduces his exclamation and subsequent apology for cursing the Verde Gay de Verdegay gang suggests that their self-presentation in public is shocking enough to justify the omission of its description or labeling. The use of the word *gang* (*pandilla* in the original) to describe the Verdegays emphasizes the insularity or sect-like nature of the group, while the repetition of the label *Verde Gay*, which reinforces the phrase's symbolic importance as a meaningful descriptor, implies illicit sexuality.

Although the phrase *Verde Gay* (from *Vert Gai*) literally refers to a bright hue of green, the word *green* has been figuratively and etymologically associated with homosexuality since at least the Byzantine Empire, when Emperor Justinian and subsequently Empress Theodora used accusations of homosexuality as a pretext for the torture and murder of members of a rival political faction identified with the color green.[52] Although the Byzantine Greens were not necessarily gay, the color green seemed to have been an important, symbolic color for gay men between the seventeenth and early twentieth century, when green hats or suits seemed to be one of the public—albeit coded—ways of communicating a man's sexual orientation.[53] In Hispanic culture per se, the embeddedness of this relationship between green and homosexuality can be surmised not only by the general association of the color green with obscenity, but also by the semantic field of *marica*, which according to the eighteenth-century *Autoridades* is a synonym of a green bird called the *curraca*. Although we cannot say for certain that the Verdegays that Padre Calancha described were *gay* in the modern sense of the word, the conspicuous and repeated use of the symbolically-loaded color green, in conjunction with the author's implication that these men engage in cross-dressing, suggests that male effeminacy in mid-nineteenth-century Mexico could signal same-sex desire. By the same token, an 1871 description of a dandy as wearing a verdegay tie implies that the color green may have been appropriated for the purposes of coding sexual desire in public by some "Clothes-wearing" men in Mexico.[54]

Padre Calancha's use of the word *gay* may be significant as well. The earliest meaning of *gay* in English refers to color, but beginning in the seventeenth century it also took on the meaning of illicit pleasure and immorality.[55] In the nineteenth century, *gay* became a code for same-sex desire and sex acts as early as the 1860s, as evidenced by the double entendres and ribald comedy of the North American burlesque theater, which often starred showily dressed and androgynous "swells" (yet another nineteenth-century variant of the "Clothes-wearing" man).[56] The use of the word *gay* in this sense became more common among gay people by the end of the century, but it did not enter print and mass culture until the 1930s.[57] More research is required to establish whether or not Padre Calancha's 1842 disparagement of the Verde Gay de Verdegay gang deserves to be read as one of the earliest uses of the word *gay* to signify homosexuality, but it is certainly an intriguing possibility that follows logically from the cultural meanings of the word green.

Thirty years after Padre Calancha's reference to the Club Verdegay, *El siglo diez y nueve* published an article called "Mal los trata el progreso" (Progress Treats Them Poorly), which details how pollos disrupt heterosexual custom by refusing to dance with women at dances. The brief article conjures up the image of a sect of affected and effeminate men who, rather than participate in the heterosexual ritual of dancing, withdraw into a conspicuously visible and self-sufficient clique of their own:

> Imagine that in every dance hall a large group of those parodies of Adonis is formed, and while there are a multitude of young ladies, lovely as the sun, seated without having danced, they stare unmoved at the hall. Some dancers, passing by, ask them, "Why don't you dance, so and so?" Because of my heart palpitations, answers this one in an effeminate voice; and you, why don't you dance? As you know I can't waltz because I get dizzy; and you? I don't want to dance because Miss so and so did not come and she gets angry if she finds out that I have danced. This is what is heard from that original group, and sometimes, in gatherings, women have danced with each other and the pollos let it happen and do not move. Tell us if we are correct in saying that those unfortunates have degenerated.[58]

By noting that "progress" promotes the disruption of heterosexual practice and ritual, and referring to *pollos* as effeminate "degenerates," the nameless author of this chronicle anticipates the arguments of Max Nordau's *Degeneration* (1892), which made the term *degeneration* de rigueur in European and New World discussions of the effects of modernity and industrialization on human physiology. Yet, unlike most representations of the *pollo* and his brethren in Mexico, which treated him as a curiosity or as an annoyance, this chronicle's bitter tone and mocking construction of the *pollo*'s physical weakness and ambivalence toward women dramatically underscore the continuities between him and his descendant, the turn of the century *marica*. The chronicle suggests that the degenerate pollo is more than a fool whose dress and love of fashion likens him to woman in appearance and vanity, he is a member of a community of men distinguished by behavioral and physiological markers of weakness and by a lack of interest in women. In this frame, the leap from degenerate *pollo* to the concept of sexual deviancy is a short one.

However, the continuities between the *pollo* and the sexual invert are most dramatically illustrated by a theater review by Altamirano in which a pollo is incontrovertibly outed as a sodomite. The linchpin of this public outing of the pollo is a nahuatl word for beetle, *mayate*, that was used in late nineteenth-century Mexico to signify the active partner in a sexual relationship between men.[59] Altamirano's 1868 article opens with an extravagant description of a "Clothes-wearing" man that he calls a *dandy*, *petimetre*, and *pollo*. Then Altamirano transcribes a dialogue between a serious, baldheaded man and the bejeweled pollo who says something shocking to him. The conversation begins when the pollo stretches out a gloved hand and greets the baldheaded man:

> "Man," my friend [the baldheaded man] responded, "you are made up like a coleopteron in those clothes and jewelry. Do you know what a coleopteron is?"
>
> "No, but it interests me little; speak in Castilian or I will get angry."
>
> "Well, man, you look like one of those brilliant insects that lives in the maize fields and meadows in this rainy season, and that naturalists nail into their boxed collections with a pin."
>
> "A *mayate*, you mean to say. . . . Well, thanks for the compliment and let's speak of something else. Were you in Valero last night?"
>
> The bald-headed man trembled in anger: I saw him smile as if he had just heard an epigram and then his cranium got . . . red, red and he directed an extremely ferocious look at his interlocutor. I thought he was going to respond with an abomination; but no, he contained himself and contented himself with responding, "I do not understand what you mean to say with that 'Have you been in Valero': pardon me, but I can't figure out what that could mean."
>
> "Oh really, it's not hard," responded the dandy, "it's a phrase everyone uses and it means, 'Have you been to see Valero or to the theater in which he is performing?' It's just that we suppress some of the words for being useless and to abbreviate."[60]

The pollo moves on and the baldheaded man and Altamirano continue to speak, quite innocuously, about the failings of Mexico's youth and the Mexican theater. And yet, through irony and a play on words, Altamirano confirms that codes like *pollo*, *mayate*, and *sodomy* were indeed related to one another during the Restored Republic, a full thirty years before explicit notions of sexual degeneracy were associated with "Clothes-wearing" men at the turn of the century.

Pollos and the Genealogies of Modern Mexican Masculinity

Despite his ubiquity in mid-nineteenth century Mexico, the Mexican *pollo* is a transitional figure linking eighteenth-century notions of male effeminacy to the construction of the *homosexual* at the dawn of the twentieth century. Like his predecessors, the *pisaverde* and *currutaco*, and his descendants, the Forty-One, the *pollo* embodied a nonproductive form of masculinity predicated on imitation, narcissism, and the consumption of luxury goods. As a social type, he was not the hardworking and loving husband (whom José María Villasana also immortalized in a caricature in *México y sus costumbres*); he was not a thoughtful, nation-building intellectual like the prominent chroniclers of social life and mores of the Restored Republic, Ignacio Manuel Altamirano and his friend Baron Gostkowski (who both ridiculed the *pollo* in their writings); and he was not a good citizen, sacrificing himself to the greater good through a life of service. Instead, at a time when nationalist thinkers were enshrining the austerity of the ideology of liberalism over the aristocratic excesses of political conservatism and its foreign allies, the *pollo* frivolously consumed luxury goods and publicly promoted their social value by aspiring to be "the *Sílfide* of Plateros Street."

The *pollo* may have been a product of Mexican modernity insofar as he was—or pretended to be—the arbiter of transatlantic literary, cultural, and fashion cosmopolitanism. But as a "Clothes-wearing" man he was hardly the exclusive invention of the nineteenth century or any of its periods; rather, as this chapter has sought to demonstrate, he is woven into a long-standing tradition of effeminate, extravagantly dressed men in Western and Hispanic cultures. The study of the *pollo* within this tradition reminds us that although modern Mexican homophobia was indeed a product of the fetishization of the dandiacal body in Porfirian political culture (and its rejection by the working-class penny press), there was also a set of earlier cultural precedents and genealogies that paved the way for the vilification of the *homosexual* as a frivolous, weak, and virtual woman. The world of the *pollo* may be hard to discern and reconstruct from the vantage point of the very categories of sexual identity that made him an anachronism in the fin de siècle, but his ubiquitous and extravagant presence in narratives of nineteenth-century Mexican masculinity make him essential for an understanding of the construction and historical roots of modern Mexican homophobia.

NOTES

I would like thank Juan Carlos González Espitia, William G. Acree Jr., John Charles Chasteen, Christian Zlolninski, Manuel García y Griego, Doug Richmond, A. Ray Elliott, Antoinette Sol, Joy Calico, Ana Peluffo, and especially Desirée Henderson for offering insights, suggestions, and encouragement. I am deeply grateful for the assistance of Christian Kelleher and the staff of the Rare Books Department of the Nettie Lee Benson Collection at the University of Texas at Austin. I also appreciate the monetary support and professional encouragement of several departments at the University of Texas at Arlington: the Office of the Provost, the College of Liberal Arts, the Department of Modern Languages, and the Center for Mexican American Studies.

1. See Carlos Monsiváis, "The 41 and the Gran Redada," 150, and Robert McKee Irwin, "The Centenary of the Famous 41," 169, in *Centenary of the Famous 41: Sexuality and Social Control in Mexico, c. 1901*, eds. Robert McKee Irwin, Edward J. McCaughan, and Michelle Rocío Nassar (New York: Palgrave Macmillan, 2003).

2. See Martin Nesvig, "The Lure of the Perverse: Moral Negotiations of Pederasty in Porfirian Mexico," *MS/EM* 16, no. 1 (2000): 8.

3. In Rugeley's and Day's chapters in this book, we learned about other elements of Porfirian political culture. Robert Buffington amply demonstrates the contrasting connotations of bourgeois and working class homophobia in his detailed study of effeminacy and homosexuality in the penny press, "Homophobia and the Mexican Working Class, 1900–1910," in *Centenary of the Famous 41*, 204, 212.

4. For a detailed discussion of the meanings of the number "41" in twentieth-century Mexico, see Monsiváis, "The 41," 164; Buffington, "Homophobia," 211–12; and Irwin, "Centenary," 177–78. Also, see Irwin, *Mexican Masculinities* (Minneapolis: University of Minnesota Press, 2003).

5. Irwin, *Mexican Masculinities*, 5. Other perspectives on several of these works can be found in Wright's chapter in this book.

6. *Oxford English Dictionary Online, www.oed.com.*

7. One of the most famous meditations on the *beau* was written by Joseph Addison and published in the satirical English newspaper *The Spectator* in 1712. In this essay, commonly anthologized as "The Dissection of the Beau's Head," Addison describes the discovery of essence and orange-flower water in the beau's pineal gland, as well as "a kind of Horny Substance, cut into a thousand little Faces or Mirrours, which were imperceptible to the naked Eye, insomuch that the Soul, if there had been any here, must have been always taken up in contemplating her own Beauties." See "Addison on the Dissection of a Beau's Brain" in *The Commerce of Everyday Life: Selections from "The Tatler" and "The Spectator*," ed. Erin Mackie (London: Bedford/St. Martin's Press, 1989), 528–31.

8. Domna Stanton, *The Aristocrat as Art: A Study of the* Honnête Homme *and the* Dandy *in Seventeenth- and Nineteenth-Century French Literature* (New York: Columbia University Press, 1980), 55.

9. Rebecca Haidt, *Embodying Enlightenment: Knowing the Body in Eighteenth-Century Spanish Literature and Culture* (New York: St. Martin's Press, 1998), 108.

10. Dorothy Noyes, "La maja vestida: Dress as Resistance to Enlightenment in Late 18th-Century Madrid," *Journal of American Folklore* 3, no. 440 (1998): 202.

11. Joan Corominas, *Diccionario Crítico Etimológico de la Lengua Castellana* (Berna: Editorial Francke, 1954).

12. Stanton, *Aristocrat as Art*, 33.

13. Vernon A. Rosario, "Inversion's Histories/History's Inversions. Novelizing Fin-de-Siecle Homosexuality," in *Science and Homosexualities*, ed. Vernon A. Rosario (New York: Routledge, 1997), 90.

14. Quoted in Haidt, *Embodying Enlightenment*, 117.

15. Federico Garza Carvajal, *Butterflies will Burn: Prosecuting Sodomites in Early Modern Spain and Mexico* (Austin: University of Texas Press 2003), 62.

16. Jennifer M. Jones, "Repackaging Rousseau: Femininity and Fashion in Old Regime France," *French Historical Studies* 18, no. 4 (1994): 943.

17. According to the *OED*, *chicken* is used to refer to human offspring as early as the fifteenth century, and was used by Shakespeare. The feminine *chick* continues to be used in the present in the United States. The eighteenth-century *Diccionario de Autoridades* cites Quevedo as using *pollo* to mean "young man."

18. *Poulet* appears in the *OED*; its first use in English as "love note" is dated 1848, in Thackeray's novel *Vanity Fair*.

19. Juvenal, "Charla de los Domingos," *El monitor republicano*, 6 April 1873, 1.

20. Pierre Larousse, *Grand dictionnaire universel du XIXe siècle: Français, historique, géographique, mythologique, bibliographique, littéraire, artistique, scientifique, etc.* (Genève: Slatkine, 1982).

21. This is worth considering because of the word's association with ducks, male effeminacy, and most importantly, its similarity in sound and spelling to *curruca*.

22. Ed Madden, "Flowers and Birds," in *Gay Histories and Cultures*, ed. George E. Haggerty (New York: Garland Publishing, 2000), 333.

23. Ibid. For a discussion of the term *chicken* in North American gay slang, see Philip Herbst, *Wimmin, Wimps and Wallflowers: An Encyclopaedic Dictionary of Gender and Sexual Orientation Bias in the United States* (Boston: Intercultural Press, 2001), 49–50. See also Jonathan Ned Katz, *Love Stories: Sex Between Men Before Homosexuality* (Chicago: University of Chicago Press, 2001), 138.

24. See J. M. del C. V., "Un recuerdo," *El monitor republicano*, 21 February 1869, 1. In the story J. M. del C. V. describes one of his protagonists as "un dandy, un petimetre, un lioncito, una maravilla," all of which are French variations on *dandy*. Also see Baron Gostkowski, "Humoradas Dominicales," *El monitor republicano*, 5 December 1869, 2. Gostkowski mocks another journalist by referring to him as a *dandy*, a *pollo*, and a *sportsman* (a reference to the English leisure class that was the model for French dandyism). Further examples of how these terms were used interchangeably can be found in Juvenal, "Charla de los Domingos," *El monitor republicano*, 6 April 1873, 1 (*pollos, liones*); and 4 July 1875, 1 (*dandy, pollo*). For a discussion of variants of *dandy* in French culture, see Stanton, *The Aristocrat as Art*, 50–57.

25. See Vicente Del Rey, Untitled, *El monitor republicano*, 20 May 1883, 2.

26. See Ovoned Leuman, "El caballo del amor," *El monitor republicano*, 4 January 1885, 3. Leuman writes, "Pollo de espetado ceño, / sietemesino o gomoso / pálido, flaco, ojeroso, / falto de salud y sueño." For the interchangeability of

catrines and *pollos*, see José Tomás de Cuéllar, *Ensalada de pollos* (Mexico City: Porrúa, 1982).

27. See "Gran Teatro de Santa Anna," *El monitor republicano*, 4 February 1852, 4. The program reads, "'La ensalada de pollos.' Chistosísima comedia en un acto, última composición del autor de '¿Quién es ella?,' en la que abunda la sátira más picante y los chistes más salados que ha escrito el Sr. D. Manuel Bretón de Herreros." The print version of the play is referred to in the "Catálogo de libros que se hallan de venta en el despacho de esta imprenta," *El monitor republicano*, 12 September 1856, 2; and "Estracto del catálago de los libros que se hallan de venta en la Editorial Universal, esquina de las calles del Refugio y Puente del Espíritu Santo," *El monitor republicano*, 25 August 1861, 3.

28. "Disección de la cabeza de un petimetre y del corazón de una coqueta. Versión del inglés de Mr. Addison remitido para El Siglo XIX por Don Luis Neyro, cónsul Mexicano en Harre," *El siglo diez y nueve*, 21 November 1845, 6.

29. See Joseph Addison, "Addison on the Dissection of a Coquette's Heart," in Mackie, *Commerce of Everyday Life*, 533.

30. Ibid., 534.

31. The references to *La traviata* and *Norma* are significant here. The protagonist of *La traviata* was a courtesan, and Norma was a pagan priestess and traitorous woman.

32. Cuéllar, *Ensalada de pollos*, 46.

33. Ibid., 31–32.

34. Baron de Gostkowski, "Humoradas dominicales," *El monitor republicano*, 5 December 1869, 1. Gostkowski writes, "Roberto [Esteva] es un lindo jovencito, aclarinetado, fresco, rizado y de una blancura de leche. Una sombra lijera germina apenas sobre su labio infantil, y su mirada lánguida, es más a propósito para hacer soñar a las pollas, que para hacer temblar a los tiranos. Vestido con un chic supremo, se le puede ver treces por semana rigiendo en el Paseo, y con un airecito de Faeton, un carro que no es precisamente el del sol. Roberto hubiera podido ser en lugar de un poeta, de un fastidioso novelista, o de un pésimo periodista, un delicioso dandy, un perfecto sportsman, un alegre compañero."

35. Manuel Fernández y González, *Los pichones y los sietemesinos (Memorias de dos señoras impresionables)* (1874), 52.

36. See José Martí, *Política de Nuestra América*, with a prologue by Roberto Fernández Retamar (Mexico City: Siglo Veintiuno, 1977), 37. Martí writes, "A los sietemesinos, sólo les faltará el valor. Los que no tienen fe en su tierra son hombres de siete meses. Porque les falta el valor a ellos se lo niegan a los demás. No les alcanza al árbol difícil el brazo canijo, el brazo de uñas pintadas y pulsera, el brazo de Madrid o de París, y dicen que no se puede alcanzar el árbol."

37. Thomas Carlyle, *Sartor Resartus: The Life and Opinions of Herr Teufelsdrockh in Three Books*, with an introduction and notes by Roger L. Tarr (Berkeley: University of California Press, 1999), 201.

38. The multipaneled caricature appears in the 25 July 1872 issue of *México y sus costumbres* on page 8.

39. The *pisaverde* is a seventeenth-century effeminate type. According to

Corominas, "Así dicho porque anda de puntillas, como el que atraviesa los cuadros de un jardín." See Corominas, *Diccionario*.

40. Spectacles were an accessory of Mexican "Clothes-Wearing" men, as evidenced by the early novel *Don Catrín de la fachenda* (1820) by José Joaquín de Lizardi, in which the titular protagonist makes a point of buying spectacles along with his other garments. For a discussion of this novel, and to compare an 1822 illustration of Lizardi's protagonist with Villasana's pollo, see Nancy Vogeley, *Lizardi and the Birth of the Spanish American Novel* (Gainesville: University Press of Florida, 2001), 184, 234–55.

41. Cuéllar, *Ensalada de pollos*, 145.

42. Ibid., 141. In the novel, a pollo takes the stance of a sfogatto tenor and cries out, "Miserable!"

43. Similarly, the notion of the overly theatrical youngster is taken up by a writer called Pipí in 1868, who recreates a conversation that he overhears at the theatre: "—¡Perico! What are you doing?—I am supremely bored.—Well, what's wrong with you?—Nothing; I am bored with life; I am tired of living." See Pipí, *El monitor republicano*, 13 December 1868, 2.

44. Haidt, *Embodying Enlightenment*, 141.

45. See Mark S. Micale, "Charcot and the Idea of Hysteria in the Male: Gender, Mental Science and Medical Diagnosis in Late Nineteenth-Century France," *Medical History* 34 (1990): 376–77.

46. Ibid., 380.

47. Rosario, "Inversion's Histories/History's Inversions," 93.

48. Frida Gorbach, "From the Uterus to the Brain: Images of Hysteria in Nineteenth-Century Mexico," *Feminist Review* 79 (2005): 89.

49. Cuéllar, *Ensalada de pollos*, 97.

50. For an analysis of how dandiacal fashion was appropriated by the Porfirian establishment, and the sexual ambiguities it led to, see Víctor M. Macías-González, "The Lagartijo at the High Life: Masculine Consumption, Race, Nation and Homosexuality in Porfirian Mexico," in *Centenary of the Famous 41*, 227–50.

51. El Padre Calancha, "Variedades: Teatro," *El siglo diez y nueve*, 1 September 1842, 3. Calancha describes the verdegays as "hombres-ecos, que repiten lo que oyen, o que palmotean lo que ven palmotear."

52. See Alan Cameron, *Blues and Greens at Rome and Byzantium* (Oxford: Clarendon Press, 1976), 173.

53. For mention of the use of the color green in Elizabethan "molly houses," see Alan Bray, *Homosexuality in Renaissance England* (New York: Columbia University Press, 1995), 87. For a discussion of the color green among North American gays and *fairies* at the beginning of the twentieth century, see George Chauncey, *Gay New York: Gender, Urban Culture, and the Making of the Gay Male World, 1890–1940* (New York: Basic Books, 1995), 52.

54. "Era un pollo finísimo: sombrerito ahuevado color café, con ala de seda: levita cola de pato con dos botones: pañuelito de seda azul enseñando la punta: corbata verdegay: chaleco amarillo . . . zapatito de charol y paño blanco. El dandy es un colorista consumado." See Juvenal, "Charla de los Domingos," *El monitor republicano*, 4 July 1875, 1.

55. See Scott Speirs, "Gay," in Haggerty, *Gay Histories and Cultures*, 362–63.

56. Michelle Durdin, "Not Just a Leg Show: Gayness and Male Homoeroticism in Burlesque, 1868 to 1877," *Thirdspace* 3, no. 2 (2004): 8–26.
57. Speirs, "Gay," 363.
58. "Mal los trata el progreso," *La orquesta*, 26 February 1870, 3.
59. In *Los criminales en México: Ensayo de psiquiatria social* (México: Tipografía el Fenix, 1904), Carlos Roumagnac notes the use of the word *mayate* in Mexico's prisons (102).
60. Ignacio Manuel Altamirano, "El teatro," *El monitor republicano*, 6 September 1868, 2. Because of the importance of this passage, it is worth including the original Spanish here: "—Cómo va, dijo al calvo, alargándole una mano enguantada. / —Hombre, le respondió mi amigo, está Ud. Hecho un coleóptero con ese vestido y con esas joyas, ¿Ud sabe lo que es un coleóptero? / —No: pero poco me interesa, hable Ud. castellano o me enfadaré / —Pues hombre, me parece Ud. uno de esos insectos brillantes que se crían en las milpas y en los prados, en este tiempo de aguas, y que los naturalistas clavan con un alfiler en sus cuadros de colección. / —Mayate querrá Ud. decir . . . vaya, gracias por el cumplido y hablemos de otra cosa, ¿ha estado Ud. en Valero anoche? / El calvo se estremeció de cólera, le vi sonreir como si acabara de escuchar un epigrama y luego se le puso el cráneo . . . rojo, rojo y dirigió a su interlocutor una mirada ferocísima. Creí que le iba a contestar una abominación; pero no, reprimióse y se contentó con responder. / —No entiendo qué quiere decir Ud. con ese ha estado Ud. en Valero: perdone Ud. pero no me doy cuenta de lo que pueda significar eso. / —¡Oh pues, no es difícil, contestó el dandy, es frase que todo el mundo usa y quiere decir: que si ha estado Ud. a ver a Valero o en el teatro en que representa Valero, solo que suprimimos algunas palabras por inútiles y para abreviar."

IO

Unveiling the Mask of Modernity

A Critical Gendered Perspective of *Amistad funesta* and the Early Chronicles of José Martí

Patricia Lapolla Swier

> Oh, it is in those markets where young generous men, who are in search of blue birds, usually bind their lives to pretty cups of flesh who after a short time, under the first hot tempers of life, reveal the sly fox, the venomous serpent, the cold and impassible cat that lies within their soul!
>
> —José Martí, *Lucía Jerez*

On the cover of the 1840 French translation of Hieronymus Fracastorius's poem "Syphilis," a vignette features a masked woman with her handsome courtier kneeling in front of her.[1] From the side angle, only a spectator could see that beneath the masked face of the beautiful woman lies the disease and corruption of the prostitute. The man kneeling before her, mesmerized by her beauty, is ignorant of the consequences of engaging intimately with the diseased woman, and is thus portrayed as a potential victim. This revealing image captures the essence of popular nineteenth-century ideologies that regarded the pathology of woman as the decadent force that threatened not only man's well-being but also that of the nation. In the previous chapter, we saw a similar understanding of the *pollo* (the effeminate man often seen as a degenerate invert); in the following chapter, links between syphilis and the role of women are explored in depth. Here, I will explore the pathological traits attributed to women that are manifested in the female protagonist of José Martí's only novel, *Amistad funesta* (Fatal Friendship), showing the imminent danger of the inevitable union between the betrothed couple Juan and Lucía Jerez. I further argue that the intimate union between these two protagonists reflects Martí's avid warnings to Latin American nations of the pending dangers of entering precipitously into trade relations with the United States at the end of the nineteenth century.

Revolutionary, writer, and intellectual, José Martí became a mediator between his country and the metropolis of New York City during his years of exile in the United States (1881–1895). In his chronicles, he not only informed his fellow Latin Americans of the progress of that great nation, but also constructed a sense of *Latinoamericanismo* from his place of exile.[2] However, Martí also reveals a growing sense of apprehension about the expansionist nature and imperialist drive of the United States, which he later refers to as the "seven-league giant." While most critics note that the apogee of Martí's anti-imperialist rhetoric is expressed in the 1891 "Nuestra América" (Our America), I argue that Martí's warnings of anti-imperialism begin as early as 1881 and are evident in many of his earlier writings and in *Amistad funesta*.

This chapter addresses the period between 1881 and 1885, when Martí composed a series of writings and promoted a sense of nationalism that is manifested and reproduced through gendered language. Together with Juan Montalvo, Martí is one of the earliest writers who was concerned with modernity and took a broad view of Latin American relations with the United States and Europe. Although he represents the national voice of Cuba, a country struggling to free itself from the grips of colonialism, through his many writings he directs his narrative to a panorama of Latin American nations emerging into an era of modernity as they are confronted with the imperialist advances of the United States. This Cuban patriot was a point of reference for Latin American intellectuals who resisted the blind appropriation of external ideologies. In many of his works, he employs the use of gender codes in his projection of the ideal Latin American subject, while at the same time warning political leaders of the imposing hegemonic presence of the northern neighbor. Juan, who is initially groomed as an ideal national subject in *Amistad funesta*, is unaware of Lucía's hysteric disorder. His engagement to her serves as a threat to his character and well-being, which thereby serves as an admonition to Latin American countries as they embark on relations with the United States. Although the principal objective of this chapter is to reveal the ways in which Martí's preoccupations with U.S. and Latin American relations between 1881 and 1885 are mirrored in his novel, a broader goal is to explore his strategic use of gender in his formation of a unified Latin American identity—one that is in constant conflict with the basic tenets of modernity and that, according to Martí, would compromise the spiritual integrity of Latin Americans. Furthermore, I will show that Martí's manipulation of gendered language in his writings illustrates the transitory status of gender and its relation-

ship to power, and ultimately results in the unexpected formation of bi-
gendered and even androgynous characters in his novel.

The Use of Gendered Language
and the Reversal of the Axis of Power

During the post-independence years, while Latin Americans struggled
to form new, national identities, many were faced with the negative stereotypes and depictions of their countries offered by well-known philosophers, travel writers, and prominent politicians from more powerful nations (this point is detailed in González-Stephan's chapter in this volume).
Immanuel Kant's hierarchy of national character based on differences in
gender allocated the civilizing qualities of reason to a select minority of
elite Caucasian men, while Georg Wilhelm Friedrich Hegel expounded
on the "immature" status of Latin American countries in their perceived
relationship to nature. According to Michael Aronna, advocates of the
discourse of degeneracy in Latin America and Spain produced a series of
essays that "accounted for underdevelopment through psychological and
medical explanations which found their nations to be too sick, immature,
un-evolved and 'feminine' to possess the rational and moral qualities necessary for national progress."[3] Due to geographical and racial factors, Latin
American people and nations were cast into the realm of the feminine as
they were held up against the rationalizing qualities of more progressive
nations.

Travel writing also helped to shape attitudes about Latin America
and its people and was largely responsible for the negative view towards
many Latin Americans during the nineteenth century. The impressions
and experiences of popularly read writers such as Alexander von Humboldt contributed to the feminized depiction of the Americas, described
for their abundance and luxuriance.[4] Denoted for its excess and lack of
boundaries, this imagery is associated with the feminine as opposed to the
rationality and reason of Kant's "civilized" man. According to Mary Louise
Pratt, Humboldt's depiction of Latin America as the "new continent," as
well as his construction of this primal world of nature as an unclaimed
and timeless space, recalls former mercantile voyeurism dating back to the
first European inventors of America, including Columbus, Vespucci, and
Raleigh.[5]

In the United States, politicians, writers, and national leaders were
also forging new ideals of masculinity in their formation of a national
citizenry in the decades following the Civil War. In *Fighting for Ameri-*

can Manhood, Kristin Hoganson shows how gender and gendered roles helped shape the imperialist discourse of U.S. politics in the late nineteenth century, exercising a keen focus on the rise of jingoism and its role in the Spanish-American and Philippine-American Wars.[6] Interestingly, Martí's perspective on gender both contrasted and intersected with late nineteenth-century jingoism. The jingoes, who equated war with masculinity, were concerned with the rise of an effeminate generation of men whose comfortable lifestyles and engagement with a "genteel style of politics based on intelligence, morality and self-restraint" would produce a weak nation.[7] Like Martí, they criticized the emergence of soft men who were a product of the conveniences and facile lifestyles afforded by the riches of modernity. Relying heavily on concepts of honor and valor, jingoes maintained that a more aggressive politics and war would strengthen American democracy by building manly character in the nation's male citizens.[8] Martí also invoked a sense of honor and valor in his writings that was strongly linked to the patriotic values supporting the project of liberating Cuba as well as maintaining sovereignty in Latin American nations. A significant difference between Martí and the North American jingoes was the former's insistence on the development of the soul in the national image that would transcend the materialistic tendencies characteristic of modernity.

Although jingoism did not become fully manifest until the onset of the Spanish-American War, the evolving posture of U.S. foreign policy during the last quarter of the century maintained many of its rising characteristics, including a virulent imperialist drive framed in racist perspectives towards the people and nations of Spanish America.[9] In fact, Beatrice Pita notes that there was a concerted effort within the United States during this time period to represent Latin American countries as black or Indian, as violent, as childlike, and as female.[10] As a political exile in New York, José Martí was very much aware of these conceptualizations of Latin America, which were often published in popular periodicals. He became one of the chief opponents of this negative image, while at the same time constructing a sense of the new modern Latin American—one who rises above the base materialism and greed that progress had engendered. Gender plays a key role in both the negative depiction of Latin American identity and in Martí's retaliation to this denigrating dominant discourse.

It is important to note that conceptualizations of gender and their relationship to the rational being had shifted considerably by Martí's time from how they were portrayed at mid-century—largely due to the displacement of the artist and the intellectual in an era of modernity—as well as to the emergence of new forms of hegemony. As a guide to progress, the intellectual was in a transitional position as a result of the importance given to positivism and modernity, which discounted aesthetic aspirations celebrated in previous generations. The scientific findings of the nineteenth century gave precedence to rationalization, utilitarianism, and the development of the individual, while the importance of art was waning. Cathy Jrade notes that many critics overlook the political nature of modernista discourse and the subtle origins of early nationalist writings within this movement. According to Jrade, the modernists searched for a language with which to communicate "their epistemological insights and ethical standing in their confrontation of the radical changes brought about by the modern world economy and their formulation of alternative paths of national development."[11] Although Martí is most widely known for fusing artistic form with his political aspirations, other artists (including Julián del Casal, Manuel Gutiérrez Nájera, José Asunción Silva, and Rubén Darío) also expressed their frustration with the sterile codes of modernity and progress, thereby contributing to nationalist agendas.

According to Jrade, Manuel Gutiérrez Nájera was one of the earlier modernista writers who noted the limitations of language and advocated greater artistic freedom in his works. His famous poem "La duquesa Job" draws on the cultural riches imported from Europe and ends with the affirmation of the poetic speaker who remains true to himself despite the abundance of riches characteristic of the modern world.[12] At a moment when artists were being displaced due to the shift in economies, many intellectuals became critical of the vulgarity of the utilitarianism of society.[13] While Rubén Darío's "El rey burgués" offers a satiric critique of society's dependence on material goods, Silva's novel *De sobremesa* provides an exemplary document of the frustration of the modernista artist and his relationship to national and global concerns.[14]

Like many of his contemporaries, Martí reacted against the cold, impotent atmosphere produced by modernity. His fourteen-year residence in the United States gave him a front row seat to the negative consequences of technological advances and the importance given to economic gains. In many of his writings, he addresses the deterioration of the soul of his North American neighbor, which was an aftereffect that he wanted to avoid in his utopian projection of the male national subject. Like the jingoes who would soon emerge on the U.S. national stage, Martí celebrated the attributes of honor and patriotism; however, an essential ingredient for this Cuban patriot was the incorporation of nurturing the soul, which was a trait that the United States had forgone.

In his prologue to Juan Antonio Pérez Bonalde's "Poema del Niágara" (1882), Martí claims that "spiritual liberty" is in jeopardy and that "the first task of man is to reconquer it."[15] The dichotomy of virile men and feminine men in his construction of a utopian Latin American identity can be seen in this prologue, where he posits the "natural" man against those other men who "like women, weak women . . . are likely to exhaust the honey sweet wine that seasoned the festivals of Horace."[16] During this "age in ruins," men are like "certain damsels, who latch onto certain virtues only when they see them praised by others."[17] These perceived virtues that Martí condemns in what he refers to as "feminized" men refer to the appropriation of ideologies and epistemologies that overlook the true nature of people and ignore the riches brought about by literature and aesthetic beauty.

In his writings, Martí utilizes gendered language as a means of instilling a heightened sense of masculinity in Latin Americans and strongly criticizes—and even emasculates—those who do not adhere to his standards.[18] In an essay published in *La América* (1883), he belittles those Latin Americans who are seduced by the greatness of the United States and France—who, like starry-eyed young lovers, do not know the value of their own worth: "So love-stricken we are with other countries that have few ties and no kinship to ours!"[19] Martí expresses his disdain for "weak men" in *Amistad funesta*, where he condemns those who blindly adopt foreign ideologies in order to appear more important. The intellectual elite in the novel are depicted for the weakness manifest in their bad management of the natural resources of their countries. Those governmental leaders are described as being "loaded with ideas from Europe and North America" and are thus considered "sterile among us because of their misguided direction."[20] Masculinity for Martí is the ability to separate oneself from the blind appropriation of learned ideologies, as well as to behold a heightened level of spirituality that transcends the decadence of materialist acquisitions promulgated by modernity.

While residing in the United States, Martí wrote for several periodicals and journals, and continued to write essays, poetry, short stories, and correspondence for publications across Latin America. Many critics note that at first he was duly impressed with the sense of freedom in his host nation. However, as Susana Rotker and Philip S. Foner have pointed out, he reveals a rising sense of anxiety about the United States that becomes evident in the early 1880s.[21] Rotker lists three significant stages in Martí's experience in the United States, beginning with his arrival to the country in 1881 when he expressed a sense of awe and admiration, and ending with "his full radicalization," referring to his goals of independence as well as maintaining Cuban sovereignty.[22] *Amistad funesta* was written during the second stage, when Martí had gained a heightened critical perspective of his host nation and began to see the inequity of U.S. foreign relations, as well as noting the excesses of materialism in New York.

In his many writings, Martí reverses conceptualizations of superiority and inferiority as he utilizes feminine imagery of excess and lack of boundaries in his description of the United States, a characterization that had been formerly assigned to Latin America. In this way, he seeks to reverse the axis of power that threatens him.[23] In an 1884 essay, he attacks the concepts of protectionism, which he regarded as a corrupt, evil system that resulted in the rich accumulating wealth.[24] Martí refers to the United States as a "colossal industrial nation," describing its factories as "Herculean mills" that resembled "hollow mountains turned upside down." He notes that because of protectionism, the U.S. economy was in a state of peril: "The market was glutted, imports increased with the mad desire for luxury, the country needed no more domestic articles than it had, and what it would need would be far less than the factories produced."[25] This description points to uncontrollability, lack of boundaries, and greed, and begins to show feminine signs of pathology as opposed to the logical masculine signs of reason. Although the illusion of pathological femininity is cast onto a mere system, and not men, Martí will later direct his invective at those who orchestrate and propagate this system, including U.S. officials dedicated to establishing trade relations with Latin America in order to dump surplus goods.

Two of these officials were James Garfield and James G. Blaine. David Healy notes that both President Garfield and Secretary of State Blaine were interested in developing trade relations with Latin America, and they were concerned about Great Britain's political penetration and interest in that region. Both men realized that Latin America sold the largest share of their exports to the U.S. market but bought the majority of its manufactured goods from Europe.[26] Furthermore, Blaine and Garfield sought a secure political climate in Central America so they could further their plans for trade relations and gain control of the isthmus.[27] Although Blaine's goals were thwarted due to Garfield's assassination in 1881, during his time in office he instigated several aggressive moves to establish trade relations with Latin American countries, including his interference in a boundary dispute between Guatemala and Mexico, and his involvement in the postwar resolutions between Peru and Chile following the War of the Pacific.[28] Martí dedicates many of his writings to Blaine, depicting him as a charismatic yet seductive individual desirous of gaining complete control in the Americas. His portrait of the Secretary is indeed lacking the qualities that Martí holds in high esteem, and is seen in accordance with the more feminine depictions of pathology that circulated in Europe during this period. One scholar noted that by the mid 1880s, Blaine had come to represent for Martí all the evil and corruption in U.S. politics.[29] Martí decries Blaine as a man who was "purchasable; who, true to his character, buys and sells in the market of men"; and a man who sought "under the pretext of treaties of commerce and peace, the wealth [from other nations] of which the economic eras of the Republican Party had begun to deprive the nation."[30]

One of Martí's principal objectives in many of the chronicles written during this time is to inform his readers of the nature of U.S. imperialism so that when they engaged in Latin American-U.S. economic relations, they would realize their own worth and not be blinded by the more enticing aspects of modernity. The chronicles in the collection *Escenas norteamericanas* (North American Scenes), for example, range from Martí's impressions of such trivialities as holidays, vacation spots, and biographical sketches, to more serious topics related to protectionism, U.S. foreign policy, and elections. Many times, Martí's deepest thoughts about U.S. imperialism, the disparity of modernity, and his position as an outsider in political exile are couched within very unassuming essay topics.

In the chronicle entitled "Las Pascuas," published in 1881, Martí provides an informative treatise about the hustle and bustle of the Christmas season in New York. Within this sketch of the holidays, he introduces the opportunist activities of U.S. officials and businessmen in Central America and Blaine's indecorous dealings. In the middle of a detailed description of riches, food, Tiffany's, and the generosity of Santa Claus, Martí alludes to the "monstrous conceptions" of a Peruvian company that "maintains that the North Americans have the rights to all the gold and riches of South America in payment for an adventurer's credit. Peru shall open all of its mines to the avaricious claimants, their streaks of gold, their veins of silver, their sources of guano, and, to guarantee the contract, their ports and railroads."[31] Martí then shifts to what must be a fabricated perception of a Christmas celebration in the White House, including President Garfield, who sits at the head of the table, and Senator Hawley, who boastfully conjectures, "And when we have taken Canada and Mexico, and we reign without rivals over the continent, what kind of civilization will we have in the future?"[32] Martí then focuses his attention on Blaine, whom he presents as one of the chief U.S. caudillos on the Spanish American stage during this time. His description of the former secretary of state positioned at the foot of the isthmus's mountains, with his arms spread wide, refusing European countries entrance into the canal territory, is reminiscent of his covetous stance towards the rights to the canal during his term of office.[33] In this and in many other chronicles, Martí responds to the aggressive stance of the United States and warns his fellow Latin Americans that they are slowly yet systematically being taken over by their northern neighbor.

The fears and preoccupations about Blaine and U.S. foreign policy expressed by Martí in these writings are reflected in the impetuous female character of Lucía in his novel. She is described for her tendencies towards hysteria, for her irrational behavior, and her desire to completely dominate Juan. Like many of Martí's chronicles and essays, the novel aims to instill a sense of virility in the Latin American national subject by provoking a sense of responsibility and accountability in national leaders. Juan's weak demeanor and submission to Lucía in the novel is an admonition to Latin American leaders and intellectuals to clear their starry-eyed gazes and beware of the seductive advances of U.S. officials in this crucial period of industrialism and expansionism.

In a January 1885 essay concerning Central America, Martí expresses that his deepest fear—that of the appropriation of Latin American territory by the United States through a series of treaties—is indeed coming to pass: "Cuba has celebrated with the U.S. government a commercial treaty that so absolutely binds the existence of the island to the United States . . . perhaps it will result, to the deep sorrow of many a Latin soul, in the loss for Spanish America of the island that should have been her bastion."[34] In this chronicle, the author condemns those Latin Americans who are eager to develop and modernize their countries "even at the cost of the nation's freedom in the future." He gives the example of Nicaragua, which had already signed a contract giving the United States the rights to territory where they had initially planned to build a canal.[35]

Time and time again, Martí alludes to the covetous desires of the United States towards the isthmus and to the pacific manner in which this modern nation acquires control over the territory that it desires. This methodical means of pursuing something and acquiring it is manifested in the seductive yet pathological behavior of Lucía Jerez in the novel. Yet Juan is not inculpable in his actions, or lack of actions. Although Juan encompasses many of the celebrated virtues that stand out in Martí's narrative, including his elevated spirit, his kindness, and his priest-like qualities, his inability to stand up to Lucía results in the death of the female character Sol del Valle, who represents the spirit of Latin America. The gendered characteristics of both Lucía and Juan are manipulated in order to achieve the ultimate goal of the novel: to reveal the unexpected consequences that will arise when Latin American leaders—represented by Juan in this case—precipitously engage in relations with the "colossus." In other words, Martí hopes to unveil to his readers the more pathological traits of modernity that otherwise seem desirable.

The Novel

During the nineteenth century, Émile Zola's *Nana* became the hallmark of naturalism in Europe, a literary movement that incorporated scientific studies and Darwinist ideas as a means of objectively examining the basest of social environments, which would then serve as metaphors for the nation. Madness or hysteria was a common illness used in novels such as Argentine Eduardo Holmberg's *Nelly* (1896), where the ills of the female body and psyche were portrayed as an allegory for the disorder and chaos of the nation.[36] The medical condition of hysteria, which was closely linked to madness, was popularized by Jean-Martin Charcot. In 1882, Charcot established a neurological clinic at the Salpêtrière Hospital in Paris where he visually exploited the different manifestations of hysteria in the amphitheater during his weekly discussions of the illness. These scientific theories and investigations positing the "abnormal" woman as degenerative influenced many Latin American writers who would link gender, race, and pathology to their nation's slow progression into modernity. Although Martí's novel is not considered a naturalist text, critics have argued that it responds to the dominant characteristics of the naturalist novels of its generation.[37] Martí's objective—to inspire the reader and form a sense of appropriate behavior for the national subject—reveals the didactic nature of his many writings, thus disqualifying him as an objective observer. However, like naturalist writers, he does employ the pathological psyche of Lucía in order to reveal the baser characteristics of modernity.

Amistad funesta was first published under the pseudonym of Adelaida Ral in the New York journal *El Latino-Americano* between 15 May and 15 September 1885. This serial novel has traditionally been considered a didactic novel or a sentimental novel like those studied in Chapter 3 of this book, available for the most part to the female audience of *El Latino-Americano* and serving as a model of how "good" and "proper" women should *not* behave.[38] Lucía's bold behavior stands out as particularly peculiar compared to the more virtuous female protagonists in the novel, including Ana, Sol del Valle, and Adela. As a result, her more masculine qualities have led to a variety of interpretations by contemporary critics, including the creation of a feminist model and a model for the Cuban independence movement.[39] My analysis of the novel complements those of recent scholars who explore the various implications of the ambiguously gendered makeup of the protagonists. I argue that Lucía reflects the discourse of degeneracy sparked by the profusion of scientific studies about gender and pathology during the nineteenth century. Her future intimate relations with Juan—much like the ignorant courtier introduced at the beginning of this chapter—will prove to be detrimental both on a personal and a symbolic level. Because Lucía reflects both the positive and negative characteristics of a modern industrial nation, she becomes a unique figure that defies traditional classifications of female characters in fin-de-siècle literature.

In a 1883 essay, Martí incorporates the word *intimidad* (intimacy) in his reference to the inevitable union that would take place between the United States and Latin American nations.[40] Martí admits that there would be benefits from this association, but he also warns Latin Americans "to stand up, look, and speak out." He utilizes the intimate relationship between Juan and Lucía as an allegory to warn fellow Latin Americans of the possible consequences of U.S.-Latin American relations. The pathological depiction of Lucía in the novel not only alludes to the precipitous conduct of U.S. foreign policy between 1881 and 1885, it also reveals the deleterious effects that modernity could inflict upon Martí's projection of his ideal subject, Juan. Furthermore, the third character introduced in the novel's love triangle, Sol del Valle, embodies the spiritual essence that Martí hopes to instill in the Latin American subject.

Lucía's opposition to Sol del Valle in the text echoes Martí's previous depictions of the materialism of citizens of the United States. In his essay "A Glance at the North American's Soul Today," he criticizes the U.S. educational system for producing materialistic men.[41] He argues that this system produces a "spiritual crudeness" that afflicts the expansive "delicate minds" of U.S. citizens. In the same essay, he urges his Latin American readers to "feed the lamp of light and reduce the beast."[42] In this analogy, Martí employs the metaphor of light in reference to the idealistic qualities that he celebrates in the Latin American subject and, conversely, that of the beast indicating the feminized, underdeveloped spirit of the North American soul. This strategy is used in like fashion in his novel, especially in reference to Sol del Valle and Lucía. Juan is confronted with the possibility of engaging with either of the two women, yet his complacent choice to stay with Lucía is quite enigmatic. Like the Latin American leaders to whom Martí refers in his chronicles, Juan is bedazzled by Lucía and ignorant of the chaos that she will provoke.

Lucía is well-regarded by many critics for her unique character and for her refusal to adhere to the status quo. She is first introduced at the beginning of the novel during a Sunday gathering with Adela and her sickly friend Ana. From the outset, Lucía defies traditional concepts of the feminine, as she is seen as active and energetic and wearing a red silk dress.[43] In addition, she stands out in contrast to the other two women since she does not adorn her summer dress with flowers, for as the narrator notes, "the flower that she liked was still unknown in the gardens: the black flower!"[44]

Throughout the text, Lucía is portrayed as an obstacle to the spiritual endeavors of Juan. Like Martí in his prologue to "Niágara," Juan alludes to the spiritual heights that one can reach in the quest to elevate the soul by separating one's self from the "tempest," or the base wants of materialism. In chapter 3, Juan cites the poem "Excelsior" by Henry Wadsworth Long-fellow in reference to the great heights he wants to achieve with Lucía at his side. "Higher," he cries, simulating the poetic voice of this inspirational poem. However, not knowing that she is meant to accompany him, Lucía cries out, "Oh no! You will not separate yourself from me. I'll take the flag from your hands. You'll stay with me. I am the highest point!"[45] The image of moving on to a higher plane with the flag in hand speaks to the lifelong patriotic mission of Martí—achieving Cuba's independence from Spain and maintaining sovereignty in Latin American nations. Lucía's incessant need to control every aspect of Juan's life is evident in her desire to thwart Juan's journey by taking the flag from his hand. In doing so, she forces Juan to choose between a spiritual ascension (Sol del Valle) and a materialistic course (Lucía), insisting that she is the more desirable goal.

In *The Female Malady*, Elaine Showalter refers to the period between 1870 and World War I as the "golden age" of hysteria because the so-called female malady had become the focus of English, U.S., French, and German physicians.[46] A significant characteristic of madness or hysteria is said to occur by "the acting out of the devalued female role or the total or partial recognition of one's sex-role stereotype."[47] In the novel, Lucía deviates from traditional codes of femininity by encompassing masculine characteristics that are revealed in her physical description, her more active demeanor, and her bold behavior. In chapter 1, she appears tall, which according to the narrator is a physical characteristic not typical for her years or her gender.[48] Similarly, Lucía's rocking chair is described as pushing more towards the front than the back as it changed position, following the energetic gestures of its owner.[49] There are numerous indications in the novel that attest to the more virile qualities of Lucía, all of which stand out in their opposition to the traditional passive role of the female hero-ine. Her egocentric behavior, however, aligns Lucía with the materialis-tic qualities of the United States described by Martí and that places her within nineteenth-century conceptions of madness or hysteria.

Lucía's egocentrism is bound to the attention she demands from Juan. This need is linked to expressions of hatred and death: "I hate a book if you are reading it," she proclaims, "and a friend if you are going to see him, and a woman if they say that she is pretty and you can see her. . . . I die of envy towards everything that you may want and that may want you."[50] Accord-ing to nineteenth-century studies on hysteria, women suffering from this disorder abandoned traditional roles of self-sacrificing daughter or mother and demanded service and attention from others.[51] The passage quoted in this paragraph exemplifies Lucía's manic need to control Juan by demanding his full attention. This situation is further aggravated by the threatening presence of the beautiful Sol del Valle, who becomes a rival of Lucía.

Sol del Valle is the poetic muse in the novel, ephemeral and free-floating. Martí refers to her as a "pearl chalice," recalling a poem of his that portrays the union of the poetic speaker with the female muse in a metafictional journey towards the creation of poetry. Although he later compares her beauty to "a cup of spirit," others would consider her "a juicy apple."[52] In this example, Martí alludes to the "uncivilized" male gaze of one that is oversexed, thus putting this gentle spirit in jeopardy. Lust, like the negative traits of materialism, poses an imminent threat to the young innocent girl.[53] Sol's elevated spirit, which is an esteemed attribute for Martí's Latin American subject, needed to be protected from the male gaze, or from the imperialist advances of the "colossus."

In contrast, Lucía's gender is once more compromised as she is indirectly associated with the lustful male gaze. Her relationship with Sol throughout the novel is dualistic in that she both desires and rejects Sol. On the one hand, she is put in the position of mentor for Sol, as she is entrusted by the schoolmaster to lead her into the social circles of society. On the other hand, the questionable erotic tensions between the two protagonists reveal the covetous representation of the imperialist advances of the United States Many critics have commented on Lucía and Sol's first encounter, when the former accidentally pricks the young Sol during an embrace, causing her to bleed.[54] The injurious effects of this initial contact not only speak to the bittersweet effects of modernity, but also serve as a forewarning of the novel's climax, when Lucía kills Sol at gunpoint. Although Juan remains loyal to Lucía throughout the novel, the reader suspects that he would have been better matched with Sol del Valle because of their shared elevated spirit. However, given the pedagogical nature of the novel, Juan is unable to break away from Lucía. While in many ways he maintains the qualities of the ideal national subject, his choice to stay with Lucía results in the annihilation of Sol, as Lucía's desire to completely control Juan is satisfied.

The parallels between this problematic love triangle and Martí's preoccupations about the imminent union between the two continents are telling. As her mentor, Lucía is responsible for Sol's well-being and her acceptance into society. Similarly, the economic advantages of the United States and its proximity to Latin America in the late nineteenth century made it a leading nation that could guide Latin American nations into an age of modernity through reciprocal trade treaties and the implementation of a modernized infrastructure. Lucía, as a member of the upper middle class, reflects the rise of the United States during an age of industrialism and expansionism, while Sol, although highly educated, is a member of the lower class, mirroring the economic devastation many Latin American countries suffered after independence.[55] Instead of a rational progression into social circles, Lucía's precipitous actions and irrational behavior prove to be deleterious to Sol's position. Acting out a fit of enraged jealousy, Lucía murders Sol, thus stifling the spirit of Latin America.

At the end of the novel, the reader is left somewhat in the dark, not knowing if Lucía will be punished for her aggressive actions. Instead of reacting to this heinous crime, Juan needs to be held up by Pedro so that he does not faint.[56] Juan, who in many ways represents the ideal man in Latin America, lacks one very important quality—a backbone, or at the very least, the adequate knowledge necessary to deal effectively with his *prometida*. Like those Latin Americans whom Martí depicts as being mesmerized by the modernity and progress of the United States, Juan is ignorant of the pathological nature of the "tempest" and will therefore suffer from the negative implications of engaging in relations with her. The climax of the novel thus exhibits one of Martí's main objectives in his many writings about Latin America and the United States—namely, to insist that nations know each other. In his more skeptical writings about the possible aggressiveness of the United States toward South America, he advocates that the leaders of different nations know what they are dealing with so that they can make appropriate transactions and treaty agreements.[57] Martí's message to his readers, through Juan's unfortunate experience, is to "stand up, look, and speak out" before engaging with this modern and aggressive nation.

The Emergence of Bi-Gendered Subjects

The United States became the object of Martí's gaze during his residency in different parts of the country. In his many writings, he employed the use of gendered language as a strategic means of both disturbing and reversing traditional perceptions of power, thereby revealing the transitory status of gender and its relationship to power in turn-of-the-century Latin America. While gendered language proved to be a successful strategy in his essays and chronicles, it produced ambiguously gendered characters when used in his novel. Many critics have noted the transcendence of Lucía's character, whose sense of individuality and autonomy defies traditional codes of femininity during that time period. González Espitia attributes Lucía's masculine qualities and her defiance of nature as factors that result in her androgynous features, enabling her to contribute to Cuba's revolutionary cause. Keja Lys Valens focuses on the homosocial relations within the love triangle, arguing that *Amistad funesta* is a national romance gone awry.[58]

My analysis stems from and points to the gendered characteristics of the main characters. Why would José Martí create such ambiguously gendered protagonists in a novel that seems to try to be a national romance? I have shown that Martí deployed gender codes for the purpose of denigrating the negative aspects of the imperialist nature of the colossus in his chronicles in order to warn his readers of the aggressive stance of U.S. foreign policy at the end of the nineteenth century. He was dedicated to unveiling the mask of seduction and revealing the more pathological traits of this modern nation par excellence. While this persuasive technique proved to be very effective in his chronicles and essays, it produced surprising results when employed in his novel. It is possible that the questionable gendered identity of its hero is precisely the reason for its failure as a national novel, which is also a contributing factor to why it constitutes such a rich and valuable reading in its production of ambiguities for today's reader.[59] The use of gendered language in the novel disrupts dichotomous views of gender, where the male is active and the female passive. Lucía succeeds in being a strong and powerful female and breaks the mold for female protagonists in genres of this type. In addition, with the exception of the significant flaw of not standing up to bullies, Juan proves to be an ideal national figure that embraces both feminine and masculine qualities, making him a unique male protagonist in Latin American narrative.

In many ways, Martí's projection of an ideal national subject is an amalgamation of the more positive characteristics of all three characters: the honest, priest-like and feminine qualities of Juan; the aggressive, virile character of Lucía; and the elevated spiritual essence of Sol del Valle. Therefore, a reexamination of this novel based on an exploration of the importance of bi-gendered subjects is indeed in order. In any case, gender codes, which were formerly used against Latin Americans, have been recoded by Martí in order to shift the axis of power as Latin American nations emerged into an era of modernity. During his years in exile, Martí heralded positive aspects of the United States, such as freedom, growth, and perseverance. He also boldly criticized what he saw to be grossly lacking. What rings strikingly familiar is the intrusive nature of U.S. foreign policy.

NOTES

This material appears in somewhat different form in Patricia Lapolla Swier, *Hybrid Nations: Gender Troping and the Emergence of Bi-Gendered Subjects in Latin American Narrative* (Madison, NJ: Fairleigh Dickinson University Press, 2009).

1. Veronese physician Hieronymus Fracastorius (1483–1553) published "Syphilis" in 1530 when he first introduced this epidemic disease in verse form. The image on the cover of the 1840 French translation of this poem is found in Sander L. Gilman, *Difference and Pathology: Stereotypes of Sexuality, Race, and Madness* (Ithaca: Cornell University Press, 1985), 106.

2. Julio Ramos argues that in the prologue to Juan Antonio Pérez Bonalde's poem "Niágara," Martí identifies the privatization of art with an exile from the polis, and thus "supercedes through the invention of new interventions and reterritorializations." Through the forging of these new spaces, we begin to see the nature and creation of a sense of *Latinoamericanismo* that becomes a recurring theme in his later writings. See Julio Ramos, *Divergent Modernities: Culture and Politics in Nineteenth-Century Latin America*, trans. John D. Blanco (Durham: Duke University Press, 2001), xxxvii.

3. In *Pueblos enfermos: The Discourse of Illness in the Turn of the Century Spanish and Latin American National Essay* (Chapel Hill: University of North Carolina Press, 1999), 16–21, Aronna argues that the discourse of degeneration emerged as a result of the scientific and philosophical theories about gender and race that culminated in the ideas of Kant and Hegel.

4. Mary Louise Pratt, *Imperial Eyes: Travel Writing and Transculturalization* (London: Routledge, 1992), 126.

5. Ibid.

6. Kristin L. Hoganson, *Fighting for American Manhood: How Gender Politics Provoked the Spanish-American and Philippine-American Wars* (New Haven: Yale University Press, 1998).

7. Ibid., 15.

8. Ibid., 15–16.

9. For racist and Darwinian elements of jingoism, see ibid., 12–13, and 36.

10. Beatrice Pita, "Engendering Critique: Race, Class, and Gender in Ruiz de Burton and Martí," in *José Martí's "Our America": From National Hemispheric Cultural Studies*, eds. Jeffrey Belnap and Raúl Fernández (Durham: Duke University Press, 1998), 137.

11. Cathy L. Jrade, *Modernismo, Modernity and the Development of Spanish American Literature* (Austin: University of Texas Press, 1998), 15–16.

12. Ibid., 37.

13. Ibid., 18.

14. Ibid., 18, 54.

15. Quoted in Ramos, *Divergent Modernities*, 310.

16. Ibid., 304.

17. Ibid., 304–5.

18. This strategy is also used later in "Nuestra América," where Martí emasculates those who are ashamed of their Indian heritage by calling them "sissies." See Ramos, *Divergent Modernities*, 296.

19. José Martí, *Obras completas*, vol. 2 (Havana: Editorial Lex, 1946), 277.

20. José Martí, *Lucía Jerez*, ed. Manuel Pedro González (Madrid: Gredos, 1969), 70–71.

21. Philip S. Foner, ed., *Inside the Monster: Writings on the United States and American Imperialism* (New York: Monthly Review Press, 1975), 41; and Susana Rotker, *The American Chronicles of José Martí: Journalism and Modernity in Spanish America* (Hanover, NH: University Press of New England, 2000), 85.

22. Susana Rotker, "The Political Gaze," in *Re-Reading José Martí: One Hundred Years Later*, ed. Julio Rodríguez-Luis (Albany: State University of New York Press, 1999), 69.

23. Susana Rotker shows how José Martí reverses the axis of colonizing/colonized through writing: "It is worth noting that the observing gaze exercises power over what is observed (the object), as it imposes the rules of its ideological game." See Rotker, *American Chronicles of José Martí*, 95.

24. José Martí, "The Fruits of Protectionism," in *Inside the Monster*, 248–52.

25. Ibid.

26. David Healy, *James G. Blaine and Latin America* (Columbia: University of Missouri Press, 2001), 17–20.

27. Ibid.

28. In the dispute between Mexico and Guatemala, he revealed his favoritism towards Guatemala, thus jeopardizing strong foreign relations with Mexico at the time. Later, he supported Peru against Chile, arguing that Chile's military aggression was encouraged by Great Britain. Blaine's intervention in the settlement treaties between the countries strongly influenced Chile's decision to accept money funded by the French bonds company Crédit Industriel. He was later accused of making this decision out of personal interest and gain. Shortly after Garfield's assassination, he resigned as secretary of state.

29. Foner, *Inside the Monster*, 42.

30. Quoted in ibid.

31. Martí, *Obras completas*, vol. 2, 1416

32. Ibid.

33. Ibid., 1417. Both the United States and England eagerly sought the rights to the Canal Zone in Central America, and Blaine had tried to eliminate the rival from the picture. During his term, he proposed a modification of the Clayton-Bulwer Treaty that had been signed between Great Britain and the United States in 1850, designed to prevent the monopoly or exclusive rights of either country to the Canal Zone. In his correspondence with the British government, Blaine consistently tried to exclude England from rights to the construction of a canal. See David M. Pletcher, *The Awkward Years. American Foreign Relations under Garfield and Arthur* (Columbia: University of Missouri Press, 1962), 63–68.

34. Martí, *Obras completas*, vol. 2, 323.

35. Ibid.

36. Francine Masiello, *Between Civilization and Barbarism: Women, Nation and Literary Culture in Modern Argentina* (Lincoln: University of Nebraska Press, 1982), 89.

37. See, for example, Cedomil Goić, *Historia de la novela hispanoamericana* (Valparaíso: Ediciones Universitarias de Valparaíso, 1972).

38. Nuñez Rodríguez claims that although this periodical was considered a family

magazine directed primarily towards a female audience, its circulation to twenty two countries in Latin America and the Caribbean reflected a much broader audience, given its coverage of Latin American topics. See José Martí, *Lucía Jerez,* ed. and with a prologue by Mauricio Núñez Rodríguez (Guatemala City: Letra Negra, 2001), 10.

39. See Olga Uribe, "La mujer como invención de lo posible," *Revista de critica literaria Latinoamericana* 15, no. 30 (1989): 25–38; in "Lucía: ¿funesta?" Memorias de la Conferencia Internacional "Por el equilibrio del mundo," *150 aniversario del natalicio de José Martí,* vol. 6 (Mexico City: Sociedad Cultural José Martí, 2003), 89–106, Juan Carlos González Espitia explores the political implications of Martí's intention of changing the novel's title from *Amistad funesta* to *Lucía Jerez* and signing the novel with his own name.

40. See Pedro Pablo Rodríguez, "Definir, avisar, poner en guardia . . . Visión martiana de Estados Unidos en La América," in *José Martí y los Estados Unidos* (Havana: Centro de Estudios Martianos, 1988), 81.

41. Blanche Zacharie Baralt, *El Martí que yo conocí* (Havana: Centro de Estudios Martianos: Editorial Pueblo y Educación, 1990), 198.

42. Ibid.

43. Enrique Anderson Imbert, "La prosa poética de José Martí: A propósito de Amistad funesta," in *Memoria del Congreso de Escritores Martianos: Febrero 20 a 27 de 1953* (Havana: Comisión Nacional Organizadora de los Actos y Ediciones del Centenario y del Monumento de Martí, 1953), 570–616.

44. Martí, *Lucía Jerez* (1969), 61.

45. Ibid., 143.

46. Elaine Showalter, *The Female Malady: Women, Madness, and Culture in England, 1830–1980* (New York: Pantheon Books), 1985.

47. Phyllis Chesler, *Women and Madness* (New York: Avon Books, 1973).

48. Martí, *Lucía Jerez* (1969), 81.

49. Ibid., 85.

50. Ibid., 146–47.

51. Showalter, *Female Malady*, 133.

52. Martí, *Lucía Jerez* (1969), 72.

53. Ibid.

54. Ibid., 156.

55. Sol's family had enjoyed some wealth when her father was still alive, but faced financial crisis after his death. Although Cuba had not yet achieved independence, after the Ten Years' War (1868–1878) the island lost former sugar markets and suffered an economic depression that would continue into the 1880s. See Louis A. Pérez Jr., *Cuba and the United States: Ties of Singular Intimacy* (Athens: University of Georgia Press, 2003), 55–56.

56. Martí, *Lucía Jerez* (1969), 202.

57. In "Washington Pan-American Congress," published in *La nación* in 1889, Martí states, "Dangers must not be recognized only when they are upon us, but when they can be avoided. In politics the main thing is to clarify and to foresee. Only a virile and unanimous response, for which there is still time without risk, can free all the Spanish American nations." Quoted in Foner, *Inside the Monster,* 340–42.

58. Uribe, "La mujer como invención de lo posible"; González Espitia, "Lucía:

¿funesta?" 89–106; Keja Lys Valens, "Between Women: Desire in Caribbean Literatures" (PhD diss., Harvard University, 2004).

59. In his preface to the novel, Manuel Pedro González states the following about the protagonist Juan: "Without realizing it, Martí portrays himself in Juan Jerez who, despite the author's intentions, reveals his alter ego. The virtues, the talent, and the nature of this character are the same esteemed by Martí himself. This identity weakens the novel and diminishes [the character of] Juan Jerez, who does not begin to measure up to his creator, but cannot be separated from him by the knowledgeable reader" (42). In *La prosa poética de José Martí* (Havana: Comisión Nacional Organizadora de los Actos y Ediciones del Centenario y del Monumento de Martí, 1953), 58, Enrique Anderson Imbert also comments on the disapproval that Martí felt for his novel, reflected in the opinions of critics.

II

A Brief Syphilography
of Nineteenth-Century Latin America

Juan Carlos González Espitia

Ideas of construction, building, and foundation are recurrent in the study of nineteenth-century Latin America. The processes of independence and the implementation of republicanism are generally presented under the positive light of agglutination and progress. In this sense, discussing ideas about a debilitating disease during the period could be seen as a marginal study—one perhaps more related to medicine and sanitation than to identity, nation building, history, or culture. This sort of inquiry into an illness could be further rejected if the name of the disease is *syphilis*, and not, for example, the less taboo *malaria* or *yellow fever*.

In this chapter, nevertheless, I will study ways in which the literary and social implications of syphilis indeed make it the most representative disease of nineteenth-century Latin America, in the same way that tuberculosis (then also known as *consumption*) functioned in Europe during the same period. Syphilis is the metaphoric Latin American malady. One of the reasons for my claim is the very origin of the disease, a source of heated debate even today between those who argue that it was brought to the indigenous people by the conquerors (together with horses, swords, and religion) and those who maintain that it was the itchy gift given by the indigenous people to the Europeans, who carried it (at the same time as parrots, pineapples, and gold) in their wooden vessels back to their countries.[1] The contested starting point of syphilis amplifies the ambivalent position of Latin American thinkers after independence: an idealized identity of clean and fructiferous origin was absolutely necessary in order to found the new nations, but their romanticization of the aboriginal past was doomed from its inception by sores and pustules.

As I will show, syphilis is also representative of Latin America in that understanding and treatment of the disease mirrored the manner in which the recently independent republics, in their search for autonomy beyond liberation, depended on modes of rationalization elaborated in and exported by European countries. Medical technology, official regulation, and literary production related to syphilis replicated the problems that resulted from the desire to attain the progress and modernity shining on the other side of the Atlantic. As I will discuss below, syphilis epitomizes how nineteenth-century Latin American societies developed a discourse of internal stratification and differentiation—not necessarily based on a specific idea of racial delineation, but more out of fear for the fate of their nations as a consequence of moral depravity. Likewise, syphilis reveals the ways in which feminine roles were assigned during this period (which we learned about in Chapter 10) and how these roles changed over time, especially in relation to the division between private and public life.

This assessment of syphilis in Latin America allows for a distinct peek into everyday life not found in many of the general studies of nation formation. With this in mind, nation conformation can be seen as the answer to specific problems such as the eradication of disease, links between illness and commerce, and ways to control female prostitutes. An approach of this sort requires a comprehensive study that goes beyond the scope of the present chapter, in particular because it entails an examination of what I call the "profane trinity" of commerce, sexuality, and disease. Maintaining its metaphorical qualities, I propose here to isolate different stages of the presence of syphilis and show, with the help of literary examples, how they relate to the nexuses of dependence, social change, and cultural production.

From Private Embrace to Public Disease

Syphilis was already present (although in a hidden fashion) at the moment of independence. In general, new republican governments approached each case of syphilis in the same way that it had been handled by colonial authorities—that is, as an individual, isolated contagion to be treated by particular doctors, and not subject to direct, official regulation. There were timid changes in the containment of prostitution, more because of the need to hide the indecent presence of prostitutes in the streets than because of syphilis itself.[2] Treatment was the radical use of mercury in its many presentations (ointments, concoctions, infusions, fumigations, tints), which produced in patients loss of hair and teeth, severe digestive problems, and—on more than one occasion—death. Doctors did not know the difference between syphilis and gonorrhea, and therefore the treatment for both diseases was practically the same.[3] The sexual origin of the disease indirectly produced a kind of leniency for its male victims; it could be said that the scars of syphilis were somehow seen as manly scars received in the "war of love." Respectable women were not supposed to enlist in that sort of combat, so syphilis for them was synonymous with exile from society.

That syphilis was connected with the expected masculine exercise of sexuality is possibly the reason why there has been a lot of veiled giggling associated with—but not much condemnation of—the claim that some of the most revered founding heroes suffered from this venereal disease. Such would be the case of General Manuel Belgrano (1770–1820), no one less than the creator of the Argentine national flag, victor of the battles of Tucumán (1812) and Junín (1813) against Spanish troops, and a man who acquired syphilis before 1796.[4] Current history textbooks prefer to avoid the stinging subject of syphilis and leave the cause of death of this founding father to the more historically acceptable and vague hydropsy known today as edema, which actually is not a disease in itself but the consequence of malfunctioning internal organs. Also lost in mythical shadows is the claim that Simón Bolívar had syphilis. Some assert that he acquired the disease in one of the frequent skirmishes with women in his liberating journeys; others allege that he was the victim of hereditary syphilis.[5] Beyond the truth or falsehood of these claims, what is important to note is that the perception of syphilis during the first half of the nineteenth century—as embodied by these two prominent characters—isolated the disease from its social consequences, indirectly approved of masculine sexual behavior out of wedlock, and deemed it not dangerous enough to be confronted with strict civil regulations.

In Latin America, syphilis became the center of debate, fear, and anxiety only when its consequences trespassed the realm of the private or the individual. In other words, syphilis gained its symbolic prominence when its consequences erased the threshold between private and public. The introduction of scientific evidence showing that syphilis was a disease with hereditary consequences radically changed its appreciation.[6] If the first half of the century had been devoted to the creation of cohesive symbolism that would serve as a *foundation* for the nation (as we saw in the first section of this book), the presence of syphilis serves as a clear example of how during the second half the prevailing endeavor was a quest to protect the nation's endangered *future*. Once syphilis was shown to infect descendants—when it threatened the nation's embodied future—the governmental and societal machinery started moving to protect the national community. The hidden first stages of the disease that would later be manifested in the form of horrible and fetid wounds became rapidly associated with the ideas of degeneration and doom portrayed in Émile Zola's Rougon-Macquart saga (1870–1893), which had been widely read by Latin American intellectuals.[7]

Latin American writers expressed the fear of degeneration related to syphilis, too. An excellent example comes from one of the characters of Brazilian author Aluísio Azevedo's naturalist novel *O mulato* (The Mulatto) (1881). Gustavo de Vila Rica is a sixteen-year-old character in the novel; he is a light-skinned descendant of Portuguese parents whom "the climate of Maranhão had not yet managed to destroy. Always in good spirits, he prided himself on his unflagging appetite and on never having fallen sick in Brazil."[8] But the clean, light, European features of the youngster are eventually shadowed by the deteriorating effects of the disease acquired, no doubt, in a hospitable bed of inhospitable Brazil: "Gustavo had in fact completely lost his lovely European coloring; his face was now mottled with syphilitic scars. He was about to marry the girl at his side, one of old Serra's daughters."[9] The reader will not know whether the wedding ever took place. What we know for sure, though, is that the offspring of this couple walking in the middle of the heat will not have a promising future. The environment and the disease—understood now as the product of reproachable sexual contact—are a source of fear.

There is not much that can be done to mitigate the character of the environment, save trying to tame it through "civilization." That said, disease is much more feared because it can remain hidden, away from the assessment of the naked eye, and ready to prey on future generations. It is precisely the champion of civilization against barbarism, Domingo Faustino Sarmiento, who makes connections between the past, disease, and the environment. In *Conflict and Harmony of the Races in America*, published in 1883, Sarmiento points out the long history of excesses of the Spanish church and state against the population that he thinks the former colonies have inherited. The image used by Sarmiento could not be more telling of the fears of his time: "We must have sufficient impetus in order to avoid the relapses, to uncover the fetid sores of our history, and the infections of which we are not cured yet, in the same way that syphilis remains latent in the blood, although its ravages are not apparent."[10] Under the seemingly normal exterior of the body—and here more specifically of the national body—looms the secret disease that may consume it without remedy. Under the deceptive charms of an enticing woman, men may well find certain death. Under the apparent beauty of foreign ideas or neighbors may reside the treacherous disease that will choke the liberty of the new nations.

Beyond recognizing the presence of disease in the male body—and, by extension, in the national body—as dangerous for the continuation of the nation, the next step was to identify the polluting source. Women, in fact, were the center of attention, often considered part of the problem and thus key to stopping the latent sickness. But not all women could be overtly blamed, for the overwhelming majority were fulfilling the obedient, homely, weak, and passive roles that had been assigned to them. The obvious group to be blamed was, of course, one in the margins of society: prostitutes.

There is no shortage of literary treatments of female prostitutes and disease. With a tongue-in-cheek appearance that is not sufficient to hide the poetic voice's fear of women who made commercial sexuality their profession, Colombian poet José Asunción Silva (1865–1896)—the renowned author of the extensively anthologized "Nocturno"—shows in "Enfermedades de la niñez" (Childhood Illnesses) the connection between the traditional early male sexual initiation with prostitutes, disease, and the disarrangement of the social structure:

> The body he embraced when his ardent
> desire enticed his anxious flesh
> was the body of a vile old courtesan,
> an untiring Juana of the human troops.
> And the divine ecstasy
> of which he dreamt in delight
> left him melancholic and predisposed
> when the lascivious caress was over.
> He did not feel the intense magic of love
> and instead he contracted . . . a good blennorrhagia.[11]

In major cities across the continent, the handling of these courtesans of the human troops mimicked the social dynamics of the time. The problem of syphilis was not a problem of many men having sexual relations with prostitutes while at the same time fulfilling their roles as fertile family patriarchs, but rather one of infected prostitutes not being duly controlled by the authorities so they could safely serve their clientele. The measures to contain prostitution clearly show how the society of the second half of the nineteenth century was stratified in a ruling class fearful of infection, a middle class with the constant desire to climb to higher positions through commerce and professionalization, a working class suffering health problems in the slums, and a marginalized group of prostitutes offering their services in dark street corners and glittering exclusive clubs to the whole spectrum of society. Being a disease that thrived especially in urban environments, syphilis stressed the traditional gap between rural and urban areas. It also provided a set of tools to articulate the role of women either as mothers and wives, or as prostitutes and lost souls. Furthermore, syphilis outbreaks led governments to shape further their politics of controlling the private sphere through education in order to attain national (public) goals of productivity.[12]

The implementation of regulations governing the exercise of prostitution was generally placed in the hands of the government branch in charge of public health and sanitation. As Diana Obregón states in her study of venereal diseases and prostitution in Colombia, the medical profession during the second half of the nineteenth century gained respectability and power as efforts to contain the disease became more successful.[13] As a result, doctors were the arbiters of how to handle the national body, so to speak, which had to be treated as a diseased body. Of course, the best remedies at hand were to be used, and in general, the remedies, regimens, and prescriptions for the ailing Latin American patient were to be found in Europe. The fight against syphilis replicated old terms of dependency and awkward relations between Latin America and European powers. Families who had the means to do so sent their young to study in Europe—particularly in France, which was not only a literary mecca but also a dynamic center of studies in medicine, with its own well-established population of diseased men and prostitutes for the study of syphilis. Brandishing titles from European universities, these new professionals then returned to their countries of origin to open their own practices or to share their knowledge in national medical schools. In the Latin America of the time, the great majority of books on the treatment of syphilis were either translations or original texts written in French or English, and as a result could be interpreted only by those who had had the means to learn those languages or who had studied in French- or English-speaking countries. This is not to claim that there was no research done by Latin American doctors; in fact, there are a strong number of dissertations evidencing the interest in observation of the disease in public hospitals and private practices, but the way in which this autochthonous research was done followed the patterns established by European academics.[14]

A telling example of the omnipresence of the European influence in the implementation of syphilis-related matters is that of the naming of the disease. Many documents related to syphilis in Latin America name the patients as *averiados*, which in Spanish means "broken" or "spoiled." Derived from the Arab word 'awār (defect, vice), its origin is not Spanish but French. During the nineteenth century, the French called syphilis *avariose* (Gustave Flaubert's favorite word for the disease that he suffered in his own flesh)—a term that ended up translated for its use in Spanish-speaking countries as *averiado* or *avariosis*.[15] José Asunción Silva, in his recurrent use of themes related to syphilis and gonorrhea in his early poetry, attests to the French influence on the Spanish language in "Filosofías" (Philosophies):

> And if from *avariosis* you were freed
> by the wise prophylaxis,
> coming to age forty, you will begin to feel
> the first stages of ataxia.[16]

These "wise" prophylactic measures implemented in the treatment of the physical disease and its supposed source were, as can be imagined, brought from Europe.

The European connection to syphilis was manifest in other ways, too. The struggle to contain the disease mirrors the amply debated ambivalent processes of modernization in Latin America in which governments tended to follow the ways that cultural and material production had been organized by the "developed" countries that previously had been their colonial masters. The process of following the pre-established pattern was complicated by autochthonous reality. As a consequence, the new nations negotiated autonomous modes of appropriation and regulation. The actions regarding brothels and prostitution in cities like Mexico, Buenos Aires, and Bogotá, for example, used French legislation as a model of cutting-edge prevention against the spread of the disease. From a literary perspective, perhaps the text that best portrays the way in which prostitution as a vector of syphilis was regulated is *Santa*, a novel by Mexican writer Federico Gamboa, first published in 1903.[17] Although its publication was relatively distant from the initial regulatory measures of the late 1870s, Gamboa's novel does give a sense of reality and perspective to what in the documents appears as remote legal jargon (or as a verbatim reproduction of the French model). For instance, it illustrates the compulsory registration of prostitutes by showing Santa's madam taking her to a sanitation exam:

> Pepa, in a very serious and severe way, warned her, "You better not contradict me, you hear? I will answer whatever needs to be answered, and you, let them do what they want . . ."
> "Let them do what they want? . . . Who? . . ."

"You ass! It is nothing bad, but the doctors may insist on examining you, do you understand?"

"But I am good and healthy, I swear to you."

"Even if you are healthy, idiot, this is what the authorities demand and it is necessary to yield to it. I will try to arrange for them not to examine you. Down! Go . . ."

Afterward she could not remember what the doctors had done, even though there had been an exceptional effort to avoid the exam. She could better remember a lithographic portrait in a varnished wood frame of a very strange gentleman in a military suit with a handkerchief tied around his head; she remembered the eyeglasses of one of the doctors, incessantly slipping down his nose; she remembered the vulgar appearance of a male nurse watching her, watching as if he wanted to eat her. . . . Of the examination itself, she remembered nothing; only that they made her lie down on a sort of table, covered with somewhat dirty rubber; that they poked her with a metal device, and . . . nothing else, no, nothing else. . . . Also that the room smelled very bad, like what they put underneath the bed of the dead, to . . . what was it called? . . . *ioto, iolo* . . . Oh! "iogroform," a stinking and sweet-smelling thing that nauseates and grips the throat.

What she could remember perfectly was that, when she got up and fixed her dress, the doctors spoke to her with extreme familiarity and even made annoying jokes about her that caused great laughter in Pepa but made her angry. She did not know what right those gentlemen had to make fun of a woman.[18]

The establishment of sanitation offices and specialized hospital wards, the compulsory periodical examination of prostitutes by governmental medical personnel, the enforcement of *zonas de tolerancia* (lenience zones)—what in English is known by the euphemism of "red light districts," the use of photographic documentation to follow medical cases, and the incipient gathering of statistical data regarding prostitutes—these are a handful of the European models implemented in Latin America.[19] Of course, the authorities made use of local inventiveness to control specific cases, as in Colombia, where authorities—not content with the weak action of assigning parts of the city to commercial prostitution—radicalized the scheme of containment by placing prostitutes in a penitentiary colony in Medellín and sending them to populate an experimental settlement far removed from Bogotá.[20] Not surprisingly, there were also many endemic obstacles that made the execution of the seemingly neat European models difficult, such as the negative reaction of the Catholic church (which would have preferred the idea of prohibition over the idea of tolerance) or, in the realm of economic reality, the lack of funding to accomplish the goals legislators had set on paper.

The implementation of European models of syphilis control in Latin America also served as a catalyst that revealed many hidden social dynamics. In Mexico City, the rules to keep brothels in check (and established to watch for any suspicious activity against decency) did not provide instructions for what to do when the prostitute in question was a man. Katherine E. Bliss states that "the *Reglamento's* assumption of heterosexuality meant that sanitary legislation completely overlooked and failed to regulate the apparently large number of male prostitutes willing to exchange sex with other men for money."[21] The fact that these prostitutes were out of the bounds of official regulation did not mean necessarily that they were not carriers of the disease; what it meant was that the law was "discovering," quantifying, and publicly uncovering the exercise of non-sanctioned sexuality. It is possible that the very same law enforcers that found syphilitic male prostitutes in the zócalo were related to those who in November 1901 arrested the infamous forty-one men caught dancing (some dressed in women's clothing) who have become the iconic founding figures of the discourse on homosexuality in Mexico.[22] With regulation, many of these secret activities (as veiled as the initial stages of syphilis) became obvious; this exposed that the pristine, solid image instituted to create national cohesion was rotting from the inside out. In a similar manner to the measures to control homosexual prostitutes in Mexico, the supervision of syphilis and prostitution in Colombia revealed that the masculine heads of the family—deemed by republican tradition to be exemplary, magnanimous mirrors of rectitude and devotion—were actually not living up to either of these attributes. Obregón reports that "according to the records of the 'service for syphilitic women' in the six years it functioned, 2,333 women had been registered, with the majority referred by the police, as well as some housemaids who had registered voluntarily. In fact, the housemaids (mainly farmer immigrants from the Boyacá and Cundinamarca regions) were the victims of seduction, abuse, and subjugation at the hands of the bosses—usually the honorable heads of the family and their sons."[23] These instances from Mexico and Colombia exemplify the decisive moment in which Latin American society began elaborating a new perspective of itself, pushed by the multiple forces that in more recent scholarship we have catalogued as the contradictory process of modernization.

Commerce and the Treatments for Syphilis

One of the best indexes of the course of modernization in nineteenth-century Latin America is commerce, and more specifically the publication of product announcements in periodicals. Modernity can be measured not only in machines, trains, eugenics, and evolutionism, but also in the development of an economic system looking for new markets. Prior to the discovery of arsphenamine and penicillin in the early twentieth century the treatment for the French disease was essentially mercury and patience.[24] There were nevertheless many other treatments that boasted their complete effectiveness in all manner of advertisements, and that capitalized on the known negative secondary effects of mercury by clearly stating they were not related to the traditional treatment of syphilis.

The medium of choice for placing ads was newspapers, which acted as true mouthpieces of the nation, and of the nation in comparison with the world. An initial assessment of the material I have been able to study about the Mexican case shows that the indicator of modernity in these announcements is the strategy of gaining customers by defending some sort of artificial originality at a moment when originality is being dulled by vertiginous mechanical reproduction. In some cases, originality is claimed by highlighting the product being sold nationally as the result of international testing and international approval. Such is the case of an early ad published in 1851 for the "Licor anti-sifilítico y depurativo del Dr. Peters" (Anti-Syphilitic and Depurative Liquor of Dr. Peters) (Figure 11.1).[25] In addition to the aura of respect derived from a foreign last name in a Mexican context, the announcement poses as a journalistic report with the title of "Interesting Discovery"; this ad is what we would call today an "infomercial." Written as a narrative bare of images or symbols, the lengthy explanation conveys scientific weightiness by stating that the medicine is the result of extended research and experimentation in New York, France, and Spain (with no mention of Curitiba, India, or Ecuador, for example), and now selflessly offered by Dr. Peters as "the most effective and powerful means discovered to the present for the healing of all the illnesses derived from the Gallic vice." As if such a blaze of originality would not suffice, the ad ends by warning the captivated reader that this medical marvel can't be found "in any drugstore of the republic, except in the French drugstore in Puebla." Spain, France, New York, English surnames, and incredible medical discoveries can now only be found in Puebla. Modernity: the world is big and small at the same time.

The sense of originality of a product, the use of foreign names, the cure of venereal diseases, and literature are all present in a poem titled

mo, á satisfacer los deseos de diversiones que quieran los concur-
rentes y que sean conformes con la opinion y gusto de la genera-
lidad de los señores presentes á esta diversion. 319— v—8

Interesante descubrimiento.

Licor anti-sifilítico y depurativo del Dr. Peters.

El autor de esta preciosa y muy especial medicina, despues de
los numerosos esperimentos hechos tanto en Nueva-York como en
Francia y España por celebridades médicas, y de las infinitas cu-
raciones que él mismo ha conseguido con dicho medicamento, se
ha determinado á dar á conocer á los dolientes el licor anti-sifilítico y depurativo como el medio mas eficaz y poderoso hasta ahora
descubierto, para la curacion de todas las enfermedades debidas al
vicio gálico, tales como úlceras ó llagas, flujos blancos de las señoras y otras enfermedades del útero, herpes, manchas de la piel,
reumas, dolores en el periosto, vulgarmente llamados dolores de
huesos, hinchazon de huesos (exostosis) callosidades en el canal
de la orina, &c. &c., y todas las demas infinitas dolencias que ocasiona el gálico ó sifilis.

El poder estraordinario de este medicamento está tan esperimentado contra el vicio gálico, que el Dr. Peters puede asegurar
la curacion radical y completa de los enfermos que quieran curar-
se bajo su direccion viniendo á Puebla, ó llamándolo á cualquier
punto.

Al tiempo que el licor anti-sifilítico y depurativo es heróico contra las enfermedades dichas, su composicon es en tal grado inofen-
siva, que puede administrarse en la edad mas tierna, sin que las
naturalezas mas delicadas hayan jamas esperimentado la menor
indisposicion con su uso; por lo contrario, el apetito no tarda en
desarrollarse, las fuerzas aumentan, el sueño muchas veces perdi-
do se recupera, y el doliente no tarda en concebir lisonjeras espe-
ranzas de su completo alivio.

Para la curacion de una enfermedad crónica se necesitan seis
frascos. El precio de cada frasco es de ocho pesos.

En ninguna botica de la República, escepto en la Botica France-
sa de Puebla, se hallarán los frascos del licor anti-sifilítico y depurativo. Las cartas, pedidos y remesas de dinero deben dirigir-
se franco de porte al Dr. Peters en Puebla.

Cada frasco va acompañado de una instruccion sobre el modo y
tiempo en que se ha de tomar el medicamento segun la edad del
enfermo. 287—10 v—10

TIPOGRAFIA DE RAFAEL Y VILA,

Calle de Cadena núm. 13.

Figure 11.1: *El universal* (Mexico City), 9 May 1851, 4.

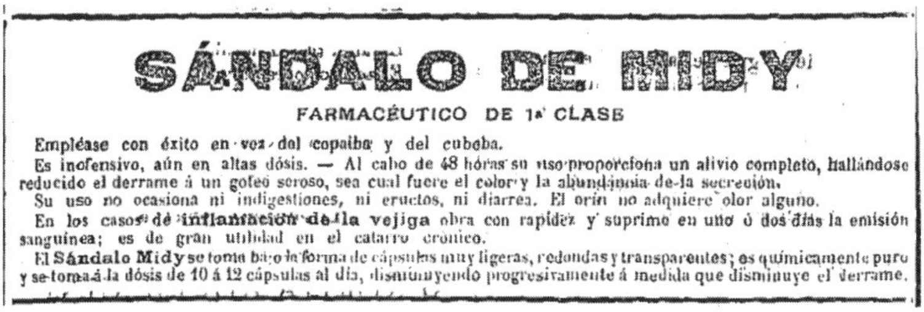

SÁNDALO DE MIDY

FARMACÉUTICO DE 1ª CLASE

Empléase con éxito en vez del copaiba y del cubeba.

Es inofensivo, aún en altas dósis. — Al cabo de 48 horas su uso proporciona un alivio completo, hallándose reducido el derrame á un goteo seroso, sea cual fuere el color y la abundancia de la secreción.

Su uso no ocasiona ni indigestiones, ni eructos, ni diarréa. El orín no adquiere olor alguno.

En los casos de inflamación de la vejiga obra con rapidez y suprime en uno ó dos días la emisión sanguínea; es de gran utilidad en el catarro crónico.

El Sándalo Midy se toma bajo la forma de cápsulas muy ligeras, redondas y transparentes; es químicamente puro y se toma á la dósis de 10 á 12 cápsulas al día, disminuyendo progresivamente á medida que disminuye el derrame.

Figure 11.2: *Diario del hogar* (Mexico City), 23 October 1885, 4.

"Capsules" by José Asunción Silva. In the poem, Silva makes reference to very specific names:

> Poor Juan de Dios. After the ecstasies
> of Aniceta's love, was unhappy.
> Three months of severe bitterness he suffered,
> and, after lingering pains,
> cured himself with copaiba and with capsules
> of Sándalo Midy.[26]

The stanza could be perfectly used as a catchphrase, but the poem ends in a suicide with a Smith & Wesson revolver, and that is not good for business. In the last verse, Silva translates from French the name of a remedy that was used for the treatment of gonorrhea and offered to the distinguished public in the form of small round pills. The product mentioned by the poet is not just any product containing a generic oil of sandalwood; it is *Santal de Midy*. In other words, the name of the product is important because it conveys the impression of imported and sanctioned effectiveness. Midy was a pharmaceutical company based in France whose products helped many a desperate and itchy man and woman from France to Canada, from Colombia to Spain, and from the United States to Mexico, where we find an ad in one of the most widely read family newspapers, the *Diario del hogar*. With this example, we can make a clear connection between the nineteenth-century commerce represented in the advertisement, syphilis as a source of fear and commerce, and poetry as a means of articulation for both (Figure 11.2).[27]

The early 1850s saw a great increase in the number of original products of the sort I just commented upon. In February 1853, the report of the *Consejo de Salubridad* (Health Council) states the denial to the petitions of sr.

Girandeau de Saint Gervai and of the professor of pharmacy D. Joaquín Guerrero to commercialize remedies against syphilis "since no secret remedy can be tested on the sick without knowing first what substance it is composed of, which is in tune with what is advised by reason and stipulated by law."[28] Some petitioners did listen to reason and to the law, such as the representatives of Anselmo Vicente, "pharmacist of the school of Paris," who sold his "New Antivenereal without Mercury by Doctor Vicente" with the clear statement that it was composed of "bicromato de potasa," and that Dr. Vicente's study on venereal diseases "has been approved [of course] as a textbook in all the Spanish universities."[29]

The ads in the 1870s show significant changes. The information is in a smaller space, with more care for the visual arrangement of the typography and more telegraphic wording. The stress on the qualities of the product signaled by the foreign names of the remedies—*Zarzaparrilla de Helmbold*, *Zarzaparrilla de Bristol*—continues to be a main selling point.[30] But, the most interesting element is the appropriation of the current scientific discourse on blood as a substance prone to be tainted and the need to maintain its purity. Of course, blood also represented the possibility of decay from one generation to the next that, as mentioned earlier, was literarily exemplified in Zola's novels from 1871 on. The idea of decaying blood and generational decomposition had already been proposed in the eighteenth century by the Count of Buffon (1707–1788) and later developed by Benedict Morel (1809–1873), Jean-Baptiste Lamarck (1744–1829), and Cesare Lombroso (1835–1909). With no exception, all of the theories elaborated by these men had been amply discussed in and appropriated by Latin American intellectual circles. The ad for the Zarzaparrilla de Bristol praises the plant's extract qualities as a "blood purifier," guaranteeing it as infallible against all the diseases derived from impurity of the blood (Figure 11.3).[31] In these ads, modernity for Latin America is presented as the need to protect or repair the prospective qualities of blood. This idea is further stressed in an 1882 advertisement for the "fluid extract of vegetable juices," which already incorporates the observations of doctors such as Jonathan Hutchinson about the hereditary character of syphilis.[32] The announcement targets the population of children who had acquired the disease by assuring their parents that the extract "is the most innocent and at the same time the most efficient BLOOD PURIFIER," and by offering directions for children under five years of age—they just had to take "five drops to a teaspoon in the same way as adults."

In many ads for syphilis cures, modernity posed in the garb of solutions bordering on the fantastic. Seen with twenty-first-century eyes, some of these announcements do not look as fantastic as they did in their day,

Figure 11.3: *Diario del hogar* (Mexico City), 2 May 1882, 4.

but appear rather as shameless hoaxes, such as a complete cure for pneumonia, pox, and syphilis via hydrotherapy.[33] Healing sun baths were also a possibility: "Syphilis and all the diseases of the blood are ousted by the system of our sun baths."[34] Or one could have tried the "Thermalume system [that] cures by cleansing pores to remove all the impurities ingrained in them."[35] There was also the possibility of preventive war against venereal diseases: "In my consulting room, one can purchase certain flasks whose liquid contents completely prevent the acquisition of any venereal disease."[36]

But some fantasies may well be true. While announcing the cure of syphilis using the classic "Ricord System," Dr. Adrián Rodríguez promoted the use of "X rays to examine the sick."[37] Rodríguez made use of the discovery that German physics professor Wilhelm Conrad Röntgen had revealed just a few years before, in 1896. This shows the great speed with which Latin America adopted new technologies while at the same time struggling with long-standing problems derived from still-rigid social and political structures. With its mix of new and old, the use of art nouveau decorative elements, and its great emphasis on images, Rodríguez's newspaper advertisements indeed represent the turning point of the turn of the century. The perception of venereal disease also changed radically from one of regulatory interest to one of methodic prevention. In contrast to the implied acceptance of syphilis in the early 1800s as a disease resulting from manly sexual drives, the last years of the nineteenth century saw

Figure 11.4: *El imparcial* (Mexico City), 16 February 1899, 4.

it as a stigma that could be passed on to new generations. That is the message implied in an announcement for the seemingly popular Antisifílitico Oriental Africano (Oriental African Anti-syphilitic), summoning "all those who suffer from Secret Diseases" to be cured like "10,000 sick [were] cured in 3 years." This marvelous "benefit to humankind" shared commercial space on the same page with the absolutely guaranteed "Hermin Hair Dye" (Figure 11.4).[38]

Diseased Nations and Literary Representations

In a course of action that parallels the problems of contemporary approaches to regulation—who should be controlled, the producer or the consumer?—Latin American governments during the nineteenth century struggled to contain what they considered the main vector of syphilis—found, as the argument went, in female prostitutes. In opposition to those debased yet necessary social actors were the mothers and wives who conformed to their homely, passive roles. The problem of syphilis got out of hand when the obedient, normalized women bore diseased children as a result of fulfilling their conjugal duties with infected husbands. Furthermore, the deeper problem was that the future of the nation represented in newborns was steadily being condemned to doom. This changing dynamic is literarily portrayed in three novels: Mercedes Cabello de Carbonera's *Blanca Sol* (1889); Federico Gamboa's *Santa* (1903), which we have already mentioned; and last, *La herencia de la sangre* (1919), written by Claudio de Alas.

Blanca Sol offers the view of a society that trapped respectable women in a conundrum of social codes that ultimately turned them—perhaps literally—into disreputable and debased beings. The protagonist supposedly falls from the heights of her name to the darkness of lust in her straying search for material pleasure. She turns to prostitution not only as revenge against the society that shaped her, but also as an escape route from misery for her and her children. Although society (that is, the nation) has failed her, the children must be preserved for the future of that nation. Cabello de Carbonera's character ironically reflects the process that marginalized her author. The cause of the alleged insanity of Cabello de Carbonera, of which many critics accused her, may well have been the last stage of the syphilis that her husband, Dr. Urbano Carbonera, infected her with.

Federico Gamboa's *Santa* shows the perspective of the underprivileged woman who is pushed by social and economic circumstances to become a prostitute. As her name suggests, Santa expiates her deviation from the path of righteousness by dying right after being cut and opened in one of the hospitals that, with its "autoclave for sterilizing instruments and bandages, a manometer, exactly like those of the machine boilers," represents newly acquired technology and progress.[39] Yet, Santa dies without progeny—in fact, while being subjected to a hysterectomy—almost as if, after careful assessment and documentation, the author meant to phase out her segment of society.

The last stage in this literary progression of the role of women, prostitution, and disease as cultural markers is represented by Claudio de Alas's *La herencia de la sangre*, the only novel of the three whose main topic is clearly syphilis and its frightful consequences.[40] Claudio de Alas is the pseudonym of Colombian writer Jorge Escobar Uribe (1886–1918), who at an early age exiled himself from his country and developed his career as a poet and journalist in Chile. In 1917, Alas decided to move to Buenos Aires in search of better opportunities for his literary career, but his expectations were rapidly answered with rejections. The poet decided to kill himself. Juan José de Soiza Reilly was entrusted with the publication of the manuscripts left by Alas; therefore his novel and most of his poetry appeared posthumously. *La herencia de la sangre* is allegedly based on real facts about the Chilean high society of Santiago, and most likely was written by Alas before 1917. Since the novel is not clearly located in a specific country, but generally situated in a developing capital city, it allows for a generalization of its broad features to all of Latin America.

The novel characterizes the destruction produced by syphilis among the high social strata and the groups that until then had been considered the trendsetters of the nation's future. Although the text does not show the affluent ranks of society as subject to economic or class downfall, they are not placed under a flattering light, either, for the venereal disease functions as an equalizer. It is likely that the sensitive topic of the bourgeoisie having syphilitic chancres may have accounted for the near-absence of literary criticism related to this work, especially with Alas's blunt style: "He repeated the words of a great 'syphilographer' of the city, whose clientele was the 'high-life'—that class in which the pustules and the bruises produced by the infection were not supposed to flourish, not under the satin corsets or under the splendid frock coats."[41]

Nevertheless, by 1920, one of the publishing houses printing *La herencia de la sangre* was on its fourth edition, and everything indicates that the novel was commercially successful and widely read. The reception of this book is parallel to that of the play *Ghosts* (1881), written by renowned Norwegian dramatist Henrik Ibsen.[42] *Ghosts* also points to the hidden disease that thrives among the rich but is constantly cloaked under the appearance of moral rectitude, good manners, feigned philanthropy, and praise for nobility and "good blood." Ibsen was heavily criticized, accused of nihilism, and of advancing a personal agenda through the speech of his characters, two indictments that certainly could have been uttered against Alas in Buenos Aires, Bogotá, or Santiago, but that he could not hear in his grave. *La herencia* appears with a difference of thirty-eight years from its European predecessor, but illustrates the same kind of hereditary horror iterated by Oswald, the Ibsen character who has inherited syphilis from his publicly respected yet privately ignoble father: "The sins of the fathers are visited on the children."[43]

Alas's book begins with what we could identify as a national couple, but unlike many of the romantic examples with which we have become accustomed, the union of these two idealized individuals happens without major obstacles. We actually see them in the suspect environment of their private room. The scene is ominous, nevertheless, since the recently married Víctor Bernal lies sick while his beautiful wife Alba tends to him. The nub of the novel is not about the hovering desire to witness the two lovers conquering every obstacle in order to be together—in other words, the desire to see them as founders—but about the uncertainty of survival of the sick man that translates into skepticism about the future of the narrated society. Aristocratic, rich, handsome, and knowledgeable, Víctor has made the almost mandatory pilgrimage for people of his status to Paris. But Paris—the city of magnificent fairs, libraries, science, and art—is the source of the disease that is exterminating him with unusual fury. The idealized metropolis is not the model to follow anymore. It is the vortex-like place that sucks life from the Latin American men willing to risk being too close to it. Paris presents the Latin American young male aristocracy with the flower of syphilis.

The feminine character, Alba, is as full of light and beauty as her name hints; she is the epitome of the woman in whose womb and on whose heart the nation rests. She is sexually appealing to her husband while devoted to her obligations as a housekeeper. She is a silent sufferer of the tests placed on her by life—just the fact that she is putting up with a syphilitic husband should suffice to convince us. She is the fertile ground to bear children that will uphold the name of the family. She seems so in accordance with masculine expectations that she is almost as dull as a blank canvas. Instead of criticizing or questioning the reasons for the venereal disease of her husband, she keeps quiet and offers him more tea. The only moment when she seems to be the owner of her self is when she seduces Víctor to have intercourse, in spite of his initial fear of transmitting the disease.

The external symptoms of syphilis in Víctor are radically treated by Alfredo Grott, the eminent doctor educated in France and Prussia, the cold observer of society and of the human condition, and the man who seems skeptical of the chances of overcoming the presence of "the great evil" of syphilis: "Yes, my friend, the evil is everywhere: you find it in the high spheres, as well as in the misery of the mob. The statistics are frightening. Eighty per cent of the country is contaminated. This can only be compared to Turkey or France. . . . If world medicine is not able to contain this great tide of rottenness, the future generations will be a pile of misery, of decrepitude and of contagion."[44] Grott has the knowledge and the technique to counteract the disease, which allows Víctor to partake of the social gatherings proper of his class once again. In these gatherings, he endures the veiled mocking comments about his scars. He endures them because he knows that every member of this society has had some sort of acquaintance with the veiled evil. Having the economic means that reward him with propriety, he knows that it is only a matter of patience before he will be back in the position of respectability he deserves.

Yet the law of inheritance that gives the title to the novel cannot be surmounted with money, status, or time. As a result of his intercourse with Alba, a child is born. The initial fear is dissipated when the baby boy does not present any sign of congenital syphilis. The future of the patrician family is apparently secured in the male offspring, "but amid that love, amid that tenderness, amid that silent tuning fork of affections and fulfilled hopes, the future was raising its foggy silhouette." Indeed, the strict law of nature takes action, and after a few days, the child shows the mark of syphilitic wounds on his face. Víctor cannot bear having transmitted the disease to his own son and kills himself. In a final letter—yes, there is the trite device of the suicide note—Víctor explains that he would have liked to kill his own son "to promote morals, to avoid the continuation and expansion of the horrible misadventure of my illness through him," but he is not brave enough to do it, and this move actually allows for the continuation of the life of the diseased through his son.[45]

La herencia de la sangre shows the belated change of perspective in regard to the role of men rather than women in the spread of syphilis in Latin America. Men, the consumers, became directly responsible for the ominous future of their countries. The book also marks a turning point in the ways in which governments tackled the problem. There was a noticeable reduction of the regulatory measures on prostitutes and an increasing emphasis on the importance of education, and prevention campaigns lasting well into the 1950s in most countries.

The other idol that this novel manages to destroy is that of matrimony. During the nineteenth century, the publicly sanctioned union was the main prescription to preserve the health of the nation. Matrimony was the means of combating masturbation, which actually was even more feared than prostitution. Matrimony was the best path to bring new blood into the economy and for the good and the strength of the nation. Matrimony was the answer to moderate prostitution, which had been considered a necessary evil for young male sexual initiation, a source of relaxation for the overworked gentleman, and a necessary escape valve to tame the sexual drive of young bachelors without money to start a family. Matrimony served the great purpose of tempering all the excesses that could harm society. The formula of matrimony had been extremely useful until the end of the nineteenth century because it led to the solidification of social bonds and the assurance of a basic structure for society embodied by family. But hereditary syphilis ruined it all. The intangible bond of matrimony stopped being sufficient to secure the future of the nation, for the social benefits of marriage dissipated the closer the husbands got to the zones officially accepted for prostitution. Víctor was married and loved by an ideal woman. He was ready to provide the nation with a child that could serve it in the future. But the ghost of syphilis was more powerful than that.

The use of the noun *ghost* to qualify syphilis in Latin America is appropriate given that the disease was both intangible and ubiquitous. Nevertheless, as with ghosts, the source of the "paranormal activity" could be traced directly to spent energy—in this case sexual energy. In spite of attempts to blame the contagion of syphilis on shared handkerchiefs, holding hands, and suddenly infected wounds, the main cause of syphilis was clearly sexual relations—most likely consensual or paid. Unlike yellow fever, for example, syphilis could not be attributed to unhealthy regions or populations of a nation, to a barbaric untamable nature inhabited by equally uncultivated people, or to polluted waters.

In this sense, syphilis escaped the structure of opposition between a civilized and progressive Western geography and a doomed, immature New World populated by societies prone to crises, as interestingly described by Benigno Trigo in his reading of European travelers Alexander von Humboldt and Gaspard-Theódore Mollien.[46] The reason why syphilis was not used as another example of inferiority is that it was also found in Europe, where it was an even more pervasive problem than in the former American colonies. Syphilis was a cosmopolitan disease, without a doubt—one that always appeared side by side with what was considered civilized. It was a disease that equalized both hemispheres; it was a degenerative menace that could not be connected to a specific Latin American racial group as a vector of decay. Thus, at the national level, syphilis was a very egalitarian, democratic, and republican ghost, and its characteristics did not provide an easy way to structure a discourse of segregation based on race. That syphilis was a problem increasingly in need of containment exposed the reality that blood was being mixed at all levels. Paradoxically and annoyingly for the whites of the time, this revelation could be seen as evidence of the supposed foundational desire for bridging differences of racial origin depicted in Latin American romantic fictions.

The physical effects of syphilis could not be racialized simply because the effects of the disease were equal for all races. The case of Gustavo de Vila Rica in Azevedo's *O mulato* is a good example of the difference between the consequences of the venereal disease and the impact of the environment where one lives. The fact that Vila Rica's skin color turns from white to grey is not because of syphilis, but because nature—tropical nature—finally takes its toll. The scars of syphilis on his face point to something different: that the offspring of his relations with the daughter of native Joaquim Furtado da Serra will be equally destined for decay, even if their skin is as light as that of his father when he was a carousing young son of Portuguese ancestors. Here it is the national race and not particular races within the nation that is under the siege of syphilis.

As I have argued, syphilis was an urban disease. It contradicted the opposition between city and countryside where the rural factor was invested with negative qualities of backwardness and regression. As a paradoxical complement to Trigo's discussion of rural disease as a menace to the "whiteness" of the country, the fashion in which syphilis spread in the urban environment opposed the idea of a supposedly inferior population—also supposedly racially inferior—inhabiting the periphery of the nation, diseasing it, feminizing it, and ultimately degenerating it.[47] Nancy Leys

Stepan's observations on eugenics explain how syphilis was more directly connected to issues of poverty rather than race: "At the same time as expectations about the control of disease increased, the diseases most often associated with poverty—tuberculosis, venereal infections, alcoholism—pushed at the limits of medical knowledge and social expertise."[48] Indeed, the need to contend with syphilis reinforced previous structures of differentiation based on class more than on race. Granted, the parallel between class and race in Latin America that we still see today has its origins in the nineteenth century, and phenomena like the institutionalization of prenuptial certificates provided a tool to control marriage among individuals alleging health reasons while implicitly keeping in check disparate class and race relationships. The move to hinder the pairing between a syphilitic and a healthy person—an idea sketched in Alas's novel—seems not to be necessarily related to the disease itself, but to the imperative of maintaining a healthy pool of individuals at each strata of society that could continue with the order necessary for progress. In other words, it seems to have been more dangerous for the desired nation to see a marital relation among individuals belonging to different social strata than a relationship between a syphilitic Víctor and a healthy Alba. In sum, syphilis played a role in the fear of degeneration, not in terms of race but in relation to the unhealthy habit of bridging social classes.

Conclusions

I have in front of me a magnified photograph of the *Spirochaeta Pallida*, the almost invisible cause of syphilis. It is entangled, convoluted, and repetitive. It fascinates me that such a small thing influenced so many segments of society and produced so many changes in the Latin American national body. Transferred in the private or secret sites of intimacy, its later public appearance could not be hidden. Its pervasiveness trespassed on the distinctions of race, class, political views, and gender that outlined the features of the nation, but at the same time the disease acted as an enforcer of the very same distinctions. The unavoidable presence of syphilis during the nineteenth century acted as a reminder of the unproductive materials that were also part of the national makeup.

Accurately traceable in its literary representations, syphilis as an expression of social and political changes constitutes a rich source of study of the interconnections between medical discourse, commerce, sexuality, and public policy. Throughout this chapter, I have composed a preliminary picture, very much like that of the *Spirochaeta* I just mentioned, in which the sinuous pattern reveals the course of *sífilis* and how public, private, and official perceptions of it shifted during the nineteenth century. The disease would survive in Latin America through the first half of the twentieth century, and there are still cases of it even today. Its iconic qualities would remain in policy making, in links to commerce, in the change of approaches to sexuality, and in the transformation of gender roles. Furthermore, the ways syphilis was addressed would be transformed during the last part of the twentieth century and what has passed so far of the present one with the surge of its perhaps more devastating corresponding disease, AIDS. But that would be material for another book: one on the third centennial of independence, on the re-rooted cultures, identities, and nations and the building of twenty-first-century Latin America.

NOTES

I want to thank William G. Acree Jr. for his great help and his almost biblical patience with revising this chapter. I am also grateful for the assistance of Diane McKenzie of the Health Sciences Library at the University of North Carolina at Chapel Hill for her help with medical references to syphilis during the nineteenth century in Europe and Latin America.

1.   For a useful introduction to the debate of the origins of syphilis, see Alfred W. Crosby, *The Columbian Exchange: Biological and Cultural Consequences of 1492* (Westport: Greenwood Press, 1972).

2.   Here I am following broadly the useful study on prostitution in Mexico during the nineteenth century by Fernanda Núñez Becerra, *La prostitución y su represión en la Ciudad de México (Siglo XIX)* (Barcelona: Gedisa, 2002). Núñez Becerra's book has been crucial to the development of the present chapter.

3.   It was not until 1838 that Philippe Ricord, in his *Traité pratique des maladies vénériennes* (Paris: Just Rouvier et E. Le Bouvier, 1838), showed the difference between the two diseases and the distinct kinds of treatment needed.

4.   Felipe Pigna, *Los mitos de la historia argentina: La construcción de un pasado como justificación del presente; Del "Descubrimiento" de América a la "Independencia"* (Buenos Aires: Grupo Editorial Norma, 2004), 373.

5.   Luis Salazar Martínez, *El parricidio de Santa Marta: Simón Bolívar asesinado* (Caracas, 1997), 29. In 1916, Diego Carbonell published *Psicopatología de Bolívar*, a positivist interpretation of Bolívar's persona in the vein of the classifications in *The Man of Genius* (1889) by Cesare Lombroso. Carbonell asserts that since Bolívar's father "was probably a megalomaniac and, as a result, with general paralysis, Bolívar should have been heredito-syphilitic, since that later disease is considered a form of nervous syphilis. Being heredito-syphilitic, it is not surprising that he was irritable, headstrong, and a restless youth. Naturally, there must have been a cause or lesion that would explain as heredito-syphilitic that restlessness mentioned by Perú de Lacroix: the scarce data taken from the practice by the physician Révérend should allow us to locate in the meningeal vessels and in the brain cortex that lesion of which we know so little." *Psicopatología de Bolívar* (Caracas: Universidad Central de Venezuela, 1965), 150. Though weak by contemporary medical standards, Carbonell's connection of megalomania to syphilis interestingly reveals a move to revise the almost

mythical qualities with which many of the heroes of independence were invested during the 1800s. I want to thank Christopher Conway for leading me to this under-studied work by Carbonell.

6. Cohesive explanation of the signs of hereditary syphilis was published for the first time in 1861 by English surgeon Sir Jonathan Hutchinson in "Clinical lecture on heredito-syphilitic trauma: and on the teeth as a means of diagnosis," *British Medical Journal* 1 (1861): 515–17.

7. Between 1871 and 1893, French naturalist writer Émile Zola published a series of twenty novels narrating the life of two strands of the same family: the Rougons—the legitimate, socially elevated side, exemplified in *Doctor Pascal* (1893)—and the Macquarts—the illegitimate, underprivileged, and debased side, epitomized in *Nana* (1880), the famous story of the street prostitute that rises to become a celebrated *cocotte*, but who finally dies of smallpox. With great detail on the influx of heredity and environment in the development of human behavior, the novels recreate the society and culture of France during the Second Empire of Napoleon III.

8. Aluísio Azevedo, *Mulatto*, trans. Murray Graeme MacNicoll, ed. Daphne Paptai (Rutherford: Associated University Presses, 1990), 51.

9. Ibid., 294.

10. Domingo Faustino Sarmiento, *Conflicto y armonía de las razas en América* (Buenos Aires: S. Ostwald, 1883), 173.

11. José Asunción Silva, *Obra completa*, ed. Héctor H. Orjuela (Nanterre: ALLCA XX, 1990), 80. The book in which this poem first appeared, *Poesías*, was published posthumously in 1908, but many of the poems related to syphilis and gonorrhea were probably written around 1885.

12. Focused studies on disease, society, and governmental regulation in particular include Diego Armus, "Tango, Gender, and Tuberculosis in Buenos Aires, 1900–1940" in *Disease in the History of Modern Latin America: From Malaria to AIDS*, ed. Diego Armus (Durham: Duke University Press, 2003); Sergio González Rodríguez, "Cuerpo, control y mercancía: Fotografía prostibularia," *Luna Córnea* 4 (1994): 73; Gabriela Nouzeilles, "Ficciones paranoicas de fin de siglo: naturalismo argentino y policía médica," *MLN* 112, no. 2 (1997): 232–52; and Jorge Salessi, *Médicos, maleantes y maricas: Higiene, criminología, y homosexualidad en la construcción de la nación argentina (Buenos Aires, 1871–1914)* (Rosario, Argentina: Beatriz Viterbo, 1995).

13. Diana Obregón, "Médicos, prostitución y enfermedades venéreas en Colombia (1851–1886)," *História, ciências, saúde—Manguinhos* 9 (2002): 161–86. Obregón's insights have been extremely helpful in my approach to the interaction of medicine and regulation with syphilis.

14. The earliest nineteenth-century document that I have been able to find related to syphilis and the need to create regulations against its spread in a Latin American city was written by the (of course French) traveler and diplomat Henri Ternaux de Compans: *Influjo del clima y de la policia sobre el ecsito de varias enfermedades reynantes en Arequipa: Referencia de ellas á un mismo genero de lesion, y efectos macsimos de los acidos minerales y el mercurio en su curacion* (Arequipa: Imprenta del Gobierno, 1829). One example of the dynamic of reproduction of European knowledge for its use in Latin America is a book titled *Instrucción popular sobre el gálico o sífilis, o su curación racional y segura con*

    los medicamentos y método del doctor H. W. Forwel (Bogotá: Imprenta de Guarín, 1877).

15. I will not delve in the other French related names for the disease such as *morbo gálico, gálico*, or *mal francés* because their origin has been traced back to the fifteenth century.

16. Silva, *Obra completa*, 89.

17. In Chapter 7, Stuart Day studied Gamboa's theater piece *La venganza de la gleba* and the performative negotiations he developed in relation to Porfirio Díaz's rule.

18. Federico Gamboa, *Santa* (Mexico City: Eusebio Gómez de la Puente Editor, 1927), 12–14.

19. Since regulations in some Latin American cities forced prostitutes to periodical examination, they provided a "captive" statistical population.

20. Obregón, "Médicos, prostitución y enfermedades," 166. In Chapter 3, Amy E. Wright points to the removal of Antonio, the main character of Justo Sierra O'Reilly's *Un año en el Hospital de San Lázaro* (1845), to a leper's colony that replicates the measures of containment applied to infected prostitutes. Things go well for Antonio, for instead of leprosy he "just" seems to be infected with syphilis.

21. Katherine Elaine Bliss, "Between Risk and Confession: State and Popular Perspectives of Syphilis Infection in Revolutionary Mexico," in Armus, *Disease in the History of Modern Latin America*, 188. Bliss's essay is especially useful on the topic of syphilis and politics in Mexico after 1900. The same gap in regulation in relation to male prostitution for the case of Buenos Aires is commented on by Donna J. Guy, *Sex and Danger in Buenos Aires: Prostitution, Family, and Nation in Argentina* (Lincoln: University of Nebraska Press, 1991), 85–86.

22. Bliss, "Between Risk and Confession," 188. For a re-rooting exploration of this crux long before the facts of 1901, see Christopher Conway's "Birds of a Feather" in this volume.

23. Obregón, "Médicos, prostitución y enfermedades," 167.

24. Sahachiro Hata discovered the anti-syphilitic properties of arsphenamine in Paul Ehrlich's laboratory in Germany in 1908; this drug was then commercialized as "Salvarsan" and "606" in 1910. In the 1920s, penicillin—the mother of all remedies against syphilis—was discovered, but it was not regularly used against the venereal disease until the late 1940s. In Rosalina Estrada Urroz, "La influencia de ultramar: Medicina y sociedad en México, siglos XIX y XX," *Nuevo Mundo Mundos Nuevos* 7 (2007), *nuevomundo.revues. org/sommaire2893.html*. The author follows how Salvarsan sparked attacks from a group of Mexican doctors who defended the excellence of the French medical academy against the supposed commercialized interests of the German scientists producing the drug known as 606. Although this is relevant to my discussion on commerce, modernity, and dependency, the fact that 606 was not used until 1910 precludes my going into further detail. While the discovery of penicillin has been attributed to the 1928 conclusions of Scottish scientist Sir Alexander Fleming, there is evidence that by 1927 a Costa Rican doctor, Clodomiro Picado Twight, had reported his study on the effects of *Penicillium sp.* on bacteria of the types *Streptococcus* and *Staphylococcus*. See Édgar Cabezas

Solera, *El onceavo mandamiento: Desconfiar de sí mismo y del prójimo; Clorito Picado y la antibiosis, contribución al conocimiento del sabio costarricense y su aventura relacionada con el descubrimiento de la penicilina* (San José: Editorial Nacional de Salud y Seguridad Social, 1993).

25. *El universal* (Mexico City), 9 May 1851, 4.
26. Silva, *Obra completa*, 78.
27. *Diario del hogar* (Mexico City), 23 October 1885, 4.
28. *El universal*, 14 February 1853, 2.
29. Ibid., 13 October 1853, 4.
30. *La voz de México* (Mexico City), 7 July 1870, 4. See also *Diario del hogar*, 2 May 1882, 4.
31. *Diario del hogar*, 2 May 1882, 4
32. Ibid., 27 October 1882, 4.
33. *El universal*, 8 October 1849, 4.
34. *El imparcial* (Mexico City), 4 April 1897, 2.
35. Ibid., 29 April 1897, 2.
36. Ibid., 2 July 1897, 4. There is a similar product advertised in *El imparcial*, 27 October 1898, 4, with the statement that "with the use of these pills, there will be no more syphilis from now on, nor venereal disease of any kind."
37. *El alacrán* (Mexico City), 16 September 1899, 3.
38. *El imparcial*, 16 February 1899, 4.
39. Gamboa, *Santa*, 339.
40. Claudio de Alas, *La herencia de la sangre* (Buenos Aires: Editorial Forjador, 1920).
41. Ibid., 26.
42. Henrik Ibsen, *Ghosts*, trans. and with an introduction by Stephen Mulrine (London: Nick Hern, 2002).
43. Ibid., 37. Europe was not immune to retrograde behavior. Ibsen's play was performed for the first time in 1882 in Chicago. Later performances in Scandinavia and the rest of Europe were not very successful because of the negative reactions of literary commentators.
44. Alas, *La herencia de la sangre*, 20.
45. Ibid., 109, 112.
46. Benigno Trigo, *Subjects of Crisis: Race and Gender as Disease in Latin America* (New Hampshire: Wesleyan University Press, 2000).
47. Ibid., 69–89.
48. Nancy Leys Stepan, *"The Hour of Eugenics": Race, Gender, and Nation in Latin America* (Ithaca: Cornell University Press, 1991), 43.

Contributors

Hugo Achugar is a poet, essayist, and Professor of Latin American literature and culture at the University of Miami. He has taught at the Universidad de la República (Uruguay), the University of California at Irvine, Dartmouth College, and Northwestern University. He is the author of numerous scholarly books and edited collections, including *Planetas sin boca: Escritos efímeros sobre arte, cultura y literatura* (2004), *Derechos de memoria: Nación e independencia en América Latina* (2003), *La fundación por la palabra* (1999), and *Poesía y sociedad: Uruguay, 1880–1911* (1985).

William G. Acree Jr. is Assistant Professor of Spanish at Washington University in St. Louis. His present research centers on print and popular cultures in nineteenth-century Latin America, especially in the Río de la Plata region. He is co-editor with Alex Borucki of *Jacinto Ventura de Molina y los caminos de la escritura negra en el Río de la Plata* (2008). Acree is currently completing a book that studies the development of print culture and its links to collective identity in Uruguay and Argentina from 1780 to 1910.

John Charles Chasteen has taught Latin American history at the University of North Carolina at Chapel Hill since 1990. He is the author, editor, and translator of numerous books. The most relevant to the study of nineteenth-century Latin America are *Heroes on Horseback: A Life and Times of the Last Gaucho Caudillos* (1995); *National Rhythms, African Roots: The Deep History of Latin American Popular Dance* (2004); and *Americanos: Latin America's Struggle for Independence* (2008). He recently completed a translation of the naturalist novel *Santa* (1903) by Federico Gamboa.

Christopher Conway received his PhD from the University of California at San Diego in 1996 and is Associate Professor of Spanish at the University of Texas at Arlington. He is the author of *The Cult of Bolívar in Latin American Literature* (2004) and the editor of Ricardo Palma's *Peruvian Traditions* (2003). His journal articles and book chapters include studies of journalism during the wars of independence, the life and times of Ignacio Manuel Altamirano, and children's literature in nineteenth-century Mexico. Conway's current research and publications focus on the United States-Mexico War.

Stuart A. Day is Associate Professor of Spanish at the University of Kansas and editor of the *Latin American Theatre Review*. His book *Staging Politics in Mexico: The Road to Neoliberalism* was published in 2004. He has also published an anthology of Chilean and Mexican plays and co-edited, with Jacqueline E. Bixler, the collection *El teatro de Rascón Banda: Voces en el umbral* (2005). Day has published book chapters on Mexican theater, as well as numerous articles, play introductions, and interviews in a variety of journals.

Juan Carlos González Espitia is Associate Professor of Spanish at the University of North Carolina at Chapel Hill. He is the author of *On the Dark Side of the Archive: Turn of the Century, Nation, and Literature in Spanish America* (forthcoming). He has published several studies on the unorthodox Colombian writer José María Vargas Vila and is currently working on a Hispanic literary history of syphilis.

Beatriz González-Stephan is the Lee Hage Jamail Chair of Latin American literature at Rice University and the recipient of the *Casa de Las Américas* Prize in 1987. Her books include *La historiografía literaria del liberalismo hispanoamericano del siglo XIX* (1987); *La duda del escorpión* (1992); *Crítica y descolonización: El sujeto colonial en la cultura latinoamericana* (with Lucia Costigan, 1992); *Esplendores y miserias del siglo XIX: Cultura y sociedad en América Latina* (with Javier Lasarte y Graciela Montaldo, 1995); *Cultura y tercer mundo* (1996); *Fundaciones: Canon, historia y cultura nacional* (2002); and *Galerías del progreso* (with Jens Andermann, 2006). She is currently working on the following projects: *Andrés Bello y los estudios latinoamericanos*; *Hispanismo: Past and Future*; and a volume on *Modernidad, emancipación y descolonización en America Latina siglo XVIII*.

Michael Kenneth Huner is a PhD candidate in Latin American history at the University of North Carolina at Chapel Hill. He is currently writing his dissertation on religion, popular political culture, and state formation in Paraguay before and during the Triple Alliance War.

Terry Rugeley is Professor of Latin American history at the University of Oklahoma. He is the author of four books, including a translation of Austrian botanist Karl Heller's 1845–1848 travels in Mexico. Rugeley's next work, a study of society, memory, and Caste War violence in nineteenth-century Yucatán, will appear in 2009.

Patricia Lapolla Swier teaches Spanish at Wake Forest University. Her area of specialization includes nineteenth- and twentieth-century Latin American narrative, women's studies, masculine studies, and French feminism. She recently completed the book *Hybrid Nations: Gender Troping and the Emergence of Bi-Gendered Subjects in Latin American Narrative* (2009).

Amy E. Wright currently teaches at Bard Early College in lower Manhattan. She earned her PhD in Hispanic Studies from Brown University in 2006 with "Subscribing Identities: The Serial Novel in the Development of Novel and Nation; Spain and Mexico from the 1840s to the 1860s." Her research and teaching reflect an array of historical and literary interests with an eye towards the margins/marginalized—in particular those figures or works that blur borders between genres, maps, and literary movements.

Index

Illustrations indicated in **bold**.